Human Aspects of Man-made Systems

The Open University Systems Group

George Barclay
John Beishon (Professor)
Stephen Brown
Rita Daggett
Bob Drozdowskij
Hal Dunkelman
Nick Easton
Malcolm Henderson
Lyn Jones
Martin Lockett
John Martin
Bill Mayon-White
Dick Morris
John Naughton
Sue Parrott
Rob Paton
Geoff Peters
Christopher Pym
Lindsay Read
Viv Risby
Roger Spear
Alan Thomas
Viv West
Bob Williams

In consultation with:

Victor Bignell (City University, Dept. of Mechanical Engineering)
Keith Cavanagh (editor)
Philippe Duchastel (OU Institute of Educational Technology)
John Groom (BBC)
Clive Holloway (OU Dept. of Psychology)
Larry Kern (OU Institute of Educational Technology)
Andrew Millington (BBC)
Tony Wright (OU Staff Tutor)

The full set of courses produced by the group so far is:
T241 Systems Behaviour
T242 Systems Management
T341 Systems Modelling
TD 342 Systems Performance

Human Aspects of Man-made Systems

Readings on: Conceptual models
Practical strategies
Design situations

Edited by Stephen C. Brown
John N. T. Martin

THE OPEN UNIVERSITY PRESS

This selection and editorial matter copyright © 1977
The Open University

All rights reserved
First published 1977

No part of this book may be used or reproduced in any manner whatsoever without written permission except in the case of brief quotations embodied in critical articles and reviews.

Published by the Open University Press.

ISBN: O 335 00047 9

Printed in Great Britain by
Staples Printers Ltd., St. Albans.

PREFACE

Although this collection of papers and articles should be of use to many types of reader, it was originally compiled for students following the Open University course *Systems Performance: Human Factors and Systems Failures* (TD 342).

The course is concerned with exploring the concept of failure and with finding ways of analysing, predicting and coping with failures in a wide variety of systems. While writing the course we were (and still are) uncertain about what constitutes a failure in any particular context, and how failures can be recognized. For example, is a divorce a failure or is it a successful way of handling an untenable marriage?

We approached this uncertainty by examining a range of case studies, from highly structured situations such as the collision between a train and a special-load transporter at Hixon level crossing in 1967, through problems of reliability engineering in a nuclear power station, to the much more intangible evaluation of the provision of mental health care.

These case studies were used as a vehicle to explore the development of an overall interdisciplinary approach to the analysis and prediction of failures or potential failures. This is achieved through the examination of methodologies, concepts and techniques borrowed from a range of different disciplines including engineering reliability, social science, human factors and general systems theory.

Although the basic philosophy of the course team is that all failures are in some sense *systemic* failures, and can only be understood in their systemic context, we also believe that all failures in systems involving people are ultimately *human* failures in cause, even if not necessarily in blame. One common feature of the failures examined in the course is the involvement of people at some stage in the design, development, operation or maintenance of the systems in which the failures occurred. Consequently, although the approach taken to the study of failures in the course units is an essentially systemic one, the human aspects of these failures are given special prominence.

By 'human aspects' we do not mean simply the relatively narrow band of study covered by ergonomists. Ergonomics (which is usually defined as the study of man in his working environment) is too narrow a subject to deal with all aspects of human behaviour and failure. It is necessary to apply knowledge and expertise from a much wider range of the human sciences to the types of problem examined in the case studies.

Nevertheless, the *Systems Performance* course is not intended to produce human-factors specialists. Human factors represents only one area of human knowledge relevant to the study of failures and our intention is to produce students who, having taken the course, will be able to conceptualize a wide variety of unstructured social and technical problems at an advanced level. For this reason, the human factors material in this Reader is not presented as a 'fait accompli', but is accompanied by a discussion of its utility and its very real limitations, to encourage a critical and intelligent approach to this area.

We hope that this form of presentation will make the Reader useful not only to Open University students, but to all those either working in human factors or related areas and those who have to deal with human-factors experts in the course of their work.

ACKNOWLEDGEMENTS

Open University academics depend even more than those in other Universities on their libraries and their secretarial staff. We are most grateful to the library staff of the Open University, and of the Senate House Library of the University of London which provided most of the material for the readings; to Sue Parrott who typed all the drafts for the original material; and Andrew Reilly of the Open University Press for editorial advice.

CONTENTS

	Page
Preface	v
Acknowledgements	vi

Part 1: Study Aids

1 Introduction	6
The aims of this book	6
The model underlying the structure of this book	7
Further general reading	14
2 Selective guides to the readings	16
Conceptual models of man and his environment	16
Practical strategies and techniques	21
Design situations and application areas	30
Assessing the practical value of human factors recommendations	36

Part 2: The Readings

3 The historical perspective	44
3.1 An historical view of the development of human factors. *S. C. Brown*	44

4	**Mechanistic views of the individual**		54
	4.1 Control design. *E. J. McCormick*		54
	4.2 Ergonomic techniques in the determination of optimum work surface heights. *J. S. Ward*		65
	4.3 Vigilance Research: Its Applications to Industrial Problems. *R. L. Smith and L. F. Lucaccini*		81
	4.4 Skilled Performance and Stress. *C. Poulton*		93
	4.5 Methods of Predicting Human Reliability in Man–Machine Systems. *D. Meister*		114
5	**Situational views of the individual**		133
	5.1 Improved Operating Procedures Manuals. *J. D. Vandenberg*		133
	5.2 Human Factors In Urban Transportation Systems. *L. L. Hoag* and *S. K. Adams*		143
	5.3 Railway Signals Passed at Danger: the Drivers, Circumstances and Psychological Processes. *D. R. Davis.*		157
	5.4 Ergonomics and air safety. *J. M. Rolfe*		173
	5.5 Design of Industrial Jobs a Worker Can and Will Do. *A. D. Swain.*		188
	5.6 The Role-set: Problems in Sociological Theory. *R. K. Merton*		200
	5.7 Social Benefit versus Technological Risk. *C. Starr*		210
6	**Organizational views**		230
	6.1 Esso London Airport refuelling control centre redesign – an ergonomics case study. *B. Shackel* and *L. Klein*		230
	6.2 Organizational perspectives in the health service. *M. Kogan* and *J. Balle*		247
	6.3 The goals of an industrial system. *J. K. Galbraith*		263
	6.4 The real threat to 'All we hold most dear'. *S. Beer*		273

7	Evolving strategies	285
7.1	Systems Design. *W. T. Singleton*	285
7.2	Human Error in Man–Machine Systems. *D. Meister*	299
7.3	Human Factors: Micro to Macro. *A. L. Porter*	325

Glossary 340

Index 346

Part 1
Study Aids

1 INTRODUCTION

The aims of this book

This set of readings has grown out of an overlapping group of areas variously known as: ergonomics, human engineering, biomechanics, industrial psychology, etc., which we will refer to collectively as human factors. Central to the collection is the basic idea that the role played by the 'human element' is critical in determining the performance and failure of man-made systems. From this it follows that it is essential for us to understand the causes of human errors if we are attempting to analyse system failures.

However, as indicated in the preface, as the editors we were not just concerned with errors and accidents in the narrow man-machine context that normally dominates these subject areas. At the same time, we did want to retain the bias towards providing a suitable technological base for people (often unselected members of the general public) rather than selecting or adjusting people to fit some particular technology. The readings therefore reflect these two constraints, and extend conventional boundaries of human factors selectively into areas such as industrial relations, organizational psychology, and even government policy making.

This chosen area falls at the intersection between academic research areas in the human sciences, and practical professional skills in planning, designing, and managing complex systems that span the range from 'hard' engineering to 'soft' social, organizational and political administration. There are therefore three groups of people who might find this reader useful: those on the intersection, and those on each wing.

Students of ergonomics and related areas are squarely on the intersection, and should find this collection central to their area of study.

On the academic wing, students of the social sciences should find sufficient theoretical material to show the essential link between their own topics and applied areas: but they will also find a critical and realistic discussion of the severe problems and limitations of applying academic ideas and philosophies to practical situations, and the changes of emphasis and strategy that this demands.

On the other side of the fence, engineers, managers, planners, administrators, etc., often need to call in, or liaise closely with, human factors specialists, of various sorts. They should find that this set of readings provides a cross-section of the wares that the human factors expert has to offer, and a discussion of their benefits and very distinct limitations, selected so that there is no need for substantial prior knowledge of specialist fields or specialist jargon. Nevertheless, we felt it important, particularly for this audience, that we should avoid pre-digested and misleading 'Noddy's guides', so the readings are almost all primary source material, mainly from professional journals or conferences.

Mathematical sections have normally been avoided, although statistical sections of experimental papers have been left in. The glossary explains the jargon we have been unable to avoid.

Apart from the readings themselves, we have provided three study aids that readers may find useful:

1   Section 2 provides reading guides to the four main areas that emerge from the model described in the next section (models; strategies; application areas; practical value), drawing out the lessons that we felt were most relevant from these papers.

2   An annotated reading list for those who want to study further is provided at the end of this section. It includes introductory text-books, manuals, major journals and major abstracting services. More references can be found in the individual papers and in Section 2.

3   Shortcuts through the reading guides are indicated in Tables 1-4, listing the minimal subsets of papers that would be just sufficient to convey the outlines of the topics covered by each guide.

The model underlying the structure of this book

Like most editors of collections of readings, we devised a conceptual model to guide our selection and to structure the book. Although there are many other ways the book can be used, some explanation of this model seems justified. The central questions considered are: 'Where do human factors experts get their information from, and why should we pay attention to them?' These are really questions about the epistemological pedigree of the subject, and so we start with the basic model shown in Figure 1 suggesting how knowledge accumulates in most applied fields. It would not satisfy all philosophers of science, but it is close enough for our purposes.

It is built round a 'knowledge resource' consisting of a collection of conceptual *models,* a collection of *evidence,* and a general awareness of the existence of *gaps* in our knowledge that need to be filled. There are two major modes of interaction with this resource area: *academic research* and *practical technology* (using the word 'technology' in its very widest sense to include all man-made systems, not just those consisting of hardware). The

INTRODUCTION

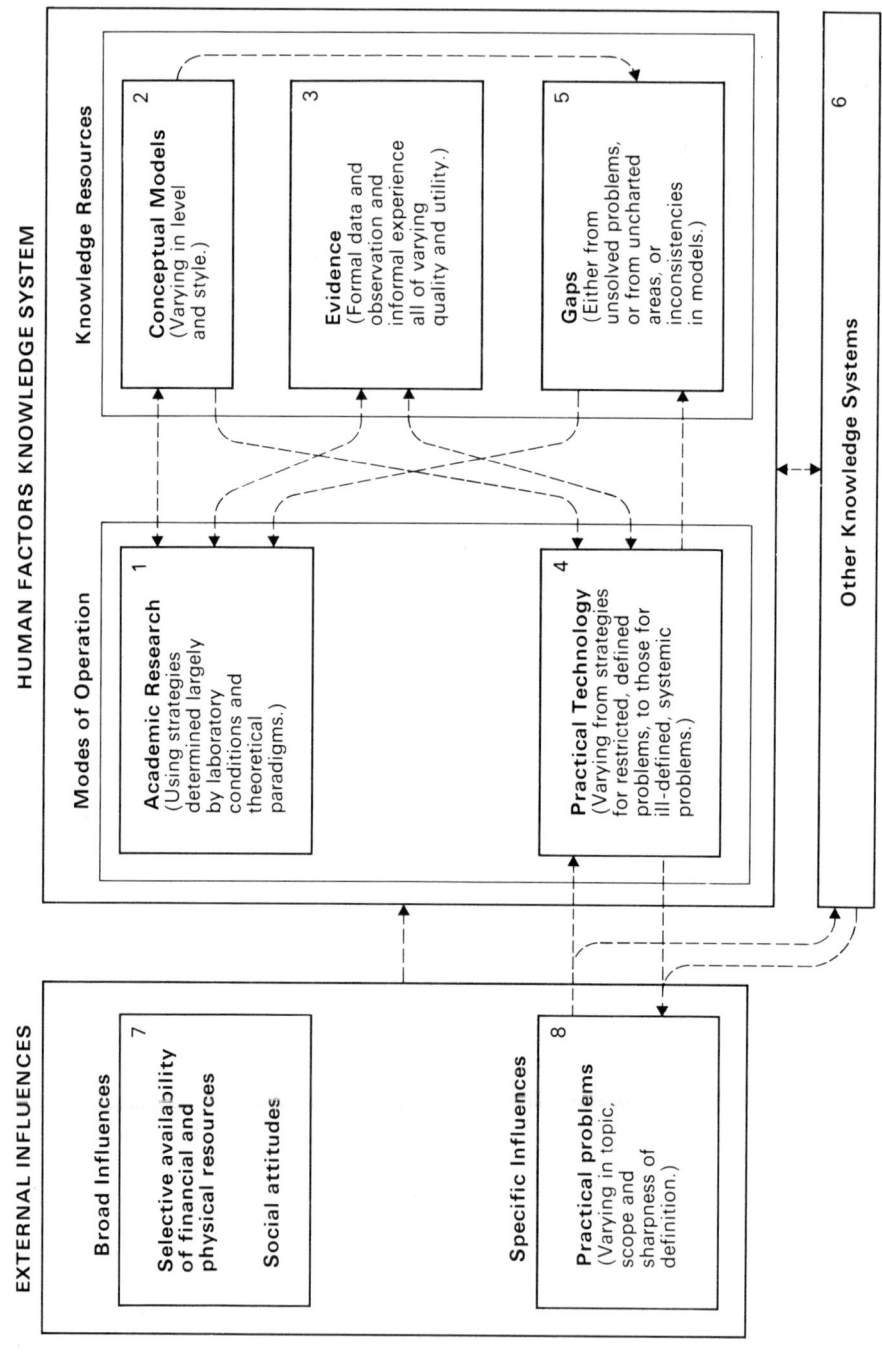

driving force behind academic research is largely the urge to resolve the contradictions and gaps in the models; that is, it is driven by an inner momentum within the existing knowledge system itself. Practical technology, however, is largely driven from outside by its input of *problems*. Both models contribute to and draw on the body of evidence. The building of fundamental conceptual models (as distinct from using routine computational models) tends to be more characteristic of academic research. Practical technology, on the other hand, probably contributes most to building up the repertoire of gaps which tends ultimately to control the direction in which the entire system moves. If you like analogies, academic research involves conceptual toolmaking, but ultimately it is practical technology that needs uses and justifies the tools. It is common to find human factors experts deliberately alternating between free-running laboratory work and specific consultancy to get the benefits of both modes, because each makes a unique contribution.

Our selection of papers reflects both sides of this dichotomy and the major factors that influence them. We have tried to provide a wide coverage in each of the following four areas, as indicated in Tables 1-4:

1   Conceptual models, in the range of styles and levels of analysis outlined in Table 1, corresponding roughly to boxes 1 and 2 in Figure 1.

2   A range of techniques and strategies typical of those involved in developing and using human factors knowledge as outlined in Table 2. These come under the practical technology mode, and correspond roughly to boxes 3 and 4 in Figure 1.

3   The range of types of design situation in which human factors can make a significant contribution outlined in Table 3 and corresponding roughly to boxes 6 and 8 in Figure 1.

4   Illustrations of the practical value and limitations of human factors studies outlined in Table 4. Obviously, this is a very general property, but it relates most to boxes 3, 5, 6, 7, and 8 in Figure 1.

These four areas are each treated in detail in the four reading guides in Section 2.

Table 1 Conceptual models of man in his environment

Classification	Paper	Author
Level 1: The individual — basic psycho-physiological functioning.		
1 The marionette — levers and pivots	4.2	Ward
2 A productive system with optimal conditions for maximum yield	*4.4*	*Poulton (Sections 3–7)*
3 The defective organism in need of servicing	5.3	Davis
Level 2: The individual — control of tasks		
4 The goal-seeking automated robot	*4.4*	*Poulton (Sections 1–2)*
Level 3: The group — inter-personal behaviour		
5 The compliant servant	5.6	Merton
6 Organization man	6.2	*Kogan and Balle*
7 Economic man — pursuit of self-interest	5.7	Starr
	6.3	Galbraith
Level 4: the group — the behaviour of complete organizations		
8 The juggler — grappling with the long-term control of society	*6.4*	*Beer*

The papers in italic are the minimal set for making reasonable sense of the notes.

Table 2 Selected papers on practical strategies and techniques in human factors studies

Classification	Paper	Author
Group 1 Restricted strategies: those that draw on experience		
Strategy 1: Codifying currently accepted good practice	*5.1*	*Vandenberg*
Strategy 2: Interviewing participants after something goes wrong	5.3	Davis
Group 2 Restricted strategies: those that rely on experimentation		
Strategy 3: Observation field studies	4.2	Ward
Strategy 4: The experimental project oriented towards one specific question	*4.2*	*Ward*
Strategy 5: Developing general principles from a body of theoretical research	4.3	Smith and Lucaccini
Group 3 Systemic strategies: upward extensions of the experimental approach		
Strategy 6: Large scale field studies	6.2	Kogan and Balle
Strategy 7: Detailed modelling of human behaviour	*4.5*	*Meister*
Group 4 Systemic strategies: those aimed at structuring the analyst's approach to his problems		
Strategy 8: Liaison, teamwork, simulation and pragmatism	6.1	Shackel and Klein
Strategy 9: Broad-based normative classification	7.2	Meister
Strategy 10: Problem-solving methodologies	*7.1*	*Singleton*
Group 5 Systemic strategies: solutions generated by social structures	—	—

The papers in italic are the minimal set for making reasonable sense of the notes.

Table 3 Selected papers on application areas for human factors studies

Classification	Paper	Author
The historical background		
General review	*3.1*	*Brown*
Group 1 Application areas at the equipment level: the man–machine interface		
1 Simple interfaces involving one person	4.2 *4.1*	Ward *McCormick*
2 Complex work-stations and work areas	5.1 6.1 5.4	Vandenberg Shackel and Klein Rolfe
3. Human factors surveys across complete systems	5.2 7.2	Hoag and Adams Meister
Group 2 Widening the boundary to include the people within the operational sub-system: the person-to-person interface		
4 Accident prevention and analysis	5.3	Davis
5 Design of jobs and organizations	*5.5* 6.2	*Swain* Kogan and Balle
Group 3 Widening the application boundary still further — policy-making beyond the operational sub-system: the society-technology interface		
6 Providing information about human behaviour as an input for policy-makers	4.2 5.7 6.3	Ward Starr Galbraith
7 The relationship between human factors, systems science and technology policy assessment	*7.3*	*Porter*

The papers in italic are the minimal set for making reasonable sense of these notes.

Table 4 The practical value of human factors recommendations

Classification		Paper	Author
Direct assessment of benefits			
1	Cost-benefit accounting for individual proposals	*6.1*	*Shackel and Klein*
		4.2	Ward
		5.2	Hoag and Adams
Some potential limitations			
2	The reliability of the basic evidence	*4.2*	*Ward*
		5.1	Vandenberg
3	The validity of assumptions made when building models	4.3	Smith and Lucaccini
		4.2	Ward
		4.4	Poulton (Sections 3–7)
		6.4	Beer
		5.6	Merton
4	Can models be generalized to new situations, and how sensitive are they to local variations?	*4.3*	*Smith and Lucaccini*
		4.5	Meister
		6.1	Shackel and Klein
5	Are human factors recommendations of a suitable form and level of precision to be usable?	4.2	Ward
		4.3	Smith and Lucaccini
		4.5	Meister
		5.2	Hoag and Adams
		7.2	Meister
		5.5	Swain
6	Acceptability, credibility, and communicability	5.5	Swain
		6.2	Kogan and Balle
		5.1	Vandenberg
		6.1	Shackel and Klein
		4.5	Meister
		4.2	Ward

The papers in italic are the minimal set for making reasonable sense of the notes.

INTRODUCTION

Further general reading

Below are listed a number of selected books that would make useful general follow-up reading to the papers contained in this Reader. There is also a list of some of the main academic journals and abstracts relevant to the human factors area. These selections are not intended to be comprehensive bibliographies, they do not even claim to represent all the most important sources. However, they should provide a useful point of entry to the human factors literature and they each contain large numbers of further references.

General introductory texts

Davis, L. E. and Taylor, J. C. (eds.) (1972)
Design of Jobs, Penguin Books Ltd.
De Greene, K. B. (ed.) (1970)
Systems Psychology, McGraw-Hill, New York.
Edholm, O. G. (1967)
The Biology of Work, World University Library, London.
Holding, D. H. (ed.) (1969)
Experimental Psychology in Industry, Penguin Books Ltd.
McCormick, E. J. (4th edn. 1976)
Human Factors in Engineering and Design, McGraw-Hill, New York.
Silverman, D. (1970)
The Theory of Organisations, Heinemann.

Handbooks for Designers
Van Cott, H. P. and Kinkade, R. G. (eds.) (Rev. edn. 1972)
Human Engineering Guide to Equipment Design, US Government Printing Office, Washington.

Handbooks for Researchers
Chapanis, A. (1969)
Research Techniques in Human Engineering, Johns Hopkins, Baltimore.
Phillips, B. S. (1971)
Social Research: Strategy and Tactics, MacMillan, New York.

Journals and Abstracting Services
Abstracting services:
    Ergonomics Abstracts
    Psychological Abstracts
Bibliographies and Reviews:
    Annual Review of Psychology
    Psychological Bulletin

Journals:
   Applied Ergonomics
   Ergonomics
   Human Factors
   Journal of Applied Psychology

2 SELECTIVE GUIDES TO THE READINGS

Conceptual models of man in his environment

Table 1 lists the papers in this selection. Those in italic show the minimum reading list required for making reasonable sense of the following notes.

These readings represent a sample of some of the different ways in which the inter-relation between man and his physical and operational environment can be conceptualized in the behavioural and social sciences.

We have called these conceptual viewpoints 'models'. We ought to make clear what this means. At its most general, a 'model' is any representation of something. This would include any verbal or symbolic description, any descriptive sketch or drawing, any representational physical construction, and so on. This is so broad that it includes not only scientific models, but also all sorts of everyday descriptions and representations, and many artistic activities.

In a scientific context, the word is used much more narrowly than this. A *scientific* model is one that deliberately sets out to represent particular objectively detectable properties of something under describable conditions, in an unambiguous and publicly accessible way. Provided you understand the jargon, you should ideally be able to work out how a scientific model has been constructed, and in what respects it is claimed to represent its original. If you do not believe this claim, or if you think you have a better model, you should be able to demonstrate this in an unambiguous and rational way. Nothing is hidden or private, so any debate is in principle a matter of balancing tangible evidence and logic, and should, therefore, be resolvable.

This is quite different from, say, an artistic description, in which the artist may be deliberately ambiguous, may set out to produce something which different people see in different ways, and may aim to be emotive and private in the imagery used.

Although the models described below are all unquestionably 'scientific' in intention, you will have little difficulty in seeing that many of them have a strong evocative element that goes a long way beyond the narrow interpretation of the idealistic scientific model described above.

Table 1 lists eight models, arranged in four different *levels of aggregation* of the analytic variables in the model, with the level of aggregation increasing towards the bottom of the table, so that the list moves from models based on single behavioural aspects of individual people to models involving long-term strategies for complete organizations.

Within each *level of aggregation* the papers show different *styles* of model. Styles vary very widely — some models are very reductionist and mechanistic, some are more richly structured and 'human' in their descriptions; some are strictly parsimonious in their approach to evidence, some are more concerned with generating a vivid image round which to organize thinking and to stimulate research; some are concerned mainly with summarizing naturalistic observations, and others with describing the formal limits that define rational behaviour in particular situations.

Level 1: The individual at the level of basic psycho-physiological functioning

From a research point of view, one of the most obvious characteristics of the higher levels of human behaviour is that they are far too complex and fluid to permit the kind of precise and rigid experimentation possible in the physical and, to a lesser extent, the biological sciences. Tightly controlled experiments can only be applied easily to human behaviour at the simpler levels, represented by this group of papers: measuring distances and forces, recognizing medical symptoms, and recording the averaged rates of output in repetitive tasks under simple laboratory conditions.

Model 1 (The marionette — levers and pivots). This is the model for the anthropometrist or applied anatomist. Man is seen as a set of levers (bones) of varying dimensions connected by various kinds of pivots (joints) and operated by ropes, springs, and pulleys (tendons and muscles), of various types and strengths. The problem is seen as the design of the physical dimensions of the world to fit this puppet-like structure. At this very general level the model is so simple conceptually that we have not included a theoretical paper on it;* however Ward's paper (4.2) shows what it can look like in a fairly simple application. An obvious achievement of this kind of approach is the vastly improved design of the best modern chairs. Notice that although these ideas are simple in concept, they are far from simple in application. Providing a model capable of describing the movements of something as complex as the human body through space and time is a formidable mathematical task†, and collecting the normative quantitative measurements so that the model can be adapted to a particular group of people is very time-consuming and expensive.

Model 2 (A productive system with optimal conditions for maximum yield). Here, the individual is seen as having an optimal level of general performance

---

**One such paper would be: P. Branton, (1969) 'Behaviour, body mechanics and discomfort'. Ergonomics, Vol. 12, (2), pp. 316–327.*

†*See for instance: Ayoub, M.A., Ayoub, M.M. and Walvekar A.G. (1974) 'A biomechanical model for the upper extremity using optimization techniques'. Human Factors, Vol. 16, (6), pp. 585–594.*

for any task, and this is best achieved by some balance of stresses, some of which can be mutually compensatory. It is very much the same kind of approach as a farmer might use: to get the best yield he must get the right balance of many factors — rain, sun, fertilizers, soil factors — not too little, not too much, but just right and with the right balance. Many biological systems have complex optima of this sort.

The second part of Poulton's paper (4.4, Sections 3-7) illustrates such a model showing how a range of environmental stresses can interact to affect the level of 'arousal' of an individual relative to the optimal level of arousal for any particular task. This paper is an excellent example of rigorous and parsimonious scientific method at work in the behavioural sciences, with every statement carefully backed by reliable experimental results representing many man-years of work, and presenting the simplest possible model consistent with those findings.

Model 3 (The defective organism in need of servicing). This is the viewpoint of the doctor or the mechanic: did the accident occur because there was something 'wrong' with the person (or machine) involved? Where recognizable diseases, physical damage, or specific drugs are involved, this concept makes sense. But in recent years its application to *mental* disorders has been strongly challenged. Again we have not attempted to provide a paper to illustrate this model in a theoretical form, but the paper by Davis (5.3) shows this very familiar approach at work. While Davis's paper is particularly concerned with psychiatric problems, clearly physical defects, and the effects of alcohol, drugs and poisons would come in the same category.

Level 2: The individual seen at the level of the cognitive control of tasks

Model 4 (The goal-seeking automated robot). Computers have played a very important role in the development of psychological theory in the last decade or so. Particularly useful have been the ideas, techniques, and structures developed by computer programmers to help them to think about the ways in which very complex tasks can be organized and controlled. These have given us insights into the requirements for co-ordinating complex functions, a common language for discussing them, and a modelling device (the computer) on which we can actually try out our ideas. This broad and loosely organized area of psychology which tends to talk in terms of 'information stores', 'serial and parallel processing', 'information channels', 'search processes', and so on, now tends to be called 'cognitive psychology'.*

**From the influential and very readable book: Ulric Neisser (1967)* Cognitive Psychology, *Appleton-Century Crofts.*

The paper we have chosen to illustrate this approach is the first part of Poulton's paper (4.4, Sections 1-2). Its basic concepts would be quite familiar not just to psychologists, but also to someone designing some kind of automated industrial robot. There is a control loop involving some kind of sensory input and mechanical output, controlled by a central computer whose memory holds a list of characteristics of potentially significant sensory events and also several alternative sets of instructions for different patterns of mechanical output. The computer can use this to recognize significant events and select suitable responses, and can modify the stored information and instructions to correct failures in the control loop. A model of this sort provides very considerable insight into skilled human behaviour, its limitations and the kinds of error it is prone to.

Notice that such models are rarely parsimonious in the strict sense of the other model in Poulton's paper (Model 2). Cognitive models do explain many findings in a very straightforward way, but often several different flow charts could all explain the known data just as well. They show how a particular writer is currently thinking about the data he is trying to explain, rather than being a logically minimal summary of it. This often makes the model much more interesting but also makes it a less secure foundation for practical decisions.

Level 3: Analysis at the level of the group — inter-personal behaviour

As we move into the areas normally covered by social psychology and sociology the character of the data, of the analytical techniques, and of the models changes. The most obvious feature is that two of the papers in this section are 'arm-chair' theories in the sense that they try to clarify and define logically the essential characteristics of very complex behaviour. Even where experiments are a significant source of new data to be accounted for in a model, acute observation and the development of a theoretical position tend to come first; formal experiments tend to follow later as attempts to confirm or elaborate the theory. This is mainly because social behaviour is so complex and changeable that experimental studies are difficult and easily invalidated, and a high degree of personal interpretation is involved. One obvious result of this is that theories at this level are particularly likely to conceal personal and ideological bias.

Model 5 (The compliant servant). We have called Merton's paper (5.6) 'the compliant servant' because he is describing behaviour that follows the social expectations set by our social slots; ignoring both our random deviations from our roles and much of our rationally independent behaviour. Compliant here does not necessarily mean 'subservient'; for instance, one of the most widely researched roles is the leadership role — the leader can respond in ways determined by our expectations while still 'leading'!

One area where role perceptions have a profound effect on technological functioning is of course in industrial relations.

Model 6 (Organization man). Kogan and Balle (6.2) formalize the role idea and use it to analyse organizational structures. In this case, the efficacy of the organization is seen entirely in terms of the way the roles of its human members are defined and interrelated. Notice that this particular point of view tends to ignore both the individual characteristics of the role-holder and the nature and purpose of the organization.

Model 7 (Economic man — the optimization of self-interest). The papers by Starr (5.7) and Galbraith (6.3) although concerned with very different topics, both rely on the classic economic model of man pursuing his own self-interest by balancing the advantages or 'benefits' and disadvantages or 'costs' of any action to get the best possible net gain. In Starr's paper, the 'cost' is the risk of death or injury, and the 'benefit' is money, a job, excitement, etc. Galbraith's paper is in more conventional economic territory, and is trying to show that conventional economists have been far too narrow in the costs and benefits they have chosen to consider, and in the ways in which they assume them to interact in large organizations.

The idea of this type of rational trade-off is very neat and attractive to the model-builder, and there are certain areas where it probably applies quite closely (negotiation, diplomacy, military strategy, and so on). However, there are many areas of human psychology that are not usefully thought of in these terms — activities that seem to occur regardless of cost, activities that are not carried out even though apparently highly beneficial, or trade-off points that seem to shift so continually and unpredictably as to be unmeasurable.

Level 4: The group: the behaviour of complete organizations

The behaviour of complete organizations is the coarsest level of aggregation we will be considering. The element of arm-chair philosophy becomes even more obvious here, and the formal manipulative experiment is only possible in the very rarest of cases; the raw data consists almost entirely of historical data, case-histories of existing organizations, official industrial and commercial statistics, and such like.

Model 8 (The juggler — grappling with the long-term control of society). Beer's paper (6.4) is written from the perspective of the decision makers trying to keep control of a complex environment containing a wide variety of factors, grouped in a complex, changing structure.

The abstraction and generalization is very marked. It is a good non-mathematical example of the type of theory typical of general systems theory — the attempt to find models whose applicability is almost independent of any specific setting, depending on system structure rather than content.

Models in general

There are several features worth noting about this series of models as a whole:

1 The complexity of a model is determined much more by the limitations of its creator or its audience than by its subject level. Although the complete world of organizations and their environments is obviously more complex than one man responding to a couple of stresses, Stafford Beer's model is no more complex than Poulton's. Conceptual models are aids to understanding, and they can be no more complex than the limitation to understanding set by the human brain.

2 However, once the validity of a conceptual model has been accepted, and it is developed into a specific, practically useful form it can become very complex indeed. Although the anthropometric idea in Model 1 is simple, its practical realization is far from simple. Meister's first paper (4.5), describing the THERP model, illustrates this sort of practical development of a theoretical model in some detail. Notice that a complex development of a simple idea is not likely to be any more valid than the original simple idea, and may be less so.

3 The higher the level of aggregation, the less likely it is that a model will be a summary of particular biologically based human characteristics, and the more likely it is that it will be a model of a *situation* which need not even be specific to human beings. This is one of the characteristics of very general systems models. For instance, the way stresses interact in Poulton's model may well apply only to people — baboons or Martians might well behave quite differently. However, the concept of variety refers to a situation or systems structure, not a particular biological organism, so it should apply to baboons or Martians as much as to human beings. The concept of 'role' (in 5.6 or 6.2) is intermediate between these two extremes — in so far as baboons or Martians have a leadership role, for instance, its situational aspects will tend to be similar to the human case.

Practical strategies and techniques

Theories for looking at the world are not much use in an applied area unless you also have practical strategies for coming to grips with the actual details of specific problems.

Table 2 (p. 11) lists the papers, and the strategies they illustrate. Those in italic show the minimal reading list required to make reasonable sense of these notes. You can see that there is an historical review and two broad clusters of strategies. The first cluster (Groups 1 and 2) are aimed at *restricted* and specific questions:

> 'How should one write procedure manuals?'
> 'How high should a kitchen unit be?'
> 'At what point in his shift is an inspector most likely to fail to detect a faulty item?'

The second cluster (Groups 3, 4 and 5) are aimed at broad, systemic questions:

> 'Where in all the different stages and levels of this project are errors likely to occur?'
> 'How can complex procedures and equipment best be integrated into this organization?'

Obviously, these are two very different situations. In the 'restricted' cluster we are in the position typical of the specialist consultant called in from outside; the environment of the problem is already largely defined for him, and is only marginally his concern. For instance, Vandenberg's paper (5.1) does not question whether something quite different from a procedure manual might not be more suitable in some particular situation, and the British Standard in Ward's paper (4.2) presumably applies only to cooking, so there is no need to think of what happens when the kitchen surface is used by children for doing their homework or by adults as a work-bench for domestic repairs, or whether it is the right height for papering the ceiling when you stand on it.

The questions in the 'systemic' cluster imply a much wider brief. They require a comprehensive and holistic approach and their problems are still in very undefined forms. Before they can be reduced to well-defined analyses there has to be a pre-analysis stage, scanning and coming to grips with a complete environment. Indeed, the pre-analysis may be by far the largest part of the job, because once the problem has been defined it can often be delegated for routine solution. This is quite often the position of a human-factors specialist who is a permanent and senior member of a design team, with very broadly based terms of reference, but it also applies to many senior problem-solving and decison-making roles which also have responsibility for the wider results of their actions.

Historically, as you can see from the review paper (3.1), the 'systemic' cluster are all recent developments, the traditional role of the ergonomist being more 'restricted'.

Group 1: Restricted strategies: those that draw on experience

Strategy 1 (Modifying currently accepted good practice). This is one of the oldest and most obvious types of strategy for any well-established type of task: find people who do it well, and write down how they do it. Vandenberg's paper (5.1) was a response to an earlier paper* pointing out how little research has been carried out on the wording of manuals, signs, and instructions of all sorts, and how disastrous this can often be. Vandenberg has simply pooled his own experience with some recommendations from other sources such as American military specifications, themselves based mainly on personal experience.† The disadvantages of this strategy are:

There is no way of finding out what weight to put on any one recommendation in any particular situation. Some of the points will be purely personal stylistic preferences by the authors; some will represent highly significant points to watch; some may even represent bad practices that have become hallowed by time; some will only apply under certain (undefined) conditions.

Obviously, this strategy will not work at all under completely new conditions where no one has any experience.

Strategy 2 (Interviewing participants after something goes wrong). This is a more formalized way of collecting experience. Davis (5.3) concentrates particularly on medical and psychosomatic factors because these are his speciality, but obviously an engineer, a manager, or a lawyer, would adapt the same process for their own use. Again this strategy is useless in completely new areas, and it only provides information after the system has been built. A more subtle problem is that, in practice, there is still a great deal of scope for the interviewer to force his observations into the mould of his own preconceptions: would an engineer interviewing Davis's train-drivers have drawn comparable conclusions?₽

An obvious upward extension of this strategy is the public inquiry where the 'interviews' occur under very formal legalistic conditions.‡

---

*Chapanis, A. (1965) 'Words, Words, Words' Human Factors, Vol. 7, pp. 1–17.

†*A well known English version of this approach is:* Gowers, E. (1970) (rev. edn.) The Complete Plain Words, *Penguin Books Ltd.*

₽*A fuller discussion of interviewing techniques, is contained in:* Phillips, B. S. (1971) (2nd ed.) Social Research: Strategy and Tactics, *MacMillan.*

Group 2: Restricted Strategies: those that rely on experimentation
Strategy 3 (Observational field studies)/Strategy 4 (The experimental project orientated towards a specific question). Ward's study (4.2) illustrates both of these approaches, since it starts with a field study involving 'sequential activity sampling' and concludes with an experimental laboratory-based study.

As in the previous two strategies, field studies still rely on existing on-going activities. However, rather than depending on unreliable and distorted memories and opinions about events, the experimenter uses more objective and controlled methods of recording the activity of the system without disturbing it.

The disadvantage is that real systems tend to be large, complex and not amenable to experimental control. This means that you have to record selectively, and your data may be seriously incomplete or misleading in other ways. An important problem is the so-called 'Hawthorne effect'* — the tendency for people to change their behaviour as soon as they know they are being observed. Other problems may arise if the recording has to be carried out by assistants, or even by people within the system itself, possibly leading to variable recording standards, misunderstandings, and even 'rigged' data.†

An obvious alternative is to narrow the question down until it becomes amenable to a specific laboratory study as in the later part of Ward's paper.

This kind of tight experimental design has many benefits: the results are quantitative, we know exactly what they mean, we know exactly how reliable they are and in some respects we know what range of the population they apply to.

However, it also has disadvantages precisely because of the way in which it has been narrowed down. For instance, in Ward's case, we cannot really generalize beyond the highly specific question about kitchen surfaces, so that all these experimental resources have gone into one question only. That makes sense when setting up a British Standard, but it would not have made sense for each of the host of minor design questions that can arise in any

---

‡*Wraith R. E. and Lamb G. B. (1971)* Public Inquiries as an Instrument of Government, *Allen & Unwin*.

*Roethlisberger F. J. and Dickson W. J. (1939) Management and the Workers, *Harvard University Press.*

†*Johnson E. M. and Baker J. D. (1974) 'Field Testing: The delicate compromise',* Human Factors, *Vol. 16, No. 3, pp. 203–214.*

particular design project — it would cost too much, and take too long. A second disadvantage is that we have limited its applicability in various subtle ways even within the original question: it is probably quite representative of kitchen activity in a suburban family semi-detached, but what about the tiny urban single flatlet; it is fine for European cooking, but what about non-European cooking;⁋ it may apply to 95 per cent of British women by height, but how does it sample other dimensions; what are we excluding when we ignore the 'others' category in Ward's Table 1?

Notice that these problems are not really criticisms of Ward's very business-like study, they are statements about what has to happen in *any* formal experiment: to devise an experimental design, carry out measurements, and interpret them you have to make many simplifications and assumptions. These inevitably limit the applicability of the conclusions.

Strategy 5 (Developing general principles from a body of theoretical research). The ideal way out of the cost implications of the narrowness of Strategy 4 is to get to such a state of general knowledge that the principles of human behaviour in a particular area are understood as general laws which apply over many different situations. This is the point where programmes of 'pure' academic research and specific applied problems should come together. Smith and Lucaccini's paper (4.3) illustrates such a process. There are more recent reviews of vigilance research,* but we have included this one because it illustrates the kind of hiatus that can develop between applied problems and programmes of supposedly related laboratory studies. Vigilance research arose originally from quite specific industrial and military problems. Early experiments related these to some theoretically interesting issues, and devised some very ingenious and elegant experimental adaptations of the original problem that were ideal for the laboratory setting. As a result, vigilance research 'took off' as a topic for laboratory-based research, in spite of the growing doubt of a few of the experimenters involved. In effect, it almost became an autonomous area of 'pure' research driven by its own problems and discoveries, with only the occasional token nod in the direction of the original applied problem. It needed reviews such as Smith and Lucaccini's to bring this contradiction into a clearer focus so that research could swing back in a more productive way. It *is* possible to discover general laws of behaviour, but the route there is neither short,

---

⁋Dhesi, J. K., and Firebaugh F. M. (1973) 'The effects of stages of chapati making and angles of body position on heart rate', Ergonomics, *Vol. 16, No. 6, pp. 811–815.*

*Childs, M. J. (1976) 'Signal Complexity, Response Complexity and Signal Specification in Vigilance Theory', Human Factors, *Vol. 18, No. 2, pp. 149–160.*

SELECTIVE GUIDES TO THE READINGS

direct, nor cheap, and you may well have difficulty knowing if you have arrived.

Paper 4.3 is the only example in the present collection of a traditional academic review paper. It illustrates clearly how misleading even the best conducted single studies can be, and how even small areas of genuinely useful progress often depend on being able to take a hawk's-eye view over large and varied collections of studies, often representing many man-years of research in many different organizations. So far very few applied problems have generated collections of studies on this scale.

Group 3: Systemic strategies: upward extensions of the experimental approach

Some of the systemic strategies we will consider later on represent a radical change from the experimental philosophy of strategies 3, 4 and 5. But first we want to look at two approaches that are multi-variate extensions of these simpler techniques.

Strategy 6 (Large scale field studies). Kogan and Balle's study (6.2) takes the basic idea of a role, and a relationship between roles, and extends it to cover complete networks of role relationships using data from large scale field studies involving many interviews. The result is an attempt to 'map' the structure of a complete organization, just as a surveyor might attempt to 'map' a piece of countryside.

The problem is that the 'map' depends on:

1 The assumption that participants can report accurately on their own actions.

2 The assumption that the relationships involved are clear and stable enough to be reported and mapped.

3 The assumption that a link that *exists* is also *effective* throughout a whole class of activities.

These requirements may be met in some levels of the formal structure of a well organized bureaucracy, but it is very doubtful whether they are met in unstructured systems, or in the informal aspects of structured systems, or in the day-to-day changes in a system.

Strategy 7 (Detailed mathematical modelling of human behaviour). *The ultimate in multi-variate approaches would be a broad mathematical model of all aspects of a substantial slice of human behaviour. Meister's first paper

---

*Related techniques are described in: Meister, D. (1973) 'A critcal review of human performance reliability predictive methods' TEEE Transactions on Reliability, Vol. R22, No. 3.

(4.5) describes a way of trying to make such a model for a situation such as the operating procedure for some particular piece of equipment. The technique is borrowed from reliability engineering. It involves two components:

(a) Building up a comprehensive data-bank of human-factors data in a standard format, in much the same way as an engineer might collect tables of failure rates of various components, or an architect might want lists of materials and their fire hazards.

(b) Devising a way of representing branching sequences of possible human actions in some particular task, in such a way that the data-bank information can be slotted in to quantify it. From knowing the probability of any particular sequence of actions, and the probability of making an error at any one step, you should be able to work out the overall probability of carrying out the process correctly. This is related to the use of fault trees in reliability engineering.

This approach obviously tends to attract engineers, because it is close to their normal style of working. However, as Meister takes care to point out, there are many very severe problems in practice. Not only is most of the data needed for the data-bank missing, very inaccurate or very unreliable, but human behaviour is so variable and complex that the model is very limited, very difficult to build and needs a great deal of skilled adjustment, interpretation, and even guesswork before it makes any sense at all. Reliability-estimating techniques, which were designed originally for things like TV sets, do not necessarily work well for human behaviour, although the discipline of attempting to make it work can itself be of value.

Group 4: Systemic strategies: those aimed at structuring the analyst's approach to his problem

The next three strategies (8, 9, 10) in this section mark a sharp change in approach. The strategies have so far reflected well defined and bounded problems, even though the boundary in strategies 6 and 7 was a rather wide one. If the boundaries are thrown right back, the position changes. The experimenter is no longer able to control and contain his problem in the tight ways we have considered so far. He is no longer bigger than the problem—the problem is bigger than him. He is less like an architect designing a house, and more like an explorer in an unknown country. He needs maps, a compass and hints about survival priorities, rather than detailed procedure manuals.

Strategy 8 (Liaison, team-work, simulation and pragmatism). Shackel and Klein's paper (6.1) illustrates what the 'unknown country' described above can look like in a fairly straightforward case. It describes one particular ergonomic project as it happened, starting from the initial negotiations and contract, and going right through to follow-up checks several years after the new system was installed. It illustrates:

(a) The range of factors that have to be taken into account beyond the hardware that is the focus of the effort.

(b) The way in which applied studies depend on a very complete integration of negotiation, research and management skills, tactful liaison and timing, and a high degree of pragmatism. It is a very long way from the academic experimenter who can confine his attention to designing and executing his experiments to his own time-table, in the light of his own theories, and then writing them up and trying to get them published in a specialist journal.

(c) The paper also illustrates the use of *simulation* to test complex interactions between people and equipment. As we pointed out in Strategy 7, there is a great deal that we cannot yet model mathematically.

One way around this is for the operators to act out their roles within a simulated workplace. Sometimes the simulation can be reduced to as little as a computer program controlling a terminal. In Shackel and Klein's case, it was a 'stage-set' mock-up of the control room. The largest simulations have cost millions of dollars to stage. Rather surprisingly, reviews of the use of simulation* have found that for research purposes they are often much less useful than their cost would suggest, although they may have a valuable role in training, or as public-relations exercises. This is partly because they are almost as difficult to control experimentally as the reality they represent, and partly for practical reasons: the operators often take the simulation less seriously than the reality; they are rarely as experienced as they would be in reality; it is very difficult to simulate the full operational complexity and variability of real systems.

Strategy 9 (Broad-based normative classification). Meister's second paper (7.2) illustrates the use of a broad-based classification scheme to structure the ergonomist's approach to his problems. It is an attempt to provide a sketch map of the 'unknown country' showing the major features that are important for his purposes. Meister lists the typical types, causes and consequences of errors, and relates them to the phases of systems development. Having set up this conceptual framework he then illustrates the main categories and discusses the ergonomist's role in each.

It is a 'systemic' approach in that it is aimed at providing a wide holistic

---

*Parsons, H. McI. (1972) Man/Machine System Experiments, *Johns Hopkins Press*.

structure within which the ergonomist can handle many different types of problem, from a broad but relevant perspective. For instance, it could provide the structure for a broad human factors database; you could imagine submitting a progress report at the end of one of his phases; you could use his terms in preparing a design-team job description; it could be used to communicate the ergonomist's role to non-ergonomists.

Notice that is very difficult to argue whether Meister's classfication is 'correct' or not — you can only decide whether or not you personally would find it useful. Other writers have provided very different classification schemes for errors* which are just as 'correct' as this one. This is characteristic of higher level strategies which are more concerned with the needs of the ergonomist himself than with the analytic requirements of a particular system under investigation, so it is much more difficult to provide objective grounds for accepting or rejecting them.

Strategy 10 (Problem-solving methodologies). Singleton's paper (7.1) shows another higher level strategy. Whereas Meister provided a static structure within which to define, classify and file things. Singleton is concerned with the order in which the ergonomist does things — his methodology.

Singleton's systems ergonomics methodology is a specialized and limited development of the much more generalized systems methodologies† which have been developed to help very much wider categories of complex problem solving and decision making. These wider methodologies have roots in several different areas: in the psychology of human problem solving; in getting machines to solve problems and make decisions; in philosophical problems about the nature of knowledge and of inquiry; and in some of the sociological aspects of decision making.

Notice that methodologies represent idealized sequences: the reality is rarely as neat and tidy, and most steps and branches of the methodology are highly iterative, being recycled again and again as the design slowly evolves. Nevertheless, the framework can still be very useful as an orderly basis for discussing how to approach a problem, writing progress reports on it, checking that no major stages have been omitted, training newcomers and communicating with other groups involved in other parts of the project. It provides an agreed language and a basic set of reference points.

Group 5: Systemic strategies: solutions generated by social structures

We have not included any readings in this final area, because it is really

---

*Singleton, W. T. (1972) 'Techniques for determining the causes of errors' Applied Ergonomics, Vol. 3, No. 3, pp. 126–131.
†See Checkland, P. B. (1972) 'Towards a systems-based methodology for real-world problem solving, Journal of Systems Engineering, Vol. 3, no. 2.

beyond the scope of human factors. But it does close the loop back to the first strategies that depended on the use of existing experience, and so it is important to remember it as at least being a theoretical alternative.

All the previous strategies have tended to be 'top-down', that is to say they have assumed that there is a system designer who is quite distinct and usually in some kind of controlling position in relation to both the builder and the user of the system. The designer's task is then seen as collecting information about what the user needs and about what the builder can build, formulating this information into a design, passing it on to the builder, and checking that the user is happy with what comes out at the other end.

However, it is perfectly possible to envisage a highly participative process where the design, construction, and use of a human system are so closely integrated in a network of suggestions, shared experience of the system and group discussions that the 'designer' role is reduced to convening meetings and collecting ideas. For instance, in recent years some town planners have found that their role has tended to move towards this 'democratic convenor' rather than 'autocratic designer' pattern and in social systems such as that of modern China this principle is apparently used very widely. Under such systems, many of the strategies we have been describing become irrelevant, or have to be transformed in very drastic ways, and the only conscious 'strategy' involved is that of building and maintaining a suitable social structure in which this evolving form of design can happen successfully. In other words, it becomes a problem of ideology rather than of design strategy as this is normally understood.

Whether design should be carried out in the top-down way, which is conventional in most Western industrialized societies, or whether the participative structure is better is a complex economic and political question which goes far beyond the scope of this book.

Application areas for human factors studies

As we pointed out in the Introduction, there is a large gulf between the very general concept of 'the human element' in socio-technical systems, and the much more limited concept of 'human factors' as reflected in current knowledge. The selection of readings described below and in Table 3 indicates a range of practical problems that have received useful inputs from human factors studies of various types, and gives some feel for the type and level of *documented* information that human factors can provide, although *informal judgments* on particular situations can often go much further.

Clearly, these readings cover only a small fraction of the application areas you might come across if you followed up the 'further reading' suggestions in Section 1.3, although they do span the areas of human factors relevant to most normal design situations. The three major constraints on the range are:

1 At the physiological end of the spectrum, we have largely excluded areas such as industrial medicine and public health. There is little on pollutants, long-term health risks, physical injury and poisoning, epidemiology, and so on, even though these are obviously important and well studied aspects of the 'human element'.

2 Towards the 'social' end of the scale, we have been much more concerned with adjusting technology to people, rather than the other way round. We have severely under-emphasized areas such as industrial training, personnel selection, consumer research, publicity, the effects of mass media, etc., although these are widely studied and are unquestionably aspects of the 'human element'.

3 The third major omission arises directly from our concentration on essentially normal day-to-day aspects of human behaviour. We have excluded the large number of studies of human behaviour in bizarre and extreme situations, mostly carried out for military and aerospace purposes, but also including areas like the psychology of sport. We exclude problems such as:
astronauts operating in zero gravity;
divers using spanners at the bottom of the sea;
orientation illusions in pilots 'flying blind';
soldiers carrying out manoeuvres in tropical jungles;
marathon runners at the limits of exhaustion;
pole-vaulters in mid-flight; and so on. It is worth pointing out that although this type of problem has in the past been one of the mainstays of ergonomics, there is now probably just as much interest in more 'normal' problems.

After the historical introduction, the arrangement of studies in Table 3 follows the same general pattern as in Tables 1 and 2, starting with small-scale applications, and moving towards much broader ones.

The historical background

Paper: 3.1 Brown

Like most applied sciences, the historical development of human factors application areas is not a neat progress of orderly social commitment, but a story of opportunities grasped wherever they came from, making use of resources wherever they seemed to be available. It depended often crucially on the interests of particular individuals or the existence of special external circumstances such as the sudden demands of major social reform, or the even more drastic demands of war.

However, as resources and people become more widely available, there are some signs that this 'frontier survival' phase is giving way to a more orderly and balanced spectrum of activities, and human factors is being treated in a more 'systemic' way.

GROUP 1: Application areas at the equipment level: The man-machine interface

The key characteristic in this group of papers is that they assume a willing and fairly undifferentiated population of users, sometimes the entire general public (as in Hoag and Adams' study of a public transport system), or more usually the whole of a particular occupational group (Ward's housewives, Rolfe's pilots, etc.). They want to do the activity, and therefore the problem is how to design the equipment so that they can do it easily, efficiently, safely and usually with only the minimum of disturbance of their normal work-patterns. A pilot may be delighted to have a better arrangement of his knobs and dials, but he doesn't want a totally new way of flying the 'plane.*

Within this broad category, we have isolated four main levels of design problem:

Application 1   Simple interfaces involving one person

Papers: 4.2   Ward
        4.1   McCormick
        5.1   Vandenberg

From the research point of view, both conceptually and in practical experimental terms, the simplest 'human factors' situation is that of one person interacting with one object — someone boiling a kettle, someone steering a car, someone operating a machine tool, someone reading a printed sheet or someone working at a desk. Such a situation is easy to set up in the laboratory, and easy to consider, e.g. as a single well defined control loop. In actual application areas, however, this research simplicity can be quite misleading, because it is only in rather limited situations that such an interaction happens in isolation. It is more likely to be part of a whole complex of actions and subject to a host of attitudinal, social and motivational factors; these may radically upset the validity of recommendations made in isolation.

For further reading suggestions relevant to this section, see the human factors handbook listed in Section 1.3.

Application 2   Complex work-stations and work areas

Papers: 6.1   Shackel and Klein
        5.4   Rolfe

Some of the more extreme over-simplifications of the narrow one-person one-object approach can be avoided if the system boundary is widened to include the more significant parts of the environment. Rather than considering one man and one lever, you consider him sitting at a complete work-station, possibly co-operating with someone else; or you can consider a complex of equipment, with groups of people passing round it. This situation is much more realistic (although still missing many potentially important personal variables). However, it is more difficult to handle experimentally, so analytic techniques still tend to involve drastic simplification, and often rely on skilled human judgements in interviews, descriptions based on experience, and so on.

Application 3   Human factors surveys across complete systems

Papers: 5.2   Hoag and Adams
        7.2   Meister

These papers are concerned with the contribution human factors can make not just in one subsystem, but across the complete spectrum of problems raised by a single large system. The problems taken individually are not very much different from those described in the earlier papers in this selection; the difference lies in the attempt to present them on a system-wide basis.

Meister's paper is presented in more generalized and systemic terms than Hoag and Adam's paper, and aims to show the types and sources of human errors at each possible stage in the development of a typical project. If you compare the two papers, you can see how this approach enables Meister to point out several major classes of errors that Hoag and Adams do not mention, although Hoag and Adams can be much more specific.

GROUP 2: Widening the boundary to include the people within the operational subsystem: The person-operation interface

Most conventional ergonomics is concerned with the question 'Can people use this device?' rather than 'Will they knowingly misuse it?', or 'Will they use it at all?'. Conventional 'knobs and dials' experiments of the kind considered so far can tell you quite a bit about the first question, a limited amount about the second and very little about the third.

The papers in this section take it largely for granted that the basic equipment design is reasonably adequate. They concern themselves more with the motions and emotions on the human side of the interface, and the way these relate to the broad operational context of the job.

Application 4   Accident prevention and analysis

Paper: 5.3 Davis

The idea that some people are more 'accident prone' than others, regardless of the hardware, has been under discussion for at least fifty years. Contrary to popular belief, there is still a great deal of scope for scientific debate as to what the term means, and whether its existence really can be demonstrated.* However, as Davis's paper implies, it does seem fairly clear that many of us do go through periods when we are accident prone, because of particular stresses, changes of life-style, medical and psychiatric conditions, etc.

Application 5   Design of jobs and organizations

Papers: 5.5 Swain
         6.2 Kogan and Balle

Swain's paper is concerned with the relation between the design of jobs and equipment on the one hand, and job satisfaction on the other: the problem of 'Will you...?' rather than 'Can you...?' He looks at the dehumanizing effect of automation, and examines various ways that have been tried to get round it, such as persuasion and propaganda, better pay, total automation, deliberate selection of low ability personnel and various job-enrichment techniques.† Kogan and Balle take a much more management centred view, considering how the job fits into the wider organization rather than how the person fits into the job.

GROUP 3: Widening the application area boundary still further: Policy making beyond the operational subsystem: The society-technology interface

All the application areas considered so far have been concerned with designing the working subsystems of organizations, that is, the people/machine and people/people combinations that form the day-to-day working basis of most productive organizations. The activities of these are constrained by the guiding policies of the organizations to which they belong, and, at an even wider level still, they are subject to constraints such as the code of conduct of professional bodies, and ultimately national legislation. The problem here is no longer 'How should I design this machine?' or 'How should I administer this group of processes?', but

---

*See: Shaw, L., and Sichel, H. S. (1971) Accident Proneness, *Pergammon Press*.
†*For wider reading in this area, see: Davis, L. E., and Taylor, J. C. (eds.) (1972)* Design of Jobs, Penguin.

SELECTIVE GUIDES TO THE READINGS

'What constraints or prohibitions should be put on the design of all such equipment or organizational structures?' At its upper limit this includes major government policy decisions as to the future development of complete areas of technology or commerce.

Application 6   Providing information about human behaviour as an input for policy-makers

Papers: 4.2   Ward
         5.7   Starr
         6.3   Galbraith

Ward's study was carried out to provide evidence on which to base a British Standard. This accounts for the careful specifying of population ranges, and the comparative data on current industrial practice and on other related standards. British Standards are not, of course, legally binding unless specified in contracts, or particular pieces of legislation, but they are often the basis for industry-wide agreements and for professional codes of good practice.

Starr's study is concerned with the very fundamental question of what levels of risk society considers 'acceptable' under different conditions. This has become important in deciding whether or not to permit new technologies to proceed (e.g. the debates over the generation of electricity from nuclear energy, or over whether or not to make the wearing of seatbelts in cars obligatory).

Galbraith's paper relates directly to major issues such as the control of economic growth, and the control of larger corporations.

Application 7   The relationship between human factors, systems science and technology policy assessment

Paper: 7.3   Porter

Porter's paper has been included to end both this selection and the whole book because it explores the potential links between human factors and other related areas, such as, systems science and technology policy assessment, that extend the human factors concern with man-machine interfaces to the much wider society-technology interface. Notice that Porter's description is made from an American point of view, Britain is some way behind the USA in these areas. He uses the term 'systems science' in the narrow sense in which people such as computer systems analysts use it, rather than in the wider sense used elsewhere in this book.

SELECTIVE GUIDES TO THE READINGS

Assessing the practical value of human factors recommendations

The main value of any applied subject is that it is useful in some practical sense (although there may be other incidental benefits). This selection of papers is intended to suggest some of the criteria for evaluating the usefulness of human factors, and some of the major limits to its usefulness.

Table 4 (p. 13) shows the six major characteristics that we are looking at, and the papers we will be using to illustrate each.

One aspect of the usefulness of the subject not included in Table 4 is the range of problem areas to which human factors studies are relevant. This is covered in the previous section.

Cost-benefit accounting for individual proposals

The accountant's ideal in project evaluation would be to be able to represent it as a simple sum:

Project benefit:	£X
Project cost:	£Y
Net gain	£(X–Y)

The closing paragraphs of Shackel and Klein's paper (6.1) are the only place in this book where this possibility is discussed directly. Notice that even though the project was carried out on a commercial basis, and was aimed at improving the efficiency of a commercial process, the operating conditions changed too radically for a straight 'before and after' comparison to be possible. Many of the main benefits could not easily be costed in cash terms, these included improved customer relations, reduced stress on the controllers, and a reduced likelihood of major catastrophic breakdowns. Similar problems would prevent detailed cost-benefit analyses of most of the other studies in this collection. This is particularly true where the project is non-commercial, how can one attach a meaningful figure to the benefit of establishing a British Standard height for kitchen surfaces (Ward 4.2) or of improved passenger comfort on a suburban train system (Hoag and Adams 5.2)?

Though strict cost-benefit studies are virtually impossible it is usually feasible to list in general qualitative terms the *types* of effects that the project is likely to have, or has had, and attach crude order-of-magnitude estimates to them.

If we cannot cost out human factors projects directly in this way, we can at least look at the bounding requirements that can act to limit their usefulness; the five remaining characteristics are of this type.

The reliability of the basic evidence

Human behaviour is so incompletely understood, so complex and multiply caused, so easily misinterpreted, so prone to be altered simply by being observed, that the risk of observations being unreliable is considerable. An observation is useless unless we can be confident that it would have been reported in the same way if it had been made by someone else, or if it had been observed from a different point of view or by a different technique. Unsupported, unjustified, once-off personal opinions must always be suspect on these ground. Where formal data collection techniques are employed the reliability of the evidence obtained can usually be estimated as a numerical 'confidence level' using routine statistical techniques.*

Ward's paper (4.2) illustrates simple routine statistical testing for reliability, although because *Applied Ergonomics* (the journal the paper appeared in) specializes in summaries of projects, rather than full reports, the details are incomplete. For instance, we do not know how many subjects there were in each group, the exact design of the experiment, which statistical technique was used for estimating the reliability of the electromyography measure or anything at all about the statistical analyses of the anthropometry and centre of weight measures.

The details of statistical analysis may seem tedious, but without them reliability can only be checked by subjective judgement and general plausibility. For instance, Vandenberg (Paper 5.1) may well be sound, but there is no way of telling where the objective and reliable stops and the subjective and idiosyncratic begins.

The validity of assumptions made when building models from evidence

Reliable evidence is essential, but it is far from being the whole story. The conclusions drawn from it must also be *valid*. It is perfectly possible to have very reliable evidence that is used in a totally invalid way. If fifty people all independently report seeing a 'Martian flying saucer' we would have to accept this as *reliable* evidence that they saw some phenomenon suggesting a flying saucer. But a real Martian flying saucer is a highly improbable event. You can only *validly* conclude that that was what the reliable evidence implied once you have eliminated all other more likely pos-

---

*Many standard texts are available. One very straightforward text is Siegel, S. (1956) Non-parametric statistics for the Behavioural Sciences, McGraw-Hill. An excellent introduction for a more theoretical approach is: Hays, W. L. (1970) Statistics, Holt, Rinehart & Winston.

sibilities: hovercraft, illusions, weather balloons, and so on. In other words, *validity* is a measure of the confidence you can place in the logical jump from reliable observations to particular conceptual explanations. Validity is more difficult to demonstrate than reliability, and it can rarely be expressed in precise numerical form. It is established by systematically examining and rejecting all reasonably credible alternative explanations that you can think of, other than the one you are offering. The success of this depends greatly on the imagination, experience and enthusiasm of the experimenter. In routine cases, the explanation of unsurprising evidence tends to be in terms of well established and widely accepted models, using stock arguments devised by earlier experimenters to eliminate the more obvious artefacts and alternative explanations. The risks of this comfortable convention are obvious, and are particularly significant where stock conclusions are being drawn in novel settings (as in many applied problems).

The risks in allowing this type of convention to develop are well demonstrated in Smith and Lucaccini's review (4.3) showing how laboratory studies of vigilance were able to develop in what appeared to be a highly consistent pattern, which eventually turned out to represent only a rather limited artefact of the laboratory setting. Earlier researchers had failed to eliminate all the alternative and simpler (if less interesting) explanations.

In the vigilance studies, the unexplored assumptions were concealed and only emerged when a wide view was taken across a whole series of studies. But validity problems can also arise even when all assumptions appear to have been stated explicitly. Ward (4.2) is very careful to state the terms of reference under which she chose her subjects and designed her tasks. However, there is nevertheless a tendency for the reader to forget, or to fail to understand, the effects of these restrictions when generalizing from the findings. For instance, the subjects represented 95 per cent of the *range of heights* of British housewives, but this is *not* the same as saying that they represented 95 per cent of British housewives in terms of all relevant variables; if you included variables such as health (including old age, disabilities and pregnancy, as well as minor illnesses), body build apart from height, and the effects of varying levels of fatigue and time of day, the sample would appear to be very much more restrictive. As far as decisions about the British Standard are concerned, they would also need to take into consideration all the other relevant kitchen surface users — men, children, other nationalities, and so on.

When models are being built for practical purposes, strict validity is obviously important. But when they are built for theoretical purposes, validity can be interpreted more widely. For instance, Poulton's second model (4.4, Sections 3–7) aims for strict validity, while Merton (5.6) or Beer

(6.4) interpret it in a much more liberal way. The latter are trying to evoke future possibilities, rather than limiting themselves to collating existing evidence.

Can models be generalized to particular applied situations and how sensitive are they to local variations?

Applied situations are almost always complex, with many local idiosyncracies, ensuring that each situation is in some respects unique. Human factors recommendations must be sufficiently robust to apply in spite of these unexpected local differences. There are usually three types of variable for any given model:

1   Those central variables which are well understood and crucial to the model. Clearly, these must match the applied setting closely.

2   Those less well understood, but probably relevant, peripheral variables, which can be ignored but *only* if they can be controlled within certain limits.

3   Finally, there are the host of other variables whose behaviour and relevance is not understood at all, but which might have some effect, as yet unknown. Because they are not known and therefore cannot be measured, all you can do is to hope that the model is relatively insensitive to changes in them.

When a model developed in a laboratory setting, is applied in a realistic setting, it is usually the second and third types of variable that cause the problems; it is obviously better to have a model that has shown its ability to apply across a wide range of settings. The Smith and Lucaccini paper (4.3) discussed earlier shows important, but concealed, differences between the laboratory situation where the model was developed and the real situation where it was to be applied.

In this book, the most explicit treatment of the relation between a model and reality is Meister's discussion of the Data Store and THERP (4.5). This model is not a laboratory theory transferred to reality, but a custom-built one designed with a specific situation in mind. In this case, the modeller is well aware of the limitations of his model, so he tries to use his skill and experience to bridge the gap between them to an acceptable approximation.

Shackel and Klein (6.1) avoid this type of problem in three ways: firstly, by being involved closely with the entire design process, so that significant variables are unlikely to be overlooked; secondly, by the use of a realistic simulation; and thirdly, by gradual implementation of the new system, so that problems can be detected and corrected as they appear.

Are human factors recommendations in a suitable form and at a level of precision to be usable?

If a designer wants to know whether there are human factors grounds for preferring a 2 cm gap between two buttons to a 3 cm gap, it is no help for him to be told: 'Pedal operated buttons should be more widely separated than manually operated ones', no matter how reliable and valid that is. He needs the right facts in the right form.

Where the problem is straightforward and clearly specified, and where time and resources are available for a full-scale experiment, then, as Ward's study illustrates (4.2), it is usually possible to deliver a useable answer. Although, as Smith and Lucaccini's review shows (4.3), 'absolute truth' may take a little longer!

However, time, resources and a tidy problem are the exception, not the rule. If you hope to rely on the existing literature for highly specific data, the situation that Altman and his co-workers (Meister 4.5) found in 1962 (only 164 reports out of several thousand were usable for data store) is still largely true. Hoag and Adams were making quite similar complaints in 1975 (5.2). Meister (7.2) discusses a number of reasons why major gaps in the data are likely to continue. However, there is a great deal of information available (see manuals listed in the Introduction), but the potential field of application is so wide that unless you happen to be interested in a popular area, you may well not find exactly what you want. Skilled interpretation will be needed to adapt information for your particular problem (see Meister's description of the way in which the modelling problems of THERP are solved, Paper 4.5). As Smith and Lucaccini (4.3) found, field data are particularly scarce, so the extrapolation will normally be from laboratory data.

At the 'knobs and dials' level, many gaps will be filled as research accumulates, although there will always be some lag because the technological base is changing all the time.

However, at the 'social' end of the spectrum, 'look-up table' recommendations may never be possible. Swain (6.5) shows how the same ideas (on job enrichment) applied in different organizations can have results anywhere between marked success and marked failure, depending on how they are interpreted and on local variations in conditions. Such ideas are best thought of as aids for understanding, rather than routine solutions.

Acceptability, credibility and communicability

In purely informational terms, the four characteristics we have looked at so far are enough to describe the factual value of a recommendation. However, in solving applied problems it is usually not enough to be factually correct.

If successful implementation of some recommendation involves the consent of other people as decision-makers, or as people affected by the resulting changes, the recommendation and its sources must be 'acceptable'. This will depend partly on local features — relations between the groups involved, prior consultation and negotiation, relative importance of other factors, etc. (See Swain, 5.5.) But it will also depend on the human factors project itself — the prestige and credibility of the people involved, the plausibility of the evidence, the simplicity and clarity of the way it is presented, and the ethical (or even ideological) acceptability of the experimental procedures and the sources of the data. If the people involved don't know you, can't understand the project, don't like the way it is done, and don't have the resources to carry it out, your project is unlikely to be implemented successfully. For instance, projects such as Kogan and Balle's (6.2) are easily destroyed if the participants do not wish to cooperate, and Vandenberg (5.1) lists in detail the problems that can interfere with one particular type of project, in this case manual writing. One way to avoid this is to be involved at all stages from problem definition to final implementation; Shackel and Klein's study (6.1) illustrates this kind of close liaison.

The communication element of acceptability is illustrated by the advantages of the close similarity between THERP (4.5) and the models of the reliability engineers involved in other aspects of those projects. The superficial credibility provided by the common modelling approach can, of course, conceal fairly fundamental differences in the nature of the properties being modelled — people *don't* behave like machines, and it may not always help to pretend that they do.

Of course, acceptability may be less of a problem where the recommendations are a response to a formal request from a related specialist group, as in Ward's study (4.2) which arose from a request from the Research and Development Group of the (then) Ministry of Housing and Local Government. Wider range problems may still arise of course, for instance, we have no idea how the public will react to Ward's suggestions, if they are implemented.

Part 2
The Readings

3 THE HISTORICAL PERSPECTIVE

3.1 An Historical Review of the Development of Human Factors
S. C. Brown

Pre-Human Factors Background

There is a limit to how far back one can go and just how much detail one can cover in an introduction of this kind. The summary presented here is necessarily brief and should be understood as such.

For our purposes, the origins of human factors can be traced back to the late nineteenth century and the emergence of experimental psychology, the oldest form of psychology as we understand it today and principally an academic (i.e. non-applied) discipline. After a brief period studying the similarities between the behaviour of individuals, experimental psychologists began to turn increasingly to the examination of interpersonal differences. Galton in 1883 published the results of his explorations into individual differences in intellect and mental imagery, and this was followed in the 1890s by Cattell's investigations into differences in sensory and motor capacities, reaction times and problem-solving abilities.

Further contributions came from educational psychologists such as Ebbinghaus and Binet who devised the first tests of differences in intellectual ability, thus laying the foundations for the later growth of vocational or personnel psychology.

While experimental psychology was developing as an academic discipline, two distinct engineering approaches to the study of human behaviour were evolving in the USA. The concept of motion study was pioneered by Frank and Lilian Gilbreth during the late nineteenth and early twentieth century as a technique for improving worker efficiency. They believed that any task could be broken down into individual motions or manipulations, and that it was the nature of these individual motions which determined overall efficiency. Frederick Taylor, a contemporary of the Gilbreths, developed an alternative approach to improving worker efficiency called time study. Taylor believed that skilled behaviour should be defined more in terms of the sequencing of motions made by an operator and the speed at which they are carried out rather than in terms of the individual units of movement themselves. Taylor's technique consisted of rationalizing a particular task into its most economical sequence of actions and determining the maximum rate for these actions which would not overtire the operatives performing them. Taken together, time and motion studies proved to be a powerful management tool for determining realistic work schedules, setting basic pay scales and generally improving the efficiency of the production process.

The outbreak of the First World War provided a stimulus for these and other rudimentary human factors studies. First, the need to expand the armed services to many times their pre-war size meant that large numbers of civilians had to be conscripted and sorted according to their abilities. Large scale testing of the suitability of conscripts for a variety of roles such as pilots, observers, drivers, telegraphists, etc., was undertaken. During the period 1917–18 the Americans tested nearly two million recruits in batches of up to 500 a time—2,000 a day at separate intelligence testing centres.

Secondly, while the men went off to the front to fight, the women took their places in the factories. Here they had to learn skilled trades extremely rapidly. In addition, they were faced with workloads which far exceeded normal capacity due to the pressure for war materials to keep the services well supplied. In Britain the demand for munitions was so great that operatives volunteered to work long periods of overtime, sometimes extending their working week to 100 hours. The unexpected result of this patriotic effort was a fall in production due to a decline in the health and morale of workers which led to strikes, absenteeism and carelessness. To combat these problems the Department of Scientific and Industrial Research and the Medical Research Council (MRC) were asked to investigate the conditions of industrial workers in 1917, and shortly afterwards the Committee on the Health of Munitions Workers (later the Industrial Fatigue Research Board) was appointed to investigate the causes of fatigue among munitions workers. Under the direction of this committee research workers from the biological sciences were called in, for the first time, to investigate the behaviour of men at work in real industrial settings.

The inter-war years were, with one or two notable exceptions, a period of slow growth for human factors studies. However, two of the most important developments during that period were the foundation of the Cambridge Psychological Laboratory in 1921 and the so-called Hawthorne studies carried out during the late 1920s and early 1930s. The Cambridge Psychology Laboratory was a non-profit making organization which aimed at continuing the collaboration of researchers and practitioners begun during the war by making the results of physiological and psychological research available to industry. The Hawthorne experiments conducted by Mayo *et al,* at the Hawthorne works of the Western Electric Company were important because although they were intended initially to determine the effects of illumination levels on performance efficiency, the results of these studies suggested that the most important factor in determining productivity was psychological rather than physiological in nature. Before these findings could be followed up the depression of the 1930s caused widespread unemployment and this in turn resulted in a plentiful and cheap supply of labour for those industrialists who managed to remain in business.

Long queues of applicants for a handful of jobs meant that employers could dispense with elaborate personnel-selection techniques. After all they could easily find a replacement for a worker who failed to meet their expectations. Methods of improving worker efficiency such as time and motion study or improving working conditions were likewise unnecessary luxuries when labour cost virtually nothing and workers were so anxious to retain their jobs that they willingly made the maximum effort anyway.

However, the Second World War reversed this situation. As was the case in the previous war, the war effort entailed allocating large numbers of people quickly and efficiently to tasks to which they were most suited and training them as quickly as possible to perform those tasks. This brought about an immediate revival of interest in both personnel-selection and training methods and in the study of the effects of environmental factors on performance capabilities and limitations. In Britain there was an acute shortage of aircraft, and to counter this in 1942 the Production Efficiency Board of the Air Ministry was set up to advise on the best means for utilizing labour in the aircraft industry. One consequence of the work of this board was the introduction of time and motion study techniques and personnel training schemes on a wide scale throughout the industry. In the field of environmental psychology and physiology the Industrial Health Research Board, (formed in 1929 from the old Industrial Fatigue Research Board), was called in to advise on working hours, rest pauses and environmental conditions in the factories. Personnel Research Committees, one for each branch of the armed services, were set up by the Medical Research Council to handle the problems of selecting and training recruits.

The problems of the armed forces were exacerbated by the fact that the conditions under which personnel had to operate and the equipment they had to use imposed much greater stresses than were experienced during the First World War. Servicemen had to function equally efficiently in desert conditions, tropical jungles or on arctic convoys while at the same time they had to use equipment which had increased considerably in complexity, such as radar, sonar, high-altitude aircraft, sophisticated weaponry, and submarines which imposed much greater demands on operator abilities.

To overcome these difficulties a number of research establishments were set up under the MRC, such as the Climatic and Working Efficiency Research Unit at Oxford, the Applied Psychology Unit (APU) at Cambridge and the Division of Human Physiology at Hampstead, to investigate and advise on the complicated medical, physiological and psychological requirements of design. Human factors knowledge at the time was still fragmentary and limited in its practical applications. The existing knowledge of fatigue was derived almost entirely from physiological studies of muscular rather than mental work. With respect to skilled behaviour, a little was known about conditioning and simple reaction times. Studies of visual perception were concerned with recognition of flat geometric shapes under carefully controlled laboratory conditions, which were very different from the contours, shapes, distance and depth clues experienced by fighting men in the field. Learning and memory studies were still in a primitive condition dominated by measurements of subjects' abilities to memorize nonsense syllables and letters.

Attempting to apply this knowledge to the problem of pilot fatigue, researchers at the APU constructed what was probably the first crude cockpit simulator and observed the performance of experienced pilots working in it for long periods.

Attempts to explain their observations in terms of what was known about the deterioration of performance of isolated muscular or mental tasks such as lifting weights or responding to flashing lights were unsuccessful. The 'Cambridge cockpit' experimenters concluded that skilled behaviour is dependent to a large extent on the arrangement and interpretation of displays as well as controls. The interest in the perceptual elements of skilled behaviour represented an important departure from conventional work study methods hitherto dominated by the consideration of motor abilities. It also marked the beginning of a change of attitudes towards the design of machines for human use. It was henceforth recognized (in some circles at least) that it may be necessary to modify the characteristics of the machine to suit the capabilities and limitations of the operator in addition to selecting and training the operator to fit the machine.

This change in design orientation represents the birth of human factors as a distinct discipline in its own right. The event was formalized in 1949 in this country with the formation of the Ergonomics Research Society* by a group of anatomists, engineers, physiologists, psychologists and industrial medical officers.

In addition to the Ergonomics Society there are a great many organizations now involved in the study of human factors throughout the world, including an International Ergonomics Association. In Britain the principal among these tend to be government sponsored, such as the Medical Research Council's Applied Psychology Unit at Cambridge, the Ministry of Transport Road Research Laboratory and the Ministry of Technology Royal Aircraft Establishment at Farnborough. The armed services have their own human factors groups, the main ones being the RAF's Institute of

---

In 1976 the word 'research' was dropped from the Society's title, reflecting a change in emphasis in its role.

Aviation Medicine and the Armed Personnel Research Establishment, both of which are also at Farnborough. Unlike the USA, there is a scarcity of independent commercial human factors consultants in this country.

For the rest of this article, I will use the word 'ergonomics' to refer to the relatively narrow formal discipline I have described above, and reserve the term 'human factors' for the very much wider field that could in principle be covered in studying the human element in technological systems.

Classical Ergonomics

Since its recognizable beginnings at the end of the Second World War, ergonomics had undergone three major phases of activity.

The first of these is classical or 'interface' ergonomics. The interface referred to is the man/machine interface of controls and displays and the principle contribution of the classical ergonomist has been the improved design of dials and meters, control knob designs and panel layouts. However, the interest of the classical ergonomist extends beyond the simple input and output functions to the design of the complete workspace, taking in the layout of equipment, the design of chairs, tables, benches and machinery, and to a limited extent to the specification of optimum ambient working environments.

Much of the early work of classical ergonomists was applied to military equipment such as aircraft controls, missile guidance equipment and submarine interiors. More recently, however, the principles of this approach have been transferred to civilian contexts in the design of manufacturing plant equipment, televisions, washing machines, automobiles and furniture.

Information on human perceptual limitations relevant to the design of displays and controls is contributed principally by the psychologist, although the physiologist has a limited contribution to make here. Anthropometrists advise on the physical limits and ranges of people, such as the forces they are likely to be able to exert on controls, the optimum distances at which controls should be set and the most comfortable heights for working surfaces, seating, etc. The physiologist can be expected to advise on the specification of physical workloads. The psychologist and the physiologist together contribute knowledge concerning the problems of dangerous and tolerable levels of environmental stressors such as noise, light, dust, heat and vibration.

The source of the ergonomics data contributed by these various experts has been almost without exception laboratory based research. Notwithstanding the generally high quality of this research, the essentially academic bias of classical ergonomics has been criticized as being impractical by those most in need of it, the manufacturers. The trouble is that laboratory research almost by definition tends to be restricted to the study and manipulation of a restricted number of variables. It is difficult to make precise generalizations of the findings of such specific research to contexts which are more complex than the original experimental situation. Thus, when faced with a particular design problem the researcher will often be able only to advise on the 'best' solution according to his experimental results without being able to predict either the likely consequences of deviations from that or the way it would change in other conditions. Alternatively, he may set up a limited number of variations in the laboratory to compare solutions, but it can be very difficult to be sure that these variations are meaningful reflections of those encountered in real life. In other words, attempts to find answers to real problems using laboratory research methods quickly become lost in self-perpetuating series of experiments designed to validate and explicate previous experiments. Manufacturers who require readily applicable solutions to pressing practical problems understandably find this a frustrating activity.

In addition, classical ergonomists have faced a number of organizational difficulties. Large manufacturing corporations find it difficult to cope with the inter-disciplinary approach of the ergonomist, ranging as it does across traditional bureaucratic boundaries. Consequently, ergonomists have found themselves being relegated to low-level organizational positions from which they are called in to advise on human factors requirements only when the design of the equipment has been finalized, or even when it has actually been built. From this position ergonomic recommendations can often take the form of expensive modifications which are not welcomed by management and which are difficult to justify in terms of gain to the firm. Opposition to such recommendations frequently comes from the design engineers who perceive them as criticisms of their own work. Interdisciplinary rivalry and misunderstanding between ergonomists and engineers have been further fuelled by communication barriers in terms of the concepts and methods employed by each. Resentment too comes from the work force. Ergonomists have been accused by the unions of destroying job skills through practices of job simplification and machine modification involving automation. The accusation is readily understood, if you consider the early history of the subject, and the fact that even today it is still largely management sponsored and controlled. Union-sponsored research is still rare, although research for consumer organizations and for organizations concerned with safety and welfare is growing.

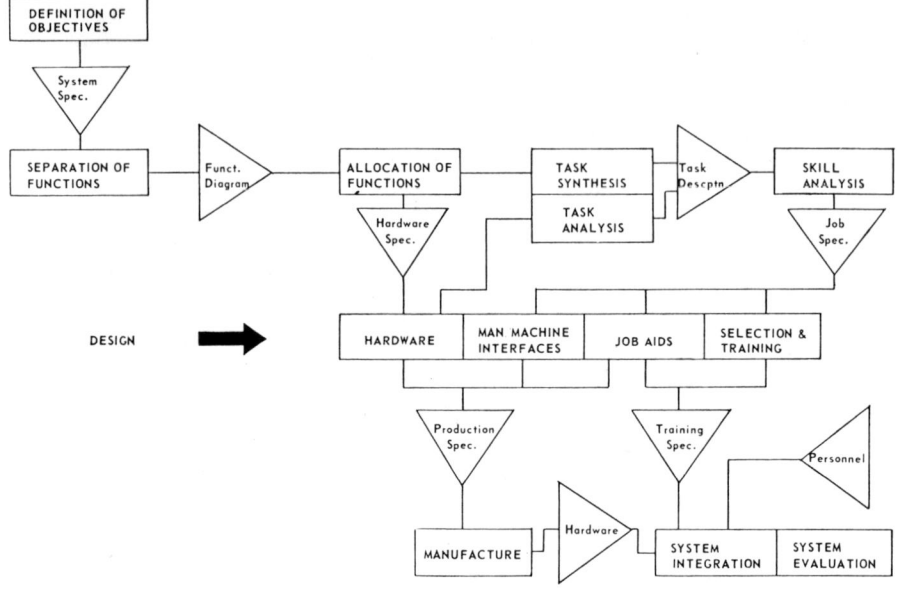

Figure 1 Decisions in the systems design approach (from Singleton 1967).

Systems ergonomics

In response to the growing dissatisfaction with classical ergonomics an alternative approach emerged from the USA in the 1950s during the 'Cold War'. Known as systems ergonomics, this approach is based on the fundamental principle that people and the machines they operate constitute one single system, and that since the design of either component must influence the performance of the other, the two must be developed concurrently and in conjunction with each other.

A typical systems ergonomics approach to man/machine systems design is illustrated in Figure 1 above. From this it can be seen that the approach is much broader in its scope than classical ergonomics. To begin with systems ergonomists collaborate with design engineers from the earliest stages of system development, establishing objectives for the proposed man/machine system, determining functions which are required if those objectives are to be achieved, and allocating these functions between the people and the mechanical components in the system on the basis of the ability and reliability of each. Following this, the systems ergonomist not only designs the man/machine interface and the workplace but develops the personnel subsystem. This is done through task analyses (analyses of *what* has to be done to achieve the specified function) and the preparation of job descriptions (descriptions of *how* the operator has to do the job). Both of these are developments of the time and motion study techniques pioneered by Taylor and the Gilbreths, respectively. Job aids in the form of instruction manuals, legend plates on equipment and increasingly automated visual display sequences are also the responsibility of the systems ergonomist as are selection and training procedures.

This approach has several important advantages over classical ergonomics. Close cooperation of the ergonomist and the engineer in the initial stages of system development ensures that wasteful duplication of effort does not occur and that costly human factors modifications are not necessary later. This cooperation also helps to overcome the interdisciplinary conflict brought about by the retrograde approach of classical ergonomists. Parallel development of personnel and hardware subsystems leads to reduced system development times, an important consideration in a competitive commercial world and one of prime importance to the original military sponsors of this approach. Inclusion of training, selection, job aid and man/machine interface design in a single process, called the personnel subsystem, helps to integrate such disparate elements as work study, anthropometrics and vocational psychology into a single systemic framework.

Unfortunately, this approach has failed to live up to its early promise. Difficulties encountered included the lack of sound criteria for allocating functions to people and machines; indeed it has even been argued that a one-to-one analogy between human beings and mechanical devices cannot be drawn (Jordan 1963). Systematic methods for conducting task analyses have similarly proven elusive because of the complexity, variability and subtlety of most human tasks. Moreover, the systems approach, embracing as it does all aspects of system development, could be regarded by some professional groups as a threat to their integrity. Thus where, for instance, personnel management subsystems are already in existence, the activities of the systems ergonomist could be viewed as an encroachment.

Error ergonomics

An alternative approach to systems ergonomics which has begun to emerge in recent years is error ergonomics, so called because of the prominence it gives to the study and explanation of human error in man/machine systems. Error ergonomists believe that system failures occur as a result of human error regardless of the type of system. Thus, even in a fully automated chemical plant, for example, breakdowns can be traced to human error at some stage of system development other than machine operation, such as installation, or repair, or design.

There are essentially two complementary approaches to error ergonomics. There is the 'zero defects' approach which assumes that human error is principally the result of inadequate motivation. The solution to problems of human error therefore lie in 'zero defects' programmes, i.e. campaigns of safety propaganda aimed at operatives with the intention of raising their performance levels. In contrast to this, adherents of the 'error data store' approach believe human error to be inevitable and ineradicable. Given this philosophy, solutions to human error problems must take the form of ways of designing systems in such a way as to minimize their occurrence and effects of errors. It is therefore necessary to be able to predict the incidence and consequences of human errors, in any given situation. To this end 'error data stores' have been compiled. These consist of data banks of error probabilities for a variety of tasks executed under various different types of conditions derived from research projects with a sound statistical basis. These probabilities can be combined in various ways to produce overall human reliability values for a variety of human activities.

Future developments

As we have shown, human factors studies have always been an essentially multi-disciplinary branch of the human sciences. Although the discipline of ergonomics was originally defined relatively narrowly, historically the range of contributing disciplines has tended to increase as the boundaries of the subject have been pushed back and redefined. In recent years, interest in questions of human motivation has added the social psychologist to the ergonomics team. More recently still, it has been asserted that ergonomists must explore still broader areas of human knowledge if ergonomics is to be relevant to society as a whole in the future. (See, for example, paper 7.3 by Porter in this Reader.) These areas might include more complex aspects of individual behaviour such as emotions, communication and personality; or they could include social interactions, organizational behaviour, political tactics and strategies, economic and geographic factors; or even value structures and religious beliefs.

The references given below, apart from those specifically mentioned in the text, are general historical works and they represent only a fraction of the material to which this history is indebted.

References

Cumming, G. and Corkindale, K. (1969) 'Human Factors in the United Kingdom', *Human Factors,* vol. 11, no. 1, pp. 75–80.

Edholm, O. G. and Murrel, K. F. (1973) *The Ergonomics Research Society: A History 1949–1970*, Ergonomics Society.

Jordan, N. (1963) 'Allocation of functions between man and machines in automated systems', *Journal of Applied Psychology*, Vol. 47, pp. 161–5.

Singleton, W. T. (1967) 'The systems prototype and his design problems'. *In* Singleton *et al.* (eds) (1967). *The Human Operator in Complex Systems*, Taylor & Francis, London.

Thompson, R. (1968) *The Pelican History of Psychology*, Penguin Books Ltd.

International Ergonomics Association (1976) *Ergonomics*, Vol. 19, no. 3. Papers to be presented at the International Ergonomics Association hosted by the Human Factors Society, University St., Maryland, USA 11–16 July 1976.

4 MECHANISTIC VIEWS OF THE INDIVIDUAL

4.1 Control Design

E. J. McCormick
Professor of Psychology, Purdue University

Types and uses of controls

Although many different types of controls have been used for various purposes, the primary types are included in the following table; these are related to the types of control functions for which they are generally used.

Type of control	Activation	Discrete setting	Quantitative setting	Continuous control	Data entry
Hand push button	X				
Foot push button	X				
Toggle switch	X	X			
Rotary selector switch		X			
Knob		X	X	X	
Thumbwheel		X	X	X	
Crank			X	X	
Handwheel			X	X	
Lever			X	X	
Pedal			X	X	
Keyboard					X

Some indication of possible uses of most of these controls is shown in Figure 1. But although a general type of control might be considered most appropriate for a given purpose, the specific utility of a particular variant of that type for some specific application is influenced by such features (if relevant) as ease of identification, location, size, control-display ratio, resistance, lag, backlash, rate of operation, and distance of movement. A discussion of some such characteristics will follow.

Acknowledgement

Reprinted from E. J. McCormick, *Human Factors Engineering*, 3rd edn. Copyright © 1970 by McGraw-Hill Inc. Used with permission of McGraw-Hill Book Co.

Identification of controls

Although the correct identification of controls is not really critical in some circumstances (as in operating a pinball machine), there are some operating circumstances in which their correct and rapid identification is of major consequence—even of life and death. For example, McFarland (1946) [pp. 605–608] cites cases and statistics relating to aircraft accidents that have been attributed to errors in identifying control devices. For example, confusion between landing gear and flap controls was reported to be the cause of over 400 Air Force accidents in a 22-month period during World War II. It is with these types of circumstances in mind that consideration of control identification becomes important.

The identification of controls is essentially a coding problem, the primary

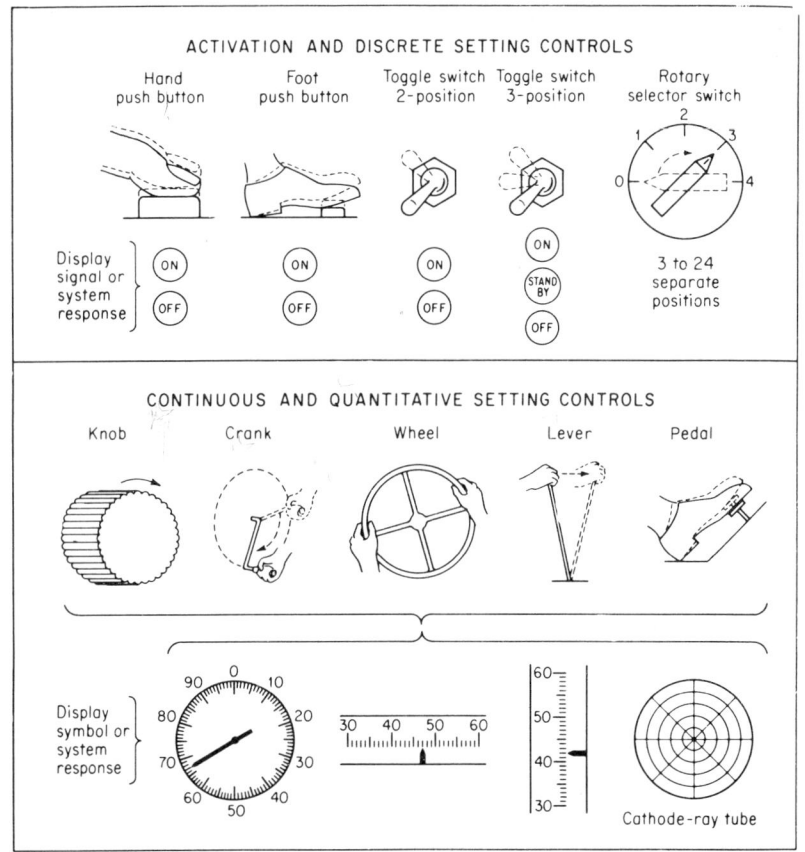

Figure 1   *Examples of some types of control devices and their uses.*

coding methods including shape, texture, size, location, operational methods, colour, and labels. The utility of these methods typically is evaluated by such criteria as the number of discriminable differences that people can make (such as the number of shapes they can identify), bits of information, accuracy of use, and speed of use.

Shape coding of controls

The primary consideration in shape coding of controls is the accuracy of identification of the controls. Two factors contribute to such identification, namely, the tactual discrimination of various shapes and the symbolic association of such shapes (if this is feasible).

Discrimination of shape-coded controls

The discrimination of shape-coded controls is essentially one of tactual sensitivity. The procedure generally used in the selection of controls that are not confused with each other is illustrated by the study by Jenkins (1947) in which he had 25 controls mounted on a rotating lazy Susan. Each subject, blind-folded, was presented with one knob which he touched for 1 sec. The experimenter then rotated the turntable to a predesignated point from which the subject went from knob to knob, feeling each in turn, until he found the one he thought was the one he had previously touched. It was then possible to determine which knobs were confused with which other knobs. While the statistical results will not be presented, it can be said that two sets of eight knobs were identified, such that the knobs within each group were rarely confused with each other. These two sets of knobs are shown in Figure 2.

Following essentially the same tack as that mentioned above, the United States Air Force has developed 15 knob designs which are not often

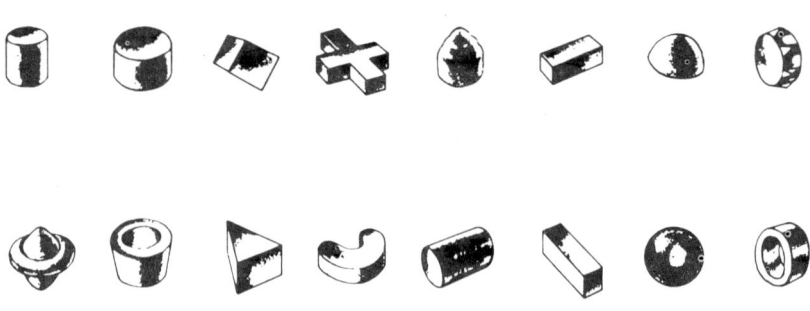

Figure 2 Two sets of knobs for levers that are distinguishable by touch alone. The shapes in each set are rarely confused with each other. (From Jenkins, 1947)

confused with each other. These designs are of three different types, each type being designed to serve a particular purpose (Hunt, 1953):

Class A: Multiple rotation. These knobs are for use on controls (1) which require twirling or spinning, (2) for which the adjustment range is one full turn or more, and (3) for which the knob position is not a critical item of information in the control operation.

Class B: Fractional rotation. These knobs are for use on controls (1) which do not require spinning or twirling, (2) for which the adjustment range usually is *less* than one full turn, and (3) for which the knob position is not a critical item of information in the control operation.

Class C: Detent positioning. These knobs are for use on discrete setting controls.

The 15 knobs in these three classes are shown in Figure 3.* In connection with sizes of knobs in these three classes, Hunt suggests that they be not more than 4 in. in their maximum dimension and not less than $\frac{1}{2}$ in. (except for class C, for which he suggests a $\frac{3}{4}$-in. minimum). In height they should not be less than $\frac{1}{2}$ in., but need not be more than 1 in.

Symbolic associations of controls

If in addition to being individually discriminable by touch, the controls have shapes that are associated with their use, the learning of their use usually is simplified. They do not then require the learning of a new code. In this connection, the United States Air Force has developed a series of 10 knobs that have been standardized for aircraft cockpits. These standard knob shapes, besides being distinguishable from each other by touch, include some that also have symbolic meaning. In Figure 4, which includes these shapes, it will be seen, for example, that the landing-gear knob is like a landing wheel, the flap control is shaped like a wing, and the fire-extinguishing control resembles the handle on some fire estinguishers.

Texture Coding of Controls

In addition to shape, control devices can be varied in their surface texture. This characteristic was studied (along with certain other variables) in a series of experiments with flat cylindrical knobs such as those shown in

---

*A few of these knobs were confused with each other, and such combinations should not be used together if identification is critical. These combinations were ab, co, cd#, do#, eg#, kp, ln, lo, np and op. Those with a number sign (#) were confused only with gloves on and were not confused without gloves.

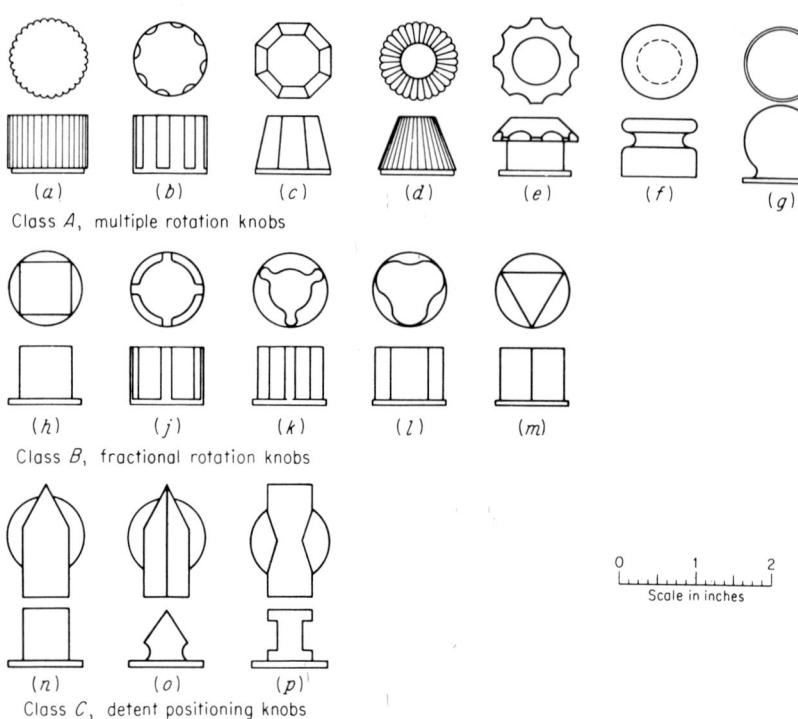

Figure 3 Knob designs of three classes that are seldom confused by touch. *(Adapted from Hunt, 1953)*

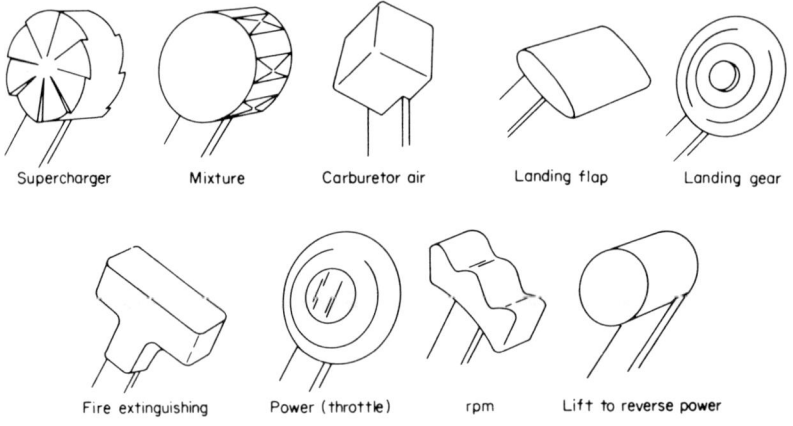

Figure 4 Standardized shape-coded knobs for United States Air Force aircraft. A number of these have symbolic associations with their functions, such as a wheel representing landing-gear control. (Personnel subsystems, 1969.)

Figure 5 (Bradley, 1967). In one phase of the study, knobs of this type of 2-in. diameter were used, and subjects were presented with individual knobs through a curtained aperture and were asked to identify the particular

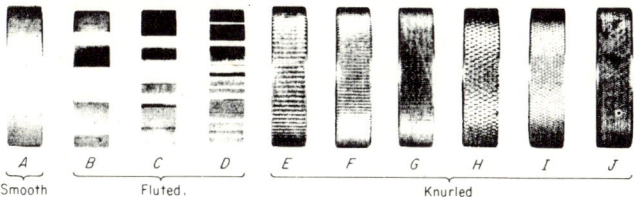

Figure 5 Illustration of some of the knob designs used in study of tactual discrimination of surface textures. Smooth: A; fluted: B (6 troughs), C (9), D (18); and knurled: E (full rectangular), F (half rectangular), G (quarter rectangular), H (full diamond), and J (quarter diamond). (From Bradley, 1967.)

design they felt. The results are shown as a 'confusion matrix' in Figure 6, this indicating the number of times each knob was identified correctly and incorrectly (and in such cases the knobs with which the one was confused).

		Smooth	Fluted			Knurled					
		A	B	C	D	E	F	G	H	I	J
	A	45									
	B		42	6							
	C		3	33	1						
	D			6	44						
	E					29	11	1	4	1	
	F					8	8	7	8	5	6
	G					1	7	27		15	9
	H					6	7		27	1	2
	I					1	7	6	5	2	18
	J						5	4	1	21	10

Column header: Knob that was felt
Row header: Response (the knob that the "felt" knob was "identified" as)

Figure 6 'Confusion matrix', showing results of study in which knobs with different surface textures were presented through an aperture to 45 subjects. (The knobs are those shown in Figure 5.) The numbers in any given column are the numbers of times each knob was 'identified' as the one that was felt by hand, when the one actually felt was the one identified at the top of the column. The numbers of correct identifications (out of 45) are those in the cells along the diagonal. (Adapted from Bradley, 1967.)

The smooth knob was not confused with any other, and vice versa; the three fluted designs were confused with each other, but not with other types; and the knurled designs were confused with each other, but not with other designs. It should be added that with gloved hands and with smaller-sized knobs (in a later phase of the study) there was some cross-confusion among classes, but this was generally minimal. The investigator proposes that three surface characteristics can thus be used with reasonably accurate discrimination, namely, smooth, fluted, and knurled.

Size Coding of Controls

Size coding of controls is not as useful for coding purposes as shape, but there may be some instances where it is appropriate. When such coding is used, the different sizes used should of course be such that they are discriminable one from the others. Part of the study by Bradley reported above dealt with the discriminability of cylindrical knobs of varying diameters and thickness. It was found that knobs that differ by $\frac{1}{2}$ in. in diameter and by $\frac{3}{8}$ in. in thickness can be identified by touch very accurately, but that smaller differences between them sometimes result in confusion of knobs with each other. Incidentally, Bradley proposes that a combination of three surface textures (smooth, fluted, and knurled), three diameters ($\frac{3}{4}$, $1\frac{1}{4}$, and $1\frac{3}{4}$ in.), and two thicknesses ($\frac{3}{8}$ and $\frac{3}{4}$ in.) could be used in all combinations to provide 18 tactually identifiable knobs.

Aside from the use of size coding for individual control devices, size coding is part and parcel of ganged control knobs, where two or more knobs are mounted on concentric shafts with various sizes of knobs superimposed on each other like the layers of a wedding cake. When this type of design is dictated by engineering considerations, the differences in the sizes of superimposed knobs need to be great enough to make them clearly distinguishable, as illustrated in Figure 7 (Bradley and Stump, 1955).

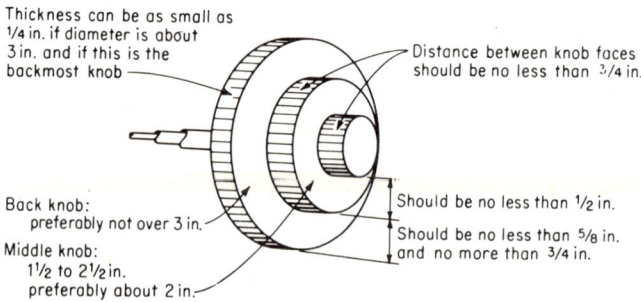

Figure 7 Dimensions of concentrically mounted knobs that are desirable in order to allow human beings to differentiate knobs by touch. (Adapted from Bradley and Stump, 1955.)

Location Coding of Controls

Whenever we shift our foot from the accelerator to the brake, feel for the light switch at night, or grasp for a machine control that we cannot see, we are responding to *location coding*. But if there are several similar controls from which to choose, the selection of the correct one may be difficult unless they are far enough apart that our kinesthetic sense makes it possible for us to discriminate. Some indications about this come from a study by Fitts and Crannell as reported by Hunt (1953). In this study blindfolded subjects were asked to reach for designated toggle switches on vertical and horizontal panels, the switches being separated by 1 in. The major results are summarized in Figure 8, which shows the percentage of reaches that were in

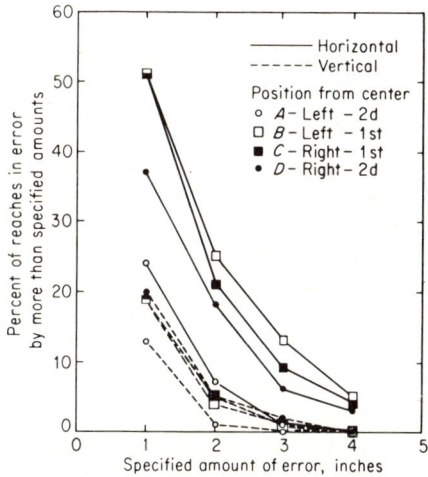

Figure 8 Accuracy of blind reaching to toggle switches (nine in a row on switch box) with switch box positioned horizontally and vertically at four locations. (Adapted from Fitts and Crannell, as presented by Hunt, 1953.)

error by specified amounts when the panels were in horizontal and vertical positions, left and right from centre. The curves indicate quite clearly that accuracy was greatest when the toggle switches were arranged vertically. For the vertically arranged locations probably a 5-in. difference would be desirable for reasonably accurate positioning. Since errors drop quite low at about $2\frac{1}{2}$ in. and since these errors are in both directions from the control, the central range of errors is double this distance, or 5 in. For horizontally arranged controls there should be 8 in. or more between them if they are to be recognized by location.

Operational Method of Coding Controls

In the operational method of coding controls, each control has its own unique method for its operation. For example, one control might be of a push-pull variety, and another of a rotary variety. Each can be activated *only* by the movement that is unique to it. It is quite apparent that this scheme would be inappropriate if there were any premium on time in operating a control device and where operating errors are of considerable importance. When such a method is used, it is desirable that compatibility relationships be utilized, if feasible. By and large, this method of coding should be avoided except in those individual circumstances in which it seems to be uniquely appropriate.

Discussion of Coding Methods

In the use of codes for identification of controls, two or more code systems can be used in combination. Actually, combinations can be used in two ways. In the first place, *unique combinations* of two or more codes can be used to identify separate control devices, such as the various combinations of texture, diameter, and thickness mentioned before (Bradley, 1967). And, in the second place, there can be completely *redundant codes*, such as identifying each control by a distinct shape *and* by a distinct colour. Such a scheme probably would be particularly useful when accurate identification is especially critical. In discussing codes, we should be remiss if we failed to make a plug for standardization in the case of corresponding controls that are used in various models of the same type of equipment, such as automobiles and tractors. When individuals are likely to transfer from one situation to another of the same general type, the same system of coding should be used if at all possible. Otherwise, it is probable that marked 'habit interference' will result (Weitz, 1947) and that people will revert to their previously learned modes of response. In connection with the use of individual control coding methods, a few general principles can be set forth, as evolving from both research and experience. Some of these are given below, with the usual words of caution about the usual exceptions to general principles:

1 Shape and texture

A Desirable features. (1) Useful where illumination is low or where device may be identified and operated by feel, without use of vision; (2) can supplement visual identification; (3) useful in standardizing controls for identification purposes.

B Undesirable features. (1) Limitation in number of controls that can be identified (fewer for texture than for shape); (2) use of gloves reduces human discrimination.

2 Location

A   Desirable features. (1) Same advantages as for shape and texture.
B   Undesirable features. (1) Limitation in number of controls that can be identified; (2) may increase space requirements; (3) identification may not be as certain (may be desirable to combine with other coding scheme).

3 Colour

A   Desirable features. (1) Useful for visual identification; (2) useful for standardizing controls for identification purposes; (3) moderate number of coding categories possible.
B   Undesirable features. (1) Must be viewed directly (but can be combined with some other coding method, such as shape); (2) cannot be used under poor illumination; (3) requires people who have adequate colour vision.

4 Labels

A   Desirable features. (1) Large number can be identified; (2) does not require much learning.
B   Undesirable features. (1) Must be viewed directly; (2) cannot be used under poor illumination; (3) may take additional space.

5 Operational method

A   Desirable features. (1) usually cannot be used incorrectly (control usually is operable in only one way); (2) can capitalize on compatible relationships (but not necessarily).
B   Undesirable features. (1) Must be tried before knowing if correct control has been selected; (2) specific design might have to incorporate incompatible relationships.

References

Bradley, J. V. (1967) Tactual coding of cylindrical knobs. *Human Factors* Vol. 9, No. 5, pp. 483–496.

Bradley, J. V. and Stump, N. E. (1955) *Minimum allowable dimensions for controls mounted on concentric shafts,* USAF. WADC. TR55–355, Dec. 1955.

Hunt, D. P. (1953) *The Coding of Aircraft Controls,* USAF, WADC, TR53–221, Aug. 1953.

Jenkins, W. O. (1947) The tactual discrimination of shape for coding aircraft-type controls. *In* Fitts, P. M. (ed.) *Psychological Research on Equipment Design.* Army Air Force, Aviation Psychology Program, Research Report 19.

McFarland, R. A. (1946) *Human Factors in Air Transport Design,* McGraw-Hill.

Personnel Subsystems, (1969) USAF, WADC Design Handbook, Series 1–0, general, AFSC DH 1–3 1st ed., Jan. 1, 1969, Headquarters AFSC.

Weitz, J. (1947) The coding of airplane control knobs. *In* Fitts, P. M. (ed.) *Psychological Research on Equipment Design.* Army Air Force, Aviation Psychology Program Research Report 19.

4.2 Ergonomic techniques in the determination of optimum work surface heights

Joan S. Ward
Institute for Consumer Ergonomics and Department of Ergonomics and Cybernetics, Loughborough University of Technology

In a previous issue of *Applied Ergonomics* (Ward, 1970) it was stated that... 'investigations to determine the amount of physiological effort (particularly that of muscle activity by techniques such as electromyography) are needed in order to ensure that the housewife performs her tasks with the minimum of unnecessary effort and maximum satisfaction...'

Such an investigation is described here, in which several ergonomics techniques were employed to solve a practical problem. The problem arose when the British Standards Institution publication BS 3705:1964, 'Recommendations for provision of space for domestic kitchen equipment', was under scrutiny with a view to metrication. This suggested the need to modify the existing dimensions for such equipment, and led to a request from the Research and Development Group of the Ministry of Housing and Local Government (now the Department of the Environment) for ergonomics data to guide any such modification.

As time did not permit the examination of every item of domestic kitchen equipment, preliminary studies were undertaken, (a) to determine the most important items of such equipment, from the point of view of the physiological cost to the housewife of working at them, and (b) to assess the validity of data upon which current recommendations for those items had been based.

Assessment of importance of items of equipment

This study involved sequential activity sampling of a number of housewives, by which observations of the tasks they performed and the related

---

Acknowledgement

Reprinted, by permission of the author, from J. S. Ward, 'Ergonomic techniques in the determination of optimum work surface heights' in *Applied Ergonomics*, Vol. 2, No. 3, 1971, IPC Science and Technology Press.

workstations in the kitchen were recorded at 15 second intervals throughout two complete days, one during the week, the other over a week-end. The mean percentage times spent at the principal workstations were calculated to be as set out in Table 1.

From this table it can be seen that, either during the week or at weekends, the greatest amount of time spent while in the kitchen is at (a) the sink and drainer, (b) the work top and/or table, (c) the cooker. The entry 'Others', also a large time-consumer, was an amalgam of activities that were observed to occur in the kitchen but which could have been pursued elsewhere in the home, ie reading the newspaper, drinking tea, attending to children.

Table 1 Comparison of mean percentage time spent at different workstations in the kitchen

	Weekday			Weekend		
	Hrs	% 24	% A	Hrs	% 24	% A
'A' Mean time awake	15·27	63·6		14·27	59·5	
'B' Mean time in kitchen	3·57	14·9	23·4	3·24	13·5	22·7
Workstations		Mins	% B		Mins	% B
1 Sink and drainer		73·5	34·4		66·5	34·2
2 Worktop*		30·4	14·2		27·6	14·2
3 Table*		31·6	14·8		27·4	14·1
4 Cooker		26·9	12·6		28·6	14·7
5 Pantry		6·2	2·9		6·6	3·4
6 Cupboards		4·1	1·9		6·2	3·2
7 Refrigerator		3·6	1·7		2·7	1·4
8 'Others'		27·8	13·0		12·8	6·6
9 Movements Entry/Exits			13·8			10·9

*Totals for both Table and Worktop usage were included although these did not occur in every study undertaken.
Overall totals will not, therefore, balance with mean time spent in the kitchen.

Current recommendations

Table 2 summarizes the main recommendations in the United Kingdom and some other countries for standing sink and work surface heights. They are not exhaustive, as they omit both references earlier than 1943 and those in which the recommended values coincide with individual values, or fall within the range of values, already in the Table.

No UK references specifically recommending heights for the cooker hob were found, presumably because this height was deemed to be set by the height recommended for the worktop. However, a survey of hob heights of some 110 gas, solid fuel and electric cookers commercially available elicited values ranging between 30 and 37 inches, (762–940 mm).

The total range of recommended heights for the three principal workstations (sink, worktop, cooker) at which the housewife spends the major portion of her time in the kitchen is thus between 30 and 39 inches (762–990 mm).

It was clear from examination of the studies enumerated in Table 2 (and others) that the recommended heights had been based largely on data obtained by two methods:

1 Anthropometry – relating static body dimensions to equipment and, in most cases, proposing an average or mean value as the optimum solution.

2 Subjective preferences and/or fitting trials – without due care being taken (as mentioned in an earlier paper, Ward 1970, and discussed more fully by Kirk and Ridgway 1971), to ensure that such methods were carefully adminstered and/or controlled.

However, it cannot be denied that tasks performed at kitchen workstations involve not only the dimensional relationship between equipment and user and the assessment by the user of the suitability of this relationship, but also a physiological effort of a greater or lesser degree in performing such tasks. It is known (Ward, 1970) that such tasks do not demand the expenditure of more than 1 or 2 calories (4–8 joules) in those muscles concerned with maintaining the body in various postures and those concerned with limb movements relevant to the task. Electromyographic techniques appeared therefore to be most appropriate to determine the type of energy expenditure.

Main investigation

Apparatus

Having determined that the range of heights for the three primary workstations in the kitchen (i.e. sink, worktop, cooker hob) to be investigated would be 30 to 39 inches (762–990 mm), special workstations were constructed (Fig. 1), capable of this range of adjustment, by placing them upon dental chair base units.

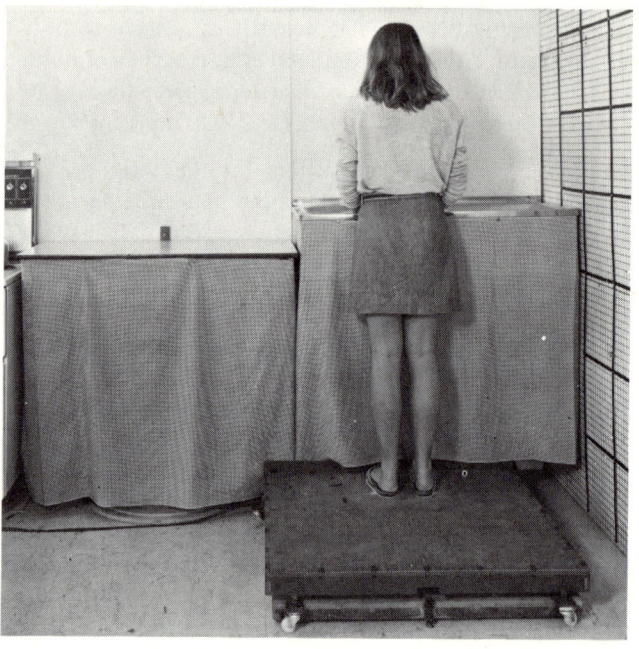

Figure 1 Specially-constructed workstations capable of height adjustment.

Subjects

To ensure that results would be applicable to 95% of adult British women (Fig. 2) three groups of subjects were selected:

(a) the shortest, representing the 2.5th percentile of the stature range – stature 59 inches (1499 mm) ± 1 inch (25 mm)

(b) the 'mean', representing the 50th percentile of the stature range – 64 inches (1626 mm) ± 1 inch (25 mm)

(c) the tallest, representing the 97.5th percentile stature range – stature 68.5 inches (1740 mm) ± 1 inch (25 mm).

DETERMINATION OF WORK-SURFACE HEIGHTS

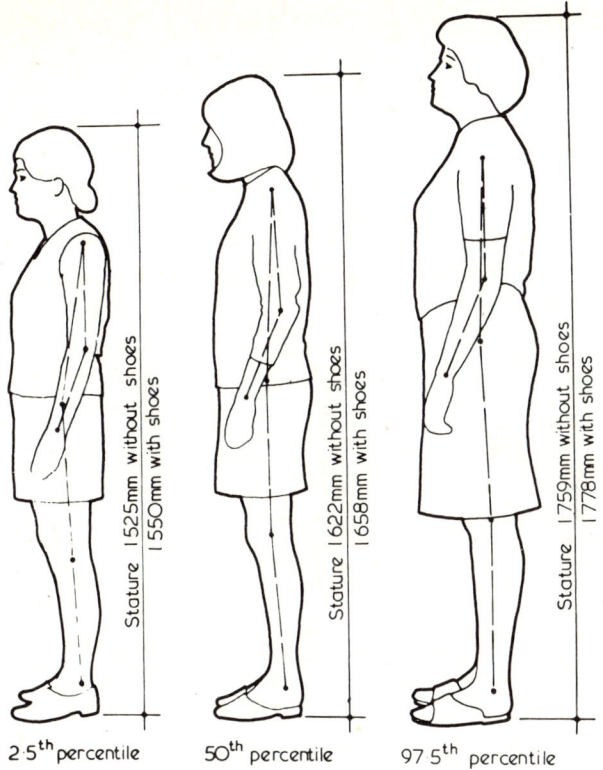

Figure 2 The three groups of subjects selected.

Tasks performed

The tasks undertaken during the investigation by each of the subjects were:

At the sink	(a)	washing up dirty crockery
	(b)	peeling potatoes
At the worktop	(a)	ironing (i.e. working above the surface)
	(b)	slicing potatoes (working on the surface)
At the cooker hob	(a)	frying rice (working on the surface
	(b)	boiling rice (working above the surface)

Each subject performed each of these tasks for two two-minute periods at each of the four standardized heights, viz., 30, 33, 36 and 39 inches (762, 838, 914 and 990 mm) at which each of the three workstations was randomly set.

Measuring methods

Three methods of assessing the physiological responses to the tasks and one method of assessing subjective preference were employed:

  1   Electromyography – surface electrodes were placed in pairs on the skin over those muscles previously determined to be predominant in maintaining standing body posture. These muscles were the soleus and gastrocnemius in the lower leg, the biceps femoris on the thigh (shown in Fig. 3) and the erectores spinae on the trunk.

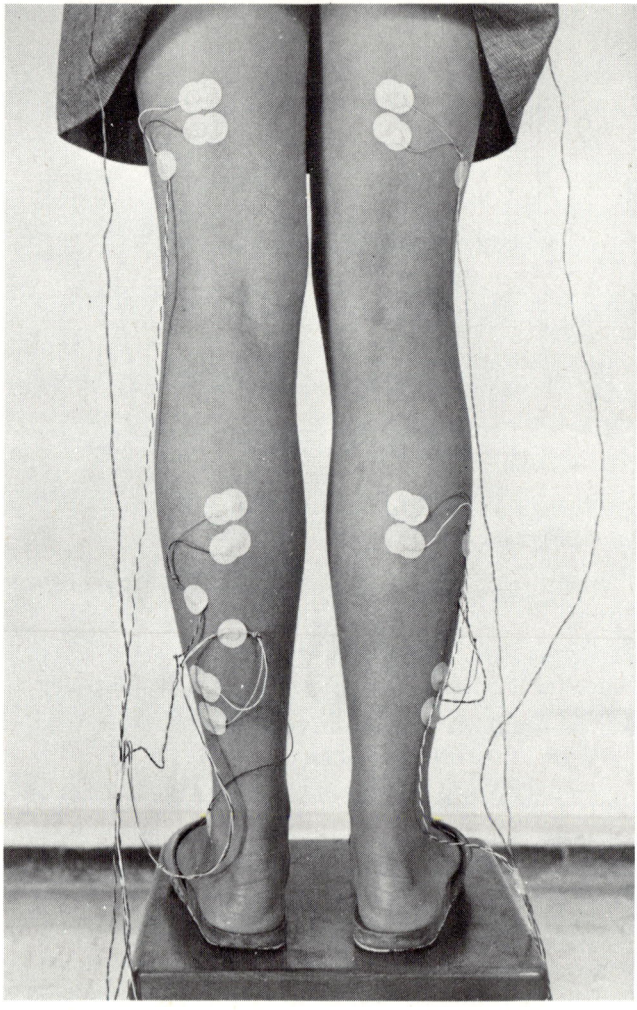

Figure 3 Electromyography – one method of assessing physiological responses to the tasks involved.

DETERMINATION OF WORK-SURFACE HEIGHTS

Electronic integration of changes in signal frequency and amplitude from the electrodes enabled fine discrimination between the degree of muscular activity consequent upon changes in posture while working at workstations set at different heights. Details of the technique are given in saville (1969).

2 Anthropometry – in addition to measurements of static body dimensions relevant to the tasks performed, i.e. stature and elbow height above floor, measurements were made from photographs of each subject against a scaled grid (Fig. 4) on the angular deviations of the main body segments as shown in the illustration. Information was thereby obtained on the postures adopted to achieve stability under varying working conditions.

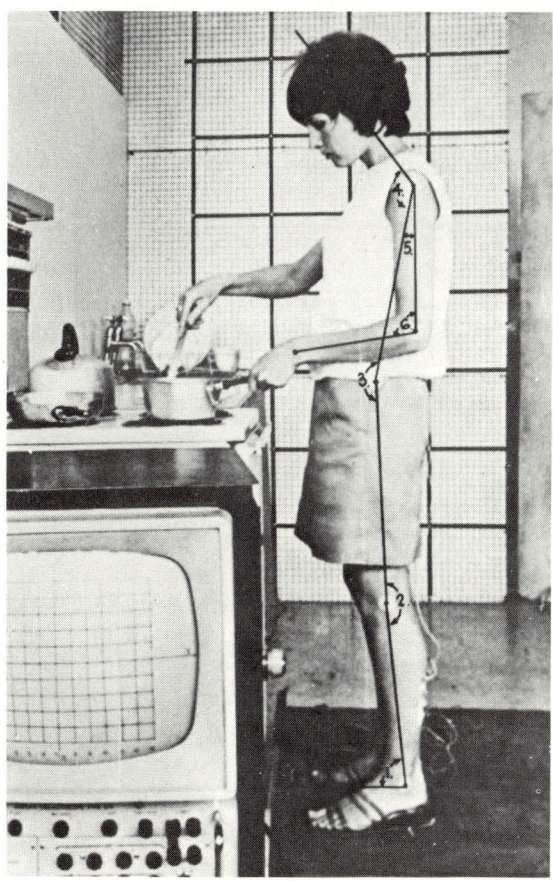

Figure 4 Subjects were photographed against a scaled grid to measure the angular deviations of the main body segments.

71

3   Centre of weight determination – the photographs taken of each subject also displayed the X and Y co-ordinations of the centre of weight recorded from a stability platform upon which subjects stood for the performance of the tasks. These co-ordinates were displayed as a single light source on an oscilloscope. The exact location of the centre of weight position relative to foot position was derived from grid lines superimposed both on the oscilloscope screen face and on the stability platform top. The location of centre of weight was determined in a pre-work comfortable stand-at-ease position, and also during the performance of the allotted tasks at each workstation at each of the four heights above the floor.

Methods two and three are, of course, not independent in interpretation, i.e. the causes of angular displacement of body segments were to be found in the shifts in centre of weight position on the stability platform, and vice versa, and both methods were of course related to the muscular activity as determined by method one. The use of all three methods, however, independently and simultaneously recorded, was intended to ensure that all the physiological parameters involved in this type of task were investigated.

4   Subjective preferences – subjects were required to asses the comfort and ease of each of the work situations (2 tasks at each of the 3 workstations at each of the 4 heights) at the completion of each task. The assessment was made on a 0 to 10 rating scale, 10 being the most comfortable, 0 a completely unacceptable height from the point of view of comfort.

Results

Electromyography

Although the degree and pattern of muscular activity varied slightly between subjects in each of the three percentile groups (2.5th, 50th and 97.5th) statistical analysis showed these variations not to be significant. The data are thus homogeneous within the three percentile groups. There were highly significant differences for percentile group electromyographic responses between conditions (i.e. heights), workstations and muscles. Overall muscle activity was highest at the sink and lowest at the cooker. Individual results elicited the interesting fact that there were highly significant differences in muscle activity between the right and left sides of the body, the dominant side contributing the greater activity.

Group responses in relation to conditions (i.e. heights) were:

2.5th percentile

At both sink and worktop, muscle activity descreased with each increase in work height. At the cooker, activity decreased similarly but only up to the 36 in. (914 mm) height; above that (i.e. 39 in., 990 mm) muscle activity increased.

50th and 97.5th percentile

At both worktop and cooker, muscle activity decreased with each increase in work height. At the sink, the muscle activity increased with each increase in height to a maximum at the 36 in. (914 mm) height; above that (i.e. 39 in., 990 mm) muscle activity decreased sharply to below the initial levels.

The effects of the different work heights upon the activity of the four muscle groups studied was that in all cases the greatest activity was recorded in the erectores spinae (trunk) followed by the biceps femoris (thigh), particularly at the lowest height (30 in., 762 mm). Activity in the gastrocnemius and soleus (lower leg) remained remarkably constant throughout.

Interpreting the electromyographic findings only, and postulating that a situation demanding least muscle activity to maintain posture is desirable, the following recommendations for optimum heights were made:-

	2·5th Percentile	50th Percentile	97·5th Percentile
At the sink			
Activity (a)	36 (914)	39 (990)	39 (990)
(b)	36 (914)	39 (990)	39 (990)
At the worktop			
Activity (a)	33 (838)	36 (914)	39 (990)
(b)	36 (914)	39 (990)	39 (990)
At the cooker			
Activity (a)	36 (914)	39 (990)	39 (990)
(b)	33 (838)	39 (990)	36 (914)

Anthropmetry

The angular displacement of body segments measured for each work height at the three workstations was calculated and compared with similar measurements taken on the subjects on the stand-at-ease position. Again, those postures most closely related to the stand-at-ease position were considered optimal. In summary, the optimum heights derived from the anthropometric data only are:-

		2·5th Percentile	50th Percentile	97·5th Percentile
At the sink				
	(a)	36 (914)	33, 36, 39 (838, 914, 990)	39 (990)
	(b)	36 (914)	39 (990)	39 (990)
At the worktop				
	(a)	36 (914)	39 (990)	39 (990)
	(b)	39 (990)	39 (990)	39 (990)
At the cooker				
	(a)	30, 33, 36, 39 (762, 838, 914, 990)	39 (990)	39 (990)
	(b)	39 (990)	30, 33, 39 (762, 838, 990)	36 (914)

Centre of weight

In the same manner as was done for the angular deviation data, the results of the centre of weight displacement determinations during tasks at the workstations were compared with those found in the previously determined

		2·5th Percentile	50th Percentile	97·5th Percentile
At the sink				
	(a)	36 (914)	39 (990)	39 (990)
	(b)	36 (914)	39 (990)	39 (990)
At the worktop				
	(a)	36 (914)	36 (914)	39 (990)
	(b)	36 (914)	36 (914)	39 (990)
At the cooker				
	(a)	33 (838)	39 (990)	39 (990)
	(b)	30 (762)	36, 39 (914, 990)	36 (914)

stand-at-ease position. Data were calculated to assess (a) the work height at which each subject's mean centre of weight position was nearest to that found in the stand-at-ease position, and (b) the work height at which the centre of weight recordings covered the smallest area on the stability platform. Again, the optimum heights on this basis were as shown opposite.

Subjective preferences

The individual preference scores (on the 0 – 10 rating scale) for each work condition were summarized in percentile groups, and optimum heights determined from a frequency analysis of the most preferred height for each condition. On this basis, recommended heights are:-

		2·5th Percentile	50th Percentile	97·5th Percentile
At the sink				
	(a)	36 (914)	39 (990)	39 (990)
	(b)	36 (914)	39 (990)	39 (990)
At the worktop				
	(a)	33 (838)	33 (838)	36 (914)
	(b)	36 (914)	36 (914)	39 (990)
At the cooker				
	(a)	33 (838)	36 (914)	39 (990)
	(b)	33 (838)	36, 39 (914, 990)	39 (990)

Analysis of variance of these data indicated a highly significant difference ($p<0.001$) between the preference of the three percentile groups for the particular heights preferred.

Integration of results

Optimum work heights assessed by the four independent methods were finally tabulated, each height being denoted numerically by 1, 2, 3 or 4 for 30 in, 33, 36, and 39 (762, 838, 914 and 990 mm) respectively, dependent upon the specific optimum indicated. This enabled statistical comparison (by product moment correlation coefficients) between the respective parameters.

In the four cases where the optimum height for any parameter was equally disposed between two or more heights, the optimum chosen was that which coincided with the majority choice of the other parameters. Table 3 gives the correlations between the heights derived from the four methods of assessment. All show a significant degree of correlation, although it will be noted that the assessment derived from anthropometric measures produced lower correlations with the remaining methods than the correlations between the electromyography, centre of weight and subjective preference. This is thought to be because the anthropometric measurement technique was too coarse to discriminate finely between the sometimes slight postural changes that were recorded electromyographically and on the stability platform.

Table 2 **Recommendations for standing working heights in the kitchen (in)**

Source	Sink	Worktop
'Work in the Home', Steidl & Bratton (1968)	32 – 33	$31\frac{1}{2} - 36\frac{1}{2}$
'Space in the Home', MOHLG Bulletin No. 6 (1965) (Reprinted)	36	34
'Provision of Space for Domestic Kitchen Equipment', BS 3705 (1964)	36	34
'Kitchen Storage & Working Heights', J. Long (1964) Thesis Birmingham School of Architecture	30 – 39	28 – 39
'Woningbouw', Bouwcentrum, Holland (1963)	$35\frac{1}{2} - 36\frac{1}{2}$	$35\frac{1}{2} - 37$
'Council of Scientific Management in the Home', (1961)	36	33
'Kok' Planering Inredning Swedish Consumer Institute (1960)	$35\frac{1}{2}$	$33\frac{1}{2} - 35\frac{1}{2}$
'The Kitchen', Joan Walley (1960)	general 36	
'Management in the Home', Gilbreth (1956)	38	34
'The Kitchen Book', R. R. Hawkins, USA, (1953)		32 – 36
Birmingham Anthropometric Survey (1951)		33
'Kitchen Fitments & Equipment', BS 1195 1948)	general 36	
Gas Industry (1945)	36	32 – 36
Ascot Limited (1943)	general 33 – 39	
Overall ranges:	30" – 39"	28" – 39"
Difference:	9"	11"

On the above basis thus described, the final recommendations given in Table 4 were drawn up. A number of general points may be made.

In general the measure of agreement between the different parameters was far less for the cooking tasks than for those at the sink or at the worktop, indicating that for the former, the optimum heights were less critical.

There appeared to be no difference in optimum work height for either of the two tasks performed at the sink. The recommended height of 42 in. (1066) mm) given in Table 4 for the 97·5th percentile group of women is derived from the projection of the values found for the other two percentile groups: supporting evidence is adducible from individual electromyographic and centre of weight assessments, which indicated that optimum levels were not actually achieved at the ceiling of 39 in. (990 mm).

There was no material difference in optimum heights for the two tasks carried out at the cooker. The difference in handle height between saucepan and frying pan was adjusted to by minor adjustments of shoulder, elbow and forearm.

Table 3 **Correlation of Parameters**

Parameters correlated	Correlation	Significance
Electromyography: Anthropometry	+0·515	$p<0·05$
Electromyography: Centre of weight	+0·828	$p<0·001$
Electromyography: Subjective preferences	+0·745	$p<0·001$
Anthropometry: Centre of weight	+0·471	$p<0·05$
Anthropometry: Subjective preference	+0·408	$p<0·05$
Centre of weight: Subjective preferences	+0·751	$p<0·001$

Application of results

The heights recommended directly from this study require modification in terms of conversion to their metric equivalents. The 3 inch increments used (on the basis of earlier findings and recommendations) do not equate readily to a metric equivalent or coincide with existing modular dimensions. In accordance with the 100 mm module (suitable for division into a 50 mm grid) the equivalents for the heights recommended are 850, 900, 1 000 and 1 050 mm. Table 5 illustrates the conversion, and gives the recommended heights in terms of ranges to suit 95% of the adult British female population.

The height of the rim of the sink is more critical than either of the other work stations: this was shown by the higher values of electromyographic activity exhibited by subjects at the sink tasks and by the subjective assessments. It would clearly therefore be of great advantage for the sink to be adjustable within the total range specified in Table 5. This is perfectly feasible technically: various ranges of fittings are marketed in Scandinavia which allow such adjustment, and methods of adjustment produced by manufacturers in this country could well be extended to cover the ranges given here. Flexible service connections need present no difficulty. If, however, it is not feasible, or not considered desirable, to provide flexible adjustment, it is suggested (as shown in Table 5) that adjustment should be provided to allow at least 4 heights within the total range of 900 – 1 050 mm.

The height of the worktop is less critical than that of the sink and, as indicated in Table 5, should follow a range of values some 3 in. (50 mm) lower than the range for the sink. The same is true of the cooker hob, which, for additional safety reasons, should be set by the height of the adjacent worktop.

It will not be thought surprising that these recommendations should come out so strongly in favour of flexibility and adjustability – common observation tells us that we come in different sizes and shapes and that therefore one solution to a dimensional problem is unlikely to suit everyone. The fallacy has been to suppose that a compromise (or 'average') answer will be equally

Table 4 **Final recommendations (in inches and mm)**

Workstation task	2·5th Percentile	50th Percentile	97·5th Percentile
Sink			
Wash up	36 (914)	39 (990)	42 (1066)
Peel potatoes	36 (914)	39 (990)	42 (1066)
Worktop			
Iron	33 – 36 (838–914)	36 (914)	39 (990)
Slice potatoes	36 (914)	36 – 39 (914–990)	39 (990)
Cooker			
Fry	33 (838)	39 (990)	39 (990)
Boil	33 (838)	36 – 39 (914–990)	39 (990)

satisfactory to all. This investigation illustrates the magnitude of this fallacy.

The practical application of the findings in the present study poses problems. For those whose business it is to design equipment or to install it in kitchens, suggestions for ways of obtaining the flexibility proved essential from this investigation are available (Sheppard and Mahaddie, 1970). The implementation of flexibility should be a challenge, particularly in this technological age, and not dismissed as impractical because it poses problems.

Table 5 **Recommended heights for 95% of adult, British female population**

Work station	Task	Optimum height for 95% range of female population (in)	Proposed metric equivalent mm	Comments
Sink	Wash up Peel Potatoes	36 – 42	900 – 1050	4 height range
Work-top	Iron Slice Potatoes	33 – 39 36 – 39	850 – 1000 850 – 1000	
				3 or 4 height range
Cooker	Fry Boil	33 – 39	850 – 1000	

References

Ascot Ltd. (1943) 'Kitchen planning: outline of findings and suggestions for further investigation', (2nd Ed.).

Birmingham University Department of Anatomy (1951) 'The best height of the working-plane and work bench for use by women when standing', unpublished report.

British Standards Institution (1948) 'Kitchen fitments and equipment', BS 1195.

British Standards Institution (1964) 'Recommendations for provisions of space for domestic kitchen equipment', BS 3705.

Bouwcentrum (1963) 'Woningbouw', Rotterdam.

Council for Scientific Management in the Home (1961) 'Preferred depth and height for kitchen sinks', Report to British Standards Institution.

Gas Industry and Drew, J. B. (1945) *'Kitchen Planning'*. Gas Industry, London.

Gilbreth, L. M., Thomas, O. M., and Clymer, E. (1956) *'Management in the home'*. (Rev. 1959) Dood, Mead, New York.

Hawkins, R. R. (1953) *'The kitchen book of planning and remodelling'*. Van Nostrand, New York.

Kirk, N. S. and Ridgway, Susan (1971) Ergonomics testing of consumer products 2. Techniques. *Applied Ergonomics*, Vol. 2.1, pp. 12–18.

Saville, B. F. (1969) Optimum domestic work heights – a postural analysis. Ph.D. thesis to University of Technology, Loughborough.

Sheppard, N. and Mahaddie, C. (1970) *The Architects' Journal*, 30 Sept., pp. 787–790.

'Space in the home' (1965) Ministry of Housing and Local Government Bulletin, HMSO.

Steidl, R. E. and Bratton, E. C. (1968) *'Work in the home'*, Wiley & Sons, London.

Walley, Joan E. (1960) 'The Kitchen' Queen Elizabeth College University of London. Constable, London.

'Kok' (1960) Planeringinredning, Konsumentinstitutet, Sweden.

Ward, J. S. (1970) Ergonomics in the home, *Applied Ergonomics*, Vol. 1.4, pp. 223–227.

4.3 Vigilance Research: Its Application To Industrial Problems[1]

Russell L. Smith, *Integrated Sciences Corporation, Santa Monica, California,* and Luigi F. Lucaccini, *Education Research Branch, Dental Health Center, U.S.P.H.S., San Francisco, California*

Introduction

During the past two decades, few man-machine tasks have received more attention than the vigilance task. The authors are aware of more than 300 vigilance studies which follow the Mackworth (1950) tradition in terms of experimental conditions, constraints, and objectives. While many of these studies have been oriented toward industrial problems, such as quality control inspection, the bulk have been directed toward specific military tasks, such as radar and sonar monitoring. Regardless of orientation, however, most have been concerned with the same problem as Mackworth, the ability of human observers to detect brief, low intensity, and non-recurring or nonpersistent signals over extended periods of time. Mackworth found performance (1) to be relatively high during the first thirty minutes of the task, (2) to decline rapidly during the second thirty minutes, and (3) to remain relatively low and stable thereafter. This sharp decline, termed the vigilance decrement, has been the prime concern of most vigilance experiments conducted to date.

The imposing collection of research results now available is unfortunately of limited value with respect to understanding the causes of the decrement or to providing practical means of preventing it. Before considering what might be the potential of the vigilance performance data now accumulated for application in the improvement of performance in industrial (and military) tasks, a closer look should be taken at the vigilance decrement itself.

The Decrement: Fact or Fantasy

One of the most important questions about vigilance research which has

---

Acknowledgement

Reprinted, by permission, from R. L. Smith and L. F. Lucaccini, 'Vigilance research : its application to industrial problems' in *Human Factors,* Vol. 11, No. 2 © 1969 The Johns Hopkins University Press.

---

[1]*Based on a paper presented at the 12th Annual Meeting of the Human Factors Society, Chicago, October, 1968.*

been raised in recent years is whether the laboratory decrement has a parallel in industrial and military monitoring tasks. If it does, the problem of applying laboratory results to the field is one of practicality rather than validity. If not, the data collected in the laboratory setting would appear to be contaminated by the processes which underlie the decrement and, as a result, can be generalized to the field only with extreme caution.

What, then, is the evidence for the appearance of the decrement in the field? Formalized evidence is generally lacking, although there are a few studies with some bearing on this point. With respect to military tasks, Mackworth (1950, p. 12) cited studies of anti-submarine watches during World War II in support of his experimental work. He maintained that the records showed evidence of performance decrements by military watchstanders in the form of a sharp decline in the number of successful radar contacts after the first half hour of the watch period. An unstated assumption was, apparently, that the true rate of signals or possible contacts was stable across the average watch period. Further, Mackworth did not state how 'successful radar contacts' were verified.

In contrast to Mackworth's report, Elliott (1960, p. 357) claimed that the decrement had 'never been found in any closely simulated radar or asdic search'. Elliott was apparently referring to British Admiralty studies of military recruits or military watchstanders but did not clarify the basis for the statement.

There is apparently only one case in the extant literature which actually presents detailed results of a study which closely simulated an operational radar setting. The study was conducted by Veniar (1953) with the purpose of validating the early laboratory work of Lindsley, *et al.* (1944) and Mackworth (1950). As in actual combat information centres (CIC), Veniar's subjects (actual radar operators) participated as a team wherein detection, communication, and plotting were part of the total task. The CIC mockup included an IP-48 console and an APA-56 remote radar indicator. Nine new targets appeared each half hour but operators were also instructed to detect course changes, IFF signals, and fades as well as to detect the new targets. Results of his study revealed a lack of decrements during continuous four-and-a-half hour vigils over five consecutive days. In fact, performance actually increased within sessions and from day to day. Although Veniar's experiment was an extremely sophisticated one, compared to most vigilance research, to the best of our knowledge it has been ignored in the vigilance literature.

With respect to the industrial setting, there is even less evidence for the existence of decrements in inspection tasks. McCornack (1961) found in reviewing the literature that only 16 field studies were concerned with inspection accuracy and, of these, only four provided usable quantitative data (Ayers, 1942; Kelley, 1955; Lawshe and Tiffin, 1945; Tiffin and Rogers, 1941). Unfortunately, none of these or subsequent related studies presented performance as a function of time.

The apparent lack of interest in performance decrements in the industrial literature is itself interesting. Does it signify a failure on the part of investigators to consider temporal aspects of performance or simply the lack of a significant temporal decline in the data accumulated? Baker (1964) apparently assumed the former and cited the results of Wyatt and Langdon (1932) as evidence of a decrement in an industrial setting. He replotted their original data over time and found a 'marked decrement' in the performance of four cartridge inspectors. However, the scale chosen by Baker seems to exaggerate the actual decline. Further, the significance of the decline which did occur – a drop in rejections from 3 to 1% of the total number of cartridges inspected – is hard to assess without knowledge of the actual number and distribution of defective items. If that data were plotted on a scale more typical of vigilance results, that 'decrement' would appear to be a slight linear decline over time, a trend which is not unlike numerous industrial work curves.

In summary, the case for the existence of the decrement in actual industrial or military monitoring tasks is much weaker than one might wish. This question is one which deserves immediate attention. Those who possess field data on the question would do well to make them available in the literature.

Decrements and Motivation

Although the foregoing review raises considerable doubt about the existence of the decrement in the field, the vigilance literature abounds with examples of performance decrements in the laboratory setting. Closer consideration will be given to some of the possible mechanisms underlying the decrement in the laboratory.

One attempt to understand vigilance performance and the decrement has been through the study of individual differences. There are suggestions in the vigilance literature that individual differences may be important. For instance, inspection of laboratory data indicates that perhaps 30 to 40% of the subjects in a given study do not exhibit decrements within a test session (see McGrath, *et al.,* 1959, for a review). Also, it has been found that the performance of a given subject on a particular task shows a high inter-session correlation (e.g., Jenkins, 1958; McGrath, 1961; Mackworth, 1961;

Buckner, 1963). If individual differences related to monitoring proficiency could be found, they might serve as the basis for the selection of military and industrial monitoring personnel. However, attempts to correlate monitoring performance on a wide variety of aptitude, intelligence, and personality test scores have generally been disappointing (Bakan, 1959; Jenkins, 1958; Kappauf and Powe, 1959; McGrath, *et al.*, 1960; McGrath, 1961; Sipowicz and Baker, 1961; Ware, 1961; Smith, *et al.*, 1966; Solandt and Partridge, 1946). Further, differences in sensory thresholds do not appear to be important since the signals usually employed are well above threshold and readily detectable by an alerted subject. This is typically demonstrated by the fact that individual differences are almost always small at the beginning of test sessions and on short test sessions immediately following the main session (e.g., Baker and O'Hanlon, 1963; Buckner, *et al.*, 1960; McGrath and Hatcher, 1961).

Individual differences in terms of capability to learn to detect signals have also not been found, as improvement in performance is apparently not correlated with practice (Webb and Wherry, 1960; Baker, Sipowicz and Ware, 1961; Colquhoun, 1966; Ware, *et al.*, 1961).

What, then, is responsible for the decrement? Perhaps it would be useful to mention those cases in which decrements are not found. The first is a trivial one. Occasionally, the decrement does not occur in studies which use 'simple' displays, i.e., displays which require negligible scanning or discrimination of the operator. A decrement did not occur in a study by Sipowicz, *et al.*, (1962), for example, but did occur in other studies which used the same display (e.g. Weidenfeller, *et al.*, 1962; Baker, *et al.*, 1961; Ware, *et al.*, 1964). Such cases may simply be the result of sampling error.

The second case in which decrements are not generally found is in studies which use 'complex' displays, i.e., those that do require some degree of scanning or discrimination. Initial performance with such tasks is usually much lower than with those which use simple displays and tends to remain relatively constant throughout the vigil (Jerison and Wallis, 1957; Baker and Harabedian, 1962; Smith, *et al.*, 1966; Smith, *et al.*, 1967).

The third situation in which decrements are eliminated or significantly reduced is when motivational influences are employed. Because the position is taken that the decrement may best be understood in terms of subject motivation, or more properly, lack of motivation, evidence will be briefly reviewed which supports this position.

It is generally agreed that the vigilance task is an unusually monotonous one. In view of this, it is doubtful that the casual laboratory subject will attempt to do his best for very long unless he has good reason for doing so.

A similar position has been taken by Poulton (1960) and Dunlap (1961). Poulton felt the vigilance task is perceived by subjects to be 'pointless'; Dunlap suggested the 'do-nothing' nature of such tasks is likely to result in failing motivation. Evidence interpretable within a motivational framework can be found in some of the earliest of vigilance studies. Mackworth (1950), for example, in one of the studies in his classic series, called each subject by telephone midway during the watch period to ask him to 'do even better for the rest of the test'. Performance, which had shown a substantial decrement before the telephone message, recovered to a level higher than the initial levels. Subsequently, performance again declined. Fraser (1953) found that performance was significantly better for subjects who monitored with the knowledge that the experimenter was in the test room (although out of sight) than for subjects who monitored without such knowledge. These findings have largely been treated as curiosities in the vigilance literature. Another such 'curiosity' is the occasional finding that vigilance performance shows an end-spurt, particularly when subjects may feel that the session is drawing to a close (Deese and Ormond, 1953; Baker, 1960; Bergum and Lehr, 1963a). All of these results are open to the interpretation that laboratory vigilance subjects can and do voluntarily regulate the level of effort devoted to the task.

Other evidence comes from studies showing that vigilance performance can be substantially improved by the application of monetary rewards and punishments or coercive influences (Bergum and Lehr, 1963b; Pollack and Knaff, 1958; Ware, et al., 1964; Smith, et al., 1967; Smith and Lyman, 1968). Smith, et al., (1967) found that performances increased in proportion to the level of monetary reward attainable.[2] Also, Smith and Lyman (1968) have shown that knowledge of results (KOR), which is usually interpreted as informational and serving to guide learning, has an influence that is primarily coercive in nature in the vigilance situation. KOR, as usually employed in vigilance studies, carries the implied threat to the subject that somewhere within the mechanics of the KOR system the experimenter is monitoring his performance. Smith and Lyman demonstrated that when subjects were informed that KOR was automatized and that the experimenter would leave the test facilities, their performance was no better than controls. On the other hand, when the experimenter remained in the room, the performances of two groups of subjects, one receiving automatic KOR

---

[2]*It should be noted that Pollack and Knaff (1958), although finding a punishment condition to facilitate performance, did not find an effect of monetary incentives on performance. Also, Bergum and Lehr (1964) were unable to demonstrate a facilitating effect of monetary incentives. A possible reason for these apparent contradictions to the view taken here was given by Smith, Lucaccini, and Epstein (1967) as a case of offering subjects too small a payoff.*

and one receiving no information, were identical and significantly better than controls.

Additional evidence that vigilance performance can be manipulated by motivational factors was provided by Lucaccini, *et al.* (1968) in a demonstration showing that merely changing a single word in pre-task instructions could alter performance significantly. The word 'challenging', used in the sentence 'such tasks are usually challenging for most observers', resulted in significantly better performance than did the word 'monotonous'.

Finally, direct observations of subjects, post-experimental interview data, and experimenter inferences from a number of studies lead to the conclusion that a significant number of subjects are simply not motivated enough even to continuously observe the display. What other reason is possible when it has been reported that many subjects periodically sleep, read, write letters, move about, daydream, and assume positions incompatible with observing the display when they are supposed to be looking for signals (McGrath, 1960; Regan, 1961; Sipowicz, *et al.*, 1962; Anthrobus and Singer, 1964; O'Hanlon, *et al.*, 1965; Wiener, 1963; Montague and Webber, 1965; Smith, *et al.*, 1966; Smith and Lyman, 1968).[3] One cannot help but suspect, therefore, that the failure to follow instructions was a common occurrence for some significant subset of the subject population in most previous vigilance research.

Taken together, the various lines of evidence referred to above strongly suggest that the laboratory vigilance decrement is the result of inadequate motivation. A relatively large percentage of laboratory subjects do not attempt to maintain continuous attention to the vigilance display after ten or twenty minutes have elapsed. Apparently, however, the behaviour of such subjects, elsewhere referred to as 'periodic participators' (Smith, 1966), is amenable to simple extrinsic motivational influences.

Vigilance and Industrial Inspection

Several of the characteristics of the vigilance task appear common to industrial inspection and monitoring tasks. Both are monotonous, repetitive tasks which require little use of the intellect and do not permit variable interactions with the environment. Conditions such as these are linked to serious problems of industrial motivation and morale. Numerous industrial jobs

---

[3]*A recent visit to the Army Behavioural Sciences Laboratory in Washington, D.C., by the senior author revealed that similar behaviours were frequently observed during a series of vigilance studies.*

(e.g., assembly, sorting, packaging, etc.) include such conditions and the desirability of maintaining or increasing the motivation of personnel engaged in such activities is not new. Given that the vigilance task is an extreme case of monotonous work, it may offer a short-term test for determining methods to maintain acceptable long-term levels of motivation on less boring tasks.

Although motivation may be a critical factor in determining overall vigilance performance, its role in industrial inspection work appears to be secondary at best. Possibly the most demanding task requirements are perceptual. While subjects in vigilance studies are asked to judge whether a simple stimulus is present or absent, industrial inspectors must make far more difficult judgments regarding the quality of a complex mechanical or electronic part. At least one experimenter (Colquhoun, 1957; Colquhoun, 1964) has acknowledged that the task facing the inspector is far more complex than that facing the vigilance subject. Colquhoun (1964) emphasized that the detection of a fault in a product is highly contingent on what is defined as a fault. 'The complexity of faultiness in many products is such as to defy analysis'.

Recent field studies of inspection work indicate the nature of the judgmental complexities facing the modern inspector (e.g., Harris, 1964; Harris, 1966; Chaney and Teel, 1967; Teel, et al., 1968). In some cases, the components of a single product to be inspected number in the thousands (Jamieson, 1966) and defective products may be missed simply because of the large number of components to be examined. In other cases, the principal inspection problem is that of making an absolute judgment which, on the whole, may be beyond the capability of most individuals. The latter situation presents a particularly challenging task to human factors specialists in that aids must be devised to reduce the inspection task to that of making a relative judgment. Aids such as unique comparison standards have been developed for some products, such as a printed circuit board overlay showing the correct placement and size of copper-runners (Teel, et al., 1968), but development of similar standards for other products may not be possible.

The foregoing requirements of inspection tasks have not been evaluated in vigilance studies to any significant degree. The fine discriminatory capability that is required to make absolute judgments does suggest that data obtained with vigilance displays that present near-threshold signals may be applicable. On the other hand, the mere lowness of signal-to-noise ratio does not by itself define the problem of inspection. As emphasized, criteria for defining defects in many products are not well established, indicating that inspectors do not always know what to look for. Thus, the inspection task, in addition to requiring difficult absolute judgments, necessitates that an inspector know a defect when he sees it. Unfortunately, there is currently reason to believe that there may be no guarantee that the individuals who overview inspectors' performances can do any better than their subordinates.

Conclusions

The fact that characteristics of radar and sonar monitoring tasks are far more complex than those of the typical vigilance task has recently led Kibler (1965), Howell, et al. (1966), and Chapanis (1967) to question the utility of laboratory vigilance research. In general, similar comments seem appropriate with respect to attempts to generalize those results to industrial inspection tasks. In fact, inspection tasks are quite similar to sonar tasks, in that signal detection appears to be based far more on discriminatory than attentive capability. While initial performance in the typical vigilance study is generally quite high and can be maintained so by motivational influences (indicating an attentive rather than a perceptual problem), the opposite seems true for inspection tasks.

It must be concluded that much of the vigilance research to date has questionable application to industrial inspection problems. Vigilance studies can and must be designed to simulate more closely the relevant conditions of industrial tasks with care being given to the total industrial context. In effect, displays must present relevant perceptual problems and attempts must be made to simulate the motivational influences normally occurring in the industrial environment. Currently, we know a great deal about the behaviour of laboratory subjects in vigilance tasks but we are not at all sure that such knowledge is of any practical (or theoretical) importance.

References

Ayers, A. W. (1942) A comparison of certain visual factors with the efficiency of textile inspectors. *J. Appl. Psychol.*, **26**, pp. 812–827.
Anthrobus, J. S. and Singer, J. L. (1964) Visual signal detection as a function of sequential variability of simultaneous speech. *J. Exp. Psychol.*, **68**, pp. 603–610.
Bakan, P. (1959) Extraversion-introversion and improvement in auditory vigilance tasks. *Brit. J. Psychol.*, **50**, pp. 325–332.
Baker, C. H. (1960) Observing behaviour in a vigilance task, *Science*, **132**, pp. 674–675.

Baker, C. H. (1964) Industrial inspection considered as a vigilance task. Paper read at International Congress of Applied Psychology, Ljubljana, Yugoslavia, August.

Baker, C. H. and Harabedian, A. (1962) A study of target detection by sonar operators. Los Angeles: Human Factors Research, Inc., HFR Tech. Rep. No. 206–16.

Baker, C. H. and O'Hanlon, J. (1963) The use of reference signals in a visual vigilance task; II Reference signals displayed when demanded and when arbitrarily programmed. Los Angeles: Human Factors Research, Inc., HFR Tech. Rep. No. 750–2.

Baker, R. A., Sipowicz, R. R. and Ware, J. R. (1961) Effects of practice on visual monitoring. *Percept. Mot. Skills,* **13**, pp. 291–294.

Bergum, B. O. and Lehr, D. J. (1963a) End-spurt in vigilance. *J. Exp. Pschol.,* **68**, pp. 393–395.

Bergum, B. O. and Lehr, D. J. (1963b) Effects of authoritarianism on vigilance performance. *J. Appl. Psychol.,* **47**, pp. 75–77.

Bergum, B. O. and Lehr, D. J. (1964) Monetary incentives and vigilance. *J. Exp. Psychol.,* **67**, pp. 197–198.

Buckner, D. N. (1963) An individual-difference approach to explaining vigilance performance. In D. N. Buckner and J. J. McGrath (Ed.), *Vigilance: A symposium.* New York: McGraw-Hill, pp. 171–179.

Buckner, D. N., Harabedian, A. J., and McGrath, J. J. (1960) A study of individual differences in vigilance performance. Los Angeles: Human Factors Research, Inc., HFR Tech. Rep. No. 2.

Chaney, F. B. and Teel, K. S. (1967) Improving inspector performance through training and visual aids, *J. Appl. Psychol.,* **51**, pp. 311–315.

Chapanis, A. (1967) The relevance of laboratory studies to practical situations. *Ergonomics,* **10**, pp. 557–577.

Colquhoun, W. P. (1957) Vigilance and the inspection problem. *Nature,* **180**, pp. 1331–1332.

Colquhoun, W. P. (1964) Recent research in the psychology of inspection. *Textile Institute and Industry,* November, pp. 252–255.

Colquhoun, W. P. (1966) Training for vigilance: a comparison of different techniques. *Human Factors,* **8**, pp. 7–12.

Deese, J. and Ormond, E. (1953) Studies of detectability during continuous visual research. USAF: WADC Tech. Rep. No. 53–8, Wright-Patterson AFB, Drayton, Ohio.

Dunlap, J. W. (1961) Human interactions. *Electro-Technology,* **67**, pp. 128–130.

Elliott, E. (1960) Perception and alertness. *Ergonomics,* **3**, pp. 357–364.

Fraser, D. C. (1953) The relation of an environmental variable to performance in a prolonged visual task. *Quart. J. Exp. Psychol.,* **5**, pp. 31–32.

Harris, D. H. (1966) Development and validation of an aptitude test for inspectors of electronic equipment. *J. Indust. Psychol.,* **2,** pp. 29–35.

Harris, D. H. (1966) Effect of equipment complexity on inspection performance. *J. Appl. Psychol.,* **50,** pp. 236–237.

Howell, W. C., Johnston, W. A., and Goldstein, I. L. (1966) Complex monitoring and its relation to the classical problem of vigilance. *Organiz. Behav. Human Perform.,* **1,** pp. 129–150.

Jamieson, G. H. (1966) Inspection in the telecommunications industry: A field study of age and other performance variables. *Ergonomics,* **9,** pp. 297–303.

Jenkins, H. M. (1958) The effect of signal-rate on performance in visual monitoring. *Amer. J. Psychol.,* **71,** pp. 647–661.

Jerison, H. J. and Wallis, R. A. (1957) Experiments on vigilance: one-clock and three-clock monitoring. USAF: WADC Tech. Rep. No. 57–206, Wright-Patterson AFB, Dayton, Ohio.

Kappauf, W. E. and Powe, W. E. (1959) Performance decrement at an audio-visual checking task. *J. Exp. Psychol.,* **57,** pp. 49–56.

Kelley, M. L. (1955) A study of industrial inspection by the method of paired comparisons. *Psychol. Monog.,* **69,** No. 394.

Kibler, A. W. (1965) The relevance of vigilance research to aerospace monitoring tasks. *Human Factors,* **7,** pp. 93–99.

Lawshe, C. H. and Tiffin, J. (1945) The accuracy of precision instrument measurement in industrial inspection. *J. Appl. Psychol.,* **29,** pp. 413–419.

Lindsley, D. B., et al. (1944) Radar operator 'fatigue'. The effect of length and repetition of operating periods on efficiency of performance. OSRD Rep. No. 3334, Office of Scientific Research and Development.

Lucaccini, L. F., Freedy, A. and Lyman, J. (1968) Motivational factors in vigilance: The effects of instructions on performance in a complex vigilance task. *Percept. Mot. Skills,* **26,** pp. 783–786.

McCornack, R. L. (1961) Inspector accuracy: a study of the literature. New Mexico: Sandia Corporation, SCTM Tech. Rep. No. 53–61(14).

McGrath, J. J. (1960) Subjective reactions of vigilance performers. Los Angeles: HFR Suppl. Human Factors Research, Inc., Note to Tech. Rep. No. 2.

McGrath, J. J. (1961) Cross-validation of some correlates of vigilance-performance. Los Angeles: Human Factors Research, Inc., Note to Tech. Rep. No. 4.

McGrath, J. J., Harabedian, A., and Buckner, D. N. (1959) Review and critique of the literature on vigilance performance. Los Angeles: Human Factors Research, Inc., HFR Tech. Rep. No. 1.

McGrath, J. J., Harabedian, A., and Buckner, D. N. (1960) An exploratory study of the correlates of vigilance performance. Los Angeles: Human Factors Research, Inc., HFR Tech. Rep. No. 4.

McGrath, J. J. and Hatcher, J. F. (1961) Irrelevant stimulation and vigilance under fast and slow stimulus rates. Los Angeles: Human Factors Research, Inc., HFR Tech. Rep. No. 7.

Mackworth, N. H. (1950) Researches on the measurement of human performance. London: Med. Res. Council Spec. Rep. Series 268.

Mackworth, N. H. (1961) Human vigilance. *Electro-Technology,* **67,** pp. 121–123.

Montague, W. E. and Webber, C. E. (1965) Effects of knowledge of results and differential monetary reward on six uninterrupted hours of monitoring. *Human factors,* **7,** pp. 173–180.

O'Hanlon, J., Schmidt, E. A., and Baker, C. H. (1965) Sonar Doppler discrimination and the effect of visual alertness indicator upon detection of auditory sonar signals in a sonar watch. *Human Factors,* **7,** pp. 129–139.

Pollack, I. and Knaff, P. R. (1958) Maintenance of alertness by a loud auditory signal. *J. Acoust. Soc. Amer.,* **30,** pp. 1013–1016.

Poulton, E. C. (1960) The optimal perceptual load in a paced auditory inspection task. *Brit. J. Psychol.,* **51,** pp. 127–139.

Regan, R. A. (1961) Facilitation of signal detection by the use of artificial signals and by the use of longer viewing time. Pittsburgh: University of Pittsburgh, Engin. Psychol. Lab. Tech. Rep. No. 3.

Sipowicz, R. R. and Baker, R. A. (1961) Effects of intelligence on vigilance: a replication. *Percept. Mot. Skills,* **13,** p. 398.

Sipowicz, R. R., Ware, J. R., and Baker, R. A. (1962) The effects of reward and knowledge of results on the performance of a simple vigilance task. *J. Exp. Psychol.,* **64,** pp. 58–61.

Smith, R. L. (1966) Monotony and motivation: a theory of vigilance. Santa Monica, California: Dunlap and Associates, Inc.

Smith, R. L., Lucaccini, L. F., and Epstein, M. (1967) Effects of monetary rewards and punishments on vigilance performance. *J. Appl. Psychol.,* **51,** pp. 411–416.

Smith, R. L., Lucaccini, L. F., Groth, H., and Lyman, J. (1966) Effects of anticipatory alerting signals and a compatible secondary task on vigilance performance. *J. Appl. Psychol.,* **50,** pp. 240–246.

Smith, R. L. and Lyman, J. (1968) The facilitating effects of knowledge of results on vigilance performance: Information or motivation? Paper read at the Western Physiological Association Convention, San Diego, California, March.

Solandt, D. Y. and Partridge, D. M. (1946) Research on auditory problems presented by naval operations. *J. Canad. Med. Serv.,* **3,** pp. 323–329.

Teel, K. S., Springer, R. M., and Sadler, E. E. (1968) Assembly and inspection of micro-electronic systems. *Human Factors,* **10,** pp. 217–224.

Tiffin, J. and Rogers, H. B. (1941) The selection and training of inspectors. *Personnel,* **18,** pp. 14–31.

Veniar, S. (1953) The effect of continuous operation on the AEW function of air control officers in the airborne CIC. Special Devices Center, SDC Tech. Rep. No. 279-3-12.

Ware, J. R. (1961) The effects of intelligence on signal detection in visual and auditory monitoring. *Percept. Mot. Skills,* **13,** pp. 99–102.

Ware, J. R., Kowal, B., and Baker, R. A. (1964) The role of experimenter attitude and contingent reinforcement in a vigilance task. *Human Factors,* **6,** pp. 111–115.

Ware, J. R., Sipowicz, R. R., and Baker, R. A. (1961) Auditory vigilance in repeated sessions. *Percept. Mot. Skills,* **13,** pp. 127–129.

Webb, W. B. and Wherry, R. J. (1960) Vigilance in prolonged and repeated sessions. *Percept. Mot. Skills,* **11,** pp. 111–114.

Weidenfeller, E. W., Baker, R. A., and Ware, J. R. (1962) Effects of knowledge of results (true and false) on vigilance performance. *Percept. Mot. Skills,* **14,** pp. 211–215.

Wiener, E. L. (1963) Knowledge of results and signal rate in monitoring: A transfer of training approach. *J. Appl. Psychol.,* **47,** pp. 214–222.

Wyatt, S. and Langdon, J. N. (1932) Inspection processes in industry. London: Med. Res. Council Rep. No. 63.

4.4   Skilled Performance and Stress

Christopher Poulton
MRC Applied Psychology Unit, Cambridge

This reading concerns much that happens in everyday life. Most of a person's activities have been well practised, and so are skilled. When a person is active, he is often under stress. The stress may be imposed upon him by his employer, who expects him to work hard to earn his pay. The stress may be self imposed. People have standards of performance which they try hard to uphold in the jobs they do. Or the environment may impose the stress. It may be too noisy or too hot. Skilled performances are often carried out under stress.

1   Two Kinds of Skill

Every activity can be said to involve deciding what to do and then doing it. In studying activities such as talking or typewriting, the principal emphasis is generally put on selecting the response. The talker has to decide which words to use; the typist has to decide which keys to press. Talking and typing require skill for their execution. The talker has to speak so that he can be understood. The typist has to hit the correct key sufficiently hard to type the letter, and not so hard that the typeface perforates the paper. But the activities are usually studied as decisions. The person's choice of a word or of a key is related to the other choices which he or she could have made.

In studying activities such as reaching for an object or steering a car, the principal emphasis is generally put on the execution of the response. In reaching for an object, the person has to move his hand the correct distance in the correct direction. The car driver has to turn his steering wheel through the correct angle at the correct time. Reaching and steering require decisions before they are carried out—the person has to decide what to reach for; the driver has to decide where he wants the car to go to. But the activities are usually assessed in terms of the speed and precision of the movement, not in terms of the choice of movement.

Acknowledgement

Reprinted, by permission, from C. Poulton, 'Skilled performance and stress' in P. B. Warr (ed.), *Psychology at Work,* Penguin Books Co. Ltd. Copyright © 1971 Peter Warr and contributors.

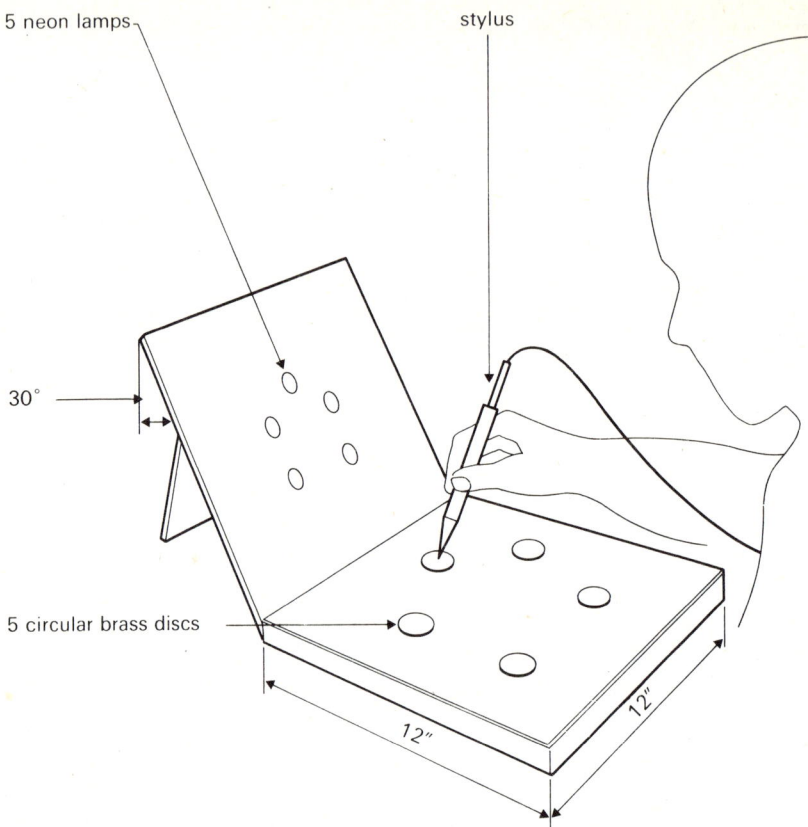

Figure 1   The 5-choice task (After Leonard, 1959)

Any one of a number of tasks can be used to study the way people *choose* the responses which they make. An example is the five-choice task of Figure 1. One of the five lamps on the left lights up. The man has to touch the corresponding brass disc with his stylus as quickly as he can. As soon as he touches a disc, the lamp goes off and another lamp comes on. Unpracticed people usually average about one tap per second. After a lot of practice the quickest people sometimes average almost two taps per second.

If the subject touches the correct disc, his response is automatically recorded as correct. If he touches one of the other four discs, his response is recorded as an error. If he does not respond for 1.5 seconds the apparatus waits until he does respond, but it automatically records a gap in his sequence of responses. Slow responding produces both gaps and also a relatively small total number of correct responses.

Tracking is the only task which has been used extensively to study the way people *execute* responses. Tracking is usually studied in the laboratory with electronic apparatus. The subject has to try to keep a moving marker superimposed upon a target marker which may or may not move (Poulton, 1966).

2   A Simple Theoretical Model for Skilled Performance

Figure 2 illustrates a simple theoretical model which shows what the brain does during skilled performances. The inputs on the left of the figure are from the eyes and ears and from the sense organs scattered throughout the body. A number of arrows are shown leading from the box labelled inputs to the working memory. This is because the eyes can take in a complete scene at a glance. The ears can receive a number of sounds simultaneously, as in listening to orchestral music. At the same time there may be inputs from a number of other sense organs.

The outputs on the right of the figure are to the muscles. A number of arrows are shown leading from the output selector to the box labelled outputs. This is because when a person moves his hand or says something, a large number of muscles are used. The rest of the connections between the boxes are by single arrows. This is to indicate the bottleneck in the brain through which all messages have to pass.

Working memory and rehearsal

The box in Figure 2 labelled working memory holds a representation of what the person is looking at, or listening to, or thinking about. The representation fades beyond recall in a few seconds unless it is maintained in some way. In looking at a scene, the inputs from the eyes keep the sensory representation in the working memory. When the eyes move to another scene, the sensory representation of the previous scene disappears almost at once (Sperling, 1960). Try it and see.

Anything which remains in the working memory after half a second or so must have been rehearsed. Rehearsal means selecting items from the scene. In the model of Figure 2, the input selector passes the items through the box labelled computer and round the rehearsal loop back to the working memory. It is not quite as simple as this, because the items are usually given names while they are being rehearsed. It is the name, not the visual image of the item, which is usually stored. Naming involves obtaining the name from the long-term memory. If items in the visual scene do not have familiar names, fewer of them can be rehearsed and stored)Eriksen and Lappin, 1967).

In listening to somebody speaking, the inputs from the ears change all the time. There is no constant sensory representation in the working memory as there can be in looking at a scene. Probably for this reason, unrehearsed sounds do not disappear from the working memory quite as quickly as visual impressions do when they are not rehearsed before the eyes move to another scene. If words are not rehearsed, it may be several seconds before they disappear completely from the working memory (Broadbent, 1957b, Experiment 2).

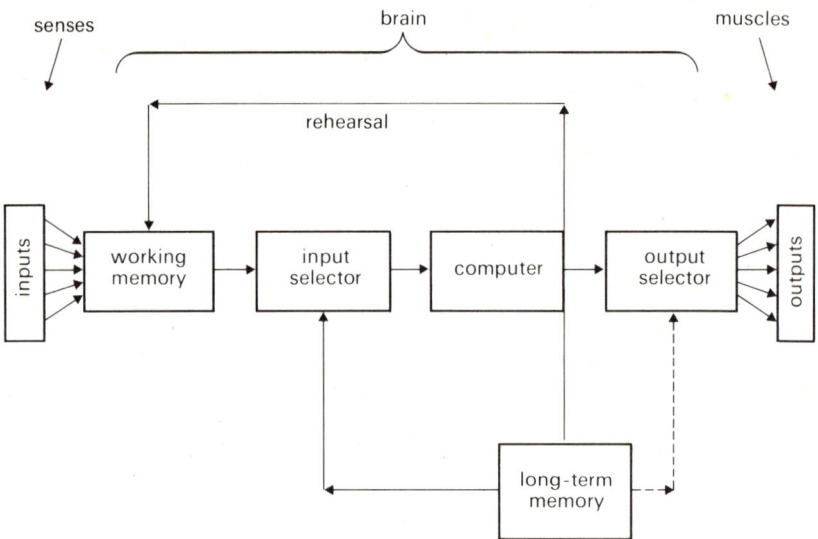

Figure 2   A simple theoretical model which shows what the brain does. (Modified from Broadbent, 1958, Figure 7)

Computer of limited capacity

The box labelled computer in Figure 2 is not like a modern high-speed digital computer. It works relatively slowly. When a task is difficult, the computer takes quite a time to carry it out. A learner driver may practise pressing the brake with his foot each time a red lamp comes on in front of him. When he is expecting the red light, he may be able to start pressing the brake pedal in about 0.2 second. Less than half this time is taken up by the message travelling to the brain from the eyes along the visual nerves, and by the messages travelling from the brain along the nerves to the muscles of the leg and foot. more than half of the time is taken by the computer in Figure 2. If there are several possible signals, each of which requires a different response, the computer may take 0.5 second, or longer to select the appropriate response. The extra time to react produces the 'thinking distance' which is travelled by a car before it can be stopped. It is illustrated on the back cover of *The Highway Code* (Ministry of Transport, 1968).

The computer's task is made more difficult if the signals are difficult to perceive, or difficult to discriminate from each other. Reaction time increases as a result. The computer's task is also more difficult if responses have to be made with great precision, as in using a slide rule, or in repairing the inside of a wrist watch. In order to achieve the extra precision, a longer average time is needed (Fitts, 1954).

The amount which can be held in the working memory is limited by the time the computer takes to rehearse. Each item in the working memory has to be rehearsed before it fades beyond recall. While items are being rehearsed, the remaining items are fading rapidly. The average person has a maximum memory span of about eight random letters or digits. If he is given more than this to remember, some are forgotten before they can be rehearsed. Try it on yourself. Undergraduates may have a maximum memory span of ten or eleven random digits.

Single-channel input selector

In Figure 2 there are a number of arrows leading from the box labelled inputs to the working memory. But only one arrow connects the working memory to the input selector, and there is a single arrow connecting the input selector to the computer. This is to indicate that only one message at a time can be selected and fed into the computer. While the computer is dealing with one message, other messages have to wait.

A person may be told to make a quick hand movement each time he hears a bell. Each time he hears a buzz, he is to make a different quick movement. After practice, he takes about 0.2 second to respond to the bell. When the buzz sounds during his reaction time to the bell, his response to the buzz takes about 0.35 second, instead of the expected 0.2 second (Poulton, 1970, Figure 5). The extra delay is not caused by having to make a second response with the same hand, because the 2 responses can involve different hands (Davis, 1957).

The period of time during the reaction to the first signal has been called the psychological refractory period. It is similar to the refractory period of the single nerve fibre, but it lasts a good deal longer. The input selector of Figure 2 feeds the first signal, the second signal has to wait in the working memory (Welford, 1967).

The delay in responding to the second signal may sometimes last one second or longer if the man is not expecting the second signal (Poulton, 1970, p.13). The input selector may not be set to select a second signal. Instead it may be set to select the sensory consequences of the first response. The person may be readjusting his hand. Or he may be waiting for the experimenter to tell him how long he took to respond. The second signal then has to capture the input selector, before it can reach the computer.

Long-term memory and the automation of skill

Each rehearsal of material in the working memory helps to establish it in the long-term memory, which is illustrated at the bottom of Figure 2. Once material has become established in the long-term memory, it remains available or partly available for hours or days. The long duration of the storage contrasts with the duration of only a few seconds in the working memory.

In talking, and in carrying out other practised movements, the input selector draws upon material in the long-term memory. The material is passed through the computer to the output selector. It also passes along the rehearsal loop to the working memory. This mechanism supplies the person with a running memory of what he is doing. He can draw upon this information when he wants to know where he has got to in his talking or his movements. If he is talking, he also receives feedback to his working memory through his ears. If he is moving, he obtains feedback from the moving parts of his body. He can also look and see what he is doing. Thus in talking and in moving the input selector and computer use in turn information from the long-term and working memories.

When a skill has become highly practised, it needs less computer time. Something like a template has been constructed in the long-term memory. The input selector has only to select the template and to pass the information through the computer to the output selector. The highly practised skill can then be carried out without involving the input selector and computer. This is indicated in Figure 2 by the broken arrow connecting the boxes labelled long-term memory and output selector. The input selector and computer are required only when it is necessary to check on how the skill is being carried out, or to change templates. Between whiles they are available for some other activity (Bahrick, Noble and Fitts, 1954).

The gradual automation of skill can be observed in teaching someone to drive a car. In the very early stages, practically the whole of the learner's attention is occupied by his control movements. A signal for action, perhaps from the road ahead, is fed by the input selector of Figure 2 into the computer. The appropriate rudimentary template has then to be found in the long-term memory. Information from the template is fed by the input selector through the computer to the output selector. It leads to a control movement.

The learner driver has then to check that he has done the right thing. He needs sensory information fed back through the input selector to the computer from his hands and feet as to what movements were made, to check whether they were correct or not. Later he needs sensory information from his eyes about the behaviour of the car. Errors are corrected by the input selector choosing a somewhat different template from the long-term memory. Information from the template is then fed through the computer to the output selector.

While the learner driver is doing all this, he may have little or no idea of what is happening in the road ahead. His computer capacity is fully occupied in attempting to control the car. At this early stage driving instructors report that they have to keep a lookout on the road ahead, to see that the car does not hit anything.

At a later stage of practice the learner driver does not need to monitor every aspect of his control movements so carefully. Appropriate templates have still to be found in the long-term memory. The information from them has still to be fed through the input selector and computer to the output selector. But once this has been done, the long-term memory and output selector can communicate directly along the broken arrow in Figure 2. The man does not need to keep a close check upon his control movements. This leaves his input selector and computer free to deal with other aspects of driving, such as what is happening in the road ahead.

At a still later stage the driver may have computer time in reserve whenever the amount of relevant information coming from the road ahead is not too great. The surplus computer time can be measured. The driver is given questions to listen to and to answer orally when he can. His score on the questions reflects the amount of unused computer time (Brown and Poulton, 1961). The scores of learner drivers have been found to increase with the number of days of training on the road (Brown, 1966b).

3   The Optimum Level of Arousal

The computer of Figure 2 works most efficiently when a person is alert or moderately aroused. The computer works less well when arousal is low and the person finds it difficult to keep awake. The computer also works less well when arousal is too high and the person is over-excited or over-anxious. The theoretical relationship between arousal and the efficiency of performance is illustrated by the unbroken curve in Figure 3. The level of arousal may increase from A_1 as to the optimum at A_2 on the abscissa. The efficiency of performance on the ordinate rises from P_1 to P_2. Arousal may continue to increase beyond A_2 as far as A_3. The efficiency of performance then starts to fall. It drops from P_2 to P_3.

The changes in arousal illustrated in the figure are accompanied by physiological changes. When a person is over-excited, he may feel his heart beating more obviously, he may sweat and his muscles may be more tense.

The position of the optimum level of arousal depends upon the nature of the task. A complex task does not require such a high level of arousal as a simple task does. You may find you can dig over the vegetable patch in your garden more quickly when you are highly aroused. But the solution to a difficult problem is more likely to come when you are not too highly aroused. It may come only when you are beginning to relax in a warm bath or in bed. For the simple task of digging, the inverted U lies further to the right, like the dotted curve in the figure. The unbroken inverted U might represent performance on the complex task of solving a difficult problem.

The point A_1 on the abscissa represents a relatively low level of arousal. Here increasing the level of arousal increases efficiency on both simple and complex tasks. The point A_3 represents a relatively high level of arousal. Here the dotted function is rising while the unbroken function is falling. Increasing the level of arousal from this point increases efficiency on the simple task. But it reduces efficiency on the complex task. This paradox is sometimes called the Yerkes-Dodson law. One of the effects of practice is to make a task more simple for the practised man. With practice the inverted U is also shifted to the right.

4 Common Kinds of Stress

A person's alertness can be influenced by stress. There are many stresses in the modern world (Poulton, 1970). Some stresses are met only in specialized jobs, but the following stresses happen to most people from time to time.

Personal threat

Most people work better when they know how well they are doing. The knowledge of results, as it is called, presents a mild personal threat. When a person finds that he is not working as efficiently as he has been working, he tries harder. He aims to maintain the standard of performance which he has set himself. The knowledge of results helps to keep a person's level of arousal at about the optimum illustrated in Figure 3.

A person may become too highly aroused if he believes that he is failing. In industry, an executive may feel that he cannot achieve what is expected of him. An experimenter in the laboratory may give his victim false knowledge of results, so that the victim is told that he is performing badly, when he is trying hard to do his best (Lazarus, Deese and Osler, 1952). The level of arousal in Figure 3 may then be well beyond the optimum. If so, the more aroused the person becomes, the worse he is likely to do. Very severe personal threats may be met by people imprisoned for political reasons in police states (Sargant, 1957).

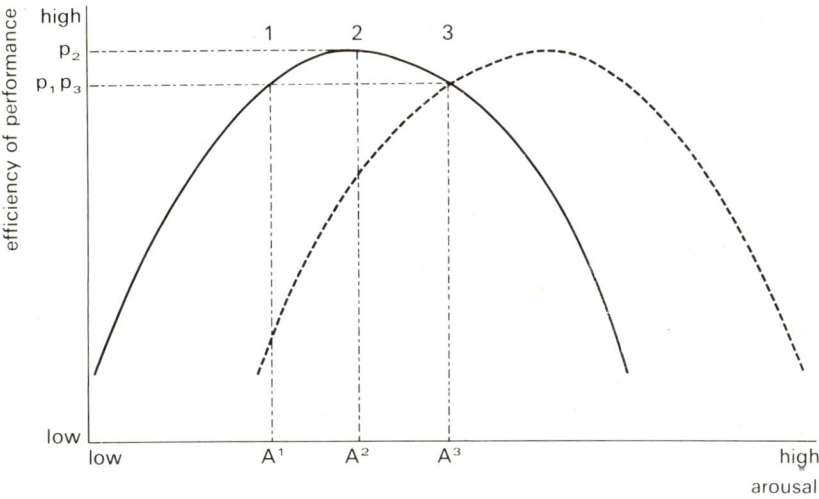

Figure 3 Theoretical inverted U curves showing the relationship between arousal and the efficiency of performance. (After Corcoran, 1965)

Too much to do at once

An executive in industry may be expected to keep track of a number of things at once. He may be in the middle of a serious discussion, when he has to answer a number of difficult questions over the telephone. Talking or telephoning while driving is another example of doing two tasks simultaneously. Each task may require the full capacity of the computer of Figure 3 from time to time. When some of the capacity is tied up with the other task, the man will not work as efficiently as he can do when he has only the one task to deal with. He is likely to work more slowly. If he continues to work at the same speed, he is likely to make mistakes.

A person who finds himself in this predicament may realize that he is not working as well as he usually does. If so, he may become too highly aroused and do still worse.

Noise

Jobs near machinery are often noisy. Noise is also met around busy airports and near crowded streets in cities. In large offices the noise may be too loud for the jobs which people have to do in them. Noise makes it difficult to hear what a person is saying. A sudden noise is distracting. A person switches his attention for an instant to the noise and loses track of what he is doing. Continuous loud noise increases a person's alertness or level of arousal. It may make him work faster. But complex work is likely to be done less accurately (Broadbent, 1957a).

Insufficient loss of heat

The human body produces heat. If the heat cannot be got rid of, the body temperature rises. This can happen near furnaces, and in the sun in hot countries. Too many clothes can also prevent the body from losing sufficient heat. When a person first enters a damp atmosphere, the heat as it were hits him in the face. This is likely to increase his alertness or level of arousal for a time (Poulton and Kerslake, 1965). As the person's body begins to warm up, his level of arousal falls below normal and his brain performs inefficiently. Eventually he becomes uncomfortably hot and over-excited (Wilkinson, Fox, Goldsmith, Hampton and Lewis, 1964). If he is unable to escape from the heat at this stage, he may soon collapse.

Loss of sleep

People may miss sleep when they work on night shift. When a person is sleepy, he has a low level of arousal and works inefficiently. He may have brief lapses of consciousness if he has to sit still listening or reading. You can sometimes notice a brief lapse in the afternoon round a committee table or at a lecture. A person's eyes almost close for a second, and his head may droop. Then he suddenly wakes up again. A sleep debt of five hours is enough to produce a reliable deterioration in performance on a prolonged inspection task (Wilkinson, 1969).

Drugs which increase or reduce arousal

Tea and coffee contain caffeine, which increases arousal. The amphetamine drugs benzedrine and dexedrine also increase arousal. If a person is feeling sleepy, these stimulants can increase his arousal to nearer the normal level. The person may then work more efficiently. The risk is that the person may unexpectedly be subjected to some stress which itself increases arousal. The person may then become too highly aroused and make a stupid error perhaps a fatal error. It can happen to a student if he takes a stimulant just before a stressful examination.

Sleeping tablets, tranquillizers and the more effective remedies for hay fever, reduce arousal. The person who takes them behaves like someone who has lost sleep.

5   Deterioration of skill under stress

A stress may either increase or decrease arousal from the optimum in Figure 3. When this happens, the computer of Figure 2 functions less efficiently. It cannot deal as adequately with a task which requires its full capacity. When arousal falls below the optimum, the computer works more slowly and makes more errors. When arousal rises above the optimum, the computer again makes more errors. If it works faster, it makes still more errors. We have seen that a rather similar effect can be produced by overloading the computer when it is working normally, by giving the person too much to do at once.

The simple picture of an overloaded computer may be complicated by strategies which are adopted to deal with the effects of the overload. The person may attempt to compensate for the fall in his efficiency by changing the strategy of the input selector of Figure 2. He may concentrate upon what he considers to be the more important aspects of the task, at the expense of the less important aspects. These effects of stress will be outlined in greater detail.

Decisions degraded by high workload

We have seen that it is not possible to make two decisions at the same time. But a routine well-practised skill can be performed while doing something else as well. The two different effects of doing two tasks at once are illustrated in an experiment carried out by Brown, Tickner and Simmonds (1969). Each of twenty-four drivers had to answer questions over a radio-telephone while deciding whether or not a gap ahead between two obstacles was just wide enough to drive the car through. Brown and his colleagues found that the driver made reliably more wrong decisions while driving and answering questions, than in a control condition while driving without questions. The driver also answered the questions reliably less correctly, and took reliably longer to do so, when he answered the questions while driving, than in a control condition when he answered the questions while the car was stationary.

The computer of Figure 2 could not make a decision about the width of the gap in the road ahead while it was occupied with answering a question. The decision about the width of the gap was a difficult one. It probably took several seconds to arrive at the best bet. Answering a question received over the radiotelephone during this period interfered with the decision. If the driver delayed his decision for too long, he had to drive through the gap whether he liked it or not, because he was not allowed to stop or swerve sharply. If the driver delayed dealing with the question until after he had decided whether or not to accept the gap, there was a chance that he had partly forgotten the question. If so, his answer could be wrong as well as late.

Routine overlearnt skills less affected

Once the driver had decided to accept a narrow gap, his skill in steering the car through the gap was not reliably degraded by having to answer questions at the same time. This is because steering the car had become pretty automatic. The result is in line with the results of laboratory experiments on tracking. Practised people can track almost as well when they have to carry out an additional task which involves listening and speaking as they can without the additional task (Garvey and Taylor, 1959). After sufficient practice, the computer of Figure 2 has only to initiate actions. Once practised actions have been initiated, they can be executed using the path between the long-term memory and the output selector which is indicated by the broken arrow. The computer is then freed temporarily for the other task. As long as the eyes are still looking at the tracking display, a critical change in the display can capture back the input selector. The input selector will then switch the computer back to the tracking task.

It is additional visual tasks which degrade tracking (Garvey, 1960; Fuchs, 1962). This is because a person cannot look in two places at once. While a driver is looking in his rear mirror, he cannot see his errors in steering. Thus they cannot attract his attention.

Decisions degraded by other stresses

An experimenter can present a subject with an unfamiliar task for the first time while he is under stress. This is a useful method of detecting the effect of a small amount of stress. An unfamiliar task is likely to be difficult. The subject has to understand what he has to do. He has to decide on the best strategy to use. The unbroken function in Figure 3 shows that an increase to only a moderately high level of arousal may reduce the person's efficiency if his arousal was previously at the relatively low optimum level required for a difficult task. Under the stress he may decide on a relatively poor strategy. He may resort to a routine overlearnt programme of behaviour which is not the most appropriate one. Unfamiliar tasks have yielded measurable changes in performance at relatively low levels of stress. The levels often lie below those at which changes in performance have been reported for practised tasks (Poulton, 1965).

Compensation by restricting attention

When a person is highly aroused he finds that he is performing badly, he may attempt to compensate by concentrating on the most important aspects of the task. Hockey (1970b) gave sixteen young sailors a tracking task to represent steering a car in traffic. The subject was told to give the task top priority.

He had also to extinguish each of six lamps whenever one came on by pressing the corresponding one of six buttons with his left hand. The lamps were arranged in a semicircle. When he was looking at the tracking display

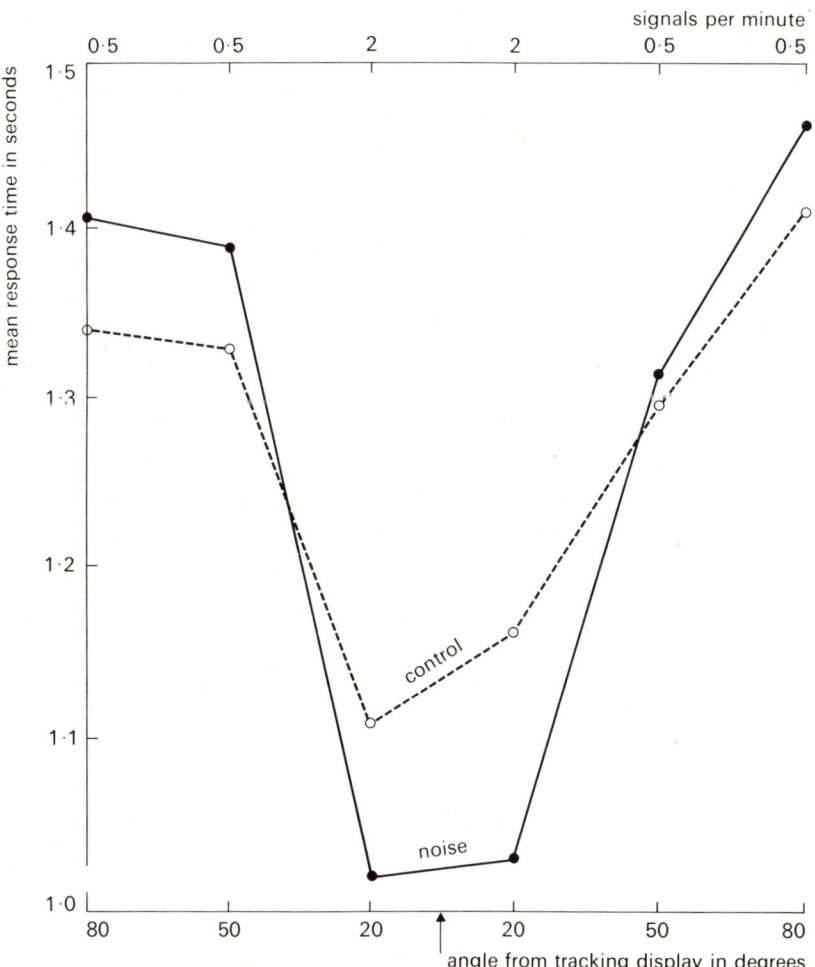

Figure 4 *The average time taken to respond in noise and in quiet to lamps fixed at different angles to the line of sight. (Results from Hockey, 1970b)*

directly in front of him, the six lamps subtended the angle to his line of sight which are shown at the bottom of Figure 4. The two lamps twenty degrees out from his line of sight each came on an average of twice per minute at irregular intervals of time. The four lamps further out each came on an average of once every two minutes. This is indicated at the top of the figure. Lamps coming on might correspond to the movements of other road users, or of pedestrians stepping off the pavement into the road.

After practice in quiet, the sailors had to perform the combined task for forty minutes, once in noise of 100 decibels and once in quiet. The average performance of both tasks was equally proficient but the averages concealed differences in the actual scores. In quiet, the average time for which the tracking task was performed accurately decreased from the first ten minutes of the task to the last ten minutes. In noise there was if anything a slight improvement over the forty minutes.

The effect of the noise on the average time taken to extinguish the lamps is illustrated in Figure 4. The lamps close to the man's line of sight as he looked at the tracking display were always extinguished more quickly on average than the lamps further towards the side. But in noise the difference was exaggerated. The sailors concentrated harder on the two nearer lamps which came on most frequently, at the expense of the four further lamps which did not come on so often.

The results can be interpreted as an attempt by the sailors to compensate for the effects of the noise. They did so by concentrating on the most important aspects of the combined task, the tracking which they had been told to give the top priority, and the nearer two lights which between them presented two-thirds of the signals. By doing so, they were able to achieve as good an average performance in the noise as they could in the quiet. When a person first enters a hot room, he becomes more alert or highly aroused. He shows a similar concentration of attention upon what he takes to be the important aspects of a task of this kind (Bursill, 1958; Poulton and Kerslake, 1965).

There appears to be no attempted compensation when a person is less aroused than usual, as after a night without sleep. Hockey (1970a) gave twelve young sailors the same combined tracking and lamps task. After practice with normal sleep, they performed the combined task twice, once after a night without sleep and once after normal sleep. At the start, the sailors performed equally well in both conditions. But soon their performance when they had gone without sleep became worse than their performance after normal sleep. After a normal night's sleep, the average time for which the tracking task was performed accurately decreased over the forty minutes of the task. The decrease was almost three times as large after loss of sleep.

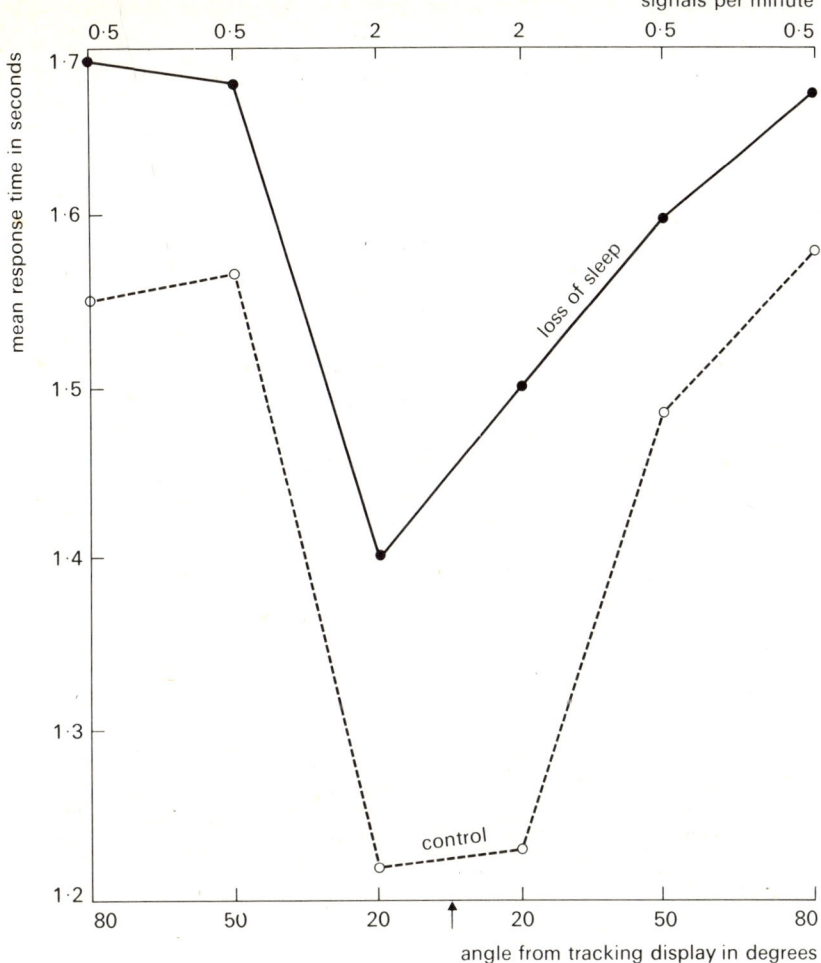

Figure 5 The average time taken to respond after a night without sleep and after normal sleep, to lamps fixed at different angles to the line of sight. (Results from Hockey, 1970a)

Figure 5 shows that after a night without sleep the lamps in every position were extinguished less quickly than after normal sleep. The effect came on gradually during the forty minutes on the task. For the first ten minutes there was little difference between the two conditions. For the last ten of the forty minutes the difference was even more marked than that illustrated in Figure 5, because the figure shows the times averaged over the whole forty minutes on the task. It was the two lamps closest to the man's line of sight as he looked at the tracking display which showed the greatest increase in response time. They were the important lamps which presented two-thirds of all the signals. Thus if anything, performance on the important parts of the combined task deteriorated more after a night without sleep than performance on the less important parts.

6 One Stress on Top of Another

Often people are subjected to more than one stress at a time. A person may have had to stand all night on a crowded ferry boat. He may have taken a tablet of hyoscine to avoid being seasick. A moderate dose of hyoscine by itself reduces arousal below the optimum. On the five-choice task of Figure 1, hyoscine reduces the rate of responding. Loss of a night's sleep by itself reduces the rate of responding, and may also increase errors on the five-choice task. When loss of sleep is combined with hyoscine, the two effects add together. The person works still more slowly. He produces about as many errors as he does with loss of sleep alone (Poulton, 1970, Tables 9 and 10).

A person may have to sleep and work in a restricted noisy place, such as an aircraft carrier while aircraft are taking off and landing throughout the twenty-four hours. The noise may prevent him from sleeping. He then reports for work in noise while he is feeling sleepy. On the five-choice task of Figure 1, noise by itself increases the number of errors. It does not appreciably affect the rate of work. Loss of a night's sleep by itself increases errors and reduces the rate of work. When noise is combined with loss of sleep, errors are not as frequent as they would be if the two effects added together. Also the person may not work as slowly as he does when he has simply lost a night's sleep.

The combined effect can be explained using the arousal model of Figure 3. Loss of sleep produces inefficiency because it lowers arousal. Noise increases arousal. When noise is combined with loss of sleep, arousal is not as low as it is with loss of sleep by itself. The person who has lost a night's sleep and works in noise, is not as inefficient as a person who has lost a night's sleep and works in a quiet place (Wilkinson, 1963).

There is a more acceptable method of reducing the effect of a night's lost sleep. Telling a person how he is performing increases his arousal. On the five-choice task of Figure 1, knowledge of results by itself increases the rate of work and reduces the number of errors. This is the exact opposite of the effect of loss of sleep. If a person is given knowledge of results after loss of a night's sleep, he does not work as slowly, or make as many errors, as he does with loss of sleep without knowledge of results. The two effects tend to cancel each other out. The deterioration in performance produced by a night without sleep is considerably larger than the improvement normally produced by knowledge of results. So giving the knowledge of results to a person who has lost a night's sleep does not fully prevent the deterioration. But the improvement produced by knowledge of results is greater when a person has lost a night's sleep that it is when he has slept normally. The combined effect can again be explained using the arousal model of Figure 3 (Wilkinson, 1961).

Giving knowledge of results is not always as beneficial as this. If a person is already highly aroused, giving him knowledge of results does not help as much as usual. This is what happens when knowledge of results is given to a person who is working in noise. On the five-choice task of Figure 1 noise by itself usually increases the number of errors, without altering the rate of work. In this particular experiment, the increase in errors was not consistent enough to be accepted as reliable. Knowledge of results by itself reduces the number of errors and increases the rate of work. When knowledge of results was given to people working in noise, it had a smaller effect than it did when it was given to the people working in quiet (Wilkinson, 1963).

This effect can also be explained using the arousal model of Figure 3. Knowledge of results increases arousal. When a person has worked once or twice with knowledge of results, he is not adequately aroused without it (Brown, 1966a). Without knowledge of results, he might be at the point A_1 in the figure. Giving him knowledge of results might increase his arousal to A_2. His efficiency therefore increases. Subjecting him to noise as well increases his arousal still further, in the direction of A_3. His efficiency is still higher than it was at A_1. But it is not as high as it was at A_2 without the noise.

7 Avoiding the Effects of Stress

A person works most efficiently when he is alert, or moderately aroused (Figure 3). If he wishes to work efficiently, he should avoid stresses which change his arousal from the optimum. Important or dangerous work should not be carried out under stresses which raise or lower arousal too much.

With the best intentions, a student may find some secluded place in which to study, well away from distractions. Unless he adopts an efficient strategy of study, his arousal will gradually but inevitably fall. Arousal will fall more quickly if the student has run up a sleep debt because he has not been sleeping well. Perhaps he is feeling sleepy because he has not fully recovered from the sleeping tablets which he took the previous evening in order to be certain of a good night's sleep (McKenzie and Elliott, 1965). As his arousal falls, his work becomes less efficient. He may suddenly realize that he has read a number of pages, but cannot recall anything in them. At this stage he may quit study. Or he may persevere, conscientiously but ineffectively.

There are a number of ways by which a student can keep himself alert when he is working alone. He can set himself targets. He can decide to learn the contents of a certain number of pages in a certain time. When time is up, he can note whether he has reached his target or not. This tells him how quickly he is working.

A student should also quiz himself as he goes along. If quizzes are not given in the textbook, he should make up his own. At the end of a section he can quickly note down the main points he has learnt. He can then check them by going through the text again rapidly. Quizzes tell him how efficiently he is working.

This method of study breaks up a prolonged period of work. Study is followed by quizzes and by quick revisions which provide knowledge of results on the effectiveness of the work. Short breaks for coffee or tea between assignments also help to break up a prolonged period of work. Discussing the work with colleagues during breaks may help to maintain interest in it. All these procedures help to keep the student alert.

8 Summary

A skilled performance involves decisions and precise movements. Figure 2 illustrates how the brain works during a skilled performance. The computer of Figure 2 is most efficient when arousal is at the optimum level illustrated in Figure 3. Stress has a marked effect upon the quality of decisions. Stress has less effect upon highly practised movements which have become partly automatic. When a person is too highly aroused, he may compensate by restricting his attention to the most important parts of the job (Figure 4). The effects of a combination of stresses can be predicted fairly well from the arousal model of Figure 3. There are ways of preventing the fall in arousal which occurs during quiet study.

Further Reading

Christopher Poulton's *Environment and Human Efficiency* (Charles C. Thomas, 1970) provides a broad introduction to stress and its effects upon skilled performance. Skilled performance is treated in A. T. Welford's *Fundamentals of Skill* (Prentice-Hall, 1967), and in *Principles of Skill Acquisition,* edited by E. A. Bilodeau and I. M. Bilodeau (Academic Press, 1969). C. Poulton's *Tracking Skill and Manual Control* (to be published in 1972) is more specialized. David Legge's book of readings *Skills* (Penguin, 1970) provides a useful introduction to the subject. Perceptual skills are treated in U. Neisser's *Cognitive Psychology* (Appleton-Century-Crofts, 1967).

References

Bahrick, H. P., Noble, M. E., and **Fitts, P. M.** (1954) 'Extra-task performance as a measure of learning a primary task', *Journal of Experimental Psychology,* vol. 48, pp. 298-302.
Broadbent, D. E. (1957a), 'Effects of noise on behaviour', in C. M. Harris (ed.), *Handbook of Noise Control,* McGraw-Hill.
Broadbent, D. E. (1957b), 'Immediate memory and simultaneous stimuli', *Quarterly Journal of Experimental Psychology,* vol. 9, pp. 1-11.
Broadbent, D. E. (1958), *Perception and Communication,* Pergamon.
Brown, L. D. (1966a), 'An asymmetrical transfer effect in research on knowledge of performance', *Journal of Applied Psychology,* vol. 50, pp. 118-120.
Brown, I. D. (1966b), 'Subjective and objective comparisons of successful and unsuccessful trainee drivers', *Ergonomics,* vol. 9, pp. 49–56.
Brown, I. D., and **Poulton, E. C.** (1961), 'Measuring the spare "mental capacity" of car drivers by a subsidiary task', *Ergonomics,* vol. 4, pp. 35-40.
Brown, I. D., Tickner, A. H., and **Simmonds, D. C.** (1966). 'Interference between concurrent tasks of driving and telephoning', *Journal of Applied Psychology,* vol. 53, pp. 419–424.
Bursill, A. E. (1958), 'The restriction of peripheral vision during exposure to hot and humid conditions', *Quarterly Journal of Experimental Psychology,* vol. 10, pp. 113-129.
Davis, R. (1957) The human operator as a single channel information system. *Quarterly Journal of Experimental Psychology,* vol. 9, pp. 119–129.
Eriksen, C. W. and Lappin, J. S. (1967) Selective attention and very short-term recognition memory for nonsense forms. *Journal of Experimental Psychology,* vol. 73, pp. 358–364.
Fitts, P. M. (1954) The information capacity of the human motor system in controlling the amplitude of movement. *Journal of Experimental Psychology,* vol. 47, pp. 381–391.
Fuchs, A. H. (1962) The progression-regression hypothesis in perceptual-

motor skill learning. *Journal of Experimental Psychology,* vol. 63, pp. 177–182.

Garvey, W. D. (1960) A comparison of the effects of training and secondary tasks on tracking behaviour. *Journal of Applied Psychology,* vol. 44, pp. 370–375.

Garvey, W. D. and Taylor, F. V. (1959) Interactions among operator variables, system dynamics, and task-induced stress. *Journal of Applied Psychology,* vol. 43, pp. 79–85.

Hockey, G. R. J. (1970a) Changes in attention allocation in a multi-component task under loss of sleep. *British Journal of Psychology,* vol. 61, pp. 473–480.

Hockey, G. R. J. (1970b) Signal probability and spatial location as possible bases for increased selectivity in noise. *Quarterly Journal of Experimental Psychology,* vol. 22, pp. 37–42.

Lazarus, R. S., Deese, J., and Osler, S. F. (1952) The effects of psychological stress upon performance. *Psychological Bulletin,* vol. 49, pp. 293–317.

Leonard, J. A. (1959) MRC Applied Psychology Research Report, No. 326/59.

McKenzie, R. E. and Elliott, L. L. (1965) Effects of secobarbital and d-emphetamine on performance during a simulated air mission. *Aerospace Medicine,* vol. 36, pp. 774–779.

Poulton, E. C. (1965) On increasing the sensitivity of measures of performance. *Ergonomics,* vol. 8, pp. 69–76.

Poulton, E. C. (1966) Tracking behaviour, in E. A. Bilodeau (ed.). *Acquisition of Skill,* Academic Press.

Poulton, E. C. (1970) *Environment and Human Efficiency,* C. C. Thomas.

Poulton, E. C. and Kerslake, D. McK. (1965) Initial stimulating effect of warmth upon perceptual efficiency. *Aerospace Medicine,* vol. 36, pp. 29–32.

Sargant, W. (1957) Battle for the Mind, (Heinemann).

Sperling, G. (1960) The information available in brief visual presentations. *Psychological Monographs, vol. 74, No. 11 (whole No. 498).*

Welford, A. T. (1967) Single channel operation in the brain. *Acta Psychologica,* vol. 27, pp. 5–22.

Wilkinson, R. T. (1961) Interaction of lack of sleep with knowledge of results, repeated testing and individual differences. *Journal of Experimental Psychology,* vol. 66, pp. 332–337.

Wilkinson, R. T. (1963) Interaction of noise with knowledge of results and sleep deprivation. *Journal of Experimental Psychology,* vol. 66, pp. 332–337.

Wilkinson, R. T. (1969) Sleep deprivation: performance tests for partial and selective sleep deprivation, in L. A. Abt and B. F. Reiss (eds.). *Progress in Clinical Psychology,* vol. 7, Grune.

Wilkinson, R. T., Fox, R. H., Goldsmith, R., Hampton, I. F. G. and Lewis, H. E. (1964) Psychological and physiological responses to raised body temperatures. *Journal of Applied Physiology,* vol. 19, pp. 287–291.

4.5 Methods of Predicting Human Reliability in Man-Machine Systems[1]

David Meister
The Bunker-Ramo Corporation, Canoga Park, California

Introduction

It can be said, without too much exageration, that the primary purpose of human factors as a technology is the prediction and measurement of human error.

To the extent that the operator is an essential component of the system, it becomes necessary to measure his potentiality for failure (which, in behavioural terms, means error). Therefore, the need to ascertain what may be called 'human reliability' (defined as the probability that a task will be successfully performed at any required stage in system operation within a criterion time period) has to be considered in the determination of equipment reliability.

Before discussing the approaches that have been taken to solving this problem, it is necessary to define error and the context in which it is to be measured. Characteristically, error has been described in terms of the traditional four-fold category: (1) performance of a required action incorrectly (i.e., its performance beyond specified response limits); (2) failure to perform the required action; (3) performance of a required action out of sequence; and (4) performance of a non-required action. While this categorization adequately describes the range of errors that can be made, it is necessary to add one qualification: the error must have a significant effect either upon the system as a whole or upon some behavioural component of the system, such

Acknowledgement

Reprinted, by permission, from D. Meister, 'Methods of predicting human reliability in man-machine systems' in *Human Factors*, Vol. 6. 1964 The Johns Hopkins University Press.

[1]This article is an integration and review of four papers presented as the Symposium on Quantification of Human Performance; the author has added certain statements and comments for which only he can be held responsible. Primary credit for much of the material in this paper must go to Drs Altman, Swain, Rook, Miller, Irwin and their collaborators, whose papers formed the basis of this review. Where subsequent reference is made to any of these individuals, it should be understood that his collaborators are implicitly included.

as a task. If, in the context of the total system, an error does not have this effect, it has no value.

For practical system operation purposes, reversible errors are irrelevant. Error will be defined, then, as any deviation from a system performance standard which is caused directly or indirectly by an operator and which has significant consequences to the system operation in which it was made.

Because the context of error measurement is the man-machine system, additional problems arise from the hierarchical nature of system organization. Where error measurement and prediction starts at an elementaristic level, e.g. the task element as defined by Miller (1962), roughly corresponding to simple visual-motor stimulus-response sequences—such measures must be combined or integrated to derive higher-order error measures for tasks, mission phases, and overall system performance. This creates a problem because it is often difficult to discern or predict the consequences of an individual error at the task level when the meaning of that error may change as a function of that task being integrated with other tasks. The precise method of integrating task errors to determine overall system error is also an unknown, although as a first approximation a simple series relationship ($a \times b \times c \ldots \times n$) has been postulated, largely because reliability engineering theory utilizes the same relationship in its product role.

In addition, the factors producing error may change as one deals with larger units of system behaviour. While it may be possible at the task element level to ignore such molar variables as stress and motivation, gross individual and situational variables may strongly affect tasks and task combinations. The problem of error measurement cannot therefore be relegated to the task element or tasks level, even though one begins there; error must now be raised, so to speak, to the system power. In this discussion of error prediction and measurement, therefore, the reader must always remember that even when error is considered at the task level, it has little meaning until it can be applied within the context of the overall system.

The various methods of error estimation that are described in this paper have certain common characteristics which were adumbrated earlier. It will, hopefully, be instructive to the reader to point out these similarities before analyzing the methods in detail.

(1) These methods all are based on a simple multiplicative probability model very similar to, if not identical with, that used in reliability engineering. Williams (1958) has suggested that if quantitative estimates of operator reliability for tasks were available, these could be readily inserted into conventional probability models and combined to

secure more complex estimates of system performance reliability. The great difficulty has been the nonavailability of basic human error rate data on which to base these estimates.

(2) The methods developed are all elementaristic, in that they begin with a detailed analysis of behavioural elements for which error probabilities are secured; these then are combined through the use of the probability model mentioned in Item (1) to form more complex task reliabilities and, ultimately, system reliability. It is important to note that the probability model through which that combination is accomplished assumes independence of task elements. Such simplifying assumptions are undoubtedly only partially correct.

(3) Although, as will be clarified later, there is a substantial subjective factor in the derivation of element and task error estimates, these methods are basically quantitative and statistical in nature. It is the quantitative basis of these methods which, despite their crudeness, excites our interest. The statistical nature of these methods means that they do not attempt to predict individual operator errors, although, of course, the latter are measured individually. These methods extend only to the development of probability predictions for a mean or distribution of population responses, and, therefore, any prediction will be itself in error to a certain extent with regard to any individual operator response.

The Data Store

The great deficiency in the development of error prediction methods has been the lack of available data. A set of human performance estimates for a large number of behavioural elements (phrased in terms of the probability of successful performance) is needed. The first (and, as far as it is known, only) effort to supply these data has come from the work of Altman and his colleagues at the American Institute for Research (1962). This work was directed toward the development of an operability index.

Three objectives were set for this index:

(1) It would be task oriented. That is, equipment design would be evaluated in terms of its compatibility with specific human operations.

(2) Scores from the operability index would be directly meaningful in terms of time and error of performance (speed and reliability).

(3) Data on speed and reliability of operator performance would be obtained, insofar as possible, from available experimental and field data.

To meet these objectives, it was necessary to establish a framework within which the kinds of information commonly found in descriptions of personnel functions and tasks could be related to human performance estimates. It was assumed that existing methods of task description would be generally adequate for the purpose of developing the index; hence, major effort was directed toward the design of a performance data store (known as the Data Store).

However, tasks, as usually defined, were considered too complex to serve as the basic unit of performance prediction. Consequently, the 'behaviour' or task element was selected as the basic unit of evaluation for the operability index. In Altman's terms a behaviour is a specific step or action in a given task. Each behaviour was subdivided into three aspects: (1) inputs or stimuli to the human senses; (2) mediating processes; and (3) outputs or responses (i.e., motor activities). These aspects generally fit the commonly accepted Stimulus-Organism-Response paradigm.

Altman identified a number of type of equipment, behavior, and equipment-behavior components likely to affect each aspect of behaviour. These components, listed in Table 1, represent a compromise between what are desirable as psychologically meaningful categories and categories for which data are available. Note, for example, the paucity of categories under 'Mediating Process'; this occurs because there is little usable information about the quantitative effects of mediating process variables on performance. At the time the index was developed, it seemed gratuitous to categorize mediating processes elaborately, and undoubtedly the situation has not changed a great deal, although some efforts are currently under way by Altman and his co-workers to develop a more comprehensive taxonomy of mediating processes.

Table 1 List of Input, Mediating Process, and Output Components

Inputs	*Mediating Process*	*Outputs*
Circular scales	Identification/ recognition	Cable connections
Counters	Manipulation	Cranks
Labeling		Disconnecting
Lights		Joysticks
Linear scales		Knobs
Nonspeech		Levers
Scopes		Object positioning
Semicircular scales		Pushbuttons
Speech		Rotary selectors
		Speech
		Toggle switches
		Writing

After breaking down behavioral aspects into components, each component was dissected into its relevant parameters. (Sample parameters for the input component 'lights' are listed in Table 2). Finally, each parameter was divided into dimensions that are either discrete categories or intervals on a continuum (Table 3). A summary of the behavioural levels involved in the Data Store is shown in Table 4.

Table 2 Parameters Affecting Performance on Lights

Component	Parameters
Lights	Size
	Brightness
	Type/function
	Number
	Presentation

Table 3 Sample Dimensions

Component: Circular Scales	
Parameter: Scale Diameter	*Parameter: Scale Style*
(Integral Dimensions) (in)	*(Discrete Dimensions)*
1–1.5	
1.6–1.8	Moving pointer
1.9–2.8	Moving scale

Human performance data. Altman and his co-workers searched several thousand research reports for data they could use to estimate the effect of design dimensions on performance. They found usable data in 164 reports. It is a sad reflection on the state of the experimental literature that Altman found it inconsistent with respect to identification, description, or treatment of independent, control, or dependent variables. Although human engineering studies yielded the most relevant information, it was difficult to establish performance standards from these studies because they were aimed at answering specific questions and were not related to any theoretical framework.

Experimental results relevant to each component were summarized in tables so that discrepancies and areas of missing data could be identified. Most of the discrepancies between the results of different experiments varying the same component came, as one would expect, from gross differences in the mediating processes required of the subjects. By analyzing the nature of these differences, it was possible in some cases to reconcile the discrepancies

Table 4   Behavioural Levels

Mission: operate fuse jammer
  Phase: prepare for operation
    Task: activate amplifier
      Behavior (or step): throw S11 to ON position
        Aspects of Behavior: (inputs, mediating processes, outputs)
          Components: (specific categories of an aspect) toggle switch as a component of output
            Parameters: (relevant characteristics of components) angle of the throw from position, as a parameter of the component toggle switch
              Dimensions: (specific values or characteristics of parameters) 40°.

---

and to arrive at comparable error rates for the component in question. To find the missing data, Altman searched the literature; where this search was fruitless, he interpolated or extrapolated from related studies. Where no experimental data could be obtained, judgment was used to establish estimated effects—sometimes supplemented by 'quick and dirty' empirical studies using members of the project staff.

To secure standard time estimates, the minimum time (sec) required for an operation (when all dimensions within a given component were optimum) was identified. This was called base time. Average time increases for the operation of a component with other (non-optimum) dimensions also were established. Therefore, to get the total time for an operation, one adds the time increments to the base time.

The resultant response time and reliability estimates were put into a central Data Store (Munger *et al.*, 1962). A sample Data Store card for the component 'joystick' is shown in Fig. 1.

Joystick
(May move in many planes)

Base time = 1.93 sec.

Time Added (sec)	Reliability		
		1	Stick length
1.50	0.9963		(a) 6–9 in
0	0.9967		(b) 12–18 in
1.50	0.9963		(c) 21–27 in
		2	Extent of stick movement (Extent of movement from one extreme to the other in a single plane)
0	0.9981		(a) 5–20 degrees
0.20	0.9975		(b) 30–40 degrees
0.50	0.9960		(c) 40–60 degrees
		3	Control resistance
0	0.9999		(a) 5–10 lb
0.50	0.9992		(b) 10–30 lb
		4	Support of operating member
0	0.9990		(a) Present
1.00	0.9950		(a) Absent
		5	Time delay (time lapse between movement of control and movement of display)
0	0.9967		(a) 0.3 sec
0.50	0.9963		(b) 0.6–1.5 sec
3.00	0.9957		(c) 3.0 sec

Figure 1   Sample data store card.

Method of using the Data Store. The application of the Data Store requires the completion of several major steps:

(1) Equipment design information and data obtained from task analyses must be analyzed into behavioral steps and sequenced by mission phases. This means that a dimension must be analyzed to its component input, mediating process, and output aspects. For each of these, a time and reliability estimate is secured.

(2) Each operation must be subdivided to its relevant components, parameters, and dimensions for each behavioral step.

(3) Each of these dimensions must be assigned a reliability estimate from the Data Store. These estimates are then used to derive scores for units of behavior, such as steps, tasks, phases, and entire missions.

In general, time scores are the *sum* of individual time estimates for each dimension. Reliability scores are the *product* of individual reliability estimates for each dimension. Thus, if there are five relevant parameters for the input, there will be five times and five individual reliability estimates. In the first case, these are added together; in the second, they are multiplied. The same process is followed with any relevant parameters of the mediating process and outputs. If these describe all relevant aspects of the step, they are added and multiplied together to derive the total step time and reliability. In the same way, similar estimates are derived for every other step, and, likewise, their step times are added together and step reliabilities multiplied to secure the total step. As is obvious, the process is one of starting at the most elementaristic level and progressively combining elements to secure a more complex output. The total output is a reliability score that is an estimate of the probability that serious operator error will not occur within the span of performance encompassed by the score.

Forms (Munger, 1962) and instructions (Payne *et al.*, 1962) have been developed for manual scoring for the Operability Index. More recently, the Data Store and scoring procedure have been computerized (Munger and Mohn, 1965) and are available on punched cards. An instruction manual for use of the computerized index has also been developed (Munger, 1965).

Data Store validity and reliability. By its very nature, the Data Store is a source of reliability estimates that can be applied to many systems and situations beyond those for which it was developed. Some of these applications shall be seen later when the study by Irwin *et al.* is examined. Because the estimates provided describe behavioral elements that are present in almost all tasks, regardless of their specific character, the natural inclination of the human engineer, searching for a source of quantitative data, is to pounce upon the Data Store and to apply it. It is therefore, especially necessary to examine the validity and reliability of the Data Store estimates.

Although the Data Store has been applied in other contexts, the only systematic tests of its validity and reliability have been conducted by its developers. The construct validity of the Data Store (its measurement of factors critical to operator performance) seems, on the face of it, to be established, because its reliability estimates were derived from an experimentally demonstrated relationship to performance time and operator error. However, these estimates involve a judgment in which laboratory-derived error estimates were weighted against estimates of overall field reliability.

The critical method of measuring the validity of a device such as the Data Store is to determine how well (based on its estimates) predictions of operator performance conform to actual performance in an operational situation. Unfortunately, because of the relative unavailability of operators and their equipment, the infrequency of errors etc., Altman and his coworkers found it impossible to obtain statistical measures of predictive validity on the Data Store. However, an attempt was made to assess the opinion of experienced operators and their supervisors with regard to the potential error associated with each of four equipments. These equipments were ranked in order of judged complexity and these rankings compared with total time and reliability scores based on application of the Data Store to these equipments.

Data Store applications. The purpose of the Data Store is to provide information for deciding upon the acceptability of a given equipment configuration. Two types of decisions can be made: (1) can required operations usually be performed within the time expected to be available? and (2) is operator reliability (as determined by Data Store estimates) sufficient for the intended mission of the equipment? In addition, it is possible to determine which of two or more equipment configurations is less susceptible to operator error and should therefore be selected for incorporation in hardware. Provided that sufficient detailed information is known about equipment, it is also possible to apply the Data Store estimates to operating procedures, either to determine whether a particular procedure will meet specified reliability and time requirements or to compare two or more alternative procedures.

It should be noted parenthetically that the author has found the reliability estimates provided by the Data Store to be far more valuable to him than the time data. The reasons for this are two-fold: (1) many tasks are not closely time-dependent (i.e., the task may be performed within very generous time limits); but more importantly, (2) reliability prediction estimates are concerned only with the binary concept of success or failure to operate; variations in performance time within an acceptable time period represent success, while performance outside this time period represents failure. Consequently, performance time estimates always must be translated into failure or error probabilities to be meaningful.

The Data Store presents perhaps its greatest potential usefulness in predesign, when empirical data (which are, of course, always preferable) are not available and the decisions noted above must be made. Here, however, one also encounters the most severe problem in the use of the Data Store; its use requires the most minute knowledge of equipment characteristics, and this information may be lacking in the predesign period.

Moreover, the Data Store seems to be primarily applicable to discrete, procedural tasks; it is hard to see its application to continuous tasks, such as tracking. In addition, nothing in the Data Store suggests the occurrence of particular *kinds* of errors, or, more importantly, their effect on the system; because the error rates describe the most elementaristic behavior level, their ultimate effect on the overall system cannot be predicted. Even with these disadvantages, however, the Data Store provides what is called a 'ballpark' estimate (which is generally better than intuitive guesses usually applied at this stage of system development).

Summary evaluation. It is apparent that if one applies rigorous standards of validity and reliability measurement commonly applied to experimental tests, the Data Store would be found seriously wanting. Even the developers admit this when they say that 'adequate validation yet remains to be done...' (Payne and Altman, 1962).

And yet, if one applies a pragmatic standard to the Data Store, it is impossible not to be conscious of the extraordinary importance of the work performed in its compilation. Even if the Data Store estimates contain major inadequacies, they are a pioneering effort whose equal has not yet been made available to us. They are in any event at least as acceptable as the equipment reliability estimates which served as their model and which have been of great value despite serious sampling and measurement inadequacies. No claim is made by the developers of the Data Store that the latter is more than a useful tool to be used as a starting point for further studies which may lead to the development of more refined human performance reliability estimates.

THERP (Technique for Human Error Rate Prediction)

The most outstanding extension of the error rate Data Store collected by Altman and his colleagues has been the development of a method for evaluating the human error contribution to system degradation. This method, which is called THERP (Swain, 1963, 1964; and Swain *et al.,* 1963), is also based upon probability theory and other methods used by reliability engineers.

THERP has been used primarily to provide quantitative predictions of system degradation resulting from human errors in association with equipment reliability, operational procedures, and other system characteristics which influence human behavior. THERP is an iterative procedure that consists of five steps which are repeated, not always in the same order, until the system degradation resulting from human error is at an acceptable level. The five steps are listed below and described more fully on the following pages.

(1) Define the system or subsystem failure which is to be evaluated.

(2) Identify and list all the human operations performed and their relationships to system tasks and functions.

(3) Predict error rates for each human operation or group of operations pertinent to the evaluation.

(4) Determine the effect of human errors on the system.

(5) Recommend changes as necessary to reduce the system or subsystem failure rate as a consequence of the estimated effects of the recommended changes.

As the originators of this methodology point out (Swain, 1964) "the steps are typical of the usual system reliability study if one substitutes 'hardware' for 'humans'." What distinguishes it from Altman's work is that the methodology that was only implied in the Data Store has now been made elaborate and systematized.

Steps in the utilization of THERP

(1) *Define the system failure.* The first step in the application of THERP is to define the system (or part-system) failure which is to be evaluated. This failure may vary from (a) such distal criteria in the life of a weapon as the probability of the weapon failing to explode within a certain area and altitude at a certain time to (b) more proximal criteria such as the failure of a component in the weapon to meet engineering specifications. The human-factors evaluation is restricted to the influences of the human element on system failure and therefore identifies only part of the total unreliability of the system. This restriction does not remove the interactions of machine and human influences from the evaluation, but it does eliminate consideration of the influences of machine variables *per se.*

(2) *List the human operations.* The next step is to identify and list all the human operations performed and their relationships to system tasks and functions. System and task analysis, a method familiar to human-factors specialists, is the basic method used in this step.

The system and task analysis presumably uncovers all those possible human actions and procedures that can enter into the evaluation. They include whatever human procedures are required in the event of equipment defects or breakdowns or to compensate for other abnormal conditions. They also include human operations which are not a part of the prescribed operating procedure but which might be substituted for the required human operations.

The task analysis is usually modeled as a probability tree (see Fig. 2). This tree is useful in applying predictions of individual error rates, predictions of various use factors (including environmental and stress influences), and predictions of the quantitative effects of errors and use factors on system and subsystem reliability goals. The branches of the probability tree represent a diagrammatic task analysis which illustrates pictorially the sequence and flow of task behaviors and other task or situational relationships. As the name "probability tree" suggests, each branch (i.e., a task behavior or other system factor) is assigned a discrete probability of occurrence.

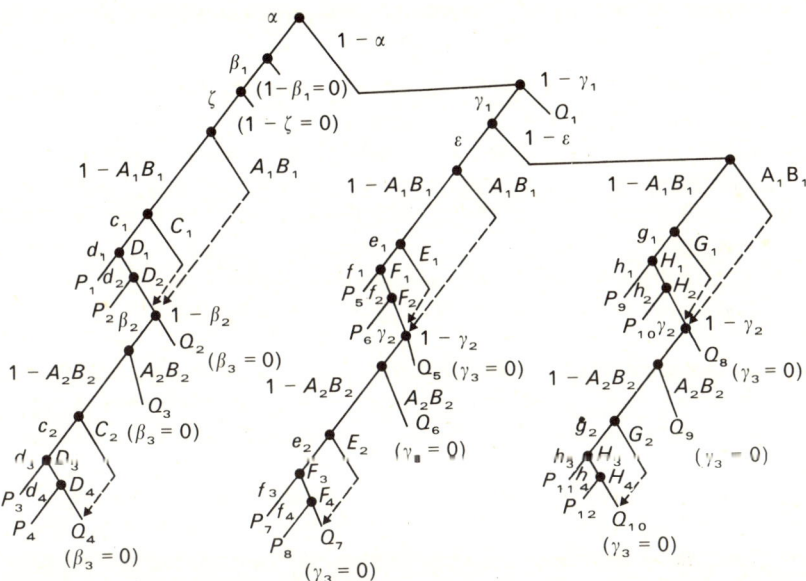

Figure 2 Probability tree illustrating branching techniques (taken from Swain, 1964). (P = success. Q = failure. Small English letters represent human successes. Capital English letters represent human failures. Greek letters represent probabilities of events not under direct control of the humans in the system.)

(3) *Predict individual error rates.* Individual error rates then are predicted by applying the Data Store to the probability tree, by generalizing from the results of simulation studies, or from error rate data on tasks comparable to the operational tasks being analyzed. These predictions are ordinarily made by a team of project engineers, operations researchers, system safety engineers, and human factors specialists.

Problems of dependence and independence of events, the effects of stress, climate, motivation, equipment malfunctions and various operational contingencies are included in the construction of the probability tree by assigning different probabilities to alternative branches which involve these conditions. Thus, much of the effort involved in applying THERP goes into the formation of the probability tree. Once this tree has been generated, application of the model follows conventional reliability prediction techniques. A computer program can be written to permit the analyst to vary his point estimates as an aid in making tradeoffs to find the optimum balance between predicted system reliability and various cost factors. The model can easily be expanded to include equipment reliability predictions to facilitate tradeoffs between allocation of system functions along continua of manual versus automatic modes of operation.

It is apparent that a probability tree for an entire man-machine system could be rather complex. In applications of THERP to date, the model has been used for limited portions of the system where it was apparent that there were serious tradeoff problems between human factors and other system considerations. In such cases, the probability tree contained no more than 50 branchings, and the appropriate equations were written manually and the computations were done on desk calculators rather than by electronic data processing.

In the application of THERP, no attempt has been made to use *distributions* of performance data, although such information could be used when available and reasonably accurate. Instead, as noted above, point estimates have been used. These usually have consisted of predictions of average error rates or average values of other system factors. In some cases, two, three, or more predicted values from a presumed distribution have been used and these have become separate branches of the probability tree. In other cases, a 'fiducial approach' has been used wherein point estimates consist of gross predictions of the high range of error rates (e.g., two or more standard deviations above the mean). The fiducial approach maximizes the deleterious effects of errors on system reliability to illustrate the "worst case". Operating times for tasks have been handled in the same manner as error rates; that is, discrete values have been used rather than a distribution of times. Thus, the model enables one to predict the probability of some event within any specified period of time. Therefore THERP can be classified as a probabilistic model using discrete probabilities.

(4) *Determine the effects of human errors on the system.* Having determined the error rates, it is necessary to determine the probability $(F_i)_2$ that each error, error class, or group of errors which has occurred will result in a failure of the system or that part of the system being evaluated. This is essentially a judgment made by experts, hopefully on the basis of empirical data. Such judgments are acceptable

only when made by highly qualified personnel and should always be checked by available data. The probability of a failure condition resulting from a single incorrect performance of a human operation of Class i is the joint probability of $F_i P_i$, where P_i is the probability that an operation can and is supposed to occur and that it will lead to an error of Class i.

In determining the effects of an error, class of errors, or group of errors on the system, two major kinds of information are needed that usually require inputs from other specialists (such as reliability or project engineers and operations researchers). The first is the probability, independent of the motivation of the operator, that certain procedures will or can be followed. The second is the effect of failure in a human operation on equipment-failure rates or system effectiveness. The first probability enters into the calculation of P_i, and the second factor is F_i.

(5) *Recommend changes to system and calculate new system failure rate.* A logical final step in applying THERP to a man-machine system is to recommend changes, if necessary, to reduce the system or sub-system failure rate to an acceptable level and then to calculate the new failure rate which results from the estimated effects of the recommended changes. The difference between the old and new failure rates can then be balanced against the various costs of changing the system.

Assumptions about human behavior. Like other models for predicting human reliability, THERP is no better than the basic data store of human behavior probabilities and the assumptions which have to be made about the interactions of human behaviors and other events in a man-machine system. Swain *et al.*, (1963) describe some of the assumptions about human behavior which have had to be made in quantifying human performance.

(1)   Given that two tasks are behaviorally similar, the standard deviations of the distributions of the error rates for the two tasks are proportional to their means.

(2)   Given the usual work situation, a monitor of another man's work has only an approximate 0.85 probability of recognizing the latter's errors if these errors occur infrequently (i.e., with a rate of about 0.01 or less).

(3)   If a man has probability p of error for an important time-critical task on which errors occur infrequently, then his probability of making an error on Trial 2 (after he has made an error on Trial 1) is $2p$; for

Trial 3 (given errors on Trials 1 and 2) it is $4p$; for Trial 4 (given errors on Trials 1, 2, and 3) it is $8p$; and so on, until the limiting condition of a 1.0 error probability is reached.

(4) Given very little time-stress or other stressful conditions, squaring one's Trial 1 error rate as an estimate of the Trial 2 error rate will not introduce any important decrease in the accuracy of a reliability analysis.

(5) Given that the tasks being analyzed are analogous to critical behaviors of Strategic Air Command (SAC) pilots in an emergency situation in military aircraft as defined by investigators from AIR (see Ronan, 1953), an estimate of 10–20 per cent error rate for such tasks is felt to be a reasonable and expedient approximation. The rationale for these assumptions, which are largely based on empirical data, is found in Chapter 2 of Swain (1963).

These are some of the assumptions that have been made (and continue to be made) with the full knowledge that the rigor behind them leaves much to be desired. The fact that such assumptions are analogous to the kinds of assumptions often made by equipment reliability specialists or operations researchers may not, as Swain (1964) has pointed out, 'necessarily diminish the rage response by some behavior scientists who do not have the practical problems to solve for which THERP was devised as an aid.' In the meantime, it is well to emphasize that THERP is strictly an empirical approach; if it enables human factors personnel to make predictions sufficiently accurate for the purpose at hand, they should use it. It should be pointed out that human reliability specialists are far from complacent about some of the assumptions they have to make. They feel, however, that using the available data is better than forcing or permitting engineers or others not trained in human factors methodology to make their own estimates of human reliability equations to continue, as most do, to assume no degradation resulting from the human element.

Summary and Conclusions

It is apparent from the studies reported that a feasible *approach* to the prediction of human performance reliability has been developed. This approach has several major advantages:

(1) It is quantitative.

(2) It is related to and can be combined with probability estimates of hardware reliability.

(3) It can be applied to a great variety of man-machine systems, at least those that are largely procedural in nature.

(4) Perhaps most important of all, the conceptual framework on which this approach is based attempts to answer the correct (that is, the truly important) questions of performance measurement. Some of these questions are: (1) What is an error and how does one predict it? (2) How does one determine the effect of an error on the task and the system? (3) How does the interdependence of task elements and tasks influence error effects? and (4) What assumptions involving individual and situational variables must one make to predict and explain error effects?

The methodology does present the following substantial difficulties (however, these are entirely understandable, considering the early development status of the methodology).

(1) It demands a body of available data, which exists at the present time only in skeletal form.

(2) The method is elementaristic, relying on the combination of task-element reliabilities to secure more complex task and system reliability estimates.

(3) The elementaristic assumption implies independence of element behaviors, an assumption that all the available psychological evidence would lead us to believe is untrue.

(4) Its application requires a much more precise taxonomy of task elements and tasks and a more sophisticated understanding of task-element, task, mission, and system relationships.

Fortunately, the developers and users of this methodology are highly pragmatic in their orientation and are fully aware of its deficiencies. They use the method when they can, modify it where necessary, and discard it when something more adequate appears.

The greatest need is for more available applicable data. Interestingly enough, the emphasis on quantification in this methodology is not in the development of sophisticated theory but, rather, on the more mundane problem of empirical data gathering (although undoubtedly the method will structure the nature of the data gathering process and what is gathered). With some effort, therefore, it should be possible to develop the relatively simple studies that would lead to these data.

It is an unfortunate reflection on the state of our experimental literature that it has provided us with utterly inadequate, piecemeal data. While it is well to develop and test highly sophisticated psychological theories, these seem somewhat trivial as long as we cannot reliably predict even the grossest of errors. One is perhaps justified in asking: What are our other researchers doing in their precise, highly polished laboratories that is so important compared with this basic need? The problem is not merely one for human factors as a technology; it is also crucial to psychology as a whole.

The work reviewed is preliminary and tentative; its value lies in what it promises rather than in what it has accomplished. Yet, it shows what can be done, even under severe handicaps, and it encourages us to believe, even if it does not make us over confident, that a truly quantitative human factors discipline is some day possible.

References

Aeroneutronic Division, Philco Corporation, Newport Beach, California, (1964) AN/MSQ-19 test assistance program: operation and maintenance tests, test procedures and results of test administration.

Altman, J. W. (1964) A central store of human performance data. *Proceedings, symposium on quantification of human performance,* pp. 97–108. Albuquerque, New Mexico, August 17–19.

Berry, P. C. and Wulff, J. J. (1960) A procedure for predicting reliability of man-machine systems. *IRE National Convention Record,* pp. 112–120.

Cooper, J. I. (1961) Human-initiated failures and malfunction reporting. *IRE Transactions in Human Factors in Electronics,* vol. HFE, pp. 104–109.

Craig, R. C. and Purifoy, G. R. Jr. (1957) Training for emergency performance, III. Preliminary Field Study of Selected Recommendations, Pittsburgh: American Institute for Research.

Dewing, D. L. (1960) Reliability handbook, Aerojet-General Corporation, Sacramento, California, RCS 60–2.

Ebel, R. L. (1951) Estimation of the reliability of ratings, *Psychometrika,* **16(4)**, pp. 407–424.

Hovland, C. I. and Sherif, M. (1952) Judgmental phenomena and scales of attitude measurement: item displacement in Thurstone scales. *J. Abm. soc. Psych.,* **47,** pp. 822–832.

Irwin, I. A., Levitz, J. J., and Freed, A. M. (1964) Human reliability in the performance of maintenance, Report LRP 317/TDR-63-218, Aerojet-General Corporation, Sacramento, California, May.

Irwin, I. A., Levitz, J. J., and Freed, A. M. (1964) Human reliability in the performance of maintenance, *Proceedings, symposium on quantification of human performance,* pp. 143–198. Albuquerque, New Mexico, August 17–19.

Meister, D. (1962) The problem of human-initiated failures, *Proceedings, 8th National symposium on reliability and quality control,* pp. 234–239.

Washington, D. C., January 9–12.

Meister, D. (1964) Unpublished study.

Miller, G. E., Maxwell, R. A., Ferguson, L., and Galbo, C. J. (1964) Human factors aspects of reliability, Aeroneutronic Division, Philco Corporation, Newport Beach, California, January.

Miller, G. E., and Maxwell, R. A. (1964) A method for predicting operator reliability, *Proceedings, symposium on quantification of human performance,* pp. 122–139. Albuquerque, New Mexico, August 17–19.

Miller, R. B., Craig, R. C., and Purifoy, G. R. Jr. (1957) Analysis of perceptual, interpretive and judgmental demands of flight personnel during aircraft emergencies. Pittsburgh: American Institute for Research, April.

Miller, R. B. (1962) Task description and analysis in *Psychological principles in system development,* (ed.) Gagne, R. M. (New York, McGraw-Hill).

Munger, S. J. (1962) An index of electronic equipment operability: evaluation booklet. Pittsburgh: American Institute for Research, January 31.

Munger, S. J. (1965) Instruction manual: computerized index of electronic equipment operability. Pittsburgh: American Institute for Research.

Munger, S. J. and Mohn, G. (1965) Computerization of the index of electronic equipment operability. Pittsburgh: American Institute for Research.

Munger, S. J., Smith, R. W., and Payne, D. (1962) An index of electronic equipment operability: data store. Pittsburgh: American Institute for Research, January 31.

Payne, D. and Altman, J. W. (1962) An index of electronic equipment operability: report of development. Pittsburgh: American Institute for Research, January 31.

Payne, D., Altman, J. W., and Smith, R. W. (1962) An index of electronic equipment operability: instruction manual. Pittsburgh: American Institute for Research, January 31.

Price, A. D. (1962) Reliability analyses of the TACDEN-operator subsystem of the ARTOC. Aeroneutronic Division, Ford Motor Co., Newport Beach, California, August 22.

Ronan, W. W. (1953) Training for emergency procedures in multi-engine aircraft. Report AIR-153-53-FR-44. Pittsburgh: American Institute for Research, March.

Rook, L. W. (1962) Reduction of human error in industrial production, Report SCTM-93-62(14), Sandia Corporation, Albuquerque, New Mexico, June.

Rook, L. W. (1964) Predicting human error rates with the simple multiplicative model, unpublished study.

Shapero, A., Cooper, J. L., Rappaport, M., Erickson, C. J., Schaeffer, K. H., and Bates, C. J. Jr. (1960) Human engineering testing and malfunction data collection in weapon system test programs. Wright Air Development Division Technical Report 60–36, February.

Stephenson, W. A. (1950) Statistical approach to typology: the study of trait universes. *J. clin. Psych.*, January 26–37.

Swain, A. D. (1963) A method for performing a human-factors reliability analysis, Report SCR-685, Sandia Corporation, Albuquerque, New Mexico, August.

Swain, A. D. (1964) THERP, *Proceedings, symposium on quantification of human performance,* pp. 97–108, Albuquerque, New Mexico, August 17–19.

Swain, A. D., Altman, J. W., and Rook, L. W. Jr. (1963) Human error quantification: a symposium, Report SCR-610, Sandia Corporation, Albuquerque, New Mexico, April.

Thurstone, E. L. and Chave, E. J. (1929) *The measurement of attitude.* Chicago: University of Chicago Press.

Williams, H. L. (1958) Reliability evaluation of the human component in man-machine systems. *Electrical Manufacturing,* April, pp. 78–82.

Willis, H. R. (1962) The human error problem, Report 62–76, Martin Marietta Corporation, Denver, Colorado. Presented at American Psychological Association, September.

5 SITUATIONAL VIEWS OF THE INDIVIDUAL

5.1 Improved Operating Procedures Manuals

By J. D. Vandenberg
Lockheed Electronics Company, Plainfield, New Jersey, USA

1 Introduction

The United States' *Gemini 9* spacecraft did not achieve one of its major objectives—attachment to a target vehicle. The connection was impossible because improperly installed disconnect lanyards had not pulled a protective shroud away from the docking apparatus. This $900 000 failure (Waldron 1966) occurred because 'The written procedures used by technicians to ready the shroud were found to be insufficiently detailed to insure proper installation of the lanyards attached to the shroud separation mechanism' (Welford 1966).

This recent, widely publicized incident highlights a chronic problem: inadequate procedures manuals. Few shortcomings produce this kind of dramatic impact. However, the problem seems sufficiently widespread to justify a consideration of measures that might be taken to effect a general improvement.

Chapanis' (1965) recent article ably called attention to the problems people have with instructions and suggested avenues of research that might be undertaken to alleviate the problems. Wiedman and Ireland (1965) call attention to the fact that 'most current operator procedure documents are excessively wordy and not sufficiently keyed to the stimuli that should trigger operator actions'. Eames and Starr (1965) cite studies '... which reveal numerous inadequacies in technical handbooks at the point of use'. McLaughlin (1966) reports a controlled experiment demonstrating superiority of an improved pamphlet over an earlier one.

Chapanis and Eames and Starr do not cite publications that tell how to write a procedures manual. Wiedman and Ireland present no references at all. The mere appearance of these articles, together with the fact that none

---

Acknowledgement

Reprinted, by permission, from J. D. Vandenberg, 'Improved operating procedures manuals' in *Ergonomics*, Vol. 10, No. 2, 1967, Taylor and Francis Ltd.

contains references to writing guides or other aids, indicates that here indeed is a topic desperately in need of development.

This paper is intended as a further stimulus to such development. Accordingly, it discusses some of the attributes that a good operating procedures manual should possess. It also considers some of the practical problems that must be solved so that technical improvements can be realized. Finally, it indicates how these problems might be dealt with.

2 Desirable Procedures Manual Characteristics

The following are some desirable characteristics that procedures manuals should possess.

2.1 Provide several means of entry into the data

It is sometimes necessary for the reader to refer to material that has been read. This is especially so when some of the procedures have been memorized but additional detail is needed. Rapid information retrieval is facilitated by providing several means of entry into the data and by adequately cross referencing the material. The means of entry should be by

(a) hardware item,

(b) phase of activity,

(c) operator position, for multi-man systems.

2.2 All the characteristics of a hardware item should be described in one location

Operators will have to know what all items do in all modes of operation. They should not have to construct their own tables and lists of equipment responses. Neither should they be kept 'off balance' by having additional equipment characteristics revealed to them as they read on. If this is done, it is more difficult to memorize the material.

2.3 When cross referencing, be specific

References that simply say 'above', 'below', 'Fig. 5', 'Chapter 3' only serve to irritate the reader who will not usually accept the challenge to engage in a game of 'hide and seek'. He will ignore the information and be content with an incomplete picture. However, if the reference is specific—'Fig. 5, page 171'— the probability is much higher that the desired information will be referred to.

2.4 Where a detailed item is illustrated, its location in the larger element should be shown also

IMPROVED PROCEDURES MANUALS

It is confusing to see all the modes on a 12-position selector switch if one is unable to find the switch and relate it to other front panel items. This item is similar to item 2.7.

2.5 Illustrations should always be visible along with the written discussion dealing with them

Information transfer from the page to the reader is substantially enhanced if he does not have to flip pages back and forth to see the picture discussed by the words. Again, he usually won't do this and will learn more slowly and/or incompletely.

2.6 References to other documents should be minimized

Usually the other documents will not be readily available or not available at all. Therefore, unless the material referred to is extremely lengthy, it should be repeated in the new manuals. When references cannot be avoided, they should be specific as to page number and not merely say 'Is discussed in Technical Manual xxx–xx'. Even when the material is available, the train of thought is broken by having to find the required page in the other document. This is undesirable.

2.7 Operational statements should be made in the order in which the motions are made or the observations are taken

For example, one should not say 'Place the MODE switch on the Main Power Panel in the STANDBY position when ordered to do so by the Duty Officer'. Rather, the text should say 'When ordered to do so by the Duty Officer, go to the Main Power Panel, locate the MODE switch, and place it in the STANDBY position.' This is especially important in a multi-panel system as the operator is then spared the labour of having to rearrange the information himself into the order in which he must perform the act.

2.8 Indicate how the equipment will respond when mistakes are made by the operator or the equipment

Surprises produce consternation and responses, if they are made at all, may be inappropriate. Mistakes are much less disconcerting when the indications resulting from them are predictable. Therefore, sequential actions should contain notations of what will happen if the sequence is not followed properly.

2.9 Required operator actions should be directly related to the specific visual or auditory stimuli received either from the equipment or from other individuals

The above heading is quoted from Wiedman and Ireland (*op.cit.*). 'We need to ask ... what specific human actions we want to result from a set of instructions and in what order we want these actions to occur. Then we need to compose the instructions ... so that they will produce those actions and in the correct order' (Chapanis *op. cit.*). The small example, section 2.7, lines 3–5, is not composed in the manner we have come to expect. However, the statement is in the order in which the actions would be taken.

2.10 Simultaneous actions by several elements should be so portrayed

The text should not present such material serially so that the reader is required to visualize the parallel nature of the activity while remembering material presented earlier. This is an unnecessary burden and it will probably not be done well. Consequently, important material will not be absorbed.

This list could be expanded considerably; however, it is not intended to be exhaustive. It is presented only to illustrate some of the things that many people would like to see in a procedures manual. None of these points is startling in its originality or insight. In fact, they may seem to be obvious platitudes. But, if they are, why haven't more of them been incorporated into manuals? The following section suggests some answers.

3 Impediments to Producing Improved Procedures Manuals

'But to say that everyone wants [good procedures manuals] is equivalent to saying, in a national context, that everyone wants prosperity; the real problem is not to want it, but how to get it' (Miller, 1965). This section mentions some of the difficulties that prevent production of better procedures manuals.

As Chapanis (*op. cit.*) has indicated 'Somebody has to write that instruction manual today. We have to install that highway sign this afternoon. The label has to go on that dishwasher right now because it has to be out on the floor ready for sale tomorrow. And ... pilots have just arrived to get training on the *DC*-8 and the 707 jets which their airlines bought yesterday. This is the first reason I think human factors engineers need to get into this business. Somebody has to tackle the immediate, messy problems of the real world right now. This is what engineers, human or otherwise, typically do so well.'

Chapanis rightly recognizes the sense of temporal urgency that accompanies the preparation of procedures manuals. This and other impediments to producing desirable procedures manuals are given below.

3.1 Time is short

Time is short because one must not write until the system design is frozen.

However, it takes time to develop information, conceive illustrations, to have them rendered and reproduced, to put in specific cross references, to develop the desired action sequences, and to develop a good index. So, by the time the design is frozen, there is often precious little time to organize, write, and draw.

3.2 There may be a shortage of funds

Often enough, unexpected expenditures on earlier phases of the work may make it imperative to achieve every possible economy during the later phases. Thus the pressure to write an inexpensive manual can be great. Unfortunately, it costs money to prepare suitable illustrations, check cross references, edit material, reproduce, and bind thoroughly detailed publications. Unless the money is spent, a poor document will result.

3.3 Technical information may be lacking

This is especially true with regard to all the subtleties and ramifications of the equipments operation. The situation becomes aggravated when the equipment is complex and sophisticated. Usually, the design records available to the writer deal with the prescribed design features. They may possibly consider some of the more obvious malfunctions and errors. However, the records rarely indicate the nature of all possible system actions and reactions. Moreover, the manuals are usually being written as the system is being checked out. Minor modifications may be made at this time and/or it may be discovered that the actual operation is not quite as intended in certain small ways. These last-minute items are not documented in time to help the manual writer. Often enough, a section of the manual is finished before a discovery is made and it is simply too late to go back and change the section.

3.4 Designers may not know exactly how equipment will be employed by the user

This is particularly true of very complex systems and/or those that are highly classified from a security point of view. Consequently, the manual writer cannot be sufficiently specific concerning the operational stimuli that should result in operator actions.

3.5 Contractors cannot establish military doctrine

New equipment sometimes requires new tactical doctrine, which can only be established by duly constituted military authority. This can frequently be done only after the equipment has been field tested. The contractor's manual must be as explicit as possible while avoiding the appearance of presuming to dictate.

3.6 Personnel turnover

Not only are people likely to leave your organization but higher priority projects within your company sometimes pre-empt their services at crucial moments.

3.7 Restrictive specifications

Sometimes it is not possible to do what one would like because it is necessary to follow a specification that was prepared for a different task and is, therefore, not very appropriate to the task at hand.

3.8 Lack of management interest

It sometimes seems that management is not sufficiently interested to provide support in terms of motivation, time, money and personnel.

3.9 Detailed guidelines do not exist

Detailed guidelines on how to prepare procedures manuals do not seem to exist.† If they do, they have not received sufficiently wide distribution to have come to the attention of the writer and his colleagues, or to previous authors (Chapanis *op. cit.*, Wiedman and Ireland *op. cit.*). As a result, most writers adhere to the tried and true wordy text. It's easier that way.

To illustrate the lack of available specific guidelines, the following are excerpts from several United States government specifications that deal with manuals (Anon., 1958, 1960, 1962, 1963, 1964). In all cases, it is procedures manuals that are under discussion. Added *underlines* emphasize the orientation toward the written word.

'... the purpose and location of these controls shall be described in the *text*, with references to the related illustrations.'

'... a separate *paragraph* will be devoted to the location, description, and purpose of each control device as well as a statement of how the operator, crew, or driver uses the controls in the proper operation of the material.'

    'A separate *paragraph* will be devoted...'

    'A brief *statement* of irregular readings...'

    'A description shall be provided...'

    'A description of the basic functions shall be included...'

---

†*An excellent monograph is now known to the author, only because R. B. Miller, the originator, happened to be attending the conference at which this paper was presented. The publication (Miller, 1956) is now unfortunately out of print and not widely available.*

'Instructions to move a group of controls or accomplish a series of checks preparatory to beginning a phase of operation shall be arranged in check-list form . . .'

'The operating procedures shall be provided in terse *paragraph* form.'

4 Dealing with Impediments

Section 3 listed nine impediments to producing better procedures manuals. This section uses the previous subsection titles and suggests some ways in which each impediment might be removed.

4.1 Time is short

Several alternatives are available. First, get people who work well under pressure. Second, schedule the manual work so that there is as much time as possible to complete it. Third, resist pressure to make up schedule slippages that occurred during the earlier phases.

4.2 There may be a shortage of funds

Manual managers must obtain an early commitment concerning the funds to be allocated for the books. Higher management must resist the temptation to reduce the writing budget to make up shortages incurred earlier. Manual managers must resist such attempts if they are made.

4.3 Technical information may be lacking

First, close working relations with design engineers must be established by the writers. This will reduce delays in transmitting information to an absolute minimum. Second, the writing must not be started so soon that information is not yet available, nor so late that on-time delivery is jeopardized. It is difficult to determine just when the proper time has arrived. Finally, an attempt should be made to find those areas for which information is reasonably firm so that they can be completed first. This will allow time for more information to develop in areas that are still flexible.

4.4 Designers may not know exactly how equipment will be employed by the user

The procuring agency and the ultimate user must ensure that the contractor has the information he needs. Also, the contractor must make every effort to obtain additional information when this seems necessary. This requires some extra effort and interest on the part of all parties.

4.5 Contractors cannot establish military doctrine

Government agencies must be understanding and contractors must be discreet. All parties must understand that, in the interest of being explicit, it may occasionally appear that doctrine is being established. Clearly, doctrine is not established until certain formalities internal to the military are completed. Therefore, concern frequently expressed on this point appears to arise from especially sensitive organizational entities.

4.6 Personnel turnover

General company policy and good first line supervision will minimize the problems of having people leave for positions elsewhere. The only solution to the loss of personnel to higher priority jobs is to ensure that the priority for the current task is maintained until the manual is complete. Pressure from the procuring agency can help in this respect.

4.7 Restrictive specifications

Exceptions to, or modifications of, specifications should be sought when it is apparent that the specification was written with another system in mind.

Procuring agencies should be amenable to overtures to tailor procedures manuals to the task at hand and should not demand slavish adherence to an inappropriate document. This was done with outstanding success in at least one instance (Ireland, 1966). Of course, it would be even better if the procuring agency suggested a more suitable manner of presentation in the first place.

4.8 Lack of management interest

This is a substantial key to the whole problem of procedures manuals. Some engineering managers just do not think much effort should go into them. Many engineers deride them as unimportant pieces of paper generated to make work for people. Chapanis has the solution. Government agencies should insist on better workmanship. He says (*op. cit.*), '... I think it would be a worthwhile adventure to see many reports summarily returned to their sources with curt notes saying: ... "Final payment on this contract is being held up until a readable report is received".' And what an adventure it would be! It is still true that money talks and management especially understands that language. There is no problem with information transfer when these terms are used.

4.9 Detailed guidelines do not exist

Wiedman and Ireland (*op. cit.*) present some excellent ideas that should serve until something more comprehensive comes along. What seems to be needed is a document that could be included as a chapter in the *Human*

Engineering Guide to Equipment Design (Morgan *et al.,* 1963) and in the *Human Engineering Guide for Equipment Designers* (Woodson and Conover', 1964). The latter already contains some excellent but brief suggestions, but they are limited primarily to graphic presentation. *Specification MIL–M–24100* (1964) is a pioneering effort in the maintenance area and tests indicate that documents meeting its provisions produce much better performance than documents following more conventional forms (Stein, 1963). Something like it is needed for procedures manuals. Miller (1956) has prepared a useful guide which could well be reprinted to make it more freely available.

5 Some Closing Remarks

Chapanis (*op. cit.*) and Easterby (1967) have outlined some technical work that might be undertaken to improve the written material that accompanies equipment. This must be done. However, parallel actions in the non-technical sphere must also be taken. Writers of manuals and others concerned with the technical aspects of manual production can never do the whole job. Sincere interest and action on the part of supervision and management in procuring agencies, using arms of the military, and in contractors plants is required to remove some of the impediments to attaining good procedures manuals.

References

Anon. (1958) Military Specification Manuals: Flight. MIL–M–7700A14.
Anon. (1960) General Specification for Preparation of Operator's Guides for Synthetic Training Systems, USNTDC 422–220.
Anon. (1962) Army Regulation Air 310–3, Military Publications.
Anon. (1963) Manuals, technical, FBM weapon System, General Specification for MIL–M–21548A (WEP).
Anon. (1964) Manuals, Orders and other Technical Instructions for Equipment and Systems, MIL–M–24100 (SHIPS).
Chapanis, A. (1965) 'Words, words, words', *Human Factors,* vol. 7, pp. 1–17.
Chapanis, A. (1965) 'On the allocation of functions between men and machines', *Occup. Psychol.,* vol. 39, pp. 1–11.
Eames, R. D. and Starr, J. (1965) 'Technical publications and the user', *Human Factors,* vol. 7, pp. 363–369.
Easterby, R. S. (1967) 'Preceptual organization in static display for man-machine systems', *Ergonomics,* vol. 10, pp. 195–205.

McLaughlin, G. M. (1966) Comparing styles of presenting technical information. *Ergonomics*, Vol. 9, pp. 257–259.

Miller, J. D. B. (1964) *The Nature of Politics,* Encyclopedia Brittanica Press.

Miller, R. B. (1956) A suggested guide to the preparation of handbooks of job instructions. Maintenance Lab. Air Force Personnel and Training Research Centre, Lowry Air Force Base, Colorado, ML–TM–56–15.

Miller, R. B. (1962) 'Task description and analysis'. In Psychological Principles in System Development, ed. by R. M. Gagné, Holt, Rinehart and Winston.

Miller, R. B. (1967) Task taxonomy: science or technology, *Ergonomics,* vol. 10, pp. 167–176.

Morgan, C. T. *et al.* (eds.) (1963) *Human Engineering Guide to Equipment Design,* McGraw-Hill.

Stein, A. (1963) One of the new horizons in technical manual preparation. Address delivered to 10th Annual Convention of the Society of Technical Writers and Publishers, Boston, Mass.

Waldron, M. (1966) Gemini study set by space agency, *The New York Times,* June 18, 11.

Welford, A. T. (1966) The ergonomic approach to social behaviour, *Ergonomics,* vol. 9, pp. 357–369.

Wiedman, T. G. and Ireland, R. H. (1965) A new look at procedures manuals, *Human Factors,* vol. 7, pp. 371–377.

Woodson, W. E. and Conover, D. W. (1964) *Human Engineering Guide for Equipment Designers,* University of California Press.

5.2 Human Factors In Urban Transportation Systems

Laverne L. Hoag, *School of Industrial Engineering, University of Oklahoma, Norman, Oklahoma, and* S. Keith Adams[1], *School of Industrial Engineering and Management, Oklahoma State University, Stillwater, Oklahoma*

Introduction

The demand for improved urban transportation in the United States has created challenging research opportunities for the entire spectrum of human factors engineering. It will very likely cause the creation of new industrial and technical specialties within the overall human factors engineering design area.

The construction of the BART system in the San Francisco area, the new rapid transit system in Washington, D. C., and the introduction of the Metrolines and Turbotrain in the Northeast Corridor, together with numerous improvements in commuter rail service equipment in many major cities, are the beginning of a new era of expanded public transportation. BART is the first railroad-type system designed and built for urban public transportation since the first decade of this century. In the intervening 60 years, changes in the culture, psychological makeup of the population, and the expectations of the U.S. citizenry have changed the requirements of any transportation system. The combination of convenience, flexibility, costs, and social and psychological effects of the mass-produced automobile is the greatest single cause of this change. The consequences are illustrated by the BART system. BART has met with only moderate success and will have an uphill struggle for user preference for some time to come. The future success of intraurban transportation systems being built or planned is highly questionable at present. Why should this be so in view of available technology and experience in designing systems for man and in view of the present chaos, congestion, and distressing experiences brought on by excessive automobile traffic in major cities?

Acknowledgement

Reprinted, by permission, from L. L. Hoag and S. K. Adams, 'Human factors in urban transportation systems' in *Human Factors*, Vol. 17, No. 2, © 1975 The Johns Hopkins University Press.

---

[1]*Now at Iowa State University.*

The basic problem lies in the human factors engineering information available to the designers of urban transportation systems. What is it and where is it? A literature search reveals little data taken from or applicable to the urban population. Except for data on noise, vibrations, and cabin air quality, there is little overlap between the data needed for public systems and that needed for military and commercial airline applications. Also, much of the existing data describe design requirements for the vehicle operator, not the passenger. Thus, the answer to the latter question is that there are little or no data.

To return to the first question—what sort of data is needed upon which to base the design of a successful urban transportation system? First, it is necessary to recognize that human factors must be considered for both the user (passenger) of the proposed system and the nonuser (at a given time) who must live or work within the overall system-created environment. Second, it is apparent that, when considering the user, many factors must be considered which are not discernible in terms of laboratory experiments or current handbook data. These include a large set of psychological, social, and economic conditions which must be satisfied to get the user into the vehicle in the first place. Even when he is finally aboard, there are many gaps in the knowledge of how to create physically acceptable conditions which accommodate the variations among individuals and their travelling circumstances. Stations and terminals also present a challenge in this report.

Bauer (1970) presented the human factor requirements for vehicle interior. A NASA-sponsored study (Millar, 1972) presented a more detailed list of requirements for vehicle interior design, as shown in Table 1. In addition to the factors listed in Table 1, there are other costs and benefits affecting both users and nonusers. Examples of these factors are: direct costs to the user; disutilities to the nonuser; revenue and tax structures; public financing, subsidies, and investment; dislocation costs; economic growth potential; and land values and urban growth.

While cost factors are very important in planning any transportation system project, they will not be discussed in detail in this paper. This emphasis is not intended to imply a lesser role for these factors. They are simply outside the areas of expertise of human factors specialists.

Examination of the factors listed in Table 1 reveals that the greatest information need exists in the areas of: (1) the physical size, strength, and mobility of various groups in the urban population; (2) the psychological preferences and the social profiles of the user (or potential user); and (3) subjective evaluations of specific features of public transportation systems by the user (or potential user) population. Significant gaps in knowledge exist in each of these areas.

Table 1 Overall Classification of Human Considerations in Urban Public Transportation (adapted from Millar, 1972)

Major Areas of Consideration	Illustrative Problems within Area
Vehicle and Station Interior	Space and Seating Entrance and Exit Package and Baggage Handling Speed, Acceleration, and Vibration Noise Illumination Air Quality—Temperature, Humidity, Movement, and Odors
Convenience and Mobility	Time—Trip Time, Waiting, Walking, Transfer, and Terminals Operations—Availability and Frequency of Service, Schedule Reliability Information—Intelligibility of Signs and Messages Related to Routing Schedule, Locations, and Vehicle Recognition Problems for Handicapped Individuals
Safety and Security	Accident Risk—Real and Perceived Emergency Provisions—Breakdown Recoverability Maintenance Crime and Vandalism Health and Sanitation
Social Factors	Desirable and Undesirable Groupings Freedom to Choose Travel Companions Personal Space, Privacy, and Crowding
Psychological State	Boredom Self-esteem Perceived Safety and Security Anxiety and Uncertainty Sense of Personal Control of Conditions Esthetics Comfort and Ride Quality
Environment-System Interaction	Congestion Pollution—Air, Acoustic, and Visual Harmony with Surroundings

Present Data and Research Needs

Anthropometric and Strength Data

One very basic consideration in vehicle design is the sizing of the vehicle to the population. 'Sizing' refers to the design of entrances, exits, seats, aisles, and storage areas in a vehicle to fit the passenger. Two problems exist in this area: (1) selection of appropriate design criteria, i.e., the segment of the population to be used as a basis of design and the compromises to be made; and (2) existence of appropriate anthropometric and strength data. Existing literature on anthropometry represents an almost exclusive sampling of military personnel. Since all military organizations are selective and are made up almost entirely of individuals between the ages of 18 and 40 (the majority being between 18 and 25), the data may not be well suited to designing for the general urban population.

A recent study (White, 1972) contains compiled data from a large number of military anthropometric surveys conducted in the United States, many western nations, and in middle eastern and far eastern allies. Nearly all of these data are limited to basic static anthropometry. Dynamic anthropometric studies conducted by the U.S. Army, Navy, and Air Force are limited to considerations for the equipment operator. In most cases, and especially in aviation, this represents an even more specialized subgroup of male military personnel.

Urban studies are far more limited in number and scope. One early survey was conducted between 1939 and 1940 by the Bureau of Home Economics of the U.S. Department of Agriculture (O'Brien and Shelton, 1941). They surveyed 15,000 women to estimate sizes and patterns for women's clothing. A fairly recent study was taken of 3,000 men and 3,500 women from the urban population of the United States (Stoudt, Damon, McFarland, and Roberts, 1965; 1970). Measures in the first study included weight, height, and some selected body dimensions. The second contains data on skinfolds, body girth, biocromical width, and other indices. A European study (Ward and Kirk, 1967) presents static anthropometric measurements of 178 elderly women.

In addition to anthropometric differences, the older citizens have other important limitations that influence their ability to use public transportation. Older citizens often require the use of a mechanical or supportive device. Steps on present-day transportation vehicles are poorly designed, in many cases, to accommodate even the young and fully capable adult, much less the elderly and the ambulatory aids. Once on the vehicle, there are narrow aisles and narrow spacing between seats. The dynamics of getting into and out of seats on public vehicles have received little or no attention in human factors research. Elderly people move more slowly as they enter and leave public vehicles, thereby creating an impedance to the movement of other passengers. Besides contributing to the reduction in speed of loading and unloading of the vehicle, the older person may feel uncomfortable in this situation. Such a situation could contribute to a dislike of public transportation by older citizens.

Another segment of the population which is totally excluded from our present mass transportation system includes those people who are temporarily or permanently handicapped, especially those in a wheelchair. None of our buses, subways, or other forms of public transportation were designed for use by the individual confined to a wheelchair. Most vehicles require passengers to ascend or descend stairs either prior to entering the vehicle or upon entering the vehicle. Once on the vehicle, no space has been designed where the wheelchair can be affixed to the vehicle to prevent movement of the chair while the vehicle is in motion. Like the elderly, the handicapped individual would be an obstruction to the normal smooth loading and unloading of a bus and, as such, represents a significant reduction in the overall speed of a transportation system.

Two examples will be presented to illustrate the type of research data that need to be collected and the compromises that must be made using such data. The particular examples presented were selected for their illustrative value without evaluation of whether they represented the most important problems in the anthropometry-strength area.

If people are to replace their automobiles with public transportation, then provision, other than vacant seats and passenger laps, must be made for storage of packages carried by passengers. Such a provision requires that questions of security of packages and location of storage areas be answered. The location of storage has two aspects: convenience to seating, and usability by people of different heights. The latter illustrates the need for additional human factors information.

The height of the storage area will determine the ability of people to utilize the area. Martin and Chaffin (1972) presented lifting strength data for young men and women for various combinations of horizontal and vertical displacements. Figure 1 is drawn from the information presented in their article, but the information presented should be treated as only a crude approximation to actual strength, since the data were interpolated from a graphical presentation of static strength. It is obvious from Figure 1 that the weight that can be lifted depends on the height of the lift and the percentage of people included in the group capable of lifting the weight. Several limitations exist for the type of data presented by Martin and Chaffin: (1) they represent only the strength of young men and women; (2) they are for static

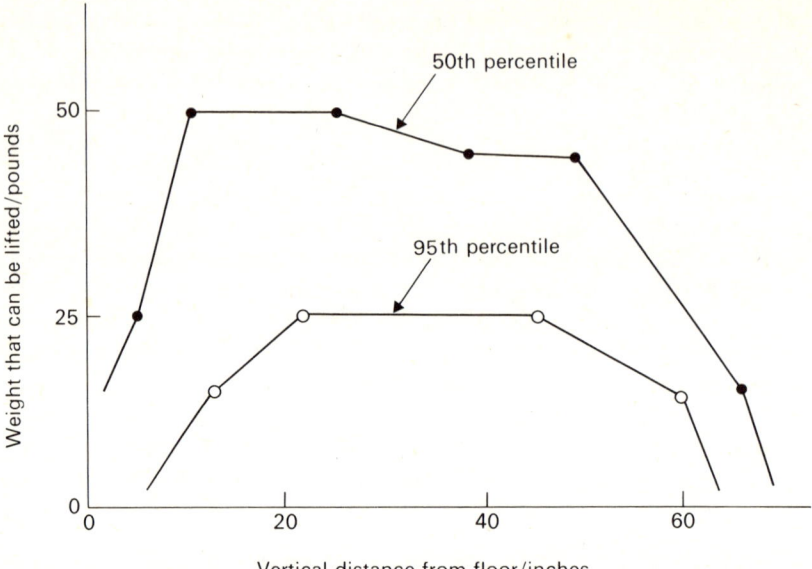

Figure 1   Lifting strength of females as a function of distance from the floor (for a horizontal distance of 10 in. (25.40 cm) in front of ankles).

muscular effort which is greater than dynamic muscular effort; and (3) they do not include the effects of different styles and weights of clothing, e.g., winter clothing could easily restrict the range of movement, and short dresses or skirts might reduce the willingness of women to lift a package very high.

The second example, the selection of a seat height, would appear to be a trivial example in view of the extensive work in the seating area. But Shackel, Chidsey, and Shipley (1969) show that it is still difficult to design comfortable chairs for a large population of users. Our concern is not the comfort of the seat, *per se,* but to quickly review a compromise (and the required data) that is necessary in selecting the seat height. Table 2 shows the effect of seat height on both short and tall women. Short women suffer a problem when the seat height is greater than their popleteal height because there is pressure on their thighs which reduces blood flow and causes discomfort. At the other extreme, the tall person encounters difficulty when the seat height is substantially lower than his popleteal height. Table 2 shows the knee extension for 99th percentile women at the different seat heights, and Table 3 presents the maximum static forces at each angle.

Notice in Table 3 that, as the angle increases, a woman is using a greater percentage of her maximum strength to rise from the seat, i.e., this is a more strenuous task for her. This increase in difficulty of rising from the seat is probably not important, except for elderly passengers, passengers carrying children, passengers carrying packages, or passengers whose muscular strength is lower than normal because of disease, injury, or physical handicap. The information presented in Table 3 is limited by the same factors as the data on lifting strength.

Table 2 Relationship between Seat Height and the Size of Women

Seat Height inches	Female Population Too Short for the seat %	Knee Extension for the Tallest Women degrees
15	5	100
16	40	96
17	85	93
18	98	90

Table 3 Maximum Static Force for Various Levels of Knee Extension (For College Men)

Knee Extension degree	Maximum Force lb
25	90
50	137
66	155
75	148
100	120

The improper design of storage facilities or selection of the 'nonoptimum' seat height will not necessarily cause people not to use public transportation. But the examples illustrate the need for serious consideration of the sizes and strengths that are represented in the population for whom we are designing the vehicle. It is no longer acceptable to ignore the characteristics of the population and design for a mythical man and woman. Responsive compromises must be made based on reliable data on strength and size of all potential users, young and old, under conditions that prevail when people use public transportation, not on situations that are convenient for the experimenter. Only when the subjects are dressed in a representative manner for the climatic conditions that exist in the four seasons, and measurements are made while the subjects are burdened with packages or are carrying a child, can we expect to obtain realistic data which will be useful in designing passenger compartments.

Neither of the examples included the effects upon passenger compartment design of physical or situational handicaps of potential users. This topic is of sufficient importance that it is presented in its own section.

The Handicapped as a User Population

It is important to define the handicapped in terms of classifying the functional nature of their disabilities and in terms of the number of individuals who are handicapped when traveling. A handicapped individual is usually regarded as being rare or exceptional, but available statistics reveal that a substantial portion of the traveling population is permanently or temporarily handicapped. These may be functionally categorized (Gutman, 1968) as:

(1) Aged who need physical assistance.

(2) Those with visual, auditory, or vocal deficiencies.

(3) Those with neural or coordinative problems such as palsy.

(4) Semiambulatory persons requiring crutches, canes, braces, or who wear artificial legs. Also, those with spastic, cardiac, or arthritic problems which limit walking and climbing.

(5) Nonambulatory persons who use wheelchairs.

Mobility of these users is affected by the design of vehicles, terminals, and transfer facilities. There are many mobility barriers to the handicapped to which practical solutions have yet to be worked out, but only a few specific design problems and recommendations will be presented in this paper.

The size of the handicapped population is more than sufficient to warrant its being considered as a major portion of the traveling public and a group for which data can and should be compiled. Estimates developed by the National Center for Health Statistics (U.S. Department of Transportation, 1970) show that nearly 6 million physically handicapped persons have severely limited mobility as a result of a chronic, semipermanent, or permanent medical condition.

In addition, there are about 15 million elderly persons who frequently experience difficulties with public transportation. Many of these also have a chronic medical condition which affects their mobility. There are also about 4.6 million people, on the average, whose mobility is limited as the result of a temporary illness or injury. Pregnancy constitutes another common cause of problems for many travelers. Then there are some individuals who are inconvenienced because of being too large or small for facilities designed for small deviations from the average-sized person. Totalling all of these groups yields a figure of 44 million or more individuals whose mobility (and therefore opportunity for social, cultural, and economic participation) is severely limited.

When first considering design standards to accommodate the handicapped, one tends to assume that in meeting the requirements for handicapped persons, one must sacrifice compatibility of design for the nonhandicapped. An examination of recommended standards for both groups (Damon, Stoudt, and McFarland, 1966; McFarland, 1969; Stoudt, *et al.,* 1965) reveals that in nearly all cases, designing to accommodate the handicapped almost invariably improves the design for the nonhandicapped. Cases of direct conflict involving additional inconvenience to the nonhandicapped appear to be quite rare.

One area of possible conflict is that of vehicle acceleration. In this case, the handicapped have reduced means of coping with the problem, even if additional hand-hold areas are provided or warnings are given. Assurance of seating for them may be the only way to provide a high degree of protection from jerk, lateral sway, or sudden deceleration.

Psychological Problems

As was true in the case of physical anthropometric data, psychological human factors data are heavily weighted toward military studies and vehicle operator requirements; the majority of studies have been designed to have direct application to aircraft or missile control systems. When the user of an urban public vehicle is considered, a far greater number of variables emerges, most of which are difficult, if not impossible, to quantify. One very important factor, for example, is personal space (Sommer, 1969). Personal space is an invisible envelope or bubble around an individual which he regards as private. Several variables affect personal space: the proximity of other people, visual contact, odors, conversation, etc. The automobile is very effective in protecting personal space by providing a shell of steel and glass which encapsulates personal space.

Another problem is derived from the heterogeneity of groups of people using the system. Passengers might be of different ethnic and racial stocks, different age level, and, to some extent, different socioeconomic classes. Research shows that people dislike and seek to avoid other people who differ in terms of socioeconomic class, attitudes, and values (Byrne, 1971; Freedman and Doob, 1968; Schacter, 1959).

Perception of safety and security is another factor which has become very important in recent times. While accidents and crimes do occur, their frequency of occurrence is not as great as people believe. However, what people believe is often more influential than reality. The President's Commission on Law Enforcement and Administration of Justice (1967) found that the belief that public transportation was crime-ridden had resulted in a drop-off in public transportation use. A study of public transportation users in Chicago (Misner and McDonald, 1970) revealed that less than 0.5% of the total number of passengers were either victims of or witnesses to crime. Yet 70% of the riders felt that crime was either very likely or somewhat likely to occur. Nearly 25% of the passengers reported they had declined to ride a city bus out of concern for crime.

Many other psychophysical and physiological variables interact to form what is known as 'vehicle ride quality'. These include acceleration, vibration, noise, lighting, visual field, flicker, odors, and seat comfort. Considerable work has been completed in this area because of its importance to the commercial air transportation industry. A recent symposium (Symposium on Vehicle Ride Quality, NASA, July, 1972) provided a comprehensive overview of the information in this area.

The importance of the esthetics of vehicle and station have received little attention from the designers of transit systems (Millar, 1972; Tehan and Wachs, 1972). The authors indicate that esthetics is treated as an afterthought and not as an important factor in the design. Millar states the importance of esthetics as 'It cannot be overemphasized that no new or improved transportation systems, vehicle, or facility is likely to succeed in the engineering or economic sense unless it first satisfies certain social, cultural, and esthetic values.'

If esthetics is of such importance, why has it been neglected? The apparent reason is the difficulty of translating the concepts of esthetics into design principles which are easily and economically applied to the design of transportation systems. For example, how can the individual's preferences for colors and patterns be used to improve the acceptance of the transportation system? Tehan and Wachs (1972) conclude, 'Surely, the task is not a simple one, but it seems to be a worthwhile effort, especially if it helps to increase transit patronage and provide viable alternatives to the automobile.'

User Evaluation

How will users of a proposed public transportation system accept it? Can this be anticipated in advance? What system and vehicle design features do they consider to be important and how much are they willing to pay for them? Examples of factors which can be and are analyzed in small surveys are: easy entry/exit, arriving when planned, lower fare, having a seat, choice of pick-up time, riding in privacy, room for baby strollers or wheelchairs, adjustable seats, easy fare payment, etc. The ranking and scaling of such factors following a stratified survey of potential users is vital as a planning tool.

Golob, Canty, Gustofson, and Vitt (1972) presented the results of a survey of potential users of a public transit system. The purpose of the survey was to evaluate the importance of system attributes. The information was divided into the major user groups: elderly, low income, and under 20 and single. There is good agreement among these groups on the important features. The following 8 items were among the 10 most important features for each of the groups: having a seat, no transfer trip, lower fares, arriving when planned, less wait time, less walk to pickup, shelters at pickup, and calling without delay.

The major limitations of this study, and similar studies, are the size of the test population and a lack of a test of validity of the results. These limitations were imposed by the resources and available research techniques. But before we can place too much significance on the results in this study, or similar studies, we must have measures of validity and reliability. For example, the study indicates that the cost of the transportation system is of primary importance to people surveyed. But if one compares the cost of using a public transportation system, one would quickly realize that even at a fairly high rate the public transit system will be considerably cheaper than the personal automobile. Apparently, people do not place the same evaluation on the cost of purchasing, maintaining, buying gasoline, paying parking expenses, and paying taxes for their personal automobiles as they do on taking money out of their pocket and placing it in the fare box of a transit vehicle.

Surveys, like the one above, usually indicate that costs of public transit systems, such as fares, are very important, or at least moderately important. Yet Lansing, Marans, and Zehner (1970) found when they asked people to list the costs of using a private automobile, 50% of those interviewed included only gasoline, oil, and grease. Three percent added parking and tolls. Twenty-five percent added depreciation and repairs. Only 6% included license and insurance costs. None indicated any taxes to support roads, signals, law enforcement, and other right-of-way expenses or placed any value on his personal time. Is the commuter indeed rational? If so, then one major problem is that of educating the public with respect to the actual costs of using alternative modes.

It is likely that demand for trips into the city is elastic and that transportation costs are significant in determining the location of economic growth areas (Moses, 1968). Thus, it may be possible to reduce congestion in cities by increasing the cost of going into them. If people value both time and money, they might consider both (a total of two effects) in choosing a transportation mode and respond according to the ratio of the total to wages or salaries. Extensive studies of such factors, combined with an engineering economic analysis and total cost estimates of various systems, could provide urban transportation planners with progressive and even innovative systems without high economic risks. The problem seems to be one of educating and of understanding the commuter.

Conclusions

(1) Human factors data describing the anthropometry, strength, and perferences of the intra-urban populations of the United States are needed for planning public transportation systems.

(2) The physically handicapped constitute a large portion of the traveling population. Therefore, their physical abilities and limitations must be evaluated and considered in designing transportation vehicles.

(3) Designing for the physically handicapped usually results in attaining a higher level of human engineering for the nonhandicapped.

(4) Subjective factors are as important as objectively measurable factors in determining vehicle and system conditions necessary for public acceptance, and methods must be developed for including them in the design of the systems.

(5) The use of dynamic modeling and programming to predict user-vehicle or user-facility compatibility can be an effective method of identifying significant combinations of design features, especially if combined with the use of existing standards as guidelines.

(6) Improved procedures for evaluating user acceptance of new design concepts need to be developed.

(7) Informing and educating the public with respect to the true total costs of public and private urban transportation will be necessary if rational consumer perception of costs is to be expected.

References

American Standards Association, (1961) Making buildings and facilities accessible to, and usable by, the physically handicapped, A117.1-1961.

Barkla, D. M. (1961) The estimation of body measurements of British population in relation to seat design. *Ergonomics, 4,* pp. 123-132.

Barkla, D. M. (1964) Chair angles, duration of sitting, and comfort ratings. *op. cit., 7,* pp. 297-304.

Bauer, H. J. (1970) Public transportation and human factors engineering. Warren, Mich.: General Motors Research Laboratories, GMR-982.

Branton, P. and Grayson, C. (1967) An evaluation of train seats by observation of sitting behavior. *Ergonomics, 10,* pp. 33-51.

Byrne, D. E. (1971) *The attraction paradigm.* New York: Academic Press.

Damon, A., Stoudt, H. W., and McFarland, R. A. (1966) *The human body in equipment design.* Cambridge, Mass.: Harvard University Press.

Eysenck, H. J. (1941) A critical and experimental study of color preferences. *American Journal of Psychology, 54,* pp. 385-394.

Freedman, J. L. and Doob, A. N. (1968) *Deviancy.* New York: Academic Press.

Golob, T. F., Canty, E. T., Gustofson, R. L., and Vitt, J. E. (1972) An analysis of consumer preferences for a public transportation system. *Transportation Research, 6,* pp. 81-102.

Gruen, V. (1968) No more offstreet parking in congested areas. In Smerk, G. M. (ed.) *Readings in urban transportation.* Indiana: Indiana University Press.

Gutman, E. M. (1968) *Wheelchair to independence.* Springfield, Illinois: Charles C. Thomas.

Lansing, J. G., Marans, R. W., and Zehner, R. B. (1970) *Planned residential environments.* Report prepared for U.S. Department of Transportation, Bureau of Public Roads. Ann Arbor, Mich.: University of Michigan, Survey Research Center, Institute for Social Research.

McFarland, R. A. (1969) Human factors in high speed ground transportation with special reference to passenger comfort and safety. In *Proceedings of Carnegie-Mellon conference on high speed ground transportation.* Pittsburgh, Pennsylvania.

Martin, J. B. and Chaffin, D. B. (1972) Biomechanical computerized simulation of human strength in sagittal-plane activities. *AIIE Transactions, 4,* pp. 19-28.

Millar, A. E. (ed.) (1972) *The motion commotion, human factors in transportation.* NASA-ASEE Report, Contract NGT 47-003-028, Langley Research Center and Old Dominion University Research Foundation.

Misner, G. E. and McDonald, W. F. (1970) Reduction of robberies and assaults on bus drivers. Vol. II: The scope of the crime problem and its resolution. Dept. of Transportation Demonstration Project, CAL-MTO-11.

Moses, L. N. (1968) Economics of consumer choice in urban transportation. In Smerk, G. M. (Ed.) *Readings in urban transportation*. Indiana: Indiana University Press, pp. 162–171.

O'Brien, R. and Shelton, W. C. (1941) Women's measurements for garment and pattern construction. Washington: U.S. Department of Agriculture, Miscellaneous Publication No. 454.

The President's Commission on Law Enforcement and Administration of Justice. (1967) Task Force Report: Crime and its impact—an assessment. Washington: U.S. Government Printing Office.

SEPACT 1: Commuter railroad service improvements for a metropolitan area. Report to the U.S. Department of Transportation on mass transportation. Project No. PA-MTD-1, Southeastern Pennsylvania Transportation Authority.

Schacter, S. (1969) *The physiology of affiliation*. Palo Alto: Stanford University Press.

Smerk, G. M. (1968) Three experiments in urban transportation. In Smerk, G. M. (Ed.) *Readings in urban transportation*. Indiana: Indiana University Press, pp. 275–285.

Sommer, R. (1969) *Personal space*. Englewood Cliffs, New Jersey: Prentice-Hall.

Stoudt, H. W., Damon, A., McFarland, R. A, and Roberts, J. (1965) Weight, height, and selected body dimensions of adults—United States 1960–1962. Public Health Service Publication No. 1000, Series II, No. 8. Washington: U.S. Department of Health, Education, and Welfare.

Stoudt, H. W., Damon, A., McFarland, R. A., and Roberts, J. (1970) Skinfolds, body girths, biaviomial diameter, and selected anthropometric indices of adults—United States, 1960–1962. Public Health Service Publication No. 1000, Series II, No. 35. Washington: U.S. Department of Health, Education and Welfare.

Tehan, D. and Wachs, M. (1972) The role of psychological needs in mass transportation. PB-216, 161. Springfield, Virginia: National Technical Information Service.

New and novel transportation systems: Planning principles, operating characteristics, and costs. Special Report, Berkeley, California: University of California, Institute of Transportation and Traffic Engineering, 1970.

U.S. Department of Transportation (1970) Travel barriers, PB 187–237. Springfield, Virginia: National Technical Information Service.

Ward, J. S. and Kirk, N. S. (1967) Anthropometry of elderly women. *Ergonomics, 10*, pp. 17–24.

White, R. M. (1972) Anthropometry and human factors engineering. Paper prepared for presentation at the NATO International Symposium on National and Cultural Variables in Human Factors Engineering, Oosterbeek, The Netherlands, June 19–23.

5.3 Railway Signals Passed at Danger: the Drivers, Circumstances and Psychological Processes

D. Russell Davis

Department of Mental Health, University of Bristol

1 Introduction

Do those railway drivers who have passed signals at danger differ from their fellows? Or do their errors arise out of the circumstances? Or both? The first step in an attempt to answer these questions is to arrive at hypotheses about the ways in which the drivers or circumstances might differ. The second step is to test the hypotheses in systematic investigations.

This paper is concerned with the formulation of hypotheses about the psychological processes leading to errors, and not with the formal testing of the hypotheses. The viewpoint is that discussed in a previous paper on transport accidents (Davis 1958). The method was that of medical examination and clinical interview of a particular sample of drivers who had passed signals. None of the incidents had resulted in damage to stock or injury to persons.

2 Composition of the Samples

The investigation was carried out in 1960–61 at the Medical Department of the Eastern Region of British Railways. The request was made that all drivers passing a signal at danger in the area served by this Department should be referred for medical examination. Forty drivers were so referred, two drivers appearing twice. After the medical examination, each driver was asked to submit to an interview. Five men refused. Four—one driver twice—had made up their minds to refuse before they arrived, for reasons which are not known. One refused because, not unreasonably, he thought the incident too trivial. The remainder participated of their own free choice. Thirty-four interviews were carried out, one man being interviewed twice.

Acknowledgement

Reprinted, by permission, from D. R. Davis, 'Railway signals passed at danger: the drivers, circumstances and psychological processes' in *Ergonomics*, Vol. 9, No. 3, 1966, Taylor and Francis Ltd.

The interviews occurred on the average nine days after the incident, the range being from 3 to 25 days.

The number of drivers not referred as requested is not known. Certainly there were some, and the sample was not complete. There is no evidence of any systematic bias, but it would be unwise to suppose the sample to be fully representative.

A second sample of 31 drivers was interviewed. These were drivers attending the Medical Department for routine examination on reaching a certain age. Twenty-seven of these 31 were 55 or more years old, and they (*Control* drivers) have been compared with the 23 of the 34 drivers (*PSD* drivers) who had passed signals, and who were of similar age.

The distribution of ages of the *PSD* drivers was an odd one, although not dissimilar in most respects from that of the whole population of drivers for British Railways at that time.

The sample divided into two groups: 23 old drivers, the youngest of whom was 56 years old, and 11 young drivers, the oldest of whom was 43. The lack of cases in the range 45–54 years, and the excess in the range 25–34 years, are worth noting.

3 Procedure

Routine tests of visual acuity and colour vision and a medical examination were usually carried out before the interview, at which the driver was asked about the incident, his medical history, recent health, health at the time of the incident, family, career, interests and social situation and any other matters having a bearing on the incident.

Any reluctance to discuss the incident, shown in a few cases at the start of the interview, soon passed, and answers were usually given freely and apparently without evasion. There was seldom any doubt about what had happened. The driver's version of how and why it had happened was sometimes less certain and consistent. More than a third of the drivers said that they had been worried or perplexed by the incident and were glad of the opportunity to discuss it and try to find an explanation for it. A few only gave dull, inadequate or uncritical accounts. Independent reports of the incidents in 15 cases confirm that the information obtained at the interviews was reasonably accurate and complete.

The incidents were arbitrarily classified, with the results shown in Table 1.

Table 1 Classification of incidents

Shunting signal	5
Running signal	
(i) fog: over-ran or failed to see	0
(ii) mistook another signal	6
(iii) failed to see in clear weather	4
(iv) saw but over-ran	14
(v) misread signal aspect	5

On the basis of the interview findings, an explanation of each incident was formulated as a conjecture, taking into account the several factors which appeared to be relevant. The manner in which this was done is illustrated by *Cases* 1 and 24.

Case 1

Incident. He was working a sleeper train towards London in February, and the incident occurred about half way. He misjudged his approach speed and was unable to bring his train under control to stop at the *home* signal, over-running by 155 yards. The 'Automatic Warning System ($A.W.S.$)' worked normally. He brought the train under control after seeing the *distant* on, cancelling the $A.W.S.$ as he did so. The misjudgement occurred when he was drawing up to the *home*.

Findings at the interview. Six months previously he had suffered from a relatively severe depression, for which he had been treated in hospital by electroplexy (eight treatments); he had still not made a full recovery, and the anxiety symptoms persisting were thought to amount to definite illness. He also gave a history of a depressive illness in 1937 when he was off work for seven months for 'neurasthenia'. The incident occurred on the exact anniversary of a serious accident, which had played an important part in the causation of the recent depression. He had been apprehensive that something untoward would happen on the anniversary, but was relieved that things were going well; fog, which had been troublesome, had cleared, and he was on time. He was not fully confident on diesels.

Explanation. One may suppose that he was unduly anxious and apprehensive during the first part of the journey, because of the psychiatric illness, the anniversary, some mundane annoyances before he started, the fog and the lack of confidence on diesels, and that he then became relatively inattentive as a result of relaxation and relief of anxiety when things seemed to be going well. The psychological processes concerned appeared to be 'relaxation after stress' and 'timing error'.

Case 24

Incident. Waiting at the country end of a platform at a London terminus, he was to remove an empty passenger train to the sidings. He moved against the starter signal at danger.

Findings at the interview. He reported a variety of psychiatric symptoms not amounting to definite illness, and he was excitable and of anxious personality. His accident record was rich and varied, and he was 'always the unlucky one who carries the can'. For instance, in an incident a few weeks previously, the electrically operated doors of the shed had been open when he got in to the wrong end of a diesel to move it out of the shed. After 'getting the air', he 'blew the brakes off' and moved back, but in the meantime someone had closed the doors and he ran into them. Also, he had recently run into the stops at the terminus because of oil on the rails. He had shown a similar lack of control on other occasions. His sight was bad, his visual acuity being 60.60.60. The light at the time of the incident was relatively poor (heavily clouded at dusk).

For reasons which are irrelevant, he was a few feet ahead of the starter signal, which was out of sight, and he was awaiting a hand signal from the signal box. He said that he was 'keyed up' and made a 'false start' in response to what must have been a casual wave from a porter going across to the box.

Explanation. Of anxious personality and accident prone, he misinterpreted and responded to a signal which did not apply to him. This signal was like one he was keenly expecting, and occurred at approximately the right place and time. His perception was possibly faulty because of his poor sight and the poor illumination. His error was thought to be a 'response to the wrong signal'.

4 Medical Factors

Many of the the men impressed as being very fit. Thus seven out of the 23 drivers who were 55 years old or more were judged to be in robust health, compared with 11 of the 27 control drivers of similar age. However, there were a few cases in which medical factors were thought to be relevant.

Eyesight

Only in *Case* 24 was eyesight regarded as a relevant factor. In *Case* 20 colour vision was found to be defective, but was not regarded as relevant. This driver had passed in daylight in clear weather a semaphore signal at danger, which was in view for at least a quarter of a mile. He saw the signal as 'on' when it came into view, but expected it to be pulled 'off' as he approached it. He had got it into his mind that this would happen, perhaps because it had happened on the previous trip earlier that day. He was distracted by men working on the line and over-ran the signal by six coach-lengths. The psychological processes were thought to be 'false expectation', 'distraction' and 'timing error'.

Hearing loss

In only one case was there hearing loss, but this was thought to be irrelevant.

Acute illness

No driver said that he had been ill at the time of the incident, with a cold or feverish illness, for instance, or any other acute illness. To questions on this point, the driver usually answered that he did not go on duty if he did not feel well. In no case was there reason to suspect hypoglycaemia. Breaks for food had been taken regularly, and there were no instances of departure from normal eating habits.

Organic dementia

There were two cases in which there was some evidence of organic dementia. This diagnosis, it should be noted, is difficult and unreliable, and the conditions of the examination did not permit attempts to confirm it. In the first (*Case* 4) the driver was aged 57 years; his blood pressure was 198/102 (165/90, 30 months previously); obese and plethoric, dull and showing emotional lability, he gave indications, on informal testing, of some unreliability in recent memory. He had passed a signal at danger twice within the previous year. The Department recalled him a year later for a repeat examination, because of the slight rise in blood pressure. Inspection of his medical card showed that his blood pressure was then 190/110, and that no other abnormality had been noted. In the second case (5), the driver, aged 58 years, was obese and plethoric, his blood pressure was 194/110. A single man living on his own since his mother died several years ago, he spent much of his off-duty time in a pub, and had the appearance typical of the heavy beer drinker. He admitted to morning sickness.

Psychiatric symptoms amounting to illness

These were reported in three cases and appeared to be relevant in all of them—*Cases* 1, 12 and 32. In all the cases of psychiatric symptoms to be discussed, there was evidence that the symptoms were present before the incident and at the time of the incident, whether or not they were exacerbated by it.

Of severely neurotic personality, *Case* 12 complained of insomnia, 'wind' round the heart, giddiness, dyspepsia, headache and excessive sweating. He showed circum-oral *herpes simplex*. He gave a history of arthritis, phlebitis, peptic ulcer (not confirmed radiologically) and nervous debility. His first marriage ended when his wife, a chronic mental invalid, committed suicide. His second marriage being unhappy, he had been looked after by a daughter of his first marriage until three months before the incident, when she had emigrated with her husband to Australia. Since then his anxiety symptoms had been much worse. Three weeks before the incident he had gone off work for a few days because of an accident, and had returned for a few days and had gone off again with 'flu. The incident occurred on his first day back.

His accident record is remarkable. The *Incident Report* records that he passed signals at danger on four occasions during the last eight years, two of them within the previous year, as well as six other driving offences and three non-driving offences. His accidents have been varied. As a boy he knocked himself out while working in a brewery, when a cask of beer fell on him. He fractured a wrist a few years ago when jumping off an engine. Recently, in addition to two collisions 'such as anyone might have had', he had overturned a train 'cannoning off another train in the sidings'. In the incident for which he was referred, he shut off power when he went past the *distant* at yellow, but being late in seeing the *home* at red, because it was raining and the wind-screen wiper was not working, he had over-run the signal by two coach-lengths.

Case 32 had suffered concussion at work four months previously as a result of a blow on the head, the retrograde amnesia being momentary, and the post-traumatic amnesia about half-an-hour. Headaches and dizzy turns had persisted, and he continued to feel nervous, apprehensive, ill-at-ease and unsure of himself; he was forgetful and bad-tempered, he said. Previously very happy in his work, he had recently felt it to be a strain, especially at night. He had passed a shunting signal.

Other psychiatric symptoms

There were eight other cases in which psychiatric symptoms appeared to be relevant, although they did not amount to definite illness.

Case 21 will serve as an example. He started on the right-away of the 'coupler-up' without looking at his signal. He was keenly aware that he was running late. He gave a history of perforated gastric ulcer, chronic duodenal ulcer, strained back muscles, and fractured ribs on two occasions. He is a man 'to whom everything happens'. He was dissatisfied with his job, and impressed as a disappointed man with strong resentments.

Table 2 Comparison of *PSD* and *Control* drivers aged 55 or more years

Number of drivers:	Out of 23 PSD drivers	Out of 27 Control drivers	Significance of difference
In robust health	7	11	—
Who had suffered from physical illness in last 10 years, involving either admission to hospital or at least one month off work—other than accidents	4	5	—
Complaining of psychiatric symptoms	8 (in 3 cases amounting to illness)	1	$p<0.05$
Complaining of recurrent psychosomatic symptoms causing a break from work	9	3	$p<0.05$
Who had sustained injuries requiring hospitalization in last ten years	4	4	—
Involved in incidents, such as *PSD*, other than that for which referred, derailments or collisions in last 10 years	8	6	—
Number of incidents	14	6	$p<0.05$

Six of the eleven drivers with psychiatric symptoms had worse accident records than any other in the series.

Comparison of the incidence of psychiatric symptoms in the *PSD* and *Control* groups of drivers of 55 or more years old shows the incidence in the *PSD* drivers to be higher, as Table 2 shows.

Recurrent psychosomatic symptoms were also more common in the *PSD* drivers, there being nine such cases, as compared with three in the *control* drivers. In every case, except one control driver, the symptoms included dyspepsia. Rheumatic symptoms were the next most common.

The physical illnesses included four operations for hernia, two in each group.

It will also be noted that the *PSD* drivers had been involved in more incidents.

5   Special Circumstances

In *Cases* 9, 29 and 33 there were special circumstances which could be held partly or wholly responsible for the incidents; in *Cases* 9 and 29 they appeared to be the sole factor.

Case 9, working a light engine, was drawing up deliberately at 5–6 m.p.h. to a signal which he had seen as 'on', when the gauge glass burst, smothering him with glass and hot water. He 'forgot himself', over-running the signal by 20 yards.

Similar was *Case* 29. The gauge glass broke and the cab filled with steam. In consequence he over-ran a signal which he knew to be 'on'.

Insufficient help from the guard was cited in *Case* 33 as a cause of a heavy goods train running away; and this was probably the main cause.

There was little fog in the London area during the period of the investigations, and there was no case in which fog was a relevant factor (except indirectly as in *Case* 1). Four drivers said that their view of the signal had been partly obscured by steam blowing down, by rain on the wind-screen, the wiper being out-of-order, by steam from a fractured manifold and by sunlight shining on the signal, but in no case did it seem that impairment of visibility was of more than marginal importance, or more than is common experience.

6   Psychological Processes

Panic reaction

There was only one case in this series in which the error could be attributed to a panic reaction. *Case* 25 was working a *Brush* diesel, pulling an 'old local' from a London terminus. Before a long down-grade to a station where he was due to stop, a bird flew into the front window. He, and his fireman, instinctively raised their hands in front of their faces, which made them laugh. Dropping his hand again, the driver began to apply the brake at the usual time and place, about a mile and a quarter from the station. He cancelled the *A.W.S.* as he did so. Gradually he realised that the train was hardly slowing from 70 m.p.h. and, with alarm, that he was going to over-run the station. He was keenly aware that the train was full of passengers, and that shunting movements commonly go on at the station. He began to whistle in order to warn the signal box. His hope was that the road would be cleared for him, but he saw that the No. 2 *distant* and *home* stayed on. Soon after he had gone past these signals, without disaster, he noticed that his vacuum gauge was still reading 20 lbs/sq in., and then that he had been applying the engine airbrake and not the vacuum brake; the two handles lie side by side.

This incident provides an excellent illustration of the inappropriate behaviour which may be elicited in an emergency. A person may then show extraordinary persistence in making particular responses—in this case, applying the air-brake and whistling—although they are seen to be ineffective; attention is fixed by these responses, and other possibilities are not explored. That the driver was of anxious personality was regarded as a relevant factor.

Panic reactions like this one are probably not common as a cause of railway accidents. Recent reports of official enquiries do not provide an example, except perhaps that on the collision at Bradford (Exchange). Much more common are failures of attention, and the essential problem is to define the conditions in which they occur. One set of conditions is that in which the driver has false expectations.

False expectations

Case 17 is an example. The driver did not look out for the signal because he confidently expected that the section would be clear. Working a diesel rail-car on a Sunday he passed at danger a signal protecting a goods-yard. There were other railwaymen with him in the cab. He knew that there was only one other train on the route, another rail-car, which with his was providing a shuttle service. The signal was only 'on', he said, because 'there were too many D.I.s doing too much jawing', *etc.*; 'he should have been verbally instructed that the signal was likely to be on'; 'the previous signal should have been dropped to warn him'; 'he should have had a clear section'.

This driver reported a number of psychiatric symptoms which were regarded as relevant, notably insomnia and dyspepsia, and gave a history of

165

recurrent fibrositis and nervous debility, and of numerous accidents, all minor.

The manner in which false expectations may arise is further illustrated by *Cases* 20, 27, 5 and 3. There were grounds for suspecting a degree of mental deterioration in *Case* 5, but similar errors have been made by drivers in good health.

Working a stopping train towards London in the early morning, *Case* 5 was expecting to cross over from the slow to the fast line. He was expecting to be checked, as he had told his fireman, to allow an express train to go through. In the event he was checked at the *home* board, but allowed forward to the *starter*. Just as he passed the *home* board, the express passed him on the fast line, and soon afterwards he opened his controller. He saw the *starter* board wrongly as 'off'. He was stopped at the next box. 'The last thing I knew about', he said, 'was that I had passed a signal'.

Travelling at 80 m.p.h., *Case* 3 saw the *down distant* and *home* wrongly as 'off'. Seeing the *starter* as 'on', he 'gave her the lot', but over-ran. Checks at this point are 'very seldom' and he was expecting to lose speed on the up-grade, where there was also a speed restriction, before running into the terminus.

There were several other cases in which a false expectation played a part: *Cases* 20, 26, 31 and 40.

Preoccupation and distraction

Three drivers told of distractions: other men on the foot-plate in two cases (11 and 17) and men working on the line in one case (20). These cannot be regarded as special circumstances, although they may have played a part in causing the error.

The combination of a minor distraction and inattention was common. In *Case* 11, for instance, a driver much troubled by his sleepiness was asked a question by one of two other drivers, who were in the cab with him because they were learning the road, and had a 'lapse of momentary observation', taking his mind off a signal at which he was intending to come to a stand; he over-ran by half a train-length. A similar combination occurred in *Cases* 12 and 20.

There were four cases (10, 15, 26 and 40) in which preoccupation with another matter played a part. *Case* 15 is an example. Working a three-unit electric train in the evening rush hour from a London terminus, the driver was preoccupied with a defective unit, which was likely to delay him. After stopping at a station, he drew forward on the guard's 'right-away' to the *starter* signal at red. He made a slow get-away, but found he could get a surge of power from the defective unit by operating the 'reset' button. When he looked up again, he saw the signal as green, but wrongly so. The sun from behind was playing on the signal. He was not surprised that he had not seen the sequence red-yellow-double yellow-green, because he had been busy and had taken his eyes off the signals.

Preoccupation with a matter of another kind was an important factor in *Case* 10. He was in a great hurry to get off duty. His daughter being ill with measles and bronchitis, he wanted to get home to relieve his wife in time for her to take the other children to school. Although familiar with the signals, he responded to the top left of four signals on a gantry, which was 'off', instead of to the top right which was 'on'.

The co-operation of several processes, in this instance, false expectation, pre-occupation and distraction, and response to the wrong signal, is illustrated by *Case* 26. He travelled as a passenger on a train from a London terminus to where he was due to relieve the driver of another rail-car. On the previous three occasions that week on which he had done this duty, the two trains had left independently, the one train by the 'slow-two' line, and the other train by the 'slow-one' line. The interval between the arrival of the one and his departure on the other was only half a minute, during which he had to take over from the other driver. As he settled into his seat, he got the 'right-away' from the guard, released the brakes and moved off. As he did so, he felt some drag on the brakes and looked over to see the pressure, which however, was rising normally. He looked up just in time to see that the board was 'on', the signal being 200 yards or so in advance of the platform, but did not stop in time to save 'cracking' the detonator. On this occasion the board was 'on' to protect the other train while it crossed over in front of him on to the 'slow-one' line. He gave an excellent account of these events, admitting that he had been preoccupied in taking over the train in haste, had responded to the two buzzes from the guard, and had been distracted by what he thought was the drag by the brakes. He had not expected the signal to be against him, and did not look at it until the last moment. Had he seen it earlier as 'on', he would probably have waited at the platform, although it was permissible to draw up.

Haste was probably also a factor in *Cases* 15 and 21; in both the driver was aware that he had lost time in the rush hour.

Response to the wrong signal

There were six cases (10, 14, 21, 24, 26 and 39) in which a wrong response was triggered off by a signal which did not apply. Two examples have been given already; *Case* 24 in which a driver moved in response to a hand signal, and *Case* 10, in which a driver in a hurry mistook the signals on a gantry. There were also two cases in which the guard's 'right-away' played a part in causing the driver to move against a signal (*Cases* 21 and 26). These errors were similar to that responsible for the collision at Staines. Of particular interest was *Case* 14, because of its similarity to the Slade Lane collision, and perhaps also to the New Mills and Waterloo collisions.

Case 14: Working a 'dropping' goods train he was running on the goods line and expecting to cross over to the slow-up. The *distant* board was 'on', and he had brought his train under control. 150–200 yards before the junction the board for the slow-up came 'off', and he opened up in response to it as if it had been the board for the goods line. The board for the slow-up line came 'off' at the time at which he was deciding whether to come to a stand.

He was a conscientious man with a very good record, who had served as the secretary of a number of railway organisations. He was very upset by his mistake.

Relaxation after stress

There were two cases in which the inattention had been preceded by a degree of stress. *Case* 1 was one of these. The other, *Case* 19, was perhaps even more remarkable. This driver was of anxious and obsessional personality, a worrier and easily upset by anything untoward. He was to work an important train to the North. The day started badly for him and continued so. His engine was not ready for him, and there were further delays in coaling and on the turn-table. Nevertheless he left London on time. From the start he was uneasy about the engine, and before long a lubricating rod had stripped. After some vacillation he decided to change engines, although he would have preferred to have gone on further. He did not regard the new engine (a *Green Arrow*) as suitable, but it proved a good steamer, and he was making up time all the way. Things went well towards the end. Going into the station, he had a *double yellow,* a *yellow* and the route indicator, and then passed a signal against him, 'the 500th and last!' He finished his account: 'One momentarily loses sight of the signal, but I ought to have checked . . . It has worried me a lot. I have not told the wife, but I am glad to have been able to talk about it'.

This driver was examined again four months later. That he was of anxious and obsessional personality was confirmed. His symptoms were perhaps severe enough to amount to definite illness, and the case might have been classified accordingly, but they appeared to be due at least in part to the incidents themselves.

On the second occasion he was working a mail train at night in clear weather when he over-ran a signal at red at a station, where he was booked to stop. He has worked this train on many occasions. He liked to be early at this station with his train, so that he could be diverted into the slow line there without holding up the train which followed him. On this occasion he had had two checks, and was keenly aware that time was short, although actually he was on time. Normally the red is 'pulled off' as the train approaches, but this did not happen, possibly because there was a relief signalman. His brakes, he said, were inefficient, and he over-ran. The signal appeared to be further away than it was ('false expectation', 'distraction').

Two days previously the boiler on a passenger train he was driving was not working and at one point a cock was found to be open, for which he feels he has been unjustly blamed.

In *Case* 19 the relaxation was related to the end of the journey, as it was also in *Case* 3, although in this case the error was made at the end of an uneventful run. In *Case* 27, too, the error was made after an easy, uneventful run. In *Cases* 10, 13, and 28 the errors were made on the way back to the shed. These cases appear to be good examples of what has been called 'specific end deterioration', which may well have contributed to such collisions as Harrow and Wealdstone, Betley Road, Milngavie and Cannon Street.

Timing errors

When the train has a relatively efficient braking system, a colour-light signal at yellow, or a *distant* signal in the 'on' position, is a warning to prepare to bring the train under control, but is not a stimulus to make an immediate response to do so, for this may be postponed arbitrarily, or until a signal at red is seen, or the *home* is in the 'on' position. At any rate, the timing of the response is a matter of judgement, which may be disturbed if the driver is inattentive, has a false expectation, or is pre-occupied or distracted. A number of examples have been given already. In *Case* 20 the driver saw the *home* in the 'on' position when some distance away, but postponed braking until too late because of a false expectation and a distraction. In *Case* 12 he shut off power when he passed the signal at yellow, but postponed braking until he saw the red, and then was too late. *Case* 11 was similar. In *Cases* 27 and 31 the driver probably left braking too late, because of a false expectation, and because he expected more of his brakes than they were capable of.

In addition to these five cases, there were eight cases in which the driver over-ran a signal which he had seen as 'on' and to which he was drawing up. In *Case* 26, it was permissible for him to draw up to the signal against him, although he was not doing so deliberately. In all these cases, the errors arose, it may be argued, because the signal did not require an immediate response of braking, but allowed the response to be delayed at the judgement of the driver, which in the event was disturbed.

7 Discussion

Medical standards

Arguments based on *Case* 24, the only case in which poor sight was a relevant factor, that more stringent visual standards are required, would be weak, although they could not be dismissed altogether. Poor sight was probably not the main factor in causing the error in this case. Similar errors have been made by drivers with normal sight. It probably played no part in the two other recent accidents reported in this case. Moreover, the driver had been kept under supervision by the Medical Department before the incident, and had recently passed a practical ('field') test of acuity. Yet his accident record became worse as his sight deteriorated, possibly because poor sight, being a handicap, led to an increase in anxiety, which impaired efficiency at work.

There are two other types of case which deserve further consideration: those in late middle life whose mental powers show some falling off, and those with psychiatric symptoms. Both types pose difficult diagnostic problems. A firm diagnosis of dementia can rarely be made, in the absence of unequivocal neurological signs, until the disease is relatively advanced, and probably long after the point at which efficiency at work has begun to decline. Cases of this kind may well be of some importance because of the age distribution of drivers on British Railways.

It has been assumed in this report that psychiatric symptoms contributed to the causation of errors in 11 cases; (perhaps this begs, the question). Psychiatric symptoms are very common. No doubt in some cases they are benign, even if in other cases they are associated with impairment of efficiency or 'accident-proneness'. To decide on clinical grounds which drivers are likely to be inefficient or sustain accidents would be very difficult in the present state of knowledge. In *Cases* 1 and 12—and possibly in *Case* 19—the drivers would have been regarded on commonsense grounds as unfit for work. The driver in *Case* 32 had been sent back to work after careful consideration. Whether they would have been regarded as unfit, had they been examined before the incidents is uncertain. These matters require further study. Practical measures are a long way off.

Errors may be regarded as the result of the combination of relative inefficiency, due in many cases to psychiatric factors, and faults in the design of control systems. These ergonomic faults become serious when drivers' efficiency has fallen off. There is no prospect at present of ensuring that every driver is fully efficient all the time. Signalling systems must therefore be designed to take account of the kinds of errors that are likely to be made when the drivers' efficiency has fallen off.

Signalling systems

The findings have been discussed so far as if the faults lay in the drivers. They might also be discussed from the complementary point of view; in what ways did the existing signals fail to elicit the required responses from the drivers, accepting as inalterable that the drivers were prone to error in certain conditions? There are at least three points to be made in answer to this question.

(1) In some cases the signal failed to gain the driver's attention altogether, or it did not do so until too late, or it was perceived incorrectly. This happened, it is supposed, when the driver was not expecting the signal to be 'on', or had some other expectation, or was simply inattentive. How could the signal have been made more emphatic?

A.W.S. would have met this need in some degree. Had it been fitted, it might have been successful in a few cases, especially 3, 17 and 27. Although working normally, *A.W.S.* failed in *Case* 1 to prevent over-running, perhaps for reason (3). In *Case* 27, the signal at red was preceded by a *double yellow* and a *yellow* well in advance of it, all well-placed, modern colour-light signals. The signals failed to gain attention, although seen clearly, perhaps for the same reason.

(2) A signal which did not apply triggered a response from the driver as if it were a signal which did apply. This happened, it is supposed, when the signal gained the driver's attention at a critical time, for instance as he was preparing to make a response, or at a time of high expectancy. How could the driver have been protected from signals which did not apply? One answer probably lies in the better screening of signals from lines to which they do not apply, as well as better positioning for the lines to which they do apply.

(3) The signal told the driver to prepare to respond, in such a way as to bring the train under control, but did not tell him *when* to respond, the timing of the response being left to the judgement of the driver. This judgement was faulty in 14 cases for the various reasons discussed above. It is questionable whether modern signalling systems give too much latitude to the driver in timing his responses, especially since the timing may be decided by expectations which are not always borne out. This point deserves further consideration both by signal engineers and psychologists.

8 Acknowledgement

The investigation was carried out by arrangement with the Medical Research Council's Committee on Human Factors in Railway Accidents.

The author is greatly indebted for the help given him by all concerned, and especially Dr J. Sharp Grant, M.D., F.R.C.S., Regional Medical Officer, Eastern Region, British Transport Commission and his staff.

References

Davis, D. R. (1958) Human errors in transport accidents. *Ergonomics,* **2,** pp. 24–33.
Ministry of Transport Reports on Collisions (1953) Harrow and Wealdstone, 8th October 1952; (1955) Betley Road, 17th November 1954; (1958) Staines, 9th August 1957; (1958) Milngavie, 7th December 1957; (1960) Slade Lane, 23rd November 1959; (1960) Waterloo, 3rd June 1960; (1961) New Mills, 12th October 1960; (1961) Cannon Street, 20th March 1961; (1964) Bradford (Exchange), 3rd June 1964, London: HMSO.

5.4 Ergonomics and air safety

J. M. Rolfe

Royal Air Force Institute of Aviation Medicine, Farnborough, Hampshire

The inter-relationships between man and machine are rarely entirely trouble free. Man has tended to design machines to extend his capabilities rather than duplicate them and the consequence is that, on occasions, the dependent inter-relationship breaks down and accidents happen. Accidents are costly in terms of the damage caused to both the human operator and complex expensive equipment. Zeller (1970) points out that no matter how important the humanitarian aspect of accident prevention is, importance must be given to recognising the impact of the loss of valuable, trained personnel and expensive equipment on the ability of organisations to fulfil their defined functions. An example of the influence of accidents on an organisation's efficiency, is provided by O'Connor (1971), who reviewed aircrew medical wastage in the RAF from 1959-1968. His study showed that 43·6% of the wastage of highly trained and skilled personnel was due to accidents. The majority of these accidents were flying accidents but road traffic accidents were also taken into account.

It is accepted that accidents do not just happen, they are caused. In transportation accidents, man himself is one of the primary causes of accidents. Human error as a causal factor figures prominently in aviation accidents statistics. The term excites strong reactions in both aircrew and administrators. Aircrew argue that it is an admission that no mechanical faults have been found to explain the accident so the blame is put upon the man nearest to hand at the time of the accident. Often he is no longer able to defend himself when the time comes for an investigation. The administrator, whilst sympathising with his flying colleagues, feels that the statistics are substantially correct, indicating that in today's high speed world man is at times the component which gives rise to the greatest concern regarding efficiency and reliability. A very readable and informative consideration of this problem is provided by Barlay (1969).

Acknowledgement

Reprinted, by permission of the author, from J. M. Rolfe, 'Ergonomics and air safety' in *Applied Ergonomics*. Vol. 3, No. 2, IPC Science and Technology Press.

The views expressed in this article are those of the author and not necessarily those of the Ministry of Defence.

Aircrew error

Aircrew error is currently the largest single cause of aircraft accidents. Percentages vary with the type of aviation being considered but annually aircrew error contributes about 55% of accidents to military aircraft and aircraft engaged in public transport; about 76% of accidents to aircraft not engaged in public transport and about 90% of accidents to gliders (this last figure is probably not surprising when it is considered how little there is to go wrong in a glider). One criticism of examining accident statistics in terms of percentages, is that the percentage gives no true indication of the actual number of accidents taking place. Black (1971) has considered current aircraft safety statistics measured in terms of passenger fatalities per hundred million passenger kilometres. Air safety measured in this way has doubled in the last decade and is six times better than it was in 1950. Aeroplanes now fly a distance equal to 5,200 times around the world before a fatal accident occurs. Despite this improvement the number of fatal accidents per year is not decreasing, as improved safety standards appear to be balanced by the increase in aviation traffic and the enlarged carrying capacity of civil aircraft. The provisional figures for 1970 show that 1,002 people were killed and 193 seriously injured flying with the world's airlines. Although such figures give no room for complacency, it deserves note that the aviation safety problem is by no means as great as that of road safety. Figures published by the United States National Transportation Safety Board indicate that in the USA road accidents kill some 35 times as many people in a year as do accidents to aircraft. On British airlines between 1961-69, the number of passengers killed averaged 88 annually. This is a tiny figure when set against the average of 7,500 people killed on the roads each year in Britain or the figure of deaths from accidents in the home which every year hovers between 7,000 and 8,000, (Board of Trade 1970).

Man and the aeroplane

With the advent of larger aircraft and higher traffic density the lives of more and more people depend upon the error free performance of man and machine. If accident statistics are correct, they suggest that while the aeroplane itself is becoming more reliable, man is looked upon as the most suspect component of the system. Two possible reasons come to mind, man is not as reliably constructed as he has been in the past or the tasks imposed upon man today are not those in which he excels. Accepting that the latter explanation is in all likelihood the correct one, it must be asked if accident statistics are capable of giving any clue to the sources of human error. Black (1971) analysing accidents in January to October 1970 showed the prevalence of accidents during take-off, approach and landing. 'Pure' jet aircraft had a greater share of take-off accidents and these were mostly caused by engine break-up. The human error accidents tended to occur in the approach and landing phase.

Whilst the accident statistics are able to indicate the most frequent phase of flight in which accidents occur they are on occasions confusing with regard to the identification of the cause of the accident. There are two major reasons for this position. The first is that it is rarely the case that an accident can be traced to one particular causal event. Accidents are more often the result of the accumulative effect of a number of events rather than one isolated error. In aviation, accidents as a result of an accumulation of factors occur at the most basic level of flight operation.

Case study 1

A single seat light aircraft took off on an engine test flight after having been extensively overhauled. Shortly after take-off the engine stopped, the aircraft crashed and the pilot was fatally injured. The investigation of the accident concluded that the engine failed because there was an obstruction in the fuel supply line and an inadequate head of fuel. But after the engine failed the pilot attempted to turn back to the aerodrome with a result that the aircraft lost speed and stalled. This action contravened established training procedures relating to behaviour after an engine failure. Yet one further factor combined to increase the gravity of the accident. An examination of the pilot's safety harness showed that two lap strap D-rings had at some time previously fractured and instead of being replaced, they had been repaired in a manner which considerably reduced their strength. An aeromedical assessment of the accident concluded that if the harness had been in better condition, the pilot might well have survived both the engine failure and the crash resulting from his attempt to return to the aerodrome. Thus, what initially appeared to be a relatively simple accident revealed the complexity of providing an explanation and cause for the accident.

The problem of specifying the cause of an accident increases with the size of the aircraft involved in the accident, the most widely documented in recent years was the accident to the BEA Vanguard at London Airport in October 1965.

Case study 2

The aircraft was attempting to land at night in poor visibility. The aircraft, on a regular passenger flight from Scotland, had made two previous attempts to land and crashed while overshooting from its third approach. This aircraft was one of two Vanguards, which at that time had been fitted with a crash recorder. Analysis of the records from the crash recorder played an important part in the investigation of this accident. The crash recorder traces showed that during the overshoot, a lag in the response of the pressure driven vertical speed indicator was such that at 3 secs before impact it was still indicating a rate of climb of 600 feet per minute, although the aircraft had been descending for $2\frac{1}{2}$ seconds and the control column had been forward of neutral for 4 seconds. Shortly after this one of the crew had presumably seen the ground and realised that a crash was imminent, a violent pull-up was initiated but this did not prevent catastrophic impact. The report at the public inquiry into the accident, found that it was probably the result of a combination of events leading to pilot error. The causes cited were low visibility, tiredness, anxiety, disorientation, lack of experience in overshooting in fog, over-reliance on pressure instruments, position error in pressure instruments, lacunae in training, unsatisfactory overshoot pressure, indifferent flap selector mechanism design and wrong flap selection (Ford 1970).

Whilst it is accepted that accidents are most frequently the result of a number of factors, the need remains to order causes in such a way that accidents can be evaluated and compared within a constant frame of reference. One widely accepted procedure is to define as the primary cause of an accident, the last act or event in the time sequence that made the accident inevitable from that point. This form of classification provides a primary cause and, if present, contributory causes. The primary cause by implication being the more important or at least the most proximate factor.

A second problem in relation to assigning causes to accidents is that the terminology chosen to define the causes at times gives little reason for the accident taking place. Reports of accidents often refer to such factors as the misuse of controls, the mis-judgement of height or distance, failure to maintain flying speed or inadequate flight planning. In many cases these terms are not explanations of the accident but re-statements of what occurred. What is of importance is the discovery of why the pilot misused the controls, misjudged his height, or failed to maintain flying speed. These underlying factors represent the causes, and they need to be understood more thoroughly in order that safety can be improved.

As the majority of accidents appear to be caused by human fallibility, it is informative to consider the events contributing to accidents in terms of human limitations as well as aerodynamic or operational limitations. Such factors relevant to the understanding of human behaviour are:

    1   Man has limited information processing capabilities.

    2   Human behaviour is influenced to a very great extent by past experience.

3   Human performance is affected by adverse physical, physiological and psychological influences.

Limits to information handling capability

Man's participation in the operation of many contemporary systems is concentrated on the transmission and manipulation of information rather than activities involving the generation and manipulation of power. In flight, as the pilot goes through the processes of guiding and controlling the aicraft, he makes full use of his information processing capabilities. But the pilot is only human, and human factors research has indicated that man's ability to sense information is restricted: his ability to process information is limited and his capability of responding to a demand is subject to delays.

First in the chain of information processing is the task of gathering information. While the senses possessed by man are extensive, they all have limitations in terms of their range and the characteristics of the physical stimuli that will activate them. For the flight environment there are gaps in man's range of senses, and some lack of sensitivity in the senses he possesses. Man has no adequate sense of velocity, only of acceleration and he cannot sense directly altitude or direction. He has a limited sense of attitude but this sense can be distorted in a dynamic environment so that false perceptions can occur which lead to disorientation. In short, man is very much an animal equipped to operate in a stable environment. These limitations must be recognised when designing the task man is required to perform in flight.

Case study 3

A single engined aircraft was engaged in crop spraying. At the end of a run and during a low steep turn to the left, it lost height and the port wing struck the ground. The aircraft crashed and caught fire and was destroyed. The pilot was killed. The accident investigators reported that it seemed likely that the pilot lost control of the aircraft during a manoeuvre which left no margin for small errors of judgement. But why did the pilot lose control? The manoeuvre was, without doubt, a very demanding one but the pilot was also very experienced. A possible explanation arose from the operating manual prepared by the operator for the pilot to follow. The manual stated that 'in the turn, airspeed must be checked, the engine rpm, oil pressure, spray pressure and spray content noted. When safely level in the turn, immediate reference should be made to the ground marker, and if possible, the spray drift noted'. The aircraft involved in the accident was a high winged monoplane and to keep the marker in sight during a turn, it was necessary to look upwards through the transparent roof. So, if the pilot obeyed his instructions he had in the turn to look down at his instruments and then transfer his gaze upwards. This action would certainly have required some head movements. The pilot who has to move his head in a direction other than that in which the aircraft is turning, in order to carry out the necessary task, is likely to experience a potent sensation of turning which differs from the true motion of the aircraft, i.e. to become disorientated. Was the writer of the operations manual aware of this human limitation?

Of all the senses used for gathering information in flight, vision is the most important. The eyeball is capable of serving the pilot well, but it has its limitations. For example, the ability of the eye to perceive fine details is limited to a very restricted portion of the field covered by the normal eye, and in this role its efficiency is influenced by factors such as the shape of the object to be detected, its contrast with the background against which it is viewed and the length of time for which it is apparently visible. Low flying aircraft fly into high tension cables even though the pilot has been briefed that they exist on his route. The problem is that the power cables do not stand out sufficiently well from their background to be detected by the pilot. The solution is not to warn pilots to pay more attention to the cables, but either to make them more detectable by, for example, attaching clearly visible fluorescent warning markers as are employed in France or by developing a cable detecting device which can be used as an extension to the pilot's visual capability.

The above example emphasises the need to ensure the information the operator requires is compatible with the sense organs which are responsible for gathering it. The second element of the information in relation to sensing is to ensure that the right amount of information is present. Too much or too little information can both give rise to error. Too much information can cause the receiver to delay a response as he searches through the presented material in order to extract what is relevant to his needs. Too little information forces the receiver to guess the correct action, filling in the gaps in the material available to him from past experience. An example of the effect of excessive information comes from the study of the performance of airport apron controllers responsible for the turnround of aircraft (Lee 1959). This study demonstrated how delays, errors and overall system inefficiency was brought about by the turnround controller being swamped with redundant information. To overcome this situation, more authority was given to the controllers assistants who were trained to function so that the controller was informed only when a turnround procedure was deviating from a pre-set timetable. In this way the turnround of aircraft improved and the controller's communications load was reduced by nearly one third.

Aviation also provides examples of the results of too little information being available. The air traffic controllers plan position radar display has, until recently, given only a two dimensional picture of aircraft behaviour. No indication of height separation has been presented on the display. In consequence aircraft can be on an apparent collision course, although separated by thousands of feet in altitude. This lack of information has now been overcome by new air traffic control systems by providing numerical read-outs of height against the aircraft track provided by an automatic altitude transponder fitted to the aircraft's altimeter (Hopkin 1970).

Another example of potential accident situations precipitated by a reduction in information is provided by landing accidents when approaching an airfield in winter with an extensive covering of snow which reduces textural and altitude cues. Under such conditions the aircraft may land short of the runway or make a very heavy landing. Similar accidents occur at airfields where the approach is over the sea.

Case study 4

A civilian passenger aircraft was landing in conditions of poor visibility and driving snow. The pilot's external view was partially obscured by a building-up of ice and snow on the centre windscreen panel. The airfield had a covering of snow and the Captain informed Air Traffic Control that although he could see the runway lights he found it very difficult to distinguish between the runway and the surrounding snow covered airfield, as they blended together. The aircraft made one attempted landing but the Captain decided to overshoot. On the second landing attempt, the last stages of the approach was made at a very steep angle, and the aircraft touched down considerably short of the touchdown point. From the evidence of eye witnesses it was apparent that the aircraft had just started its landing rotation when it flew on to the runway. As a result of the heavy landing, the aircraft was damaged beyond repair, but only one of the 48 passengers was slightly injured. The accident investigators paid particular attention to the weather conditions, and concluded that the visual cues available to the pilot were significantly degraded to have prevented the Captain from appreciating his proximity to the ground in sufficient time to allow him to complete a normal landing manoeuvre.

In situations where the system information imbalance is likely to be present, the solution is not to be found in urging the pilot to search more diligently or to be more selective. The systems designed must define what the operator is expected to do in particular circumstances and from this description abstract the information which is needed in order to enable him to make the correct decisions and responses. Having done so, it may be concluded that man himself would find it impossible to perform the task under those circumstances and the job would be better performed by a machine. One example in aviation is the introduction of automatic landing systems which have now been demonstrated to improve the reliability of aircraft operations by facilitating landings under weather conditions where manual operation would have been totally impossible.

Being able to sense the information required is only part of the problem, for an even more restricting feature of man's capabilities is what is known as his 'single channel information handling capacity'. By this is meant that man has a limit to the number of inputs he can attend to at any one time. Whilst reading this article all of the reader's senses are no doubt functioning, but as he is attending to what he sees the majority of other inputs are filtered out of consciousness. For example, until it is mentioned, the right big toe remains anonymous. The big toe can on most occasions be neglected because it is irrelevant to the task in question. In flight however, many information inputs may be important but they may have to compete for attention. With the complexity of the flight task the limited attentional capabilities of the crew members can be stretched to the extremes. Accidents which at first sight are caused by the pilot disobeying the instructions of the air traffic controller may occur because with all the activity in the cockpit, the voice of the controller is just another big toe. Scucchi and Sells (1969) examined eight accidents to civilian passenger-carrying aircraft all of which happened during the descent approach and landing phases. They concluded that 'the accidents cited, appear to call for decisions which were either made too late or never made at all. In fact, there is no evidence that the captain was ever aware of the conditions cited as the probable cause of these accidents'.

A third factor regarding man as an information transmitter is the recognition that he is not an instantaneous responder. He has built-in lags. The length of the delays are a function of factors, such as the number of possible alternative actions the operator might be called upon to make, the frequency of the stimulus he has to respond to and the degree to which he can anticipate the occurrence of the stimulus. If man is required to make a fast response there must be no uncertainty in the situation. If there is uncertainty, he must be allowed sufficient time to process the information and make his responses. If this time is not available, then ways must be found of reducing the response time without placing undue stress upon his decision making. An example of the feasibility of such a concept is to be found in the design of aircraft information display systems. The head-up display in which information is projected on to the aircraft windshield so it appears superimposed at visual infinity on the outside world removes the need for the pilot to change his eye position and re-focus on the instrument panel in order to obtain information. It has been computed that by removing these actions, information gathering times may be reduced by 50%.

In relation to human responses, it must be stressed however, that over much reliance upon speed may result in blind unthinking behaviour. This is not the reason why man is retained in complex systems. One major airline operator's check list carries the advice 'judgement and precision are as important as speed. Activating the wrong control could cause more trouble than a few seconds delay in taking the correct action.'

The influence of past experience

No one was ever born with the ability to operate complex systems. These skills must be taught and retained by the operator. Safe and efficient operation depends upon adequate training and inherent in this statement must be the inculcation of adequate knowledge to safely operate the system, coupled with adequate opportunity to practice and maintain the skills required. Statistics relating to general aviation frequently refer to accidents which took place because the pilot undertook a manoeuvre which exceeded his ability or experience. One analysis of 41 accidents to light aircraft in this country, indicated that in 22 of them the pilot had less than 150 hours experience. This finding matches figures published by Smith, (1966) which indicated that in the Royal Air Force in 1961 pilot error accidents occurred about twice as frequently in pilots that had flown less than 100 hours in the preceding 12 months than it did in the remainder of the pilot population (Fig. 1). In relation to experience, Black, (1971) has shown that the percentage of accidents due to crew error decreases with the length of time since the aircraft was first introduced into service (Fig. 2). Taken together, the above evidence underlines the need for adequate training and practice in order to maintain efficiency.

The ability to draw upon past experience is an essential element in human skill. But human memory has its disadvantages, for unlike an electronic device man has no erase button attached to his memory. In consequence, information and actions once learnt are almost impossible to forget completely. It is important in training to see that incorrect patterns of behaviour are stopped as soon as they are detected for the more times an action has been performed in the past, the more likely it is to be performed that way in the future. Problems arise in converting aircrew from one type of aircraft to another. Some skills and responses learnt previously will facilitate conversion on the new type and a positive transfer of training will take place. Conditions can arise however, in which an old response is wrong in the new situation and will therefore transfer negatively to degrade performance rather than facilitate it. It is these responses that can cause accidents.

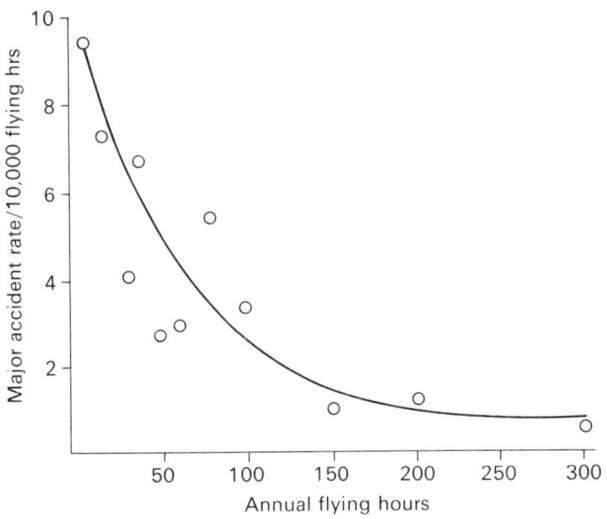

Figure 1 Accident rate pilot error against flying hours (Smith, 1966).

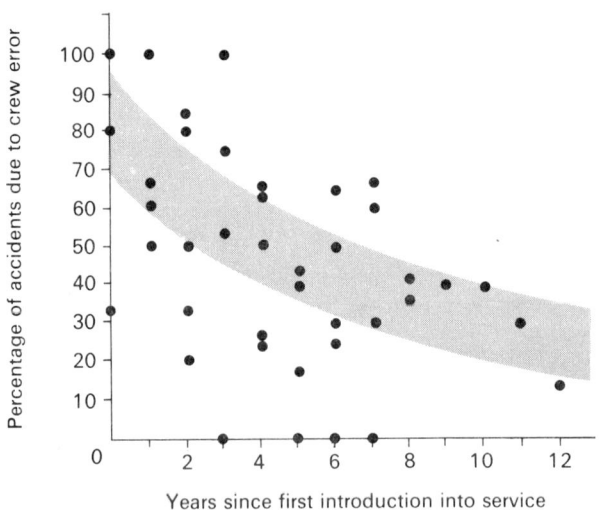

Figure 2 Percentage of accidents due to crew error, against years of service (Black, 1971).

Case study 5

A pilot was being checked out in an Auster light aircraft. Shortly after take-off the aircraft porpoised and dived steeply into the ground. The pilot undergoing a check was killed instantly and the pilot instructor died of his injuries five days later. Before he died the instructor told the investigator that after take-off the pilot under supervision, had applied excessive elevator trim with the result that after a number of violent changes of attitude the aircraft entered a steep dive from which it was impossible to recover. A possible explanation for the over use of the elevator trim came from an examination of the previous flying experience of the pilot under supervision. He had learned to fly on Austers but in the year prior to the accident, flew other aircraft, mainly the Tri-pacer. The Auster and the Tri-pacer have a similar elevator trim control, a crank handle positioned in the cabin roof. Here, however, the similarity ends for the Tri-pacer's trim control needs a number of turns before a small change of trim is obtained whereas in the Auster full nose up or full down trim is obtained in just over one complete turn of the handle. Flight tests on another Auster showed that if the trim control were handled in the corresponding way to the Tri-pacer's control the pattern of aircraft response would be very similar to that which occurred immediately prior to the accident in question.

The misleading influence of past experience, in relation to accidents, has been examined by Davis (1958). He examined a number of aircraft and railway accidents in relation to a pattern of response which he called the 'False Hypothesis'. The human observer sees the world in relation to his past experience. In consequence, what he perceives is partly determined by what he expects to see and on occasions, by what he would like the world to be. An individual, therefore, has expectations regarding what is likely to happen in a frequently encountered situation. When he acts in a way which follows expected patterns of behaviour rather than actually demanded responses, a false hypothesis situation has occured. Davis has cited five occasions when false hypothesis behaviour is likely to occur, namely:

(a) When an expected event is very probable.

(b) When the operator is anxious.

(c) When the operator's attention is being distracted.

(d) During a period of reaction following a time of high stress.

(e) When a set pattern of interpretation and action has been held for a long time.

It is interesting to note that in aviation a number of accidents fitting the false hypothesis situation can be found to occur. These frequently are related to the misinterpretation of transmitted information.

Case study 6

The Captain of an aircraft who on the take-off run looked across at his depressed First Officer and told him to 'cheer up', was dismayed to find that his First Officer though he had said 'gear up' and raised the undercarriage.

Case study 7

The Captain of a four-engined aircraft noticing that number four engine was on fire, and asking the Flight Engineer to 'feather four' was appalled when he discovered that the engineer had feathered all four engines.

One observation which must be made in relation to this type of accident is that language can be notoriously ambiguous. This fact has been acknowledged and in complex situations such as aviation, specialist and restricted vocabularies have been developed. In order to avoid ambiguity and misinterpretation, communication, particularly during periods of high activity, should be confined to messages which are relevant to the task and which can be transmitted unambiguously using the previously agreed specialist language.

Misinterpretation can also occur in relation to unspoken commands.

Case study 8

A two-pilot passenger aircraft was taking off in a rather strong cross wind. Because of the cross wind the Captain maintained control of the throttles during the take-off run until take-off speed was reached. He then indicated to the First Officer that he should take over and he transferred his hand to the control column. The First Officer having observed that take-of speed had been reached, misinterpreted the Captain's indication to mean 'raise the undercarriage' not take over the control of the throttles. He raised the undercarriage but at the same moment realised his mistake and managed to fly the aircraft off the ground just avoiding an accident.

The influence of adverse environments

Allnut (1971) has pointed out that in addition to the obvious stresses occurring in flight, such as heat, noise, acceleration, there are the more subtle stresses of sleep loss and disruption of circadian rhythms, and even more subtle stresses, such as fear, worries engendered by domestic problems, and on occasions inter-personal stresses arising from conflicts in attitudes and personalities between individual crew members. Reaction in emergency is determined to a very great extent upon the influence of these stress factors. As so much training for emergency situations is undertaken in synthetic devices such as flight simulators, it becomes necessary to ensure that the training situation, as far as possible, includes those factors inherent in the actual situation which can degrade performance. The story is told of a young embryo actor who received his first speaking part in a play. He had to enter in period costume and say 'Hark I hear a cannon'. After many weeks rehearsing his line he made his entrance on to the stage, there was a loud explosion and he said 'My God what was that?' The emergency situation, when it occurs, may well contain factors which have not been present in the training situation. These factors can degrade performance so much that relatively straight forward emergencies are not coped with effectively, and accidents happen. For example, because of the high risk engendered in practising engine failure emergencies in flight, training for this condition is undertaken in the flight simulator (Rolfe and Huddleston, 1971). Civil aircrew are given frequent and comprehensive opportunities to practice and maintain their emergency drills using flight simulators. Despite this emergency training in the simulator, at least two accidents have occurred to British civil aircraft in recent years, where an engine emergency condition was not dealt with as effectively in the air as it should have been. A similar observation must be made in relation to the drills and emergency procedures that are expected after an emergency has happened. Survival equipment which can be readily deployed in the training situation, has on occasions been found to be almost impossible to use when a real emergency has taken place.

Case study 9

A helicopter was on a night flight to an oil rig in the North Sea. During the flight, power was lost from both engines and the Captain was forced to make an emergency landing in a very rough sea. The crew then experienced great difficulty in undertaking the emergency drills which had been practised previously. On a dark, wet, cold and turbulent night, the crew found it extremely difficult to launch the life raft. The nylon lanyard attached to the life raft was so thin that the co-pilot and passenger had difficulty controlling the dinghy with cold, wet hands. A sharp edge on the aircraft's structure cut through the life raft's upper compartment and the crew were forced to cast off the life raft in order to prevent further damage. When the crew came to operate the emergency radio beacon, they found it was unusable, probably because it had been stepped on during the process of boarding the life raft. When an opportunity came to use the distress rockets and flares, partly because of the life raft's movement and partly because the crew had never had an opportunity of firing a rocket of this type before, it was fired incorrectly. The crew also found that the protective polythene pack around each distress signal was so tough that it could not be opened with cold hands and a knife was required. Despite these setbacks the two crew and one passenger were uninjured and rescued by a passing ship. The outcome of this accident was that both the crew members involved and the investigating team made recommendations which it was considered, improved the emergency training, to enable crews to perform adequately under adverse conditions.

Conclusions

This paper in no way attempts a comprehensive or thoroughly objective assessment of the factors which influence human behaviour in the flight environment. When accidents happen, their causes are rarely clear cut. What has been attempted is to demonstrate that the human factors scientist can contribute to an understanding of the accident situation by pointing out the limitations which exist in human abilities and by utilising this information, to ensure that these limitations are taken into account when tasks, equipment and environments are designed for human use. This application of behavioural data is only part of the task of reducing accidents. The users themselves must be made aware of their own limitations and the importance of knowledge, training and discipline in the maintenance of flight safety standards.

In this context, the Royal Air Force has for many years arranged courses in Aviation Medicine and Human Factors at the Institute of Aviation Medicine. These courses are specially prepared to introduce aircrew and flight safety representatives to human factors problems and to keep them informed of current advances in the application of the behavioural sciences to aviation. In September 1972 the University of Loughborough is arranging a two week course on human factors in transport aircraft operation. This course is designed specifically for personnel closely concerned with the design and operation of transport aircraft.

References

Allnut, M. F. (1971) Human Factors: their significance in an investigation. Paper presented at a Department of Trade and Industry Seminar on Aircraft Accidents.
Barlay, S. (1969) *Air Crash Detective*. Hamish Hamilton.
Black, H. C. (1971) Objectives and Standards for Air Safety. *Aeronautical J. of the R. Aero. Soc.*, Vol. 75, pp. 551–559.
Board of Trade (1970) Safety in the air. *Board of Trade Journal*, 3 June, pp. 1–11.
Davis, D. R. (1958) Human errors and transport accidents, *Ergonomics*, vol. 2, pp. 24–33.
Ford, T. E. (1970) Modern aviation profits by its past mistakes. *Design Engineering,* Sept., vol. 15, pp. 53–55.

Hopkin, V. D. (1970) Human factors in the ground control of aircraft. Advisory Group for Aerospace Research and Development, AGARD-AG-142-70.
Lee, A. M. (1959) Some aspects of a control and communication system. *Op. Res. Q.,* vol. 10, pp. 206–216.
O'Connor, P. J. (1971) Psychiatric casualties among aircrew of the Royal Air Force of Great Britain for 10 Years, 1959–1968. Advisory Group for Aerospace Research and Development, CP–89–71.
Rolfe, J. M. and Huddleston, H. F. (1971) Behavioural factors influencing the use of flight simulators for training, *Applied Ergonomics,* vol. 2.3, pp. 141–148.
Scucchi, A. D. and Sells, S. B. (1969) Information load and three main flight crews. An examination of the traditional organisation in relation to current and developing airliners, *Aerospace Med.,* vol. 40, pp. 402–406.
Smith, E. M. B. (1966) Pilot error and aircraft accidents, *ZBL. Verkehrs-Med.,* vol. 12, pp. 1–13.
Zeller, A. F. (1907) Accidents and safety, chapter in Systems Psychology. Edited by De Greene, K.B., McGraw Hill.

5.5 Design of Industrial Jobs a Worker Can and Will Do

Alan D. Swain

Sandia Laboratories, Albuquerque, New Mexico, USA

Job simplification and worker motivation

Much of the effort of ergonomists, or human factors specialists, in the United States has been, and still is, directed at the design of prime equipment, support equipment, and related procedures used by military personnel to operate or maintain military equipment and systems. One of the goals of the ergonomist expressed most often is to provide inputs to the design process which are intended to ensure the development of systems, equipment, and procedures which are compatible with the capabilities and limitations of the people who will use them. Frequently, achieving this goal for military systems has meant that the equipment and procedures are designed to simplify the skills and knowledge that the operating or maintenance personnel need to perform the job. In short, the emphasis is on designing equipment and procedures a man can use reliably.

Along with this job simplification, the ergonomist has often (perhaps usually) assumed at least an 'average level of motivation,' though this expression has not often been defined. Perhaps with the personnel redundancy often found in military organizations, this assumption has not been unrealistic since there are frequently at least a few highly motivated individual performers who can make up for those who have poor motivation. Moreover, under the leadership of a no-nonsense sergeant, or in a time of operational stress (e.g., combat or emergency situations) the involvement of most military personnel in their job situation could be expected to be enhanced, though not always in a desired direction.

The human factors man who begins to devote his efforts to the design of industrial tasks and products may find that if this same type of reasoning about job simplification and worker motivation is applied to the industrial setting, his efforts may well degrade system efficiency and effectiveness

---

Acknowledgement

Reprinted, by permission, from A. D. Swain, 'Design of industrial jobs a worker can and will do' in *Human Factors,* Vol. 15, No. 2, © 1973 The Johns Hopkins University Press.

rather than enhance it. In his research on motivation of the worker through the design of the work itself, Ford (1969, p. 136) offers a criticism of ergonomists which, though rather sweeping, cannot be lightly dismissed:

> Many observers say that human factors men do not consider the work itself when equipment is being designed. Their job is usually to see that pieces or configurations of equipment *can* be used conveniently by average employees. They ask questions like this: Can an employee run this typewriter with spaces of this width between keys which offer this many grams of resistance while averaging fewer than X errors per hour?
>
> But we are raising a long-run question: *Will* he continue to do it? This question may force us to inquire into a *total* work process. Is the employee viewed merely as someone who types or keypunches whatever someone else brings him? In the design of total work systems, human factors men must see the vast social responsibility which is theirs. Then they are less likely to think of themselves as physiologists or physiological psychologists alone and may also see themselves as social psychologists and humanists, concerned not only with what an employee *can* do but with what he is *striving* to do with his life.

One need only read magazines such as *Fortune, Time,* and *Newsweek* to note the concern over the rising costs to management (and thus to the consumer) of absenteeism, turnover, strikes, and sabotage from dissatisfied workers. Civilian workers (including former military personnel) are not the same as military personnel; they have different expectancies and demands, especially the younger ones. As stated succinctly by a Western Electric senior staff engineer (Hird, 1972):

> The 'workers to be' (our kids) want to get some *life* out of their work. They find it increasingly difficult to accept the idea that they must become *measured* men who have been *robotized* for the sake of production efficiencies. The thought of being hired for the sole purpose of burning up their calories to meet some predetermined production schedule is fast becoming repulsive. Consequently, if this is all work has to offer, then they will demand the highest possible pay for being kept in mental solitary confinement while they are on the job.

Regardless of how any manager might feel about the present generation of workers, they are what they are. They are the raw human material he has to use and it is not cost-effective to teat them in ways that they will not accept. For many jobs in American industry, there needs to be some rapprochement between what workers want out of a job and what management is providing them. That is, the job must be made more attractive in some way if workers are to stay on the job or to produce at a reasonable level. In short, the question is one of coping with the dehumanized job problem.

The dehumanized job problem

The dehumanized job, so eloquently parodied in the Charlie Chaplin movie 'Modern Times', has perhaps reached an apex in some automotive plants. In August 1971, the Columbia Broadcasting System televised some worker interviews conducted in an automobile plant. Management in that plant had complained about absenteeism, turnover, sloppy work, and poor worker attitudes. One of the interviewed workers installed front bumpers day after day. There was a deadening sameness about it that only a person with limited intelligence might find interesting or challenging. As the worker interviewed stated, 'I don't even get to work on rear bumpers.'

The problem of the dehumanized job is, of course, not restricted to automobile production plants. It is present in varying degrees in many industrial concerns. There are several ways management in various companies has used to cope with the dehumanized job problem. Following is a list of management approaches, arranged in order from probably least effective to probably most effective—both from the standpoint of work efficiency and cost effectiveness.

1. Discharge the worker if his job attitude adversely affects his performance.

Comment: The power of unions, changing times, and changing worker personalities (especially the worker under 30 [Hird, 1972]) has outmoded this approach as a cost-effective approach. Fear of losing a job is not the stimulus it once was, and it never was a rational or effective long-term approach to improving the quality of production. Nevertheless, some managers continue to employ threats as an important part of their 'worker motivation program' and to blame the personality of the new worker (Gooding, 1970a).

2. Inaugurate a motivational program to reward the best workers and to persuade all workers to do better work.

Comment: Purely persuasive programs, such as early and some present-day 'zero-defects' programs which reward a few for unusual excellence, do not reach most workers and have resulted in increased worker resentment against management (Swain, 1972, Chap. V). Such a program does not get to the heart of the problem of dehumanized jobs. 'The "poppa knows what's best for you" approach is not appropriate for today's higher educated and sophisticated worker' (Hall, 1971a, quoting Charles E. Hill, senior vice-president, U.S. Envelope). Some zero-defects programs have had a measure of success because they dropped the purely motivational approach and the insistence that perfection is possible if only the worker tries hard enough (Air Force Systems Command, 1965), and instead incorporated various job-enrichment and worker-participation techniques (Swain, 1972a). As originally defined by the U.S. Air Force System Command, a zero-defects program runs counter to what is known about worker motivation and needs (Rook, 1965; Swain, 1972).

3. Provide higher pay and more benefits.

Comment: Several studies have suggested that this approach is not a good long-term solution; after a certain level of pay and benefits has been reached, more of the same has little effect on turnover, absenteeism, and grievances (Herzberg, Mausner, Peterson, and Capwell, 1957).

4. Automate the job—remove the worker and let machines do the work.

Comment: For some jobs automation can be used to advantage by eliminating dehumanizing tasks and leaving the remaining work force more highly skilled duties which tend to be inherently motivating (Ford, 1969, p. 103). On the other hand, serious labour problems resulting from worker dissatisfaction can result if automation is used without due consideration of the nature of the remaining tasks to be given the workers. Such misuse of automation might occur if the designer automates all aspects of a job which can be automated and the remaining workers are given only those tasks which cannot be economically automated. For example, the tasks to be performed by workers at one highly automated automobile assembly plant are considered to be highly repetitious and unchallenging (Salpukas, 1972). The result has been turnover, absenteeism, grievances, strikes, sabotage, and, in general, a labour-management relationship which is inimical to productive work. It is reported that 'the over-all management strategy so far has been one of toughness—of hoping that the smaller paychecks resulting from workers being sent home early when there is a slowdown and of foremen disciplining workers through sending them home without pay will have their effect' (Salpukas, 1972). But labor problems and poor-quality output in this automobile plant are still in the news.

5. Select workers with limited mental or other capabilities for jobs requiring few capabilities and challenges, i.e. avoid 'over-training' and 'over-selection.'

Comment: Whether or not a job is considered a dehumanizing one is obviously a function of the worker's perception. Therefore, consideration could be given to selecting workers whose skills and needs match simple jobs. The main problems can perhaps be summed up in just three statements (Swain, 1972, Chap. IV):

(a) The content for selection and training programs is not often based on a thorough job and task analysis. Too often, it appears that the content of these programs is based on unverified generalizations from job titles. Rarely does a job analysis also include specific information related to the will-do aspect of work, that is, the reinforcement potential of a given job and the job hierarchy in which it is embedded (Hackman, 1969, p. 150).

(b) The validity of selection and training programs is seldom checked on a continuing basis. Management often assumes that these programs accomplish what they are supposed to do whereas systematic checks on their validity might well reveal that much of the content of these programs is irrelevant and some of it may actually have a negative weighting.

(c) There is a strong tendency to overselect and overtrain, resulting in motivational problems when the worker finds himself in a job which has little merit from his point of view and his prospects of advancement are dim. Were selection and training criteria more job relevant, persons of lesser qualifications and abilities could be successfully employed and trained. A man with an I.Q. of 70 might not aspire to work on rear bumpers.

The methodological difficulties in using this fifth approach to the dehumanized job problem cannot be glossed over. Nevertheless, it seems surprising that this approach is so seldom used despite the documented success of employment programs which emphasize use of persons of limited abilities. One report (Tinkham, 1971) describing the successful use of handicapped persons in various industries noted, 'Slight mental retardation . . . often enables a person to do tedious work which would handicap a 'normal' worker because of monotony.'

6. Use horizontal job enrichment, i.e. task diversification.

Comment: Some companies, such as Metaframe (Hall, 1971b) and even some automobile plants such as Volvo and Saab-Scania (Factories . . ., 1972) have trained their operators to operate several different types of machines as a means of providing rotation for the workers to avoid the boredom of continually doing just one task. In the CBS television program on automobile plants (previously referred to) some workers believed their jobs would be less boring if they could change tasks on some periodic basis, but management did not believe this type of horizontal job enrichment would be cost effective. Of course, if cost accounting includes only the immediate costs of production, horizontal job enrichment would appear to be undesirable from an economic point of view. On the other hand, if a broader view of costs is taken, including costs of absenteeism, turnover, and other such factors which could be reduced by using horizontal job enrichment, it might be demonstrated that the cost of training personnel to perform several different types of tasks is well worthwhile. How many different types of tasks a worker should be trained for is a problem requiring on-the-job research and is probably unique to any given industry. Furthermore, some workers dislike rotation and prefer to perform the same tasks; therefore, horizontal job enrichment should not be applied without consideration of the individual's needs. It seems reasonable to postulate that the advantages of horizontal job enrichment would be enhanced it it were combined with approach number 5, above.

7. Employ worker participation whereby the worker assists in 'engineering' his own job.

Comment: In describing the thoughts of James F. Lincoln, president, Lincoln Electric Co., Taylor (1971) states: 'If you want to find the person who can create the greatest cost-reduction progress on any particular operation, talk to the man now doing the job.' That applies whether the task is design, manufacturing, shipping, or any other phase of the operation. The man directly involved is the one who can innovate, create progress, and increase productivity, because there isn't anyone who knows better what the operation is all about.

The ergonomist in the military area has long recognized the value of information obtained from 'subject-matter experts.' When a competent ergonomist performs a task analysis, one of the best sources of information he finds is the GI who is performing the job or a similar one.

Although 'full-scale job enrichment for blue-collar workers, with real commitment from management, is still comparatively rare in the U.S. . . .,' at least 40 companies have recognized the value of some form of worker participation in designing jobs (Gooding, 1970b). Among these firms are Motorola (Hays and Saballus, no date); Lincoln Electric (Taylor, 1971); Corning Glass Works, Donnelly Mirrors, Inc., Precision Castparts Corp., Non-Linear Systems, In., R. G. Barry Corp., Texas Instruments, IBM, AT & T, Proctor and Gamble, and Polaroid (Gooding, 1970b); U.S. Envelope (Hall, 1971a); Metaframe (Hall, 1971b); several Japanese industries (Hird, 1972); and Smith Kline Instruments, Inc. (Tuttle, 1971a). In addition to finding that employees are subject-matter experts who can help improve production efficiency, these companies have also realized gains in positive employee attitudes toward the company. Calling upon a worker to engineer his job (either as an individual or, usually more effectively, as a member of a team) apparently does increase worker satisfaction and is accompanied by reported decreases in rates of turnover, absenteeism, and grievances—this, despite the fact that not all workers choose to join a worker-participation program and some of those who do join are coerced into joining.

This approach to the dehumanized job problem can create some challenge even in a simple job, particularly if combined with vertical job enrichment (approach 8).

A companion article by Swain (1973) to the one in this issue of *Human Factors* describes one worker-participation approach, an 'error-cause removal program', which draws heavily on the worker's knowledge of his own job and his usual willingness (in some cases even eagerness) to use this knowledge to improve the effectiveness of his job performance.

8. Create vertical job enrichment whereby the worker's job encompasses some meaningful whole, to give him a sense of responsibility and pride in his output.

Comment: This approach is akin to the old craft-type of job (e.g. a worker making a complete pair of shoes) as distinguished from the more modern job fractionation (or rationalization) (e.g. each worker making one part of a shoe and other workers on an assembly line each putting on one part as the shoe passes them). The history of industrial progress offers ample justification for the job rationalization approach; it was more efficient and did reduce costs. It is only fairly recently that many managers (see the references cited above) have realized that job rationalization has been carried to the extreme of creating the dehumanized job problem. (See Fitzgerald [1971] for an interesting viewpoint of a General Motors executive on the changing of worker attitudes from respect for work and plant authority to one of 'what's in it for me?')

Vertical job enrichment is illustrated by the Bell System's 'Work Itself' approach (Ford, 1969). It was adopted by the Bell System to reduce a serious problem of labour turnover of telephone operators, linemen, installers, and repairmen. Changing from an emphasis on job fractionation to one of allowing an individual worker to perform a related series of tasks with meaningful and satisfying closure resulted in greater worker satisfaction and fewer labour problems. Moreover, the extra training costs, plus costs of perhaps taking a longer time to accomplish individual job elements, reportedly was more than compensated for by savings in cost of turnover, absenteeism, and other labor problems. In short, when a total (or systems) view was taken of cost effectiveness, vertical job enrichment was a worthwhile investment.

Vertical job enrichment has been successfully applied to assembly-line work in diverse plants such as automobile assembly work (Ending . . ., 1972) and radio-equipment assembly (Schultz, no date). It has been tried successfully in the manufacture of components for nuclear weapons. In the production of such components, assembly work has normally followed detailed, written procedures wherein every minute step in the process was specified in production travelers or associated documentation. In short, the assembly worker had little or no flexibility in what he could do. This restriction had long been considered necessary in view of the demands for extremely high product quality and reliability.

However, with the advent of miniaturization and microminiaturization, some industrial processes became more like building an instrument, or like watchmaking. Each assemblyman had to weigh different factors and make judgments in fitting parts together and making adjustments. For example, to get one component to work reliably at the minimum rated voltage, there are many things which can be done by the worker because of interacting adjustments and piece parts.

Therefore, management in the plant in question decided to give the individual assemblymen more responsibility. He could accept the piece parts he wanted and reject others even though they had been certified by some previous process as being acceptable. He was responsible for each unit he assembled; it was 'his' unit and his name was on it. Since there was a 100% inspection (due to very high reliability requirements), the individual assemblyman got feedback of any defective units and the reasons for each reject were provided to him. Interviews with these assemblers indicated that they appreciated the geater responsibility and latitude. Management at that plant considered that the workers took an interest in production problems thought to be unique for union-represented workers.

Efforts were made to quantify the success of this vertical job enrichment, but the production data at the plant were not recorded in a manner permitting a controlled comparison. However, when the above investigation was made, there had been over 7,000 coded switches built (to cite one component) and there had been only two field failures, despite the fact that up to that time this unit was the most complex unit ever built at the plant in question. This unit also had the best quality/reliability number ever assigned by the AEC for components fabricated by the plant in question. Thus, although a monetary cost-effectiveness figure is not available, the reliability figures indicate that the program has been successful.

Management reaction to participation and enrichment techniques

The worker-participation and job-enrichment techniques have been greeted with both enthusiasm and skepticism (Tuttle, 1971b). Like any other new idea, some of the proponents tend to overdo it. However, the participation and enrichment techniques do appear to be consonant with accepted theories of worker motivation and needs. These techniques are backed by the theoretical and applied work of Herzberg and his followers (Herzberg, 1966; Herzberg, et al., 1957; Herzberg, Mausner, and Snyderman, 1959), by Marlow (1943), and by McGregor (1960).

As with any new approaches, it can be expected that there will be some rather soft-headed attempts at application. One investigative writer (Gooding, 1970b) notes that some companies have embraced job enrichment overenthusiastically, often prematurely, and that the sudden interest has some of the unfortunate aspects of a fad. He quotes Herzberg as calling these faddist 'sellers of snake oil', and decrying the 'whole bunch of nondescript behavioural scientists who are selling love and sitting in groups with their clothes on.' The Gooding article goes on to describe the experience of Non-Linear Systems, Inc., which went too far in trying to get rid of very detailed tasks. The president of that firm noted that both specialization and generalization can be good things, '. . . but each one, carried to an extreme, can be the worst possible thing you can get. People doing production work can get too damn much to do.'

The experience so far with these techniques indicates that they can work but that if not used in a systematic and carefully considered manner, they can backfire. This experience then should be a challenge to the ergonomist. Here is an opportunity to do practical research in an industrial system and to demonstrate that his claim for competence in 'systems research' is warranted. There is also ample opportunity to convince old-line management that the participation, and enrichment techniques are worth considering. Some firms still employ (almost literally) the 'stick and carrot' philosophy of getting their workers to produce. Skepticism about the new techniques is expressed at high levels, as witness an article entitled 'Why Motivation Theory Doesn't Work' by a General Motors executive (Fitzgerald, 1971). Much of the skepticism is based on irrelevancies; nevertheless, it exists and must be recognized by the ergonomist who wants to introduce a program of worker participation, job enrichment, or some combination thereof to see if it can improve output and reduce costs.

Conclusions

The ergonomist transferring from work in the military area (where the outputs of his design efforts will be used by military personnel) to work in the industrial area (where the outputs of his design efforts will be used by factory and other industrial workers) has the opportunity to work on a problem of utmost significance to management and to the country. This is the problem of dehumanized jobs resulting from an emphasis to the extreme on job fractionation (or job rationalization).

The ergonomist who has worked on military problems should already know how to design equipment a man can operate or maintain, and the techniques he has mastered should serve him in good stead when he turns to designing equipment and procedures a man can use in production jobs. The ergonomist transferring to the industrial area needs to take a systems viewpoint (one which most ergonomists insist they know well) and include in his design efforts systems, equipment, and procedures which are compatible with what a man will do. Unless the ergonomist is concerned with the motivation and needs of the worker, his designs will tend toward job simplification and he may aggravate the current industrial problem of worker dissatisfaction and the resultant turnover, absenteeism, grievances, strikes, and even sabotage.

It is suggested in this paper that there is ample evidence that management programs which try to get the worker to accept his lot or which attempt to motivate him by signs, slogans, small rewards for selective excellence, and other trivia will have limited and temporary enhancing effects, if any. On the other hand, several firms have found that direct efforts to reduce the dehumanizing aspects of industrial jobs do pay off.

These direct efforts include selective use of automation, avoiding overselection and overtraining of workers, worker participation, and horizontal and vertical job enrichment. The selection of the right combination of these approaches for any given plant is surely a challenge to the ergonomist who wants to look at the whole industrial setting.

Acknowledgments

This work was supported by the United States Atomic Energy Commission. Appreciation is also expressed to the industrial managers and supervisors who attended the author's two-day seminars on 'Design Techniques for Improving Human Performance in Production,' in February-March 1972 in Great Britain, and who provided him with valuable feedback on the ideas expressed in this article. Several of the firms these gentlemen represented were trying programs of horizontal and vertical job enrichment. The seminars were sponsored by Industrial and Commercial Techniques Ltd., 30 Fleet Street, London EC4.

References

Air Force Systems Command (1965) *AFSC zero-defects program (supervisor's handbook)* (AFSCP 11-2). U.S. Air Force, Feb. 15.

Ending of assembly lines may help Volvo's workers (1972) *Albuquerque Journals*, June 23.

Factories: Disassembling the line (1972) *Time*, 99(3), pp. 58–59.

Fitzgerald, T. H. (1971) Why motivation theory doesn't work. *Harvard Business Reviews*, 49(4), pp. 37–44.

Ford R. N. (1969) *Motivation through the work itself*. New York: American Management Association, Inc.

Gooding, J. (1970 Blues on the assembly line. *Fortune*, 82(2), pp. 69–117, (a).

Gooding, J. (1970) It pays to wake up the blue-collar worker. *Fortune*, 82(3), pp. 133–168, (b).

Hackman, R. C. (1969) *The motivated working adult*. New York: American Management Association, Inc.

Hall, F. (1971) Participation ups productivity—and morale. *Machinery*, 77(6), pp. 41–46, (a).

Hall, F. (1970) Participation improves quality . . . because it changes attitudes. *Machinery*, 77(7), pp. 46–50, (b).

Hays, B. and Saballus, D. New management strategy pays off at world's largest manufacturer of two-way radio. Schaumburg, Ill.: Motorola Communications Division, undated press release (received Nov. 1971).

Herzberg, F. *Work and the nature of man.* Cleveland: World Publishing Co., 1966.

Herzberg, F., Mausner, B., Peterson, R. O., and Capwell, D. F. (1957) *Job attitudes: Review of research and opinion.* Pittsburgh: Psychological Services of Pittsburgh.

Herzberg, F., Mausner, B., and Snyderman, B. (1959) *The motivation to work*. New York: John Wiley & Sons.

Hird, J. F. (1972) What makes Japan's industry so successful? *Assembly Engineering*, 15(1), pp. 20–24.

Maslow, A. H. (1943) A theory of human motivation. *Psychological Review*, 50, pp. 370–396.

McGregor, D. (1960) *Human side of enterprise.* New York: McGraw-Hill Book Co.

Rook, L. W. (1965) ZD: Momentary or momentous. *Quality Assurance*, 4, pp. 24–28.

Salpukas, A. (1972) Trouble on GM's new assembly line, world's fastest and most automated. *New York Times News Service*, Feb. 16.

Schultz, V. Employee motivation coupled with profits inspires new manufacturing concept. Schaumburg, Ill.: Motorola Communications Division, undated press release (received Nov. 1971).

Swain, A. D. (1972) *Design techniques for improving human performance in production.* London: Industrial & Commercial Techniques Ltd. (30 Fleet St.).

Swain, A. D. (1973) An error-cause removal program for industry. *Human Factors,* 15(3), in press.

Taylor, A. J. (1971) A new-old incentive to employee productivity. *Production,* 67(6), pp. 76–80.

Tinkham, M. L. (1971) Vocational rehabilitation. *Quality Progress,* 4, pp. 12–15.

Tuttle, H. C. (1971) The shortest distance to employee ideas is . . . a circle. *Production,* 67(6), pp. 73–75, (a).

Tuttle, H. C. (1971) Solving the people problem. *Production,* 68(5), pp. 79–83, (b).

5.6 The Role-set: Problems in Sociological Theory

Robert K. Merton

The problematics of the role-set

However much they may differ in other respects, contemporary sociological theorists are largely at one in adopting the premise that social statuses and social roles comprise major building blocks of social structure. This has been the case, since the influential writings of Ralph Linton on the subject, a generation ago. By status, and T. H. Marshall has indicated the geat diversity of meanings attached to this term since the time of Maine,[1] Linton meant a position in a social system involving designated rights and obligations; by role, the behaviour oriented to thee patterned expectations of others. In these terms, status and roles become concepts serving to connect culturally defined expectations with the patterned conduct and relationships which make up a social structure. Linton went on to state the long recognized and basic fact that each person in society inevitably occupies multiple statuses and that each of these statuses has an associated role.

It is at this point that I find it useful to depart from Linton's conception. The difference is initially a small one, some might say so small as not to deserve notice, but it involves a shift in the angle of vision which leads, I believe, to successively greater differences of a fundamental kind. Unlike Linton, I begin with the premise that each social status involves not a single associated role, but an array of roles. This basic feature of social structure can be registered by the distinctive but not formidable term, role-set. To repeat, then, by role-set I mean that complement of role-relationships in which persons are involved by virtue of occupying a particular social status. Thus, in our current studies of medical schools,[2] we have begun with the view that the status of medical student entails not only the role of a student *vis-à-vis* his teachers, but also an array of other roles relating him diversely to other students, physicians, nurses, social workers, medical technicians, and the like. Again, the status of school teacher in the United States has its distinctive role-set, in which are found pupils, colleagues, the school principal

---

Acknowledgement

Reprinted, by permission, from R. K. Merton, 'The role-set : problems in sociological theory' in *British Journal of Sociology,* Vol. 8, 1957, Routledge and Kegan Paul Ltd.

and superintendent, the Board of Education, professional associations, and, on occasion, local patriotic organizations.

It should be made made plain that the role-set differs from what sociologists have long described as 'multiple roles'. By established usage, the term multiple role refers not to the complex of roles associated with a single social status, but with the various social statuses (often, in differing institutional spheres) in which people find themselves—for illustration, the statuses of physician, husband, father, professor, church elder, Conservative Party member and army captain. (This complement of distinct statuses of a person, each of these in turn having its own role-set, I would designate as a status-set. This concept gives rise to its own range of analytical problems which cannot be considered here.)

The notion of the role-set reminds us, in the unlikely event that we need to be reminded of this obstinate fact, that even the seemingly simple social structure if fairly complex. All societies face the functional problem of articulating the components of numerous role-sets, the functional problem of managing somehow to organize these so that an appreciable degree of social regularity obtains, sufficient to enable most people most of the time to go about their business of social life, without encountering extreme conflict in their role-sets as the normal, rather than the exceptional, state of affairs.

If this relatively simple idea of role-set has any theoretical worth, it should at the least generate distinctive problems for sociological theory, which come to our attention only from the perspective afforded by this idea, or by one like it. This the notion of role-set does. It raises the general problem of identifying the social mechanisms which serve to articulate the expectations of those in the role-set so that the occupant of a status if confronted with less conflict than would obtain if these mechanisms were not at work. It is to these social mechanisms that I would devote the rest of this discussion.

There is always a *potential* for differing and sometimes conflicting expectations of the conduct appropriate to a status-occupant among those in the role-set. The basic source of this potential for conflict, I suggest—and here we are at one with theorists as disparate as Marx and Spencer, Simmel and Parsons—is that the members of a role-set are, to some degree, apt to hold social positions differing from that of the occupant of the status in question. To the extent that they are diversely located in the social structure, they are apt to have interests and sentiments, values and moral expectations differing from those of the status-occupant himself. This, after all, is one of the principal assumptions of Marxist theory, as it is of all sociological theory: social differentiation generates distinct interests among those variously located in the structure of the society. To continue with one of our examples: the members of a school board are often in social and economic strata which differ greatly from that of the school teacher; and their interests, values and expectations are consequently apt to differ, to some extent, from those of the teacher. The teacher may thus become subject to conflicting role-expectations among such members of his role-set as professional colleagues, influential members of the school board, and, say, the Americanism Committee of the American Legion. What is an educational essential for the one may be judged as an education frill, or as downright subversion, by the other. These disparate and contradictory evaluations by members of the role-set greatly complicate the task of coping with them all. The familiar case of the teacher may be taken as paradigmatic. What holds conspicuously for this one status holds, in varying degree, for the occupants of all other statuses who are structurally related, through their role-set, to others who themselves occupy diverse positions in society.

This, then is the basic structural basis for potential disturbance of a role-set. And it gives rise, in turn, to a double question: which social mechanisms, if any, operate to counteract such instability of role-sets and, correlatively, under which circumstances do these social mechanisms fail to operate, with resulting confusion and conflict. This is not to say, of course, that role-sets do invariably operate with substantial efficiency. We are concerned here, not with a broad historical generalization to the effect that social order prevails, but with an analytical problem of identifying social mechanisms which produce a greater degree of order than would obtain, if these mechanisms were not called into play. Otherwise put, it is theoretical sociology, not history, which is of interest here.

Social mechanisms articulating role-sets

1. *Relative importance of various statuses.* The first of these mechanisms derives from the oft-noticed sociological circumstance that social structures designate certain statuses as having greater importance than others. Family and job obligations, for example, are defined in American society as having priority over membership in voluntary associations.[3] As a result, a particular role-relationship may be of peripheral concern for some; for others it may be central. Our hypothetical teacher, for whom this status holds primary significance, may by this circumstance be better able to withstand the demands for conformity with the differing expectations of those comprising his role-set. For at least some of these others, the relationship has only peripheral significance. This does not mean, of course, that teachers are not vulnerable to demands which are at odds with their own professional commitments. It means only that when powerful members of their role-set are only little concerned with this particular relationship,

teachers are less vulnerable than they would otherwise be (or sometimes are). Were all those involved in the role-set *equally* concerned with this relationship, the plight of the teacher would be considerably more sorrowful than it often is. What holds for the particular case of the teacher presumably holds for the occupants of other statuses: the impact upon them of diverse expectations among those in their role-set is mitigated by the basic structural fact of differentials of involvement in the relationship among those comprising their role-set.

2. *Differences of power of those in the role-set.* A second potential mechanism for stabilizing the role-set is found in the distribution of power and authority. By power, in this connection, is meant the observed and predictable capacity to impose one's will in a social action, even against the opposition of others taking part in that action; by authority, the culturally legitimized organization of power.

As a consequence of social stratification, the members of a role-set are not apt to be equally powerful in shaping the behaviour of status-occupants. However, it does not follow that the individuals, group, or stratum in the role-set which are *separately* most powerful uniformly succeed in imposing their demands upon the status-occupant, say, the teacher. This would be so only in the circumstance that one member of the role-set has either a monopoly of power in the situation or out-weighs the combined power of the others. Failing this special but, of course, not infrequent, situation, there may develop *coalitions of power* among some members of the role-set which enable the status-occupants to go their own way. The familiar pattern of a balance of power is of course not confined to the conventionally-defined political realm. In less easily visible form, it can be found in the workings of role-sets generally, as the boy who succeeds in having his father's decision offset his mother's opposed decision has ample occasion to know. To the extent that conflicting powers in his role-set neutralize one another, the status-occupant has relative freedom to proceed as he intended in the first place.

Thus, even in those potentially unstable structures in which the members of a role-set hold contrasting expectations of what the status-occupant should do, the latter is not wholly at the mercy of the most powerful among them. Moreover, the structural variations of engagement in the role-structure, which I have mentioned, can serve to reinforce the relative power of the status-occupant. For to the extent that powerful members of his role-set are not centrally concerned with this particular relationship, they will be the less motivated to exercise their potential power to the full. Within varying margins of his activity, the status-occupant will then be free to act as he would.

Once again, to reiterate that which lends itself to misunderstanding, I do not say that the status-occupant subject to conflicting expectations among members of his role-set is in fact immune to control by them. I suggest only that the power and authority-structure of role-sets is often such that he has a larger measure of autonomy than he would have had if this structure of competing power did not obtain.

3. *Insulation of role-activities from observability by members of the role-set.* People do not engage in continuous interaction with all those in their role-sets. This is not an incidental fact, to be ignored because familiar, but one integral to the operation of social structure. Interaction with each member of a role-set tends to be variously intermittent. This fundamental fact allows for role-behaviour which is at odds with the expectations of some in the role-set to proceed without undue stress. For, as I elsewhere suggest at some length,[4] effective social control presupposes social arrangements making for the observability of behaviour. (By observability, a conception which I have borrowed from Simmel and tried to develop, I mean the extent to which social norms and role-performances can readily become known to others in the social system. This is, I believe, a variable crucial to structural analysis, a belief which I cannot, unhappily, undertake to defend here.)

To the extent that the social structure insulates the individual from having his activities known to members of his role-set, he is the less subject to competing pressures. It should be emphasized that we are dealing here with structural arrangements for such insulation, not with the fact that this or that person *happens* to conceal part of his role-behaviour from others. The structural fact is that social statuses differ in the extent to which the conduct of those in them are regularly insulated from observability by members of the role-set. Some have a functionally significant insulation of this kind, as for example, the status of the university teacher, insofar as norms hold that what is said in the classroom is privileged. In this familiar type of case, the norm clearly has the function of maintaining some degree of autonomy for the teacher. For if they were forever subject to observation by all those in the role-set, with their often differing expectations, teachers might be driven to teach not what they know or what the evidence leads them to believe, but to teach what will placate the numerous and diverse people who are ostensibly concerned with 'the education of youth'. That this sometimes occurs is evident. But it would presumably be more frequent, were it not for the relative exemption from observability by all and sundry who may wish to impose their will upon the instructor.

More broadly, the concept of privileged information and confidential communication in the professions has this same function of insulating clients from observability of their behaviour and beliefs by others in their role-set.

Were physicians or priests free to tell all they have learned about the private lives of their clients, the needed information would not be forthcoming and they could not adequately discharge their functions. More generally, if all the facts of one's conducts and beliefs were freely available to anyone, social structures could not operate. What is often described as 'the need for privacy'—that is, insulation of actions and beliefs from surveillance by others—is the individual counterpart to the functional requirement of social structure that some measure of exemption from full observability be provided. 'Privacy' is not only a personal predilection, though it may be that, too. It is also a requirement of social systems which must provide for a measure, as they say in France, of *quant-à-soi*, a portion of the self which is kept apart, immune from observation by others.

Like other social mechanisms, this one of insulation from full observability can, of course, miscarry. Were the activities of the politician or, if one prefers, the statesman, fully removed from the public spotlight, social control of his behaviour would be correspondingly reduced. And as we all know, anonymous power anonymously exercised does not make for a stable social structure meeting the values of a society. So, too, the teacher or physician who is largely insulated from observability may fail to live up to the minimum requirements of his status. All this means only that some measure of observability of role-performance by members of the role-set is required, if the indispensable social requirement of accountability is to be met. This statement does not contradict an earlier statement to the effect that some measure of insulation from observability is also required for the effective operation of social structures. Instead, the two statements, taken in conjunction, imply that there is an optimum zone of observability, difficult to identify in precise terms and doubtless varying for different social statuses, which will simultaneously make both for accountability and for substantial autonomy, rather than for a frightened acquiescence with the distribution of power which happens, at a particular moment, to obtain in the role-set.

4. *Observability of conflicting demands by members of a role-set.* This mechanism is implied by what has been said and therefore needs only passing comment here. As long as members of the role-set are happily ignorant that their demands upon the occupants of a status are incompatible, each member may press his own case. The pattern is then many against one. But when it becomes plain that the demands of some are in full contradiction with the demands of others, it becomes, in part, the task of members of the role-set, rather than that of the status-occupant, to resolve these contradictions, either by a struggle for over-riding power or by some degree of compromise.

In such circumstances, the status-occupant subjected to conflicting demands often becomes cast in the role of the *tertius gaudens*, the third (or more often, the nth) party who draws advantage from the conflict of the others. Originally at the focus of the conflict, he can virtually become a bystander whose function it is to highlight the conflicting demands being made by members of his role-set. It becomes a problem for them, rather than for him, to resolve their contradictory demands. At the least, this serves to make evident that it is not wilful misfeasance on his part which keeps him from conforming to all the contradictory expectations imposed upon him.[5] When most effective, this serves to articulate the expectations of those in the role-set beyond a degree which would occur, if this mechanism of making contradictory expectations manifest were not at work.

5. *Mutual social support among status-occupants.* Whatever he may believe to the contrary, the occupant of a social status is not alone. The very fact that he is placed in a social position means that there are other more or less like-circumstanced. To this extent, the actual or potential experience of facing a conflict of expectations among members of the role-set is variously common to all occupants of the status. The particular persons subject to these conflicts need not, therefore, meet them as wholly private problems which must be coped with in wholly private fashion.

It is this familiar and fundamental fact of social structure, of course, which is the basis for those in the same social status forming the associations intermediate to the individual and the larger society in a pluralistic system. These organizations constitute a structural response to the problems of coping with the (potentially or actually) conflicting demands by those in the role-sets of the status.[6] Whatever the intent, these constitute social formations serving to counter the power of the role-set; of being, not merely amenable to its demands, but of helping to shape them. Such organizations—so familiar a part of the social landscape of differentiated societies—also develop normative systems which are designed to anticipate and thereby to mitigate such conflicting expectations. They provide social support to the individuals in the status under attack. They minimize the need for their improvising personal adjustments to patterned types of conflicting expectations. Emerging codes which state in advance what the socially-supported conduct of the status-occupant should be, also serve this social function. This function becomes all the more significant in the structural circumstances when status-occupants are highly vulnerable to pressures from their role-set because they are relatively isolated from one another. Thus, thousands of librarians sparsely distributed among the towns and villages of America and not infrequently subject to censorial pressures received strong support from the code on censorship developed by the American Library Association.[7] This only illustrates the general mechanisms whereby status-peers curb the pressures exerted upon them individually by drawing upon the organizational and normative support of their peers.

6. *Abridging the role-set.* There is, of course, a limiting case in the modes of coping with incompatible demands by the role-set. Role-relations are broken off, leaving a greater consensus of role-expectations among those who remain. But this mode of adaptation by amputating the role-set is possible only under special and limited conditions. It can be effectively utilized only in those circumstances where it is still possible for status-occupants to perform their other roles, without the support of those with whom they have discontinued relations. It presupposes that the social structure provides this option. By and large, however, this option is infrequent and limited, since the composition of the role-set is ordinarily not a matter of personal choice but a matter of the social organization in which the status is embedded. More typically, the individual goes, and the social structure remains.

Residual conflict in the role-set

Doubtless, these are only some of the mechanisms which serve to articulate the expectations of those in the role-set. Further inquiry will uncover others, just as it will probably modify the preceding account of those we have provisionally identified. But, however much the substance may change, I believe that the logic of the analysis will remain largely intact. This can be briefly recapitulated.

First, it is assumed that each social status has its organized complement of role-relationships which can be thought of as comprising a role-set. Second, relationships hold not only the between occupant of the particular status and each member of the role-set, but always potentially and often actually, between members of the role-set itself. Third, to the extent that members of the role-set themselves hold substantially differing statuses, they will tend to have some differing expectations (moral and actuarial) of the conduct appropriate for the status-occupant. Fourth, this gives rise to the sociological problem of how their diverse expectations become sufficiently articulated for the status-structure and the role-structure to operate with a modicum of effectiveness. Fifth, inadequate articulation of these role-expectations tends to call one or more social mechanisms into play, which serve to reduce the extent of patterned conflict below the level which would be involved if these mechanisms were not at work.

And now, sixth, finally and importantly, even when these (and probably other) mechanisms are operating, they may not, in particular cases, prove sufficient to reduce the conflict of expectations below the level required for the social structure to operate with substantial effectiveness. This residual conflict within the role-set may be enough to interfere materially with the effective performance of roles by the occupant of the status in question. Indeed, it may well turn out that this condition is the most frequent one—role-systems operating at considerably less than full efficiency. Without trying to draw tempting analogies with other types of systems, I suggest only that this is not unlike the case of engines which cannot fully utilize heat energy. If the analogy lacks force, it may nevertheless have the merit of excluding the utopian figment of a perfectly effective social system.

We do not yet know some of the requirements for fuller articulation of the relations between the occupant of a status and members of his role-set, on the one hand, and for fuller articulation of the values and expectations among those comprising the role-set, on the other. As we have seen, even those requirements which can now be identified are not readily satisfied, without fault, in social systems. To the extent that they are not, social systems are forced to limp along with that measure of ineffectiveness and inefficiency which is often accepted because the realistic prospect of decided improvement seems so remote as sometimes not to be visible at all.

Notes

[1] T. H. Marshall, 'A note on "status" ', in K. M. Kapadia (editor), *Professor Ghurye Felicitation Volume* (Bombay: Popular Book Depot, n.d.), 11–19.

[2] R. K. Merton, P. L. Kendall, and G. G. Reader, editors, *The Student-Physician: Introductory Studies in the Sociology of Medical Education* (Cambridge, Mass.: Harvard University Press, 1957).

[3] Bernard Barber has drawn out the implications of this structural fact in his study of voluntary associations; see his 'Participation and mass aparty in associations', in A. W. Gouldner, ed., *Studies in Leadership* (New York: Harper & Brothers, 1950), 477–504, especially at 486 ff.

[4] Robert K. Merton, *Social Theory and Social Structure* (Glencoe, Illinois: The Free Press, rev. ed., in press), 336–56. This discussion of role-set draws upon one part of Chapter IX, 'Continuities in the Theory of Reference Groups and Social Structures', 368–84.

[5] See the observations by William G. Carr, the executive secretary of the National Education Association. An address at the inauguration of Hollis Leland Caswell, Teachers College, Columbia University, November 21–2, 1955, 10.

[6] In this context, see the acute analysis of the formation of the National Union of Teachers by Asher Tropp, *The School Teachers* (London: Heinemann, 1957).

[7] See R. P. McKeon, R. K. Merton and W. Gellhorn, *Freedom to Read* (1957).

5.7 Social Benefit versus Technological Risk

What is our society willing to pay for safety?

Chauncey Starr

The evaluation of technical approaches to solving societal problems customarily involves consideration of the relationship between potential technical performance and the required investment of societal resources. Although such performance-versus-cost relationships are clearly useful for choosing between alternative solutions, they do not by themselves determine how much technology a society can justifiably purchase. This latter determination requires, additionally, knowledge of the relationship between social benefit and justified social cost. The two relationships may then be used jointly to determine the optimum investment of societal resources in a technological approach to a social need.

Technological analyses for disclosing the relationship between expected performance and monetary costs are a traditional part of all engineering planning and design. The inclusion in such studies of *all* societal costs (indirect as well as direct) is less customary, and obviously makes the analysis more difficult and less definitive. Analyses of social value as a function of technical performance are not only uncommon but are rarely quantitative. Yet we know that implicit in every nonarbitrary national decision on the use of technology is a trade-off of societal benefits and societal costs.

In this article I offer an approach for establishing a quantitative measure of benefit relative to cost for an important element in our spectrum of social values—specifically, for accidental deaths arising from technological developments in public use. The analysis is based on two assumptions. The first is that historical national accident records are adequate for revealing consistent patterns of fatalities in the public use of technology. (That this

Acknowledgement

Reprinted, by permission, from C. Starr, 'Social benefit versus technological risk' in *Science,* Vol. 165, Copyright © 1969 by the American Association for the Advancement of Science.

The author is dean of the School of Engineering and Applied Science, University of California, Los Angeles. This article is adapted from a paper presented at the Symposium on Human Ecology held at Airlie House, Warrenton, Virginia, in November 1968.

may not always be so is evidenced by the paucity of data relating to the effects of environmental pollution.) The second assumption is that such historically revealed social preferences and costs are sufficiently enduring to permit their use for predictive purposes.

In the absence of economic or sociological theory which might give better results, this empirical approach provides some interesting insights into accepted social values relative to personal risk. Because this methodology is based on historical data, it does not serve to distinguish what is 'best' for society from what is 'traditionally acceptable.'

Maximum benefit at minimum cost

The broad societal benefits of advances in technology exceed the associated costs sufficiently to make technological growth inexorable. Shef's socioeconomic study (1) has indicated that technological growth has been generally exponential in this century, doubling every 20 years in nations having advanced technology. Such technological growth has apparently stimulated a parallel growth in socioeconomic benefits and a slower associated growth in social costs.

The conventional socioeconomic benefits—health, education, income—are presumably indicative of an improvement in the 'quality of life.' The cost of this socioeconomic progress shows up in all the negative indicators of our society—urban and environmental problems, technological unemployment, poor physical and mental health, and so on. If we understood quantitatively the causal relationships between specific technological developments and societal values, both positive and negative, we might deliberately guide and regulate technological developments so as to achieve maximum social benefit at minimum social cost. Unfortunately, we have not as yet developed such a predictive system analysis. As a result, our society historically has arrived at acceptable balances of technological benefit and social cost empirically—by trial, error, and subsequent corrective steps.

In advanced societies today, this historical empirical approach creates an increasingly critical situation, for two basic reasons. The first is the well-known difficulty in changing a technical subsystem of our society once it has been woven into the economic, political, and cultural structures. For example, many of our environmental-pollution problems have known engineering solutions, but the problems of economic readjustment, political jurisdiction, and social behaviour loom very large. It will take many decades to put into effect the technical solutions we know today. To give a specific illustration, the pollution of our water resources could be completely avoided by means of engineering systems now available, but public interest in making the economic and political adjustments needed for applying these techniques is very limited. It has been facetiously suggested that, as a means of motivating the public, every community and industry should be required to place its water intake downstream from its outfall.

In order to minimize these difficulties, it would be desirable to try out new developments in the smallest social groups that would permit adequate assessment. This is a common practice in market-testing a new product or in field-testing a new drug. In both these cases, however, the experiment is completely under the control of a single company or agency, and the test information can be fed back to the controlling group in a time that is short relative to the anticipated commercial lifetime of the product. This makes it possible to achieve essentially optimum use of the product in an acceptably short time. Unfortunately, this is rarely the case with new technologies. Engineering developments involving new technology are likely to appear in many places simultaneously and to become deeply integrated into the systems of our society before their impact is evident or measurable.

This brings us to the second reason for the increasing severity of the problem of obtaining maximum benefits at minimum costs. It has often been stated that the time required from the conception of a technical idea to its first application in society has been drastically shortened by modern engineering organization and management. In fact, the history of technology does not support this conclusion. The bulk of the evidence indicates that the time from conception to first application (or demonstration) has been roughly unchanged by modern management, and depends chiefly on the complexity of the development.

However, what *has* been reduced substantially in the past century is the time from first use to widespread integration into our social system. The techniques for *societal diffusion* of a new technology and its subsequent exploitation are not highly developed. Our ability to organize resources of money, men, and materials to focus on new technological programs has reduced the diffusion-exploitation time by roughly an order of magnitude in the past century.

Thus, we now face a general situation in which widespread use of a new technological development may occur before its social impact can be properly assessed, and before any empirical adjustment of the benefit-versus-cost relation is obviously indicated.

It has been clear for some time that predictive technological assessments are a pressing societal need. However, even if such assessments become available, obtaining maximum social benefit at minimum cost also requires the establishment of a relative value system for the basic parameters in our ojective of improved 'quality of life.' The empirical approach implicitly involved an intuitive societal balancing of such values. A predictive analytical approach will require an explicit scale of relative social values.

For example, if technological assessment of a new development predicts an increased per capita annual income of x percent but also predicts an associated accident probability of y fatalities annually per million population, then how are these to be compared in their effect on the 'quality of life'? Because the penalties or risks to the public arising from a new development can be reduced by applying constraints, there will usually be a functional relationship (or trade-off) between utility and risk, the x and y of our example.

There are many historical illustrations of such trade-off relationships that were empirically determined. For example, automobile and airplane safety have been continuously weighed by society against economic costs and operating performance. In these and other cases, the real trade-off process is actually one of dynamic adjustment, with the behaviour of many portions of our social systems out of phase, due to the many separate 'time constants' involved. Readily available historical data on accidents and health, for a variety of public activities, provide an enticing stepping-stone to quantitative evaluation of this particular type of social cost. The social benefits arising from some of these activities can be roughly determined. On the assumption that in such historical situations a socially acceptable and essentially optimum trade-off of values has been achieved, we could say that any generalizations developed might then be used for predictive purposes. This approach could give a rough answer to the seemingly simple question 'How safe is safe enough?'

The pertinence of this question to all of us, and particularly to governmental regulatory agencies, is obvious. Hopefully, a functional answer might provide a basis for establishing performance 'design objectives' for the safety of the public.

Voluntary and involuntary activities

Societal activities fall into two general categories—those in which the individual participates on a 'voluntary' basis and those in which the participation is 'involuntary', imposed by the society in which the individual lives. The process of empirical optimization of benefits and costs is fundamentally similar in the two cases—namely, a reversible exploration of available options—but the time required for empirical adjustments (the time constants of the system) and the criteria for optimization are quite different in the two situations.

In the case of 'voluntary' activities, the individual uses his own value system to evaluate his experiences. Although his eventual trade-off may not be consciously or analytically determined, or based upon objective knowledge, it nevertheless is likely to respresent, for that individual, a crude optimization appropriate to his value system. For example, an urban dweller may move to the suburbs because of a lower crime rate and better schools, at the cost of more time spent travelling on highways, and a higher probability of accidents. If, subsequently, the traffic density increases, he may decide that the penalties are too great and move back to the city. Such an individual optimization process can be comparatively rapid (because the feedback of experience to the individual is rapid), so the statistical pattern for a large social group may be an important 'real-time' indicator of societal trade-offs and values.

'Involuntary' activities differ in that the criteria and options are determined not by the individuals affected but by a controlling body. Such control may be in the hands of a government agency, a political entity, a leadership group, an assembly of authorities or 'opinion-makers', or a combination of such bodies. Because of the complexity of large societies, only the control group is likely to be fully aware of all the criteria and options involved in their decision process. Further, the time required for feedback of the experience that results from the controlling decisions is likely to be very long. The feedback of cumulative individual experiences into societal communication channels (usually political or economic) is a slow process, as is the process of altering the planning of the control group. We have many examples of such 'involuntary' activities, war being perhaps the most extreme case of the operational separation of the decision-making group from those most affected. Thus, the real-time pattern of societal trade-offs on 'involuntary' activities must be considered in terms of the particular dynamics of approach to an acceptable balance of social values and costs. The historical trends in such activities may therefore be more significant indicators of social acceptability than the existent trade-offs are.

In examining the historical benefit-risk relationships for 'involuntary' activities, it is important to recognize the perturbing role of public psychological acceptance of risk arising from the influence of authorities or dogma. Because in this situation the decision-making is separated from the affected individual, society has generally clothed many of its controlling groups in an almost impenetrable mantle of authority and of imputed wisdom. The public generally assumes that the decision-making process is based on a rational analysis of social benefit and social risk. While it often is, we have all seen

SOCIAL BENEFIT Vs TECHOLOGICAL RISK

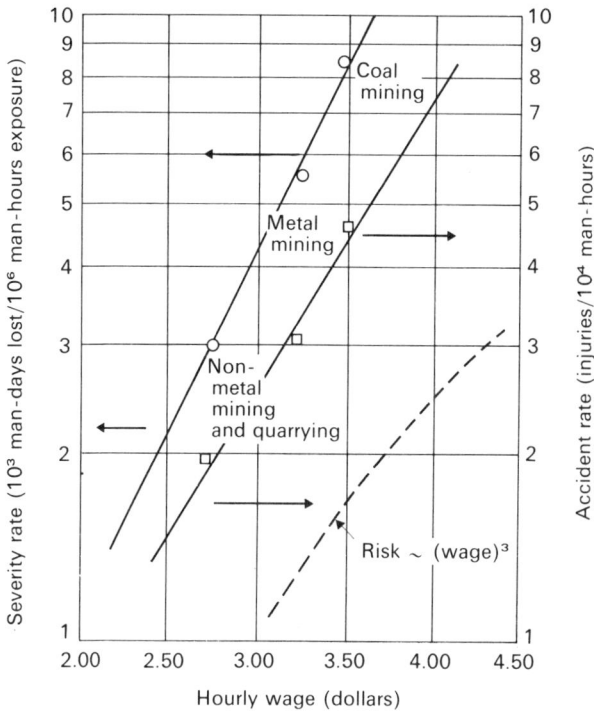

Figure 1. Mining accident rates plotted relative to incentive.

after-the-fact examples of irrationality. It is important to omit such 'witch-doctor' situations in selecting examples of optimized 'involuntary' activities, because in fact these situations typify only the initial stages of exploration of options.

Quantitative correlations

With this description of the problem, and the associated caveats, we are in a position to discuss the quantitative correlations. For the sake of simplicity in this initial study, I have taken as a measure of the physical risk to the individual the fatalities (deaths) associated with each activity. Although it might be useful to include all injuries (which are 100 to 1,000 times as numerous as deaths), the difficulty in obtaining data and the unequal significance of varying disabilities would introduce inconvenient complexity for this study. So the risk measure used here is the statistical probability of fatalities per hour of exposure of the individual to the activity considered.

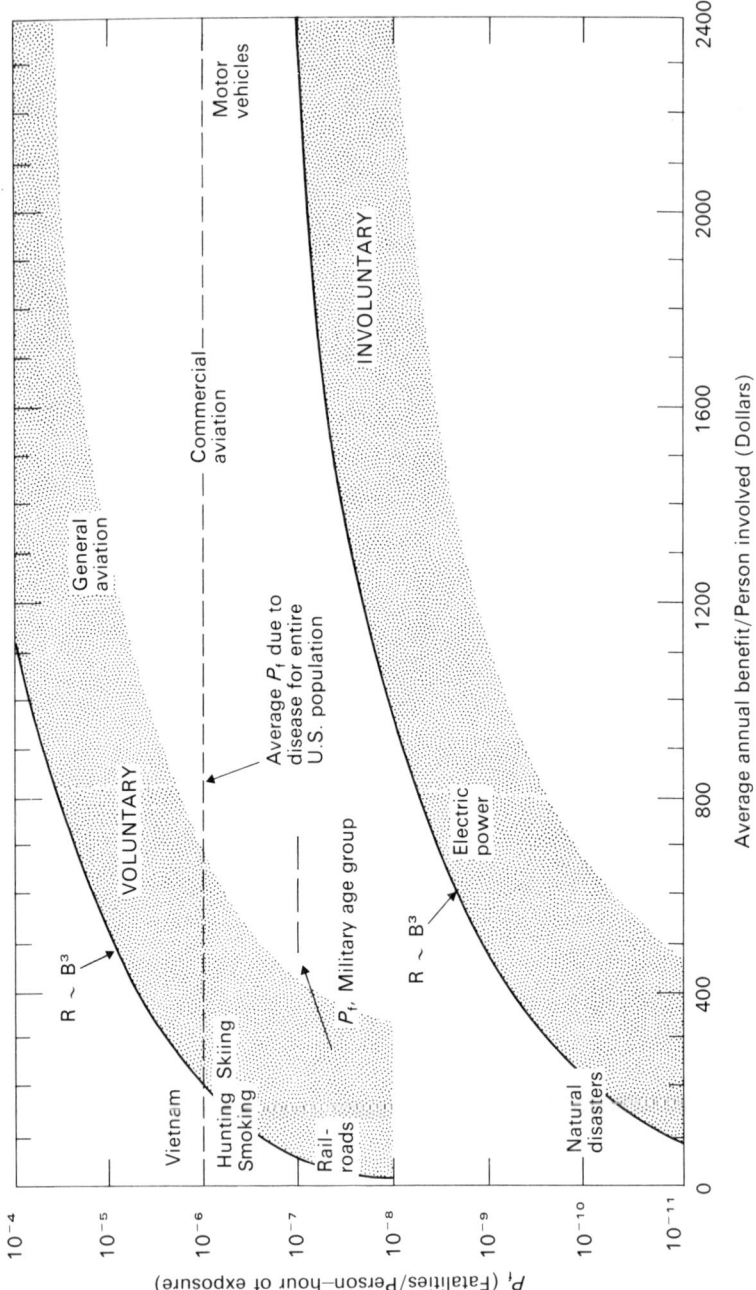

Figure 2. Risk (R) plotted relative to benefit (B) for various kinds of voluntary and involuntary exposure.

The hour-of-exposure unit was chosen because it was deemed more closely related to the individual's intuitive process in choosing an activity than a year of exposure would be, and gave substantially similar results. Another possible alternative, the risk per activity, involved a comparison of too many dissimilar units of measure; thus, in comparing the risk for various modes of transportation, one could use risk per hour, per mile, or per trip. As this study was directed toward exploring a methodology for determining social acceptance of risk, rather than the safest mode of transportation for a particular trip, the simplest common unit—that of risk per exposure hour—was chosen.

The social benefit derived from each activity was converted into a dollar equivalent, as a measure of integrated value to the individual. This is perhaps the most uncertain aspect of the correlations because it reduced the 'quality-of-life' benefits of an activity to an overly simplistic measure. Nevertheless, the correlations seemed useful, and no better measure was available. In the case of the 'voluntary' activities, the amount of money spent on the activity by the average involved individual was assumed proportional to its benefit to him. In the case of the 'involuntary' activities, the contribution of the activity to the individual's annual income (or the equivalent) was assumed proportional to its benefit. This assumption of roughly constant relationship between benefits and monies, for each class of activities, is clearly an approximation. However, because we are dealing in orders of magnitude, the distortions likely to be introduced by this approximation are relatively small.

In the case of transportation modes, the benefits were equated with the sum of the monetary cost to the passenger and the value of the time saved by that particular mode relative to a slower, competitive mode. Thus, airplanes were compared with automobiles, and automobiles were compared with public transportation or walking. Benefits of public transportation were equated with their cost. In all cases, the benefits were assessed on an annual dollar basis because this seemed to be most relevant to the individual's intuitive process. For example, most luxury sports require an investment and upkeep only partially dependent upon usage. The associated risks, of course, exist only during the hours of exposure.

Probably the use of electricity provides the best example of the analysis of an 'involuntary' activity. In this case the fatalities include those arising from electrocution, electrically caused fires, the operation of power plants, and the mining of the required fossil fuel. The benefits were estimated from a United Nations study of the relationship between energy consumption and national income; the energy fraction associated with electric power was used. The contributions of the home use of electric power to our 'quality of

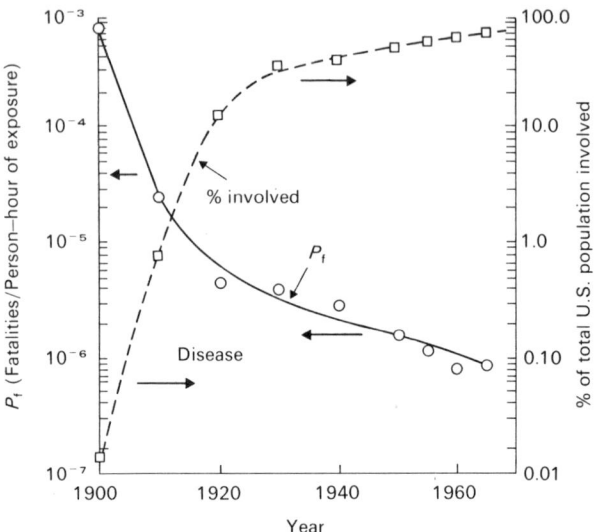

Figure 3. Risk and participation trends for motor vehicles.

life'—more subtle than the contributions of electricity in industry—are omitted. The availability of refrigeration has certainly improved our national health and the quality of dining. The electric light has certainly provided great flexibility in patterns of living, and television is a positive element. Perhaps, however, the gross-income measure used in the study is sufficient for present purposes.

Information on acceptance of 'voluntary' risk by individuals as a function of income benefits is not easily available, although we know that such a relationship must exist. Of particular interest, therefore, is the special case of miners exposed to high occupational risks. In Fig. 1, the accident rate and the severity rate of mining injuries are plotted against the hourly wage (2, 3). The acceptance of individual risk is an exponential function of the wage, and can be roughly approximated by a third-power relationship in this range. If this relationship has validity, it may mean that several 'quality of life' parameters (perhaps health, living essentials, and recreation) are each partly influenced by any increase in available personal resources, and that thus the increased acceptance of risk is exponentially motivated. The extent to which this relationship is 'voluntary' for the miners is not obvious, but the subject is interesting nevertheless.

Risk comparisons

The results for the societal activities studied, both 'voluntary' and

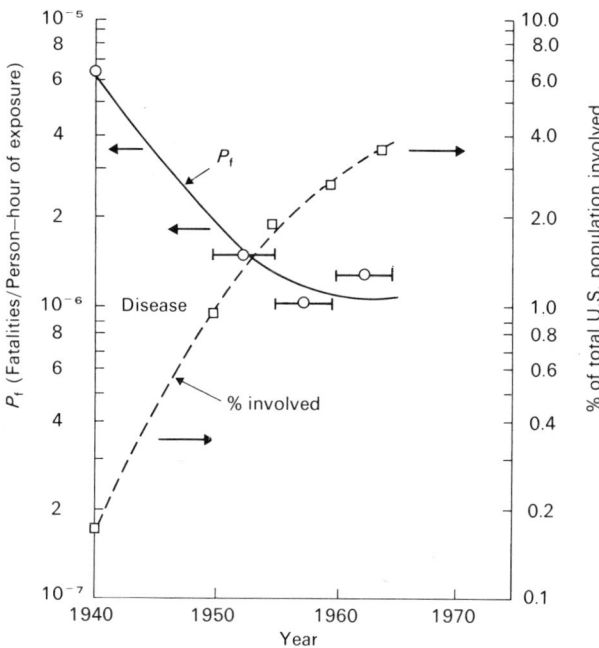

Figure 4. Risk and participation trends for certified air carriers.

'involuntary', are assembled in Fig. 2. (For details of the risk-benefit analysis, see the appendix.) Also shown in Fig. 2 is the third-power relationship between risk and benefit characteristic of Fig. 1. For comparison, the average risk of death from accident and from disease is shown. Because the average number of fatalities from accidents is only about one-tenth the number from disease, their inclusion is not significant.

Several major features of the benefit-risk relations are apparent, the most obvious being the difference by several orders of magnitude in society's willingness to accept 'voluntary' and 'involuntary' risk. As one would expect, we are loathe to let others do unto us what we happily do to ourselves.

The rate of death from disease appears to play, psychologically, a yardstick role in determining the acceptability of risk on a voluntary basis. The risk of death in most sporting activities is surprisingly close to the risk of death from disease—almost as though, in sports, the individual's subconscious computer adjusted his courage and made him take risks associated with a fatality level equaling but not exceeding the statistical

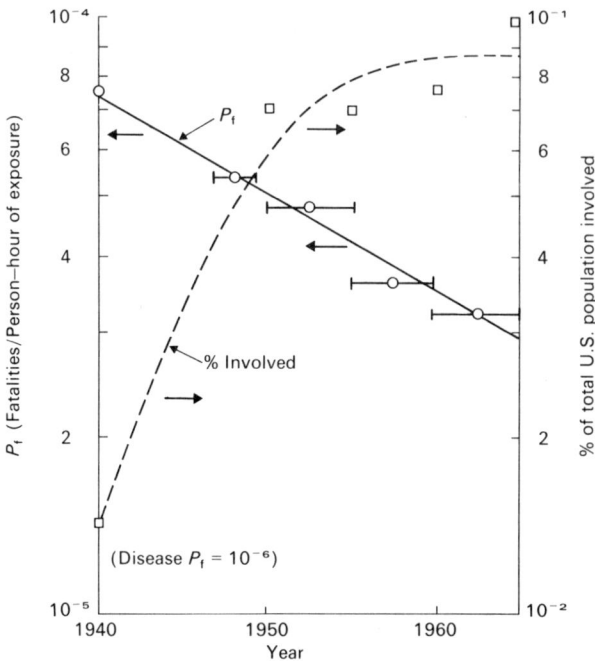

Figure 5. Risk and participation trends for general aviation.

mortality due to involuntary exposure to disease. Perhaps this defines the demarcation between boldness and foolhardiness.

In Fig. 2 the statistic for the Vietnam war is shown because it raises an interesting point. It is only slightly above the average for risk of death from disease. Assuming that some long-range societal benefit was anticipated from this war, we find that the related risk, as seen by society as a whole, is not substantially different from the average nonmilitary risk from disease. However, for individuals in the military-service age group (age 20 to 30), the risk of death in Vietnam is about ten times the normal mortality rate (death from accidents or disease). Hence the population as a whole and those directly exposed see this matter from different perspectives. The disease risk pertinent to the average age of the involved group probably would provide the basis for a mor meaningful comparison than the risk pertinent to the national average age does. Use of the figure for the single group would complicate these simple comparisons, but that figure might be more significant as a yard-stick.

The risks associated with general aviation, commercial aviation, and travel by motor vehicle deserve special comment. The latter originated as a 'voluntary' sport, but in the past half-century the motor vehicle has become an essential utility. General aviation is still a highly voluntary activity. Commercial aviation is partly voluntary and partly essential and, additionally, is subject to government administration as a transportation utility.

Travel by motor vehicle has now reached a benefit-risk balance, as shown in Fig. 3. It is interesting to note that the present risk level is only slightly below the basic level of risk from disease. In view of the high percentage of the population involved, this probably represents a true societal judgment on the acceptability of risk in relation to benefit. It also appears from Fig. 3 that future reductions in the risk level will be slow in coming, even if the historical trend of improvement can be maintained (*4*).

Commercial aviation has barely approached a risk level comparable to that set by disease. The trend is similar to that for motor vehicles, as shown in Fig. 4. However, the percentage of the population participating is now only 1/20 that for motor vehicles. Increased public participation in commercial aviation will undoubtedly increase the pressure to reduce the risk, because, for the general population, the benefits are much less than those associated with motor vehicles. Commercial aviation has not yet reached the point of optimum benefit risk trade-off (*5*).

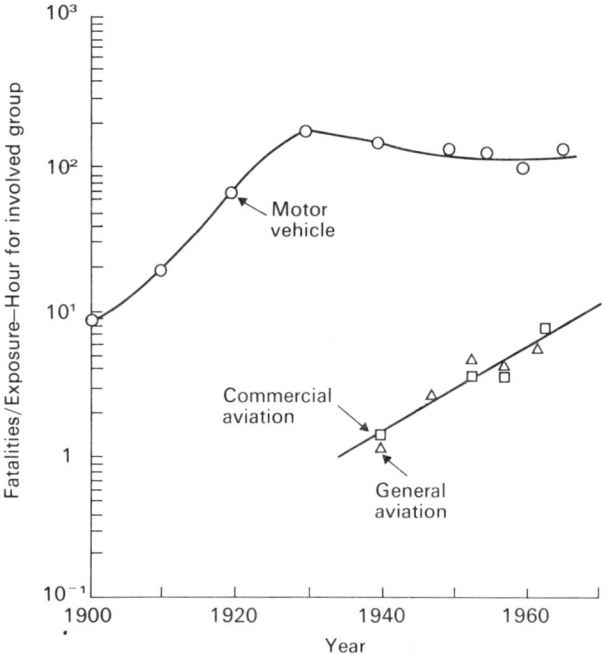

Figure 6. Group risk plotted relative to year.

For general aviation the trends are similar, as shown in Fig. 5. Here the risk levels are so high (20 times the risk from disease) that this activity must properly be considered to be in the category of adventuresome sport. However, the rate of risk is decreasing so rapidly that eventually the risk for general aviation may be little higher than that for commercial aviation. Since the percentage of the population involved is very small, it appears that the present average risk levels are acceptable to only a limited group (6).

The similarity of the trends in Figs. 3–5 may be the basis for another hypothesis, as follows: the acceptable risk is inversely related to the number of people participating in an activity.

The product and the risk and percentage of the population involved in each of the activities of Figs. 3–5 is plotted in Fig. 6. This graph represents the historical trend of total fatalities per hour of exposure of the population involved (7). The leveling off of motor-vehicle risk at about 100 fatalities per hour of exposure of the participating population may be significant. Because most of the U.S. population is involved, this rate of fatalities may have sufficient public visibility to set a level of social acceptability. It is interesting, and disconcerting, to note that the trend of fatalities in aviation, both commercial and general, is uniformly upward.

Public awareness

Finally, I attempted to relate these risk data to a crude measure of public awareness of the associated social benefits (see Fig. 7). The 'benefit awareness' was arbitrarily defined as the product of the relative level of advertising, the square of the percentage of population involved in the activity, and the relative usefulness (or importance) of the activity to the individual (8). Perhaps these assumptions are too crude, but Fig. 7 docs support the reasonable position that advertising the benefits of an activity increases public acceptance of a greater level of risk. This, of course could subtly produce a fictitious benefit-risk ratio—as may be the case for smoking.

Atomic power plant safety

I recognize the uncertainty inherent in the quantitative approach discussed here, but the trends and magnitudes may nevertheless be of sufficient validity to warrant their use in determining national 'design objectives' for technological activities. How would this be done?

Let us consider as an example the introduction of nuclear power plants as a

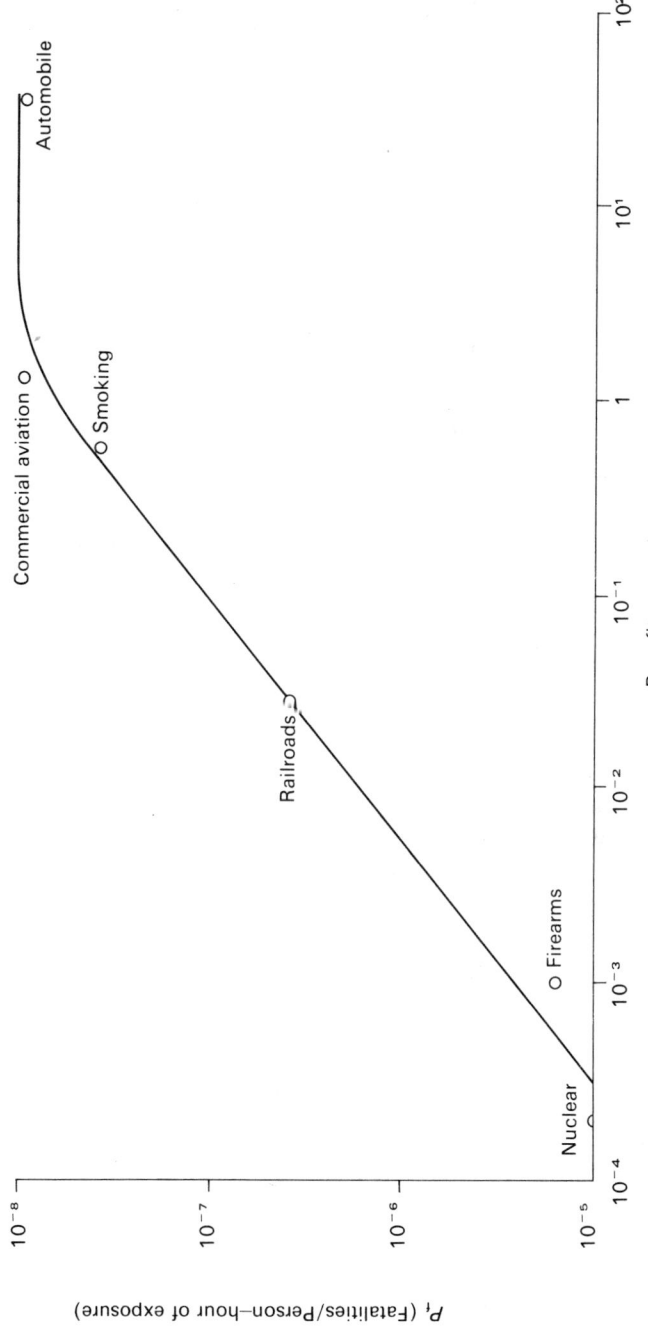

Figure 7. Accepted risk plotted relative to benefit awareness.

principal source of electric power. This is an especially good example because the technology has been primarily nurtured, guided, and regulated by the government, with industry undertaking the engineering development and the diffusion into public use. The government specifically maintains responsibility for public safety. Further, the engineering of nuclear plants permits continuous reduction of the probability of accidents, at a substantial increase in cost. Thus, the trade-off of utility and potential risk can be made quantitative.

Moreover, in the case of the nuclear power plant the historical empirical approach to achieving an optimum benefit-risk trade-off is not pragmatically feasible. All such plants are now so safe that it may be 30 years or longer before meaningful risk experience will be accumulated. By that time, many plants of varied design will be in existence, and the empirical accident data may not be applicable to those being built. So a very real need exists now to establish 'design objectives' on a predictive-performance basis.

Let us first arbitrarily assume that nuclear power plants should be as safe as coal-burning plants, so as not to increase public risk. Figure 2 indicates that the total risk to society from electric power is about 2×10^{-9} fatality per person per hour of exposure. Fossil fuel plants contribute about $\frac{1}{5}$ of this risk, or about 4 deaths per million population per year. In a modern society, a million people may require a million kilowatts of power, and this is about the size of most new power stations. So, we now have a target risk limit of 4 deaths per year per million-kilowatt power station (9).

Technical studies of the consequences of hypothetical extreme (and unlikely) nuclear power plant catastrophes, which would disperse radioactivity into populated areas, have indicated that about 10 lethal cancers per million population, might result (10). On this basis, we calculate that such a power plant might statistically have one such accident every 3 years and still meet the risk limit set. However, such a catastrophe would completely destroy a major portion of the nuclear section of the plant and either require complete dismantling or years of costly reconstruction. Because power companies expect plants to last about 30 years, the economic consequences of a catastrophe every few years would be completely unacceptable. In fact, the operating companies would not accept one such failure, on a statistical basis, during the normal lifetime of the plant.

It is likely that, in order to meet the economic performance requirements of the power companies, a catastrophe rate of less than 1 in about 100 plant-years would be needed. This would be a public risk of 10 deaths per 100 plant-years, or 0.1 death per year per million population. So the economic investment criteria of the nuclear plant user—the power company—would probably set a risk level 1/200 the present socially accepted risk associated with electric power, or 1/40 the present risk associated with coal-burning plants.

An obvious design question is this: Can a nuclear power plant be engineered with a predicted performance of less than 1 castrosphic failure in 100 plant-years of operation? I believe the answer is yes, but that is a subject for a different occasion. The principal point is that the issue of public safety can be focused on a tangible, quantitative, engineering design objective.

This example reveals a public safety consideration which may apply to many other activities: The economic requirement for the protection of major capital investments may often be a more demanding safety constraint than social acceptability.

Conclusion

The application of this approach to other areas of public responsibility is self-evident. It provides a useful methodology for answering the question 'How safe is safe enough?' Further, although this study is only exploratory, it reveals several interesting points. (i) The indications are that the public is willing to accept 'voluntary' risks roughly 1000 times greater than 'involuntary' risks. (ii) The statistical risk of death from disease appears to be a psychological yardstick for establishing the level of acceptability of other risks. (iii) The acceptability of risk appears to be crudely proportional to the third power of the benefits (real or imagined). (iv) The social acceptance of risk is directly influenced by public awareness of the benefits of an activity, as determined by advertising, usefulness, and the number of people participating. (v) In a sample application of these criteria to atomic power plant safety, it appears that an engineering design objective determined by economic criteria would result in a design-target risk level very much lower than the present socially accepted risk for electric power plants.

Perhaps of greatest interest is the fact that this methodology for revealing existing social preferences and values may be a means of providing the insight on social benefit relative to cost that is so necessary for judicious national decisions on new technological developments.

Appendix: Details of risk-benefit analysis

Motor-vehicle travel. The calculation of motor-vehicle fatalities per exposure hour per year is based on the number of registered cars, an assumed $1\frac{1}{2}$ persons per car, and an assumed 400 hours per year of average car use [data from *3* and *11*]. The figure for annual benefit for motor-vehicle travel is based on the sum of costs for gasoline, maintenance, insurance, and car payments and on the value of the time savings per person. It is assumed that use of an automobile allows a person to save 1 hour per working day and that a person's time is worth $5 per hour.

Travel by air route carrier. The estimate of passenger fatalities per passenger-hour of exposure for certified air route carriers is based on the annual number of passenger fatalities listed in the *FAA Statistical Handbook of Aviation* (see *12*) and the number of passenger-hours per year. The latter number is estimated from the average number of seats per plane, the seat load factor, the number of revenue miles flown per year, and the average plant speed (data from *3*). The benefit for travel by certified air route carrier is based on the average annual air fare per passenger-mile and on the value of the time saved as a result of air travel. The cost per passenger is estimated from the average rate per passenger-mile (data from *3*), the revenue miles flown per year (data from *12*), the annual number of passenger boardings for 1967 (132×10^8, according to the United Air Lines News Bureau), and the assumption of 12 boardings per passenger.

General aviation. The number of fatalities per passenger-hour for general avaiation is a function of the number of annual fatalities, the number of plane hours flown per year, and the average number of passengers per plane (estimated from the ratio of fatalities to fatal crashes) (data from *12*). It is assumed that in 1967 the cash outlay for initial expenditures and maintenance costs for general aviation was $\$1.5 \times 10^9$. The benefit is expressed in terms of annual cash outlay per person, and the estimate is based on the number of passenger-hours per year and the assumption that the average person flies 20 hours, or 4000 miles, annually. The value of the time saved is based on the assumption that a person's time is worth $10 per hour and that he saves 60 hours per year through travelling the 4000 miles by air instead of by automobile at 50 miles per hour.

Railroad travel. The estimate of railroad passenger fatalities per exposure hour per year is based on annual passenger fatalities and passenger-miles and an assumed average train speed of 50 miles per hour (data from *11*). The passenger benefit for railroads is based on figures for revenue and passenger-miles for commuters and noncommuters given in *The Yearbook of Railroad Facts* (Association of American Railroads, 1968). It is assumed that the average commuter travels 20 miles per workday by rail and that the average noncommuter travels 1000 miles per year by rail.

Skiing. The estimate for skiing fatalities per exposure hour is based on information obtained from the National Ski Patrol for the 1967–68 southern California ski season: 1 fatality, 17 days of skiing, 16,500 skiers per day, and 5 hours of skiing per skier per day. The estimate of benefit for skiing is based on the average number of days of skiing per year per person and the average cost of a typical ski trip [data from 'The Skier Market in Northeast North America', *U.S. Dep. Commerce Publ.* (1965)]. In addition, it is assumed that a skier spends an average of $25 per year on equipment.

Hunting. The estimate of the risk in hunting is based on an assumed value of 10 hours' exposure per hunting day, the annual number of hunting fatalities, the number of hunters, and the average number of hunting days per year [data from *11* and from 'National Survey of Fishing and Hunting,' *U.S. Fish Wildlife Serv. Publ.* (1965)]. The average annual expenditure per hunter was $82.54 in 1965 (data from *3*).

Smoking. The estimate of the risk from smoking is based on the ratio for the mortality of smokers relative to nonsmokers, the rates of fatalities from heart disease and cancer for the general population, and the assumption that the risk is continuous [data from the *Summary of the Report of the Surgeon General's Advisory Committee on Smoking and Health* (Government Printing Office, Washington, D.C., 1964)]. The annual intangible benefit to the cigarette smoker is calculated from the American Cancer Scoety's estimate that 30 percent of the population smokes cigarettes, from the number of cigarettes smoked per year (see *3*), and from the assumed retail cost of $0.015 per cigarette.

Vietnam. The estimate of the risk associated with the Vietnam war is based on the assumption that 500,000 men are exposed there annually to the risk of death, and that the fatality rate is 10,000 men per year. The benefit for Vietnam is calculated on the assumption that the entire U.S. population benefits intangibly from the annual Vietnam expenditure of $30 x 10^9.

Electric power. The estimate of the risk associated with the use of electric power is based on the number of deaths from electric current; the number of deaths from fires caused by electricity; the number of deaths that occur in coal mining, weighted by the percentage of total coal production used to produce electricity; and the number of deaths attributable to air pollution from fossil fuel stations [data from *3* and *11* and from *Nuclear Safety* **5**, 325 (1964)]. It is assumed that the entire U.S. population is exposed for 8760 hours per year to the risk associated with electric power. The estimate for the benefit is based on the assumption that there is a direct correlation between per capita gross national product and commercial energy consumption for the nations of the world [data from Briggs, *Technology and Economic Development* (Knopf, New York, 1963)]. It is further assumed that 35 percent of the energy consumed in the U.S. is used to produce electricity.

Natural disasters. The risk associated with natural disasters was computed for U.S. floods (2.5×10^{-10} fatality per person-hour of exposure), tornadoes in the Midwest (2.46×10^{-10} fatality), major U.S. storms (0.8×10^{-10} fatality), and California earthquakes (1.9×10^{-10} fatality) (data from *11*). The value for flood risk is based on the assumption that everyone in the U.S. is exposed to the danger 24 hours per day. No benefit figure was assigned in the case of natural disasters.

Disease and accidents. The average risk in the U.S. due to disease and accidents is computed from data given in *Vital Statistics of the U.S.* (Government Printing Office, Washington, D.C., 1976).

References and notes

1 A. L. Shef (1968) Socio-economic attributes of our technological society, paper presented before the IEEE, Wescon Conference, Los Angeles, August 1968.
2 *Minerals Yearbook* (Government Printing Office, Washington, D.C., 1966).
3 *U.S. Statistical Abstract* (Government Printing Office, Washington, D.C., 1967).
4 The procedure outlined in the appendix was used in calculating the risk associated with motor-vehicle travel. In order to calculate exposure hours for various years, it was assumed that the average annual driving time per car increased linearly from 50 hours in 1900 to 400 hours in 1960 and thereafter. The percentage of people involved is based on the U.S. population, the number of registered cars, and the assumed value of 1.5 people per car.
5 The procedure outlined in the appendix was used in calculating the risk associated with, and the number of people who fly in, certified air route carriers for 1967. For a given year, the number of people who fly is estimated from the total number of passenger boardings and the assumption that the average passenger makes six round trips per year (data from *3*).
6 The method of calculating risk for general aviation is outlined in the appendix. For a given year, the percentage of people involved is defined by the number of active aircraft (see *3*); the number of people per plane, as defined by the ratio of fatalities to fatal crashes; and the population of the U.S.

7 Group risk per exposure hour for the involved group is defined as the number of fatalities per person-hour of exposure multiplied by the number of people who participate in the activity. The group population and the risk for motor vehicles, certified air route carriers, and general aviation can be obtained from Figs. 3–5.

8 In calculating 'benefit awareness' it is assumed that the public's awareness of an activity is a function of A, the amount of money spent on advertising; P, the number of people who take part in the activity; and U, the utility value of the activity to the person involved. A is based on the amount of money spent by a particular industry in advertising its product, normalized with respect to the food and food products industry, which is the leading advertiser in the U.S.

9 In comparing nuclear and fossil fuel power stations, the risks associated with the plant effluents and mining of the fuel should be included in each case. The fatalities associated with coal mining are about $\frac{1}{4}$ the total attributable to fossil fuel plants. As the tonnage of uranium ore required for an equivalent nuclear plant is less than the coal tonnage by more than an order of magnitude, the nuclear plant problem primarily involves hazard from effluent.

10 This number is my estimate for maximum fatalities from an extreme catastrophe resulting from malfunction of a typical power reactor. For a methodology for making this calculation, see F. R. Farmer, 'Siting criteria—a new approach', paper presented at the International Atomic Energy Agency Symposium in Vienna, April 1967. Application of Farmer's method to a fast breeder power plant in a modern building gives a prediction of fatalities less than this assumed limit by one or two orders of magnitude.

11 Accident Facts, *Nat. Safety Counc. Publ.* (1967).

12 *FAA Statistical Handbook of Aviation* (Government Printing Office, Washington, D.C., 1965).

6 ORGANIZATIONAL VIEWS

6.1 ESSO London Airport refuelling control centre redesign—an ergonomics case study

Professor B. Shackel and Miss L. Klein

Department of Human Sciences, University of Technology, Loughborough, and the Tavistock Institute of Human Relations, London NW3. Formerly at EMI Electronics Ltd and ESSO Petroleum Co Ltd respectively.

Introduction

This paper described an ergonomic redesign of the control function and the control offices in the Esso Refuelling Control Centre at London Airport (Heathrow), which was carried out during 1967-68.

The purpose of presenting this case study is to illustrate the range of methods used for this type of problem and to give the 'flavour' of such a system redesign. The five main methods adopted were as follows:

1. Interview programme to identify the pattern of things as perceived by those involved.

2. Full appraisal of all relevant factors recorded in a set of formal 'analysis papers'.

3. Solutions developed by intuitive and analytical design procedures and presented for review (by operators also) in formal recommendation papers.

4. Simulation in full laboratory experiments to test new work methods before acceptance and implementation.

5. Evaluation of project results, by questionnaires and interviews before simulation experiments and after implementation.

The project will be described in the approximate sequence of events, after an initial review of the background and the problem.

Acknowledgement

Reprinted, by permission, from B. Shackel and L. Klein, 'Esso London Airport refuelling control centre redesign' in *Applied Ergonomics*, Vol. 7, No. 1, 1976, IPC Science and Technology Press Ltd., Guildford, pp. 37–45.

REDESIGN OF AIRPORT REFUELLING CONTROL CENTRE

The Esso refuelling service to the airlines which are its customers at London Airport is carried out from a Control Office and Truck Depot, from which men and trucks are allocated and sent out to aircraft by a Controller. By 1967 this task was becoming increasingly difficult. The growth in traffic through the airport (at a rate of between 15% and 20% per year), the expansion of the airport itself, the shortening of airline turn-around times, and the pressure to keep costs low, meant that (a) Controllers were working under considerable stress and (b) Shift Supervisors were spending much of their time in the Control Office backing up the Controller, instead of on general supervision duties. Both these factors were causing concern to Management.

Arising out of a Human Sciences Appreciation Course, Management approached the Company's Social Sciences Adviser for help. After some preliminary visits and discussions, an interview survey was carried out to obtain the perceptions of Controllers and Supervisors about the situation, and to eliminate the possibility of other problems. An ergonomic redesign of the situation was subsequently contracted to the EMI Ergonomics Laboratory.

The problem

Background to fuelling operations

After landing, the aircraft were parked at any of the approximately 100

Figure 1 Typical scene of refuelling and loading airliners at London Heathrow Airport.

stands located on the long-haul and short-haul 'aprons', see Fig.1. The turn-around time for most aircraft was about one hour, but one airline was already trying to reduce this to half an hour. In this time not only did passengers and fuel have to be loaded, but caterers, maintenance engineers, cleaners, etc, all needed to park near and work on the plane. When speed was essential, refuelling trucks travelled to the apron before the planes arrived.

Fuel was carried by pipeline from the Esso Fawley refinery through the West London terminal and fuel farm to the central airport fuelling areas. Refuelling trucks had capacities of 4,000, 6,000 and 12,000 gal (18,185, 27,280 and 54,550 l). Depending on the load required, one truck could refuel several planes during one run, or two or more trucks could refuel one plane. In 1967, Esso supplied about 135 million gal (614 million l). This amount was rising steeply and was expected to double in five years. There were peaks of demand during each day and throughout the year. Quality and safety requirements were stressed, but there was also a high priority on timing - 'a few minutes' delay and all hell is let loose'.

The manpower establishment of the refuelling operation was about 120 men. There were on shift, at any time during the day, a Shift Supervisor and five Fuelling Chiefs. The Shift Supervisor was responsible for general control of the whole shift team, subject to the Esso London Airport Manager, who also had a Deputy. The Fuelling Chiefs undertook at various times the posts of Controller, Apron Chief, Depot Chief and Bolster Man.

The job of the Controller at the desk will be considered in the next section. The two Apron Chiefs (radio code names King and Queen) supervised the actual refuelling of aircraft on the short-haul and long-haul aprons respectively. The Depot Fuelling Chief was in charge of the plant end of truck loading; he had an office next to the Controller and had to attempt to meet the Controller's need for loaded vehicles. The fifth Fuelling Chief was the Bolster Man who acted as assistant to the Controller and relieved the others during meal breaks.

The job of the Controller

For information about aircraft movements, the Controller had the arrival and departure schedules from the airlines each day, which together indicated the expected load for that day. Changes and information about the specific fuelling needs of particular aircraft were supplied by an electro-writer and by telephone links to the various airlines. Minute-to-minute information about the actual approach and arrival of aircraft was received by two tickertape machines from the air traffic control centre. For information about the men and trucks he had a list of men from the duty roster, and in racks at each side of the desk the truck logs of each available truck.

When the Controller knew the requirements of a plane he would check how many vehicles were in the Truck Depot, which ones were filled, and which operatives were available. He assigned men to a vehicle and gave them the vehicle log sheet. The operatives did the job, returned to the control centre and completed the log sheet of actual gallonage fuelled. This was then returned to the Controller who checked that the delivery was correct, stored it in the plant office and recorded the operatives on his list of men as available again. The Crewman completed delivery notes for individual loads to infrequent customers. Main customers received a general delivery note at the end of each day.

The realities of this task began to emerge from the interview programme carried out with all the Controllers and Supervisors, and from early observations by the ergonomists making an initial appraisal of the situation.

On the surface, the Controller's job was a simple control task. However, as he only had a limited number of men and trucks available, he also had a managerial problem in optimising the available resources with the demands for service. This problem was increased by the service. This problem was increased by the difficulty of predicting how long before men and trucks would become available again, because of the variability in aircraft refuelling time. He also had a supervisory problem in that he had to organise a shift of men who were doing a job which at times could be fairly unpleasant. Other difficulties were the demands made on short term memory, the relentless flow of complex information and the noise associated with it, and the constant worry of the ultimate 'crime' of causing a delay to an aircraft departure.

Pictures of the Control Room as it was before the redesign (Figs. 2a and 2b) give some indication of the conditions under which the Controllers had to work, and the complexity of the information with which they had to deal. There was also difficulty in reaching the schedules at the back and reading the tickertapes, so that the Controllers almost always stood up while doing the job, especially during peak hours. A further difficulty was that several telephones could ring at once, and it was impossible for the Controller to stop more than one of them at a time.

The interview survey was intended to find out how the Supervisors and Fuelling Chiefs perceived their work situation, especially when acting as Controllers, and to test the assumption that overload and work stress were indeed the major problems. Although some other organisation problems were mentioned, they were completely outweighed by problems due to the complexity and tension of the task itself. Motivation was high – the importance of the job was clear to all, and liked by all. They were very much identified with the success of the operation, and had many ideas about its improvement. They were also very much identified with the culture of the Airport, and wore a uniform somewhat similar to that of aircrew with rings at the cuff indicating rank. But all of them in one way or another complained of 'stress', 'fatigue', and of being 'unable to unwind'. Inevitably some informal ways of coping were being found – 'When I know I'm going to get a delay, I phone my pal who's maintenance engineer for the airline. He'll pretend there's something the matter with the engine and start pulling it to bits'.

Redesigning the system

A general consultancy contract with the EMI Ergonomics Laboratory was already in existence, and enabled preliminary work to be done. During the summer of 1967, the Head of the Laboratory and his staff paid a number of visits to the airport to collect data for analysis and began to formulate some design suggestions, together with estimates of cost and timescale. These were discussed with supervisors and local management during several cycles of development and discussion. Laboratory experiments were proposed to test the suggested solutions.

Figure 2 (a)

REDESIGN OF AIRPORT REFUELLING CONTROL CENTRE

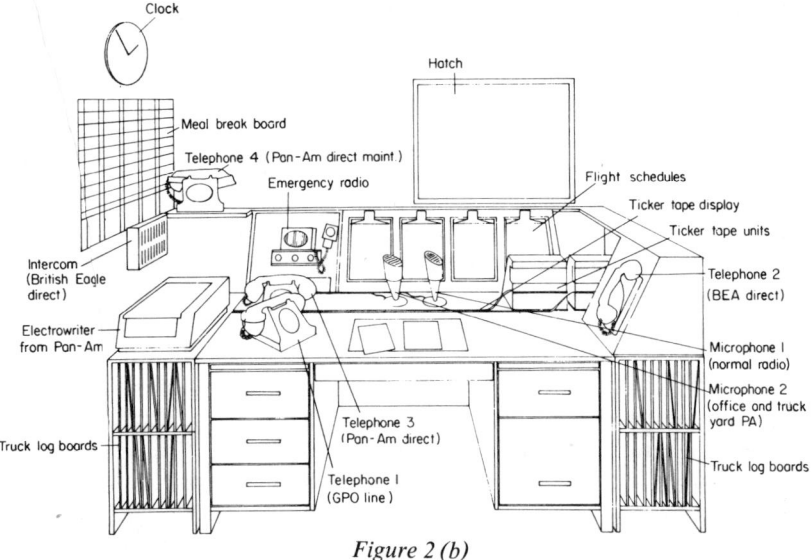

Figure 2 (b)

Figures 2 (a) and (b) show the control room and desk before the redesign project. The basic information sources for the Controller are the four aircraft schedules at the back of the desk, the tickertape, giving aircraft movements, running across the desk top, the electrowriter and direct link to Pan-American at the left, and four telephones scattered around. The clutter and difficulty is obvious.

In September, 1967, a detailed proposal was presented to Esso for the redesign of the control office and desk, and for a laboratory simulation to test them. The main stages of the project, which was agreed by Esso, were to be:

1. Thorough analyses of the system.

2. Design of building layout and general room arrangements based on the flow of people.

3. Design of control office layout in relation to the Shift Supervisor's and Depot Fuelling Chief's offices, and to the crew room.

Detailed design of the work station for the Controller's job, including both the equipment and the working method.

Analysis papers

During the information gathering visits to Esso London Airport, each member of the EMI team studied different aspects of the system. The detailed notes on these visits, together with an appraisal paper by the Social Sciences Adviser, formed the starting point for a Project Information file.

These notes provided the basic information for the detailed analysis papers which were written on all aspects of the system that were important to the Controller or which affected his task in some way. The papers included analyses of: the tickertape; the documentation in the control room; the communications with airlines; the movement of people in the control room and other rooms; the role of the Bolster Man; the shift rotation scheme; the men resources; the truck resources; and the implications for Esso of possible future changes at the airport. These analysis papers were very important in the development of the project, since they established a formal information base, checked and agreed by Esso staff, from which the proposed redesign could be developed in detail and critically evaluated.

Recommendation papers

From the information gathered and the analyses made, detailed recommendations were submitted in two formal memoranda. The first of these (EMI Ergonomics Memo No 226) detailed the design and layout of the building, control room, truck log store, and lower structure of the Controller's desk, together with recommendations for noise control, heating and ventilation, lighting and other storage facilities. Also included in this memo were lists of instruments to be ordered, and specifications in terms of detailed dimensions and layout.

The second paper (EMI Ergonomics Memo No 231) detailed the layout of the work area, the desk superstructure, the aircraft schedules, stateboard and all tags, men shift board, men tag store and colour schemes. Both memoranda were accompanied by large drawings.

It had not been intended or scheduled that the Ergonomics team should produce detailed dimensional drawings for planning the construction work. However, it was a logical consequence of the intensive approach which developed on this project. Moreover, it proved an essential contribution because Esso could not make the necessary resources available at the right time, and it was a process which was also satisfying for the project team.

Ergonomic redesign

The redesigned system is shown in Figs. 3a and 3b. The desk is now 'L' shaped, and lowered to a more comfortable height. The separate telephones have been amalgamated into one lamp and key unit which enables the Controller to 'hold' calls. The tickertape has been raised to eye level so that it is more easily readable, and the schedules have been placed within easy reach above the tickertape. The truck logs are now in a sliding store above the desk top to the Controller's left (Fig. 4), which is more readily accessible and also backs directly onto the Depot Fuelling Chief's office. Thus, both Depot Chief and Controller can handle the logs easily, in step with their work, and above all, the log of a reloaded truck, when available again, is ready in its right place, without the Depot Chief having to pass it to the Controller for him to put into the storage pigeon-hole.

A magnetic stateboard was designed to give the Controller a schematic representation of the state of his resources, see Fig. 5. It had tags representing men, trucks and aircraft. The aim was to provide a memory and planning aid for his decision task. On the stateboard, the 'men list' of the old system was replaced by a column space for men tags, a separate one for each man with his name on it, colour-coded by his current working shift. The truck tags were similarly numbered and coloured, and aircraft tags were larger white ones upon which flight numbers could be written; all stick magnetically. The Controller operated the stateboard by placing men and truck tags onto an aircraft tag, which, when the men were actually sent out, was placed in the central area of the stateboard. Thus he had readily visible the current location and duties of all the men and trucks which were available on that shift, and he was also able to use the tags to plan his allocations in advance, by building up modules ready for allocation.

Ergonomic data and methods were used to determine the actual dimensions of the desk, positioning of the schedules and angle of the stateboard, together with the other changes in design and equipment.

Both the redesign of the various rooms and the desk, and the proposed new method of working, were discussed in detail with all the Controllers and Supervisors as the potential users of the system, and their suggestions and criticisms were taken into account in the final recommendations. The importance of the potential users of the new design being involved in and contributing to the project must be stressed, since acceptability to the users is an essential criterion of system design. The Esso social science group helped with the formulation of, and took part in, the consultative approach at all levels.

It must also be pointed out that both the improved equipment and room layout, and the new systems of working with the stateboard, contributed to the effectiveness of the total redesign. Neither on its own would have been sufficient.

Simulation experiments

During January, 1968, the detailed method of working was discussed with all the Supervisors and Fuelling Chiefs. In February, 1968, a simulated control room, incorporating the new features (Fig. 6) was built in the EMI Ergonomics Laboratory, and the design of the simulation experiments was formulated. Visits were then made by Esso Management and by all the Shift Supervisors and Fuelling Chiefs, during which explanations of the equip-

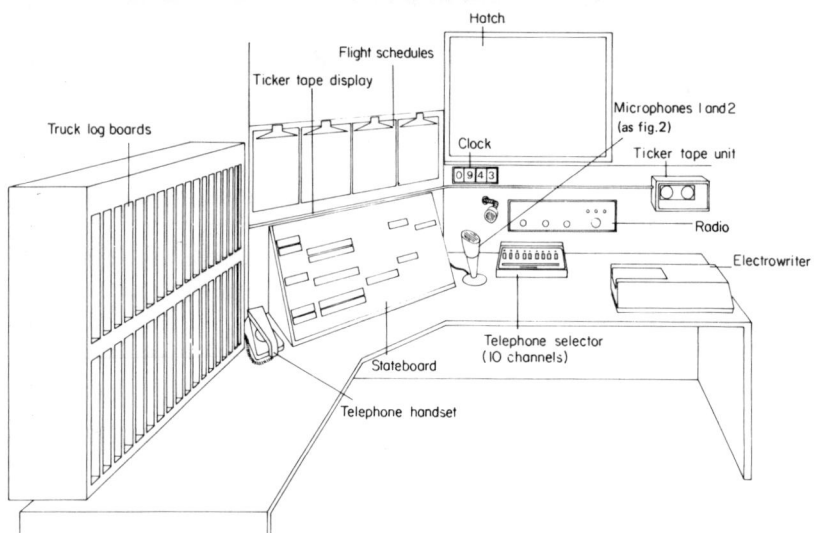

Figure 3 (a) and (b)   The Controller's desk after the project.
The Controller has his right hand near the telephone key unit through which he can select up to ten direct lines; his radio microphone is mounted on the wall. The basic information sources are now more easily visible, with the aircraft schedules and tickertape directly facing him. His left hand is pointing to the stateboard, with its men, truck and aircraft tags, showing the resources available and the location of men and trucks out on jobs. The Shift Supervisor looking over his shoulder can easily review the current situation.

ment and method were given, queries were answered and comments and criticisms were received. Questionnaires were given to the Shift Supervisors and Fuelling Chiefs immediately before they visited the mock-up, to assess their attitudes to the proposed new method and to this redesign project. The same questionnaires were presented, together with interviews, after the series of simulation experiments, and subsequently again after the redesign had been implemented at the Airport, to ascertain what changes in attitudes, if any, there were at different stages during the project.

The experiments were designed to evaluate the magnetic stateboard and tag system, and to compare the new and old working methods operated by one and two men under increasing load conditions. The detailed report of the development, running and conclusions of the experiments (EMI Ergonomics Memo No 237) was presented to management and to all Shift Supervisors and Fuelling Chiefs also; this had been agreed previously as a condition of the work.

The detailed running programmes for the simulation experiments were written (by three postgraduate students from the Department of Occupational Psychology, Birbeck College, London) from information supplied by Esso Management, Supervisors and Fuelling Chiefs, whose experience in the job was essential in presenting an accurate picture of the system. In effect these programmes were word-for-word theatrical texts for continuous three-hour plays, in which the 'actors' were happy and indeed enthusiastic to play their parts. Esso personnel also played a large part in the running of the experiments, since this was the most realistic way, for the Desk Controller, of simulating some of the roles in the system ('King', 'Queen' and Depot Fuelling Chief). The experimental sessions were of three hours' duration, and the Controller was able to walk into the replica of his office, sit down in the chair and take over the job as he would in the real situation. The realism of the situation was indicated by the fact that the Controllers needed very little explanation of what to do, other than the initial briefing with the new equipment. They found that they were able to react in very much the same way as in the real situation.

The simulation experiments were carried out in the Laboratory during February and March, 1968. In brief the main experimental conclusion was that the stateboard helped in the control of the system by relieving the short term memory problem with a visual display, but did not help with the actual volume of work. Having two men operating the system meant that a greater volume of work could be undertaken, although two men were no better at controlling the system than one. Further experiments in April showed similar results at higher load levels.

A measure of success in handling the volume of work was, for each

Figure 4 The truck log store.
To the left of the Controller, the sliding unit for storing truck logs is placed midway between him and the Depot Fuelling Chief in the office through the hatch. Both can reach the log boards easily in the pigeon-holes, which are open at both ends. The unit slides to accommodate one or two men working at the control desk.

Controller, the average number of minutes by which he allocated men and trucks to aircraft in advance of a calculated 'critical time'. A measure of the degree of control of the system was the count of the operator's rest pauses between successive jobs. It was hypothesised that good control would minimise long breaks and also very short breaks between jobs, and that good control would show a peak of breaks around 5–10 min. This was clearly achieved in the experiment when the Controllers were using the stateboard.

On the basis of the first results, a final recommendation was submitted to Esso on 1 April and a decision was made to build and install the proposed new design.

The Esso Airport Manager and Deputy Manager collaborated with the project in important ways. As well as providing the information for the simulation programmes, they arranged, despite considerable administrative difficulties, for the Controllers and Supervisors to come to EMI to participate in the experiments. These arrangements required delicate handling on occasions, since some of the men involved could not see the value of the simulation experiments and required explanation and encouragement. The full support and personal involvement of management undoubtedly contributed to the overall success of the project.

Implementation

Installation of the redesign began immediately after the decision was made in April. Structural changes were made and old equipment was gradually replaced with new. The new system was introduced in this progressive way for two reasons: firstly so that the construction and implementation should cause as little interference as possible with the normal working of the

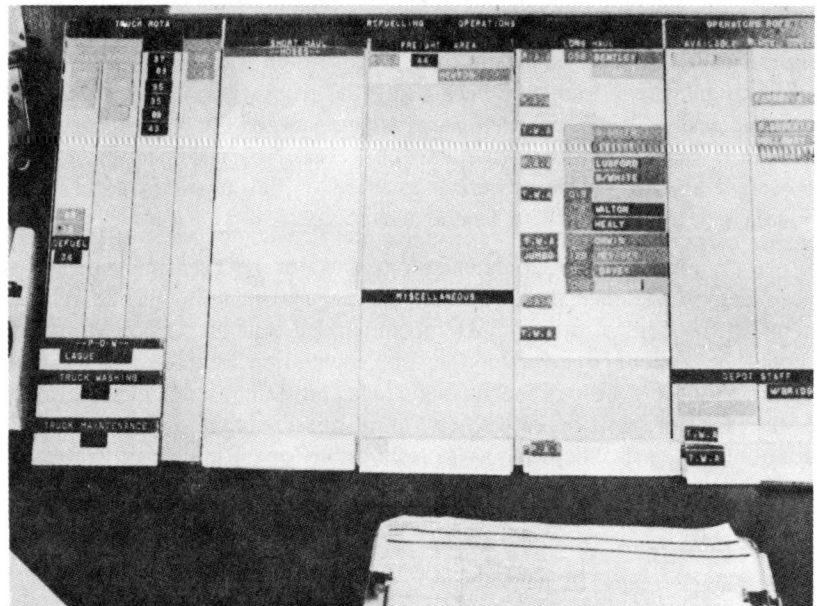

Figure 5   The Stateboard.
The tags representing men and trucks available are on the right and left. After allocation to refuel an aircraft they are mounted on aircraft tags and placed in the central area. Thus an overview of the current location and duties of all resources is always available.

system, and secondly in order that the Controllers might gradually adapt to the new equipment, so that their ability to control the system would at no time be affected by an array of new equipment. The installation proceeded very smoothly, but since the summer load increase had started unexpectedly a month earlier than in the previous year, the change to the new method of working, involving the stateboard, was postponed until after the summer peak and was planned for October. It was felt that the Controllers would not have time to become sufficiently adapted to using the stateboard under pressure by the time the peak load arrived.

Consequently it was planned that a member of the EMI Ergonomics Laboratory would go through the operational procedures with the Controllers again in October, and be present to facilitate the change-over to the new method. For many of the Controllers this would merely have been a question of reminding them of the procedures used during the simulation experiments. But in fact this arrangement proved unnecessary, since the Supervisors took the final change-over into their own hands, after the decision to implement the stateboard had been made. Within a very short time all the Controllers were using the stateboard and tag system. Not all the Controllers, however, used the truck tags until an occasion when the Esso Airport Manager came into the Control Room with a request for some information which, had they been using the truck tags, could have been supplied easily. This incident effectively demonstrated the value of the truck tags, and since then the stateboard has been in full operation. Little resistance and few problems were encountered in this implementation stage, and the new system met with general acceptance.

However, some minor recommendations had not yet been implemented a year later in October, 1969, namely the paperwork redesign and related items in the control office. EMI recommended that an 'Office Manager' should be appointed to effect this implementation, and also to be responsible for the upkeep of the magnetic tags and stateboard, and for making name tags for new operators, etc. It is possible that difficulties could arise unless one specific person was responsible for the upkeep of 'software' in this way.

Evaluation

In order to assess the effectiveness of the ergonomics recommendations, visits were made to the Control Room during and after the summer peaks in both 1968 and 1969. In both cases discussions were held with the Controllers, and in 1969 an evaluation study was made by recording relevant operational data over several days and by interviews with management and with all Supervisors and Controllers. The 1968 visits enabled an assessment of their reactions to the layout and equipment changes to be made, and the 1969 study included also the stateboard and new working methods. A full report of the validation studies was written (EMI Ergonomics Memo No 236).

The 1968 visits showed that the Controllers were especially pleased with the room layout and the new equipment, notably the telephones and truck log store. They commented that the 1968 summer peak had been 15% higher than the previous year and had lasted for a month longer at both ends of the summer. They felt that they would have been unable to cope with this unexpectedly high load without the working improvements afforded by the new layout and equipment.

The interviews and evaluation study in 1969 showed that there was unanimous approval of the new method with the stateboard and the other new equipment. Comments such as 'The stateboard helps in all respects, especially in planning and supervising', 'helps in all ways 100% – tension is somewhat less due to reduced memory work', 'it has systematised the job; anyone can now assess the current situation by looking over the Controller's shoulder', 'tension reduced by preplanning' – were common. All Controllers and Supervisors felt that the project had been valuable and all felt that they had been sufficiently consulted throughout the design.

The Airport Manager felt that the redesigned system 'had achieved everything he hoped it would'. Previously, he said, there had been no proper control over the manpower; the Supervisors had not been able easily to assess the situation and to decide upon the right level of resources. With the new system there was control over the resources, as the men could be identified; their meal breaks and overtime could also be assessed at a glance. For the first time the Manager felt that they were able to plan their manpower requirements more effectively and with greater precision.

He also observed that the Controllers were feeling less stress now. Previously the men had stood up to do the job, especially during peak load times, and sat down from exhaustion; now they sat down to do the job and stood up at intervals to stretch.

Decisions which had previously been based largely on guesswork were now based on fact since the information was in front of the Controller. The question of 'missed' or delayed aircraft was no longer a problem; there had been considerably fewer this year, but in any case the constant worry about the possibility of causing delays, which had previously added so much stress to the job, was no longer there. This was because the Controllers were now able to plan in advance on the stateboard. As well as improving relations

Figure 6   Simulated control room built in the laboratory—for experiments to test the new workstation and working methods.

with customers, this aspect could also have helped improve relations with the Crewmen, since work could now be distributed more fairly amongst them (see Fig. 7). There was a more consistent rotation of men, and their rest pauses, meal breaks and overtime were more closely controlled and therefore more evenly and fairly distributed, because the Controller had a constant record of which men had been where for how long. As a result of this fairer control, the Crewmen had never reacted against the Controller literally 'keeping tabs' on them, as the Manager had anticipated they might.

Some aspects of the redesign did not go exactly according to plan. As previously mentioned, the redesigned paperwork had not been implemented by

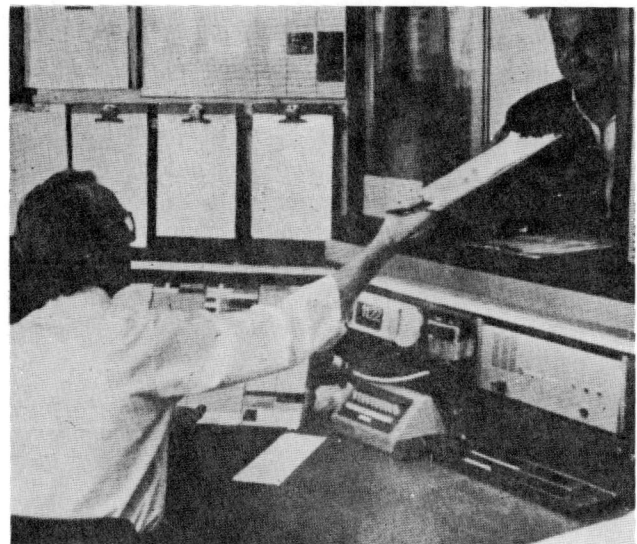

Figure 7 *Controller handling refuelling assignment and truck log to a leading operative. The crewmen as well as the controllers found the redesign beneficial.*

the time the project formally ended. There was also still a certain amount of noise in the Control Room with people coming in and out in spite of sliding doors; this disturbed the Controllers, who were however reluctant to become too strict for fear of damaging staff relations. Also the floor covering did not stand up to the movement of the Controller's chair on castors. Looking back, there is probably a case for a project team to devise and carry out a more systematic implementation programme to ensure that all the approved recommendations are installed. It is not easy for Management and Supervisors, fully involved in a 24 h operation, to ensure 100% action on the last 10% of a programme. On the other hand, it must be said that visits in subsequent years and particularly in August, 1972, revealed everything implemented and working unchanged, no magnetic tags lost, and continued high satisfaction with the system expressed by all those interviewed. The latest visit made, in September, 1975, showed the same system still in good working order and in full and satisfactory use.

It was not possible for the Manager to put an exact cash value on the redesign in terms of cost-effectiveness, for several reasons. First, as with most field studies of this nature, the operating conditions for the old and the new systems had changed, hence they could not be precisely compared. Secondly, many noticeable improvements with the new system were not directly measurable in financial cost-effective terms, although they undoubtedly were important and had an effect. For example, customer relations and service to customers had both improved, as indicated by the types of letters and telephone calls received. Similarly, 'wear and tear' on the Controllers had decreased; the Manager felt that they were better able to cope with the job. This is supported by a large majority of Controllers who, in spite of the load being greater, said in the validation interviews that they found the job easier now than they had two years before. Finally, however, he felt that, without this project and its results, there would have been a severe risk of temporary but complete breakdowns in the operation, which would have cost more than ten times the cost of the project in cash alone, apart from losses in morale, reputation and customer confidence. Thus, he considered that the effective benefits far outweighed the cost of the ergonomics project team contract of £8,500, (in 1968).

Conclusion

This case study describes a project which involved the application of simple ergonomics system design methods in an unusual industrial situation. Management and the people who operate the system are well satisfied with it (eg, see 'Esso Service at Heathrow' in *Esso Air World,* 1970, **23.3**, 70-72: 'the EMI-devised control plan has proved so satisfactory that similar plans are now being adopted at Esso's depots at Gatwick and Manchester airport; interest in it has also been shown by Esso affiliates as far away as Tokyo'). It has helped to make the operation smoother and has enabled better and fairer control of the overtime requirements and, especially, of the allocation of work and of rest pauses to the Crewmen. The full simulation experiments, which were a less usual part of the study, have been shown to be valid in successfully predicting the outcome in the real-life situation.

Many people, including some of the Fuelling Chiefs concerned, have been surprised at the simplicity of the important changes. These show the value of full and detailed analysis, but even after such analysis the design solutions are not necessarily self-evident. They can also arise out of discussion, and sometimes disagreement, between the members of a design team, and between the design team and its clients. This is an essential part of the process; time needs to be scheduled for it in the project plan.

A before and after evaluation, by questionnaire and interview, showed a high level of acceptance and support. Four and seven years after implementation, the working methods, equipment and procedures were found unchanged and still acceptable to the users. The combination of methods adopted may therefore reasonably be recommended for handling other projects of a broadly similar nature.

6.2 Organizational perspectives in the health services

Maurice Kogan and Jeanne Balle

From the Open University (1972) D203 Decision making in Britain.

1 Introduction

1.1 What this sequence is about

In this sequence the British health service is described in terms of the work it has to do and the organizations established to do the work. The discussion is in two parts:

(1) Subsection 2 discusses organization generally and defines the main elements of organization as they are found in the health services.

(2) Subsections 3 to 5 take one important part of the health service—the hospitals—and discuss their organization in terms of decision making and decision makers.

1.2 Research sources and methods of this material

Much of the material in this sequence is based on research into hospital organization carried out by the Hospital Organization Research Unit at Brunel University. The Unit was established at the request of the then Ministry of Health which wanted hospitals to be able to improve and clarify the way in which they organize their work with the help of an outside and objective research team. Brunel researchers therefore responded to requests from different hospital authorities (teaching hospitals, a regional hospital board and hospital management committees) to join with members of their staff in working out who made what decisions within the hospitals they administered. The methods used were to have interviews with individuals which the researchers then analysed and 'cleared' with the individual until there was an agreed statement of the work that the individual did, his authority or right to do that work, and the extent to which his work, and the way he did it, responded to other people's, including his managers, within the hospital. Once that statement was agreed with the role holder, it became part of the larger study in which several such statements were put together

---

Acknowledgement

Reprinted from M. Kogan and J. Balle's article in course D203 *Decision Making in Britain,* Block 5, Pts. 1–5, The Open University 1972.

by the researchers so as to make a composite, and agreed, picture of the whole hospital organization. This method is known as 'organization analysis' and is still being carried out in a large number of hospital authorities by the Brunel team.

The method of organization analysis could be used to elucidate several different aspects of organization. For example, it could show how and why people communicate with each other in hospitals. Or it could show how a particular policy came to take the form that it did. The Brunel teams, however, have mainly restricted their studies to one important dimension of organization, namely, the process of decision making. The idea is that if it is possible to see who decides what, and within which constraints, it will be possible to distinguish the differences between the various levels and roles in organization. For example, it is very easy to talk about the Department of Health and Social Security as 'deciding national policy'. The task of the researcher is to take that statement further by asking, 'What decisions are actually made by the Department?', and 'What differences can one discern between the decisions made about these two levels on identical questions such as the amount of hospital building that should be allowed within any particular region?'. By asking at each point 'What decisions are being made by whom?' it is possible to state organization in terms of what really happens, and for what reasons, and not depend on metaphors for description of organization.

This does not mean that systems of communication or descriptions of the channels through which work flows or other forms of organization study are unimportant. But it does mean that communications or work flows are tested in terms of the *status* of the communication so that it will be possible to say what authority lies behind a communications and what are the decisions that result from a communication being made.

The methods used by the Brunel team, organization analysis, are intended to enable not only those who manage the organizations, but also those who work within them, to participate in clarifying the way that the organizations should be run. In this respect, the purposes, and perhaps the methods, differ, for example, from those of management consultants who are called in by management to help make an organization more efficient in terms of the objectives laid down by the management.

2 Defining organization and its components

2.1 *How to define organization*

In describing health service organization, we must first decide 'what is organization?'. There are many definitions, and they are not always consistent with each other. In these notes we are using what many sociologists (such as A. Etzioni or Blau and Scott) would call an 'orthodox model' of organization. Our definition is: 'An organization is more than one role working towards common objectives'.

2.2 The main components of organization

The main components of organization are as follows:

(1) *Policies* are made with express judgements ('value judgements') about what an organization *ought* to do.

(2) Policies become the *objectives* (or goals—the terminology does not matter) of *organizations* when they take the form of, for example, a legal or statutory declaration in an act of Parliament or in some other *authoritative* statement such as a formal resolution of a borough council, or a central government circular.

(3) The *objectives* become meaningful organizationally when stated as the *operational activities* of the organization. These are the activities which must be pursued if the objectives are to be fulfilled. For example, it is an objective of the health service to heal the sick. It is an operational activity of the service to provide doctors who can prescribe treatments.

Other activities—non-operational activities are concerned with the control of operational activities and with the carrying through of certain specialist dimensions of operational activities. For example, a treasurer must help to ensure that hospitals do not exceed budgets. His work is essential if the hospital is not to get into serious trouble. But the hospital does not exist to make budgets—making budgets is therefore not an 'operational' task.

(4) Once operational activities are stated and agreed, it is possible to discover whether the objectives are being properly pursued by asking what decisions are being made about the carrying out of the operational activities.

(5) The activities are pursued by the creation of *executive organization* which is more than one role working together towards the fulfilment of the common objective or objectives (as in our basic definition).

(6) Each role has *authority** which can be defined as the sanctioned right to do work and to use resources in doing it (the work of subordinates being

---

**'Authority' is also used in many different ways. This need not cause problems if it is used consistently.*

part of the resources) and is *accountable* for performing the sanctioned and assigned work (*tasks*). In performing tasks, the role holder must employ *discretion* (which includes the discretion to act within the terms of the professional code or codes and the legal requirements which individual specialists or professionals must refer to), but also, more important, has to be exercised within the limits—'prescribed limits'—set by the organization.

(7) Each role is accountable for performing tasks in his role relationship to other roles within the organization.

These definitions are explained more fully as the notes progress.

(8) *Authority* and *accountability*, both properties of roles, can be seen to correspond to properties of the individuals filling the roles:

(i) personal *power* to implement the authority;

(ii) personal *responsibility* to give substance to the organizational accountability.

Thus, effective working of an organization depends on both structural factors (having an efficient role structure) and personal factors (having competent people in the roles).

2.3 Working relationships

If hospitals have a number of roles, all of which take decisions affecting the treatment of patients, there must be *working relationships* between these roles which define how the different roles will work together. The main relationships are discussed as we come to them in the text, but the most important of them, the superior–subordinate relationship, is discussed here.

2.4 Superior–subordinate relationship

Where someone has more to do than he can manage alone, other people may be assigned to help him. When he is accountable for the work of his assistant(s), there is a *superior–subordinate relationship* with the following characteristics:

(1) The superior must have minimum authority to control the assistance he receives.

(2) In some public services,* at least, the minimum authority necessary to this relationship is the authority to record an assessment of his subordinate's performance so as to affect the subordinate's career, and to

---

*The authority is different in private enterprise, and in some parts of public service (e.g. the Armed Services and the Police).

initiate transfer from role, i.e. to decide that a subordinate will be removed from his (the superior's) command.

(3) The components described above are *necessary minima of authority*. If a superior has more authority than these, such as the authority to appoint a subordinate, his control over the way the delegated tasks are performed is increased.

Other working relationships such as staff, prescribing, service giving and seeking relationships (and many others) also exist and we will define them as they emerge in this text.

3   Overview of a hospital organization

It is easiest to begin by examining how definitions of work and working relationships can be applied to one discrete sector of the health services. Let us begin with hospitals. First, what is their legal base? The 1946 National Health Act lays down that *Regional Hospital Boards* and *Boards of Governors* of teaching hospitals will be set up 'for the purposes of exercising functions with respect to the administration of hospital and specialist services' and that Regional Boards will set up Hospital Management Committees (HMCs) 'for the purposes of exercising functions with respect to the management and control of individual hospitals or groups of hospitals within the areas'.

The authority of each of these bodies in carrying out its statutory functions is laid down in the 1946 Act, in subsequent legislation, and in department circulars. The authority is the right to use resources and is expressed in such issues as level of capital expenditure, level of current expenditure, appointments, pay and conditions of service for staff, making charges to patients, providing accommodation for private patients, purchasing land, and the like. But it is left to the statutory hospital authorities to define specific *tasks* and to assign these to specific officers so that the hospital service becomes actual and effective. (By *task*, we mean a specific assignment of work, to be completed by a certain time.)

3.1   The different kinds of activities

Once a hopsital organization has authority to do work, the work must be expressed in terms of *activities*. It is possible to examine the groups of operational activities which field-work has suggested are currently being carried out in hospitals. The list is not exhaustive, and other kinds may be added, and there are many other ways in which activities can be defined:

(1) Provision of board and housing services for patients—meals, beds and other hotel facilities.

(2) Provision of general nursing services for patients (other than those specifically prescribed by a doctor).

(3) The provision of medical diagnosis, or diagnosis and prescription, or diagnosis and treatment for patients (prescribed or provided by a doctor).

(4) Some hospitals only; the provision of treatment by or as prescribed by a GP for patients.

(5) The provision of paramedical services for patients (e.g. medical social services, occupational therapy, chiropody, etc.).

(6) Mainly but not exclusively in teaching hospitals; provision of training facilities for medical students.

(7) Development—the planning of future facilities, based on assessment of current services, in relation to need.

(8) (In some hospitals) the provision of research facilities for doctors and scientific and technical staff.

(9) (In psychiatric hospitals); the provision of facilities for detaining patients compulsorily under the orders rule of the Mental Health Act, 1959.

(10) The provision of pre-registration hospital training for doctors.

(11) The provision of post-registration hospital training for doctors.

(12) The provision of pre-registration hospital training for nurses and for other professions not leading to registration as a medical practitioner.

(13) The provision of medical laboratory services to GPs and Medical Officers of Health (MOH) (e.g. pathology reports).

(14) A further operational activity is the public health education aspect of the hospital's work, if those with authority wish to make it so. It is the equivalent of sales promotion in a commercial undertaking.

3.2 The analysis of operational tasks

The analysis of operational tasks or activities in this way is useful:

(1) Because it draws attention to the separate areas where work is necessary if prescribed objects are to be effectively met. For example, hospitals are not only institutions that cure people. They are also *hotels* that can never close. This must be expressed in the list of their activities.

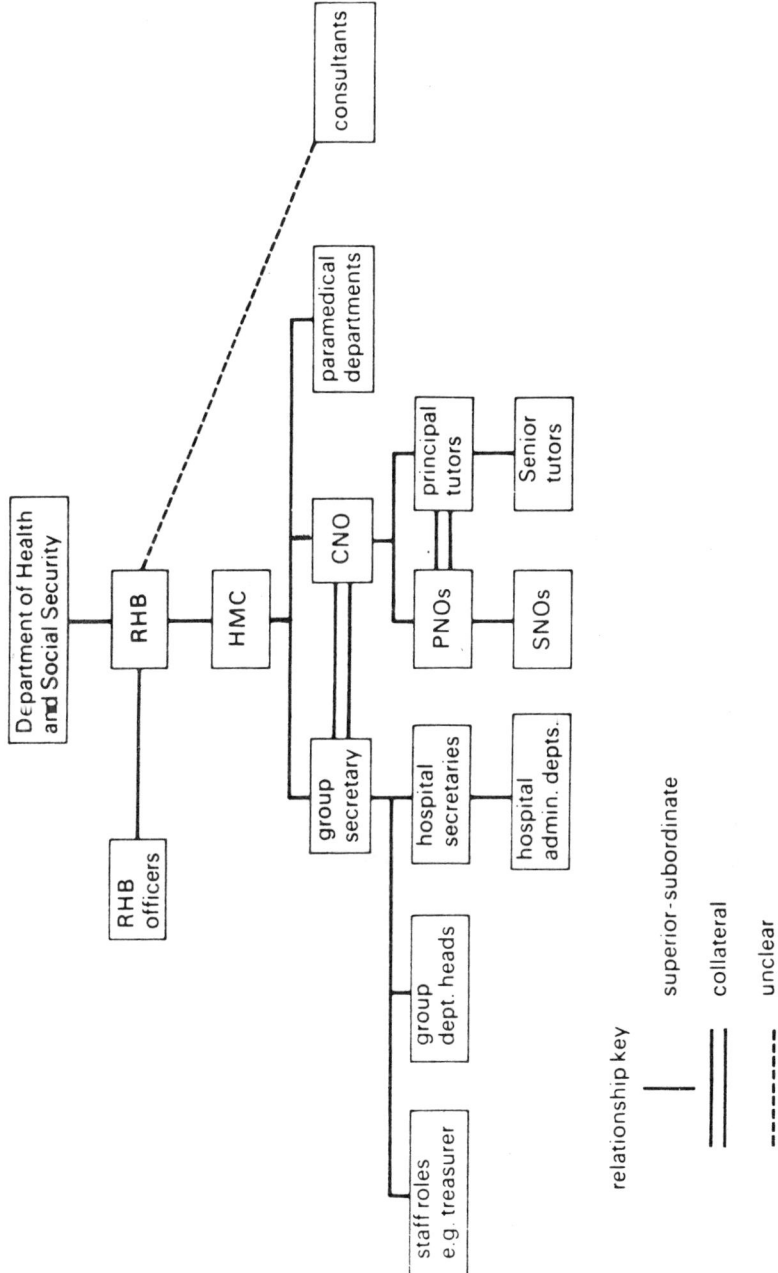

Figure 1   Chart showing main relationships in a hospital authority.

(2) Because it enables criteria of efficiency—the statements of the desired 'outputs' of the organization—to be made.

(3) In establishing requisite role relationships—who should have authority to do what—according to whether the people involved are carrying out operational or non-operational tasks.

The chart in Figure 1 is an example of how a hospital authority might delegate the performance of its tasks through the main lines of authority and accountability. To do so, *roles* are established and working relationships are established between roles.

The chart illustrates a most important fact about hospitals. A hospital can best be thought of as a complex and highly technological village in which something like twenty to thirty different professions, with all of their different equipment and types of work area, are available to help an individual patient who needs treatment and care. Of these professions, the doctor occupies a special place because he alone has legal authority to *prescribe* treatments and services for the patient. (Anybody can prescribe the treatment, but only doctors have defence in law for their prescription if things go wrong, because they are professionally qualified and legally registered to prescribe.) The prescribing authority of the doctor is one of the *working relationships* which we mentioned earlier in this sequence.

A doctor prescribes to nurses and to paramedicals what they must do (prescription), but assumes that they need not be told how to do it (discretion). In a treatment prescribing relationship, the amount of discretion given by the prescriber will vary, depending on the treatment required; this is also true of the superior–subordinate relationship but is especially significant in the treatment prescribing relationship because of the great variety of treatment situations. In some treatments a highly skilled paramedical worker might apply treatment outside the prescriber's expertise. In other cases, such as in major surgery, the theatre nurse will be under minutely administered prescription for at least part of the time.

Prescriptions may be specific instructions on the medical treatment of a particular patient, or routines in a certain area of treatment. But they all emanate from the authority to prescribe for individual patients. But note that it is not the same as a super–subordinate relationship. A prescriber is not the manager of the person carrying out the prescription.

Looking at the chart again, there is the Department of Health at the top of the hospital service. The Department of Health delegates authority to *regional hospital boards* (and governing bodies of teaching hospitals) but the day to day running of hospitals rests with the *hospital management committees*. It is they who are concerned with running the buildings, employing the nurses and, indeed, all of the professionals who work in hospitals except for the doctors. The organization of the hospital thus begins with the HMC and the hierarchies working for the HMC are the main subject of discussion in the rest of this section. At each point we are concerned to differentiate certain roles from other roles.

4 Group officers

4.1 The hospital management committee

Each HMC manages a group of individual hospitals. The body of lay managers who make up the HMCs have *subordinate* to them a number of group officers, each of whom is *accountable* for the performance of all those people within the group of hospitals who are working in a particular specialized area. For example, a group personnel officer is *accountable* for all personnel work, and a group engineer is *accountable* for all engineering work in the several hospitals which together form the group.

4.2 The group secretary

There is a chief administrator, the group secretary, who manages all administrative functions (in effect, all activities other than those controlled by doctors or nurses), and *monitors* and *co-ordinates* all areas of work carried out by the hospitals in his group. *Monitoring* and *co-ordinating* relationships contain certain elements of the *superior–subordinate* relationships which are not clarified as a direct authority and accountability. A *monitoring* relationship with staff other than his subordinate means that the group secretary has authority to:

(1) Check the standards of work produced by a member of staff (X) and his adherence to group regulations.

(2) Negotiate with X improvements in standards or in his adherence to regulations.

(3) Report to the HMC on the quality and regularity of X's work.

The group secretary has no authority to instruct X, and no authority to make formal assessments of X's overall capacity.

4.3 Co-ordinating authority

Co-ordinating authority is the authority of the group secretary (he may delegate) to approach other than subordinates, and to seek information about their work; to judge how far their performance makes the best use of resources and contributes to the achievement of the HMC objectives; and to inform the members of his judgement. If he is not satisfied that the best use is being made of resources, he can influence them to modify their activities and formulate and propose new policies and modifications to existing policies. Co-ordinative work exists mainly in the programming of resources and the maintaining of priorities, and in ensuring common standards in recruitment, selection and managing of personnel, and in organization. Co-ordinative authority may be delegated to subordinates, and in their own specialist fields, to staff officers (see 5.3).

4.4 The chief nursing officer

A chief nursing officer (CNO), accountable to the HMC, manages nursing services and nurse training throughout the group. Groups differ from one another in their organization, but in every group the group secretary and the CNO are immediately subordinate to the HMC and have a *collateral* relationship with each other. A *collateral* relationship occurs when mutual adjustment and accommodation between colleagues are necessary for each to carry out certain of his tasks but neither has authority to instruct the other. Because it may not be possible for the collateral colleagues to find a mutually acceptable solution, it is desirable that there be a role with authority over both to which they can refer a matter for decision. The first common superior in the organization above any two roles is called a *cross-over point*. The *cross-over point* for the group secretary and CNO is the HMC.

Figure 2

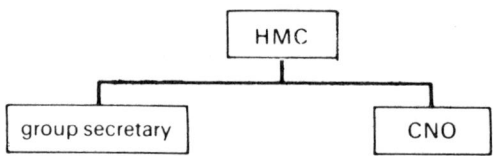

Other group officers, for example, the treasurer, group engineer, building superintendent, may also be directly *accountable* to the HMC, but they are often *accountable* to the group secretary as shown in Figure 1.

5 Administrative organization

5.1 Hospital management

Each hospital in a group has a hospital secretary who is *accountable* to the group secretary and has a role similar to that of the group secretary's but at hospital level.† The hospital secretary manages the administrative activities in this hospital and *monitors* and *co-ordinates* all hospital activities. There is also a senior nursing role in each hospital. This role may still be called the matron, or if the group has reorganized its nursing structure according to proposals made in the Salmon Report,* a principal nursing officer (PNO), senior nursing officer (SNO), or a nursing officer (NO). (Whether the senior nurse in the hospital is a PNO, a SNO, or a NO will usually depend on the size of the hospital.) The senior hospital nurse and the hospital secretary work as *collaterals*. Neither can instruct the other.

5.2 Service and staff departments

The services listed in paragraph 4.2 may have a group manager who provides the service for all the hospitals in a group; for example, a group laundry could, on one location, do laundry for all the hospitals in the group and deliver clean linen. If this is the case, the hospital secretaries and the manager of the service are *collaterals* and the centralized laundry would be in a *service-giving* relationship to hospital staff. A *service-giving* relationship is one in which one person is authorized to request a service from another who is *accountable* for providing such a service. The service-giver is required to provide service unless he has insufficient material or staff resources to do so. The service-seeker is accountable for deciding whether or not he is obtaining the service he requires and for taking steps to ensure that the service is given. There must be a role with authority over both the service-seeker and the service-giver to which problems about the quality and promptness of the service can be referred for decision.

5.3 Group departments

Group departments may occur because the group secretary finds that he needs specialized assistance in co-ordinating the work of his staff. Such specialist assistance may be needed on personnel and organizational matters, on the programming of activities and services, on the techniques to be employed and perhaps financial matters. The group secretary may in any of these dimensions establish a subordinate role (for example, group personnel officer) whose occupant has authority to interpret the superior's policy to his other subordinates and to give instructions within that policy. Such a role is called a *staff officer*. The relationship between the staff officer (SO) and other subordinates (B1, B2) is called *staff relationship*. If B1 does not agree with the staff officer's interpretation he cannot disregard it but

---

†*In the case of large mental hospitals, the single hospital is considered as a 'group'—with a group secretary in charge.*

Ministry of Health and Scottish Home and Health Department. Report of the Committee on Senior Nursing Staff Structure. HMSO (1967).

must take the matter up with A. A remains accountable for the activities of the staff officers, B1 and B2.

Figure 3

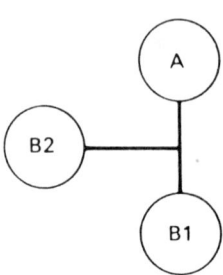

There are many examples of groups in which most of these services do not have a group manager but, instead, each hospital in the group has its own medical records officer, catering officer, supplies store, and so on, and the hospital head of the function is *accountable* to the hospital secretary.

Figure 4

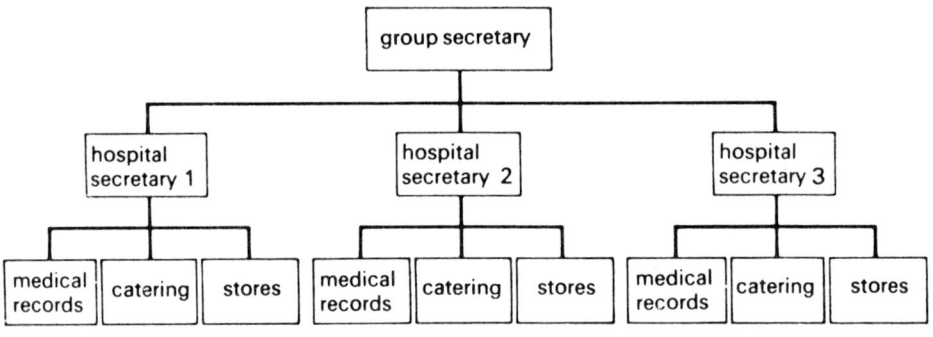

Another variation in the structure is seen in those groups where a particular function has a group officer but also has a permanent staff at each hospital. In such a case an *attachment* relationship develops between the hospital head of service, the hospital secretary and the group head of function. This is often found with engineering, where the hospital engineer is *accountable* to the group enginer, for the technical aspects of his work and *accountable* to the hospital secretary for the operational aspects.

The definition of attachment is:

(1)   When a specialist function exists at different levels of an organization

a junior specialist (BS) may be required to serve under the command of a non-specialist (B), while at the same time remaining the subordinate of a a specialist superior (AS). The junior specialist thus has two superiors who are together accountable for his work to their common superior (A). The relationship between AS and BS is called an *attachment*. The situation of attachment may be expressed as follows:

Figure 5

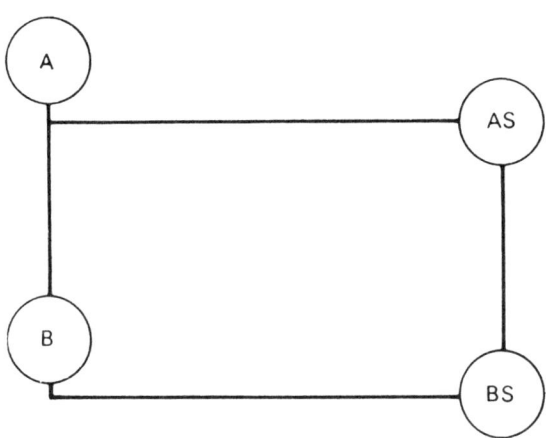

(2) Attachment assumes that the work done by the junior specialist (BS) has two components—*operational* and *technical*—and that accountability for them can be separated. The operational superior (B) allocates tasks to the subordinate and the specialist superior (AS) instructs him on the methods and techniques of executing them

If we look at a number of groups, we find many variations in the relationships between staff at hospital level and staff at group level. Within one group, some services may be organized at group level, some at hospital level, and other operated as attachments. The pattern of organization chosen by a particular group seems to depend on size of group; type of group (whether the group is dominated by one large hospital or whether it consists of a number of hospitals more equal in size); and the nature of the work in the particular field concerned. For example, it might be that a group with one large hospital and several nearby small hospitals would lend itself most readily to an organization which had most of the service located at group level.

5.4 Hospital hierarches

Because we find so many different patterns of organization, it is difficult to depict a typical hospital structure. But in each hospital (as in the group as a whole) there exist at least two *executive hierarches*, one organized under the hospital secretary and the other under the senior hospital nurse, and neither of these roles can instruct the other. An *executive hierarchy* is an executive system built upon *superior–subordinate* relationships. It therefore always has one role at the top where the occupant is accountable for the work of all those under him.

Figure 6

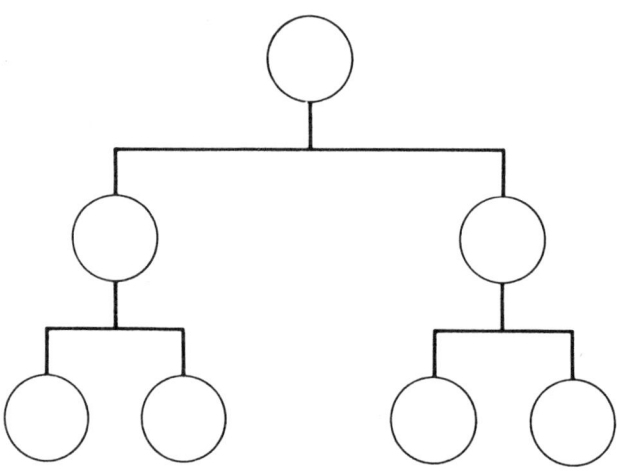

Each hospital also has medical staff working in it, and though registrars and housemen are *accountable* to consultants, *the consultants themselves are not accountable to any role within the hospital or within the group. They are employed and deployed by RHBs*. Their contracts can be terminated in cases of gross negligence, but it is questionable whether there is a full *superior–subordinate* relationship between consultants and RHBs. Consultants are not organized hierarchically. Each consultant has an individual relationship with his RHB.

There is, therefore, no one role within a hospital which is *accountable* for all the work that is going on. If a dispute arose between a consultant and a hospital secretary or a hospital secretary and a nurse, and this could not be resolved amicably within the hospital, or by group officers, it would have to be handled at HMC level. However, though the HMC serves as a *cross-over point* for administrative and nursing staff, it does not have authority over consultant staff and would not have the authority to settle a dispute between a consultant and an administrator or nurse except by instructing the administrator or nurse to change his position. (See Figure 1.) This does not cause problems most of the time because people are able to co-operate and resolve any differences which arise, but multi-managed organization does present the possibility that small inter-hospital disputes may have to be resolved outside the hospital at HMC level, and may not be settled even there if a consultant is involved.

5.5 Paramedical organization

This picture of the hospital is further complicated by the existence of *paramedical departments*. There is no accepted definition of 'paramedical'. The Professions Supplementary to Medicine Act of 1960 lists chiropodists, medical laboratory technicians, occupational therapists, physiotherapists, radiographers and remedial gymnasts. The Act provides machinery for the training and registration of these professions, but it does not define what differentiates them from, for example, the medical social work profession.

Paramedical departments can be organized in several ways. Study of hospitals reveals the following variations in the organization of paramedical work:

(1) Paramedical workers *subordinate* to an administrator.

(2) Paramedical workers *subordinate* to a consultant.

(3) Paramedical workers *subordinate* to paramedical heads of department who are not clearly *subordinate* to anyone in the hospital.

When the paramedical department does not have a medical head:

(a) Much paramedical work is *prescribed* by a doctor, though he may leave the paramedical worker a wide area of discretion.

(b) In other cases the doctor and paramedical worker may work *colaterally*.

When the paramedical department is headed by a consultant either:

(a) The prescribing consultant and the consultant in charge of the department work *collaterally,* and the paramedical workers receive instructions from their superior, the head of the department.

(b) The consultant in charge of the department *colaterally* agrees with a prescribing consultant to provide a service for him. In this case, paramedical workers are subject to the authority of the *prescribing relationship*.

5.6 A multiplicity of organization forms and divided accountability

Within an individual hospital, we thus find one *executive hierarchy* managed by the hospital secretary; one managed by a senior nurse; several paramedical hierarchies managed either by a consultant, but a paramedical head

261

of department who is not clearly *accountable* to anyone, or by a paramedical head *accountable* to the group secretary; and a group of consultants each of whom has a relationship with the RHB, but is not *accountable* within the group. This situation is unlike industry or the army or a large department store, where we can usually locate one managing director or commander who is clearly *accountable* for all the work going on within the organization and acts as a *cross-over point* for all the departments which make up the organization.

6 Conclusion

The preceding section has shown how the hospital service is structured and how discovering and clarifying working relationships can be useful in analysing the organization of the hospital. We have looked at hospital situations and described them in organizational language to demonstrate that structural relationships—let alone personal relationships—can be sources of conflict. This method is used for analysing difficulties but also for establishing more viable organizational patterns than we now find in hospitals.

The important point about this section is not so much the definitions used in it or the examples to which they are applied. It should have demonstrated to you that social science can be most helpful when it *defines* relationships and insists on adequate definitions.

References

Blau, P. M. and Scott, W. R. (1963) *Formal Organizations: A Comparative Approach,* Routledge and Kegan Paul, London.
Department of Health and Social Security (1970) *National Health Service: the Future Structure of the National Health Service,* HMSO.
Etzioni, A. (1964) *Modern Organizations,* Prentice Hall.
Ministry of Health (1966) *Report of the Committee on Senior Nursing Staff Structure* (Salmon Report), HMSO.
National Health Service Act (1946) (9 and 10 Geo. 6, Ch. 81), HMSO.

6.3 The goals of an industrial system

J. K. Galbraith

1

The individual member of the technostructure identifies himself with the goals of the mature corporation as, and because, the corporation identifies itself with goals which have, or appear to him to have, social purpose. And members seek to adapt the goals of the corporation to accord with their own with the result that the corporation accommodates social attitudes to its needs. What is deemed to be sound social purpose is a reflection of the goals of the corporation and the members of the technostructure. What remains now is to give concrete form to these relationships. We need to specify the social goals which the corporation and the members of its technostructure identify themselves. And we need to specify the goals to which, in accordance with their needs, they ascribe social purpose.

These are, we may remind ourselves once more, problems of some novelty. As economic life is ordinarily regarded, they do not arise. The sovereign consumer has wants and desires original to himself or which, at most arise by imitation from the consumption of his fellows. These wants and desires or the lack of them he manifests by his purchases or non-purchases in the market. This, with the like action of others, is the social edict. To it the corporation, and all other producers, respond and, because of their commitment to maximize return, they do so without latitude or choice. The firm is wholly subordinate to the social edict as prescribed by the consumer. So, accordingly, are the people who comprise the firm. They do not impose their imprint on the goals of society.

This is also a reassuring formula. The social will to which the business firm is subordinate is exercised in simple fashion from public master to corporate servant. The influence or power of the latter can cause no concern. If the reader senses that this may understate the social role of such evidently influential and conceivably omnipotent organizations as General Motors or Standard Oil, General Electric or General Dynamics, he will have correctly guessed the thrust of this book and he will be receptive to its argument. If he suspects that economics, as it is conventionally taught, is in part a system of

---

Acknowledgement

Reprinted, by permission, from J. K. Galbraith, *The New Industrial State*, 1967, Houghton Mifflin Co.

belief designed less to reveal truth than to reassure its communicants about established social arrangements, he will also be right.

For it is so. Modern economic belief can be understood only as the servant, in substantial measure, of the society which nurtures it. And not the least of its services to that society is to render instruction to the young which, rather systematically, excludes speculation on the way the large economic organizations shape social attitudes to their ends. Nor is the service less important for being rendered, in the main, in innocence and in the name of scientific truth. On the contrary, were it arranged and paid for it would cease to be of much effect. The wiles of the prostitute can be far more professional and superficially compelling than those of her artless competitor, but many more men succumb to the latter.

2

For any organization, as for any organism, the goal or objective that has a natural assumption of preeminence is the organization's own survival. This, plausibly, is true of the technostructure.

The first requisite for survival by the technostructure is that it preserves the autonomy on which its decision-making power depends. This means, we have seen,[1] that it must have a secure minimum of earnings. Power passes to the technostructure when technology and planning require specialized knowledge and group decision. The power remains securely with the technostructure as long as earnings are large enough to make accustomed payments to the stockholders and provide a supply of savings for reinvestment. If earnings are less than this level, it will be necessary to appeal to outside suppliers of capital. These, in turn, can ask questions and impose conditions and thus abridge the autonomy of the technostructure. And if the accustomed dividends are not covered, stockholders cannot wholly be counted upon to remain quiescent; as we have seen, struggles for control in large corporations occur all but excessively in those that are suffering losses or which have meager and irregular earnings.[2]

---

[1]*See Chapter 6 of* The New Industrial State.

[2]*There is a further and poignant reason for wanting to protect a minimum rate of return. While suppliers of capital tend to recognize at least implicitly that decision-making in the modern corporation requires autonomy—that they must not 'interfere' with management decision—investigation and study are legitimate and are invited by inadequate return. And the management consulting industry, which exists in response to this opportunity, is highly available for such tasks. It, in turn, brings the pay, position and performance of members of the technostructure under a scrutiny that most executives would wish to avoid.*

GOALS OF AN INDUSTRIAL SYSTEM

The effects of low and high earnings on the technostructure are not symmetrical. With low earnings or losses it becomes vulnerable to outside influence and loses its autonomy. But above a certain level more earnings add little or nothing to its security therein. This autonomy has become nearly absolute. This casts light, in turn, on the assumption that the mature corporation will seek to maximize its profits. By the most elementary calculation of self-interest, the technostructure is compelled to put prevention of loss ahead of maximum return. Loss can destroy the technostructure; high revenues accrue to others.[3] If, as will often happen, the maximization of revenues invites increased risk of loss, then the technostructure, as a matter of elementary interest, should forgo it.[4]

The need for protecting a minimum level of return will have, in turn, an important effect on industrial planning. While it will be desirable to achieve planned results, it will be even more important to avoid unplanned disasters. The first is pleasing; the second can be mortal. Even more important than a good price is protection against a price collapse. Even more important than a strong demand for the product is protection against a wholesale rejection. I return to the effect of these needs on the management of prices and demand in the next three chapters. [See Chapters 16–18 of *The New Industrial State*.] And we shall see, thereafter, that the relation of the mature corporation to the State—its support of steps to regulate aggregate demand and its strong encouragement of public underwriting of expensive technology—arises from the same effort to exclude any threat to minimum levels of earnings. Similar considerations will be seen to underlie modern labour policy.

---

[3]*'They [executives of the large corporation] do not receive the profit which may result from taking a chance, while their position in the firm may be jeopardized in the event of serious loss.'* R. A. Gordon, Business Leadership in the Large Corporation, Brookings, Washington, 1945, p. 324.

[4]*The importance of a minimum level of return is stressed, although not as strongly as here by William J. Baumol, in* Business Behavior, Value and Growth, *Macmillan, New York, 1959, especially pp. 48–53. What he calls the 'security' of the managerial group is a major theme of Mr Marris's analysis (Robin Marris,* The Economic Theory of 'Managerial' Capitalism, *The Free Press of Glencoe, New York, 1964). Professor Kaysen states the same conclusion as follows: 'While the firm in the highly competitive market is constrained to seek after maximum profits, because the alternative is insufficient to insure survival, the firm in the less competitive market can choose whether to seek maximum profit or to be satisfied with some "acceptable" return and to seek other "goals".' In Edward F. Mason (ed.),* The Corporation in Modern Society, Harvard University Press, Cambridge, 1959, p. 90.

3

If the principle of consistency holds, the autonomy of the technostructure should be a goal of social policy. And, as a moment's thought will suggest, it is.

The doctrine of the industrial system stresses powerfully its inherently and functionally independent character. It is the *private* enterprise system. A great gulf is deemed to divide the state from the business firm. Only in the rarest instances may there be any constraining action across this chasm. On nothing is the burden of proof so strong as on a measure—to provide standards of automobile safety, of drug advertising, of weights of packages, of health claims on behalf of cigarettes—which involves the regulation of an industrial enterprise.

The grounds on which this separation is defended are palpably bogus. It is held that nothing must interfere with the independent operation of the market mechanism to which the firm is subject. The reality in the case of the mature corporation, as we have sufficiently seen, is that the prices are substantially controlled by the firm and the latter goes on to exercise influence on the amounts that are purchased and sold at these prices. The imperatives of technology and capital use do not allow the firm to be subordinate to the market and the mature corporation so far from being separated organically from the State exists, as we shall presently see, only in intimate association with it.

Yet autonomy is necessary. The real reason why it is needed not being clearly seen, the power of the market and the allegedly deep and inherent separation between private enterprise and government are advanced in their place. Both are articles of faith. It is a tribute to the power of adaptation that it can win social attitudes favourable to the autonomy of the technostructure that have such negligible relation to reality.

And the requisite social attitudes have been secured. The right of the technostructure of autonomy, and more than incidentally to the earnings that assure it, is wholly accepted. Not for years has any serious aspirant for public office run on a platform of tighter regulation of business. Nor does anyone question the sanctity of an adequate level of profits.

There remains, indeed, a compulsive worry by businessmen over government interference which is matched by a desire by public officials to reassure that none is intended. This is much misunderstood. To the entrepreneurial corporation the State was a threat to its income. It resisted public regulation for the purpose of protecting its profits. The modern observer, noticing that the mature corporation is making a good return, is surprised to find its executives alarmed about government intrusion or asking for comfort that none is intended. 'Why are they so worried?' he asks. 'Surely they are making plenty of money.' He fails to see that the technostructure is protecting something more important than its profits—something indeed which profits themselves protect. That is its autonomy.[5]

4

Once the safety of the technostructure is insured by a minimum level of earnings, there is then a measure of choice as to goals. Nothing is so compelling as the need to survive. However, there is little doubt as to how, overwhelmingly, this choice is exercised: It is to achieve the greatest possible rate of corporate growth as measured in sales.

This goal also commends itself strongly to the self-interest of the technostructure. Expansion of output means expansion of the technostructure itself. Such expansion, in turn, means more jobs with more responsibility and hence more promotion and more compensation. 'When a man takes decisions leading to successful expansion, he not only creates new openings but also recommends himself to fill them.'[6] The paradox of modern economic motivation is that profit maximization as a goal requires that the individual member of the technostructure subordinate his personal pecuniary interest to that of the remote and unknown stockholder. By contrast, growth, as a goal, is wholly consistent with the personal and pecuniary interest of those who participate in decisions and direct the enterprise. The reader will sense once more how important profit maximization

---

[5]*I have discussed somewhat related considerations in* American Capitalism: The Concept of Countervailing Power, *Houghton, Boston, 1956, Chapter 6.*

[6]*R.Marris,* The Economic Theory of 'Managerial' Capitalism, *p. 102. Although reached by highly theoretical techniques, Mr Marris's conclusions as to the goals of the mature corporation are consistent with mine. So are Professor Baumol's (*Business Behavior, Value and Growth*) which are based partly on theoretical argument and partly on empirical observation.*

[7]*Professor Peterson has argued ('Corporate control and capitalism',* The Quarterly Journal of Economics, *vol. 74, no. 1, February 1965, p. 11) that the need for profits to finance growth means that there is little practical difference between growth as a goal and profit maximization as a goal. Growth may be the best long-run strategy for maximizing profits. This is not so. While, if one waits long enough, one may sooner or later find one strategy miscarrying and another serving its ends better, the proper test is* ex ante *not* ex post *behavior. Price, sales, cost, and other policies to maximize growth will differ within any given time horizon from those to maximize profits. Nor will profits be maximized if, as in the case of the technostructure, there is special reason to minimize risk.*

must be for the defence of traditional economic theory and specifically the rule of the market. Its use survives in competition with goals which reflect the self-interest of those immediately involved.[7]

The growth of the firm serves another important purpose for the technostructure. It is the best protection against contraction. For the firm with a small contingent of managers and supervisors and a large undifferentiated mass of blue-collar workers, a shrinkage in production presents no great difficulties. A notice is posted and men go; when needed they are called back. Those who post the notice are not personally involved.

With the rise of the technostructure, any contraction of output becomes much more painful and damaging. Costs can no longer be reduced simply by laying off blue-collar workers. A substantial share of total costs are now accounted for by the technostructure. If this remains intact, the firm will have a burdensome overhead in the form of a partially employed organization. In the technostructure men work in groups. Whole groups cannot be discharged. The discharge of individuals—or their voluntary withdrawl in response to their easily perceived unemployment—impairs the working efficiency of those that remain. Moreover, decisions for curtailment are made within the technostructure itself. They involve its own members. They do not have the agreeable impersonality which is associated with firing someone at a greater distance, or of a different social class.

All of these unpleasant contingencies are avoided by expansion. Their avoidance may even justify comparatively unremunerative expansion. This is the meaning of the frequently heard statement that business is being taken, not for its profit, but 'to hold the organization together'. It can be a highly rational course.[8]

5

The growth of the firm as a goal of the technostructure is strongly supported by the principle of consistency. No other social goal is more strongly avowed than economic growth. No other test of social success has such nearly unanimous acceptance as the annual increase in the Gross National Product. And this is true of all countries developed or underdeveloped; communist, socialist or capitalist. Japan has been deemed a successful society since World War II because of its very high rate of increase in Gross National Product; so also Germany and Israel and, latterly, France. Britain with a much smaller increase has been perilously close to being a failure.

---

[8]*In another view, as the technostructure grows the proportion of the working force that must be treated as an overhead cost grows. But it is a special type of overhead. Unlike machinery or plant it disintegrates rapidly if not fully employed.*

The communist countries have been greater or less rivals of the non-communist States in accordance with their greater or lesser increase in output. There are differences of opinion between communist and non-communist scholars on the validity of the statistics and concepts which are employed in the two worlds to measure economic growth. But there is no disagreement on the validity of the goal itself. Similarly it is now agreed that ancient cultures—India, China and Persia—should measure their progress toward civilization by their percentage increase in GNP. Their own scholars are the most insistent of all.

Given the agreement on economic growth as a social goal, the goal of the technostructure has a strong social purpose. Members can identify themselves with it in the secure knowledge that they are serving a larger purpose than their own. They seek to further the growth of their firm. This furthers the growth of the economy. Identification, as a motivation, reinforces the self-interest that is associated with such expansion.

The question inevitably arises to what extent economic growth, as a social goal, reflects adaptation. Does it reflect original social need? Has it been imposed on society by the technostructure? This question cannot be answered categorically. No doubt the emphasis on economic growth is partly grounded in man's ancient and seemingly always inadequate supply of goods. And in modern times growth has been a principal therapy for unemployment.[9] Also economic growth eases many problems of allocation in the economy—it is much easier to find resources for education or the poor by taking these from increased output than by subtracting them from the existing standard of living. But, as always, we must be alert to a two-way influence. The acceptance of economic growth as a social goal coincides closely with the rise to power of the mature corporation and the technostructure. And the latter has had every reason to value it as a social goal. It does not argue the merits of this goal. As always it proceeds by massive assumption. What other goal *could* be socially so urgent?[10]

6

Associated with growth, as a goal of the technostructure, is technological

---

[9]*Not infrequently in western countries the amount of unemployment is cited as a measure of the success or non-success of the system. But this, for nearly all scholars, is merely an indication of an insufficient output. Given a greater rate of increase in Gross National Product—a more successful economy by this standard—unemployment or most of it would disappear.*

[10]*The reader in search of verification will have a remarkably easy way of satisfying himself on this point. He will need only to examine the dominant tone of the more orthodox reviews of this volume (*The New Industrial State*).*

269

virtuosity. This also serves the needs of the members. Progressive technology means jobs and promotion for technologists. Capacity for expansion likewise depends very largely on capacity for innovation. It is by technical innovation, real or simulated, that the firm holds and recruits customers for its existing products and expands to produce new ones. Such capacity for innovation is obviously important for keeping or expanding the firm's share of weapons, space and other businesses with a high technological dynamic. But such innovation tends also to have standing in its own right. As in the Scientific work of a university, prestige adheres to successful practitioners; it is a goal with which men readily identify themselves. Here again the principle of consistency leads us to look at social attitudes. And here again we find technological *advance*, as significantly it is called, solidly enshrined as a social achievement. One would encounter less dispute, on the whole, by questioning the sanctity of the family or religion than the absolute merit of technical progress.

Technological virtuosity can be a goal of the technostructure only if it does not prejudice a minimum level of earnings. Given the costs and uncertainties associated with research and development, this can easily happen. Then this goal must be abandoned or the cost and attendant risk must be transferred to the state, that is to say, government support for the particular development, or the underlying research, must be sought. Given the high social purpose attributed to technological change, the socialization of development is strongly approved. Adaptation has paved the way. Nor need attention be paid to whether this investment of resources in technological and underlying scientific development is important in relation to alternatives. There is no need to measure the advantages of space achievements against help to the poor. In the nature of successful adaptation the absolute virtue of technological advance is again assumed.

7

Now a concession must be made to seeming orthodoxy. A rate of earnings that allows, over and above investment needs, for a progressive rise in the dividend rate will also regularly be a goal of the technostructure. This return must not be achieved by prices which would prejudice growth. Nothing better suggests the primacy of growth as a goal than the vehemence with which this would be dismissed as unsound business practice. The risks taken for such higher return, it is axiomatic, must not jeopardize the basic level of earnings. But tradition inherited from the entrepreneurial firm associates success with a rising level of realized earnings. And social attitudes, on the whole, take such an improvement in earnings over time as an indication of sound service to the community.

A secure level of earnings and a maximum rate of growth consistent with the provision of revenues for the requisite investment are the prime goals of the technostructure. Technological virtuosity and a rising dividend rate are secondary in the sense that they must not interfere with the two first-mentioned objectives. After these ends are achieved there is further opportunity for a variety of other and lesser goals. These are subject only to the limitation that they must not interfere with the two primary objectives. They are in no sense less rational or legitimate. But since these further goals will sometimes threaten minimum earnings and will not always contribute to the growth of the firm, their role will be closely circumscribed.

Building a better community; improved education; better understanding of the free enterprise system; an effective attack on heart ailments, emphysema, alcoholism, hard chancre or other crippling disease; participation in the political party of choice; and renewed emphasis on regular religious observances are all examples of such further goals. Some may also serve the primary and secondary goals—they contribute to what is called a sound corporate image and thus help recruiting and worker morale, avoid unwelcome taxes or cultivate a better public attitude toward products. But this is not necessary to justify the activity. It is sufficient that it serve goals that the technostructure (and society) think good and that it be not in conflict with higher goals.

Nearly all economists, and a great many others, dismiss pursuit of such goals as irrelevant window-dressing. This is an error. So long as their subordinate role is clearly recognized, including the limitations imposed by cost, they are a perfectly plausible expression of the goals of the individual members of the technostructure and, thus, collectively of the mature corporation. What has been called the 'social corporation' is a logical manifestation of the mature corporation and the motivation of its members.

8

At any given time the symbols of business success will faithfully reflect success in pursuit of the currently accepted goals. In the latter half of the last century, the greatest folk hero of the economic system was the elder Rockefeller. This was the era of the entrepreneurial corporation; by its goals he was the greatest success for he had made more money than anyone else.

In our time no man of wealth enjoys comparable distinction. Nor is esteem associated with individuals; by the nature of the technostructure they are submerged in the group. Esteem is associated with corporations. And among these, the first requirement is a secure earnings record. Any firm that fails this requirement is a dog. Its management is regarded with condescension, even pity. Sooner or later even subordinate employees will sense their loss of public respect and match it with a loss of self-respect. In the fashion increasingly affected by the latter-day railway employee they will conduct themselves in a slovenly and offensive manner indicating their feeling that the world in general and their customers in particular are their enemy. Or they will go elsewhere.

Given a secure level of earnings the esteemed firms are those that are large—that have a record of achieved growth—or which are growing with particular speed. Increasingly, esteem is associated with the latter. And if a firm has a reputation for technological innovation, it is additionally known as a smart outfit. Thereafter the dividend record will be mentioned. One knows little of life unless he has a theoretical system by which to interpret it. But there is little in theory that cannot be tested in life.

6.4 The real threat to 'All we hold most dear'

Stafford Beer

The little house where I have come to live alone for a few weeks sits on the edge of a steep hill in a quiet village on the western coast of Chile. Huge majestic waves roll into the bay and crash magnificently over the rocks, sparkling white against the green sea under a winter sun. It is for me a time of peace, a time to clear the head, a time to treasure.

For after all, such times are rare events for today's civilized man. We spend our days boxed in our houses, swarming in and out of office blocks like tribes of ants, crammed into trains, canned in aeroplanes, locked solid in traffic jams on the freeway. Our unbiblical concern for what we shall eat, what we shall drink, and what we shall put on is amplified and made obsessional by the pressure to consume—way, way beyond the natural need. All this is demanded by the way we have arranged our economy. And the institutions we have built to operate that economy, to safeguard ourselves, protect our homes, care for and educate our families, have all grown into large and powerful pieces of social machinery which suddenly seem not so much protective as actually threatening.

Mankind has always been in a battle with his environment. But until quite recently in history his battles were on a reasonable scale, a human scale. He could alter his house, if he would brave the weather: he did not have to take on the whole city planning department and the owners of his mortgage and his overdraft. He could dress his children as he pleased, teaching them what he knew and how to learn: he was not flattened in this natural enterprise by educational authorities, attended by boards of experts. When he fought with danger, he matched his strength and skill with another animal of similar size to his: he was not unexpectedly knocked flying by two tons of steel travelling at sixty miles an hour. And if he faced the fact of death, that also was a personal encounter, win or lose: he did not live under the stress of a remotely threatened genocide or nuclear extermination. But this is how it is for us. We do not think much about it. When things go badly, there is all of this to blame, and not ourselves: perhaps that is some sort of consolation.

Acknowledgement

Reprinted, by permission, from S. Beer, *Designing Freedom,* 1975, John Wiley and Sons Ltd.

Do we indeed even want to think about such things? I believe that people increasingly do begin to question the assumptions of our society—and not because of any characteristic that I have so far mentioned. Most people alive today in urban societies settled long ago for the role of pygmy man amidst the giants of his own institutions, and for the reason that it meant apparent advance—a higher standard of living, as measured by the gross national product per head. But in the last decade or two something has come through to public consciousness. It is the doubt as to whether the whole apparatus of our civilization *actually works* any longer. Is it beginning to fail?

The evidence for this suspicion is plentiful. I instance the decay of previously rich and healthy cities from the centre outwards, creating ghettos and all the social frightfulness that goes with them, stark inequalities, private penury, social squalor, a rise in crime, a rise in violence. I instance pollution on a world-wide scale: the poisoning of the atmosphere, of seas and lakes and rivers. Then there is the widening chasm between luxury and starvation, whereby we somehow manage to concentrate more wealth with the already wealthy, and more deprivation with the already deprived. I will not go on with this baleful list, because conscientious people are already aware of these problems. The question I would like us to address in these lectures is just *why?* Because if we can fathom that, maybe we can also conduct a fruitful search for answers.

The first point to establish is the most difficult; and it is the most difficult because it sounds so easy. It is to say that all these institutions we have been contemplating—the homes, the offices, the schools, the cities, the firms, the states, the countries—are not just things, entities we recognize and label. They are instead *dynamic and surviving systems.* Well, I did say it sounds so easy. Obviously these entities are systems; because they consist of related parts, and the relations—the connexions—between those parts. Obviously, too, they are dynamic. No-one believes that these institutions are just sitting there brooding; they are all 'on the go'. Finally, if they were not surviving, they would not be there. And having taken the point that we are talking about such systems, it is too natural to pass it by—to pass over the point, pass around the point, pass through the point—without ever grappling with the real meaning of the point at all.

Although we may recognize the systemic nature of the world, and would agree when challenged that something we normally think of as an entity is actually a system, our culture does not propound this insight as particularly interesting or profitable to contemplate. Let me propose to you a little exercise, taking the bay I am looking at now as a convenient example. It is not difficult to recognize that the movement of water in this bay is the visible behaviour of a dynamic system: after all, the waves are steadily moving in and dissipating themselves along the shore. But please consider just one wave. We think of that as an entity: *a* wave, we say. What is it doing out there, why is it that shape, and what is the reason for its happy white crest? The exercise is to ask yourself in all honesty not whether you know the answers, because that would be just a technical exercise, but whether these are the sorts of question that have ever arisen for you. The point is that the questions themselves—and not just the answers—can be understood only when we stop thinking of a wave as an entity. As long as it is an entity, we tend to say well, waves are like that: the fact that our wave is out there moving across the bay, has that shape and a happy white crest, are the signs that tell me 'It's a wave'—just as the fact that a book is red and no other colour is a sign that tells me 'That's the book I want'.

The truth is, however, that the book is red because someone gave it a red cover when he might just as well have made it green; whereas the wave cannot be other than it is because a wave is a dynamic system. It consists of flows of water, which are its parts, and the relations between those flows, which are governed by the natural laws of systems of water that are investigated by the science of hydrodynamics. The appearances of the wave, its shape and the happy white crest, are actually *outputs* of this system. They are what they are because the system is organized in the way that it is, and this organization produces an inescapable kind of behaviour. The cross-section of the wave is parabolic, having two basic forms, the one dominating at the open-sea stage of the wave, and the other dominating later. As the second form is produced from the first, there is a moment when the wave holds the two forms: it has at this moment a wedge shape of 120°. And at this point, as the second form takes over, the wave begins to break—hence the happy white crest.

Now in terms of the dynamic system that we call a wave, the happy white crest is not at all the pretty sign by which what we first called an entity signalizes its existence. For the wave, that crest is its personal catastrophe. What has happened is that the wave has a systemic conflict within it determined by its form of organization, and that this has produced a phase of *instability*. The happy white crest is the mark of doom upon the wave, because the instability feeds upon itself; and the catastrophic collapse of the wave is an inevitable output of the system.

I am asking 'Did you know?' Not 'did you know about theoretic hydrodynamics?' but 'did you know that a wave is a dynamic system in catastrophe, as a result of its internal organizational instability?' Of course, the reason for this exercise is to be ready to pose the same question about the social institutions we were discussing. If we perceive those entities, the giant monoliths surrounding pygmy man, then we shall not be surprised to find the marks of bureaucracy upon them: sluggish and inaccurate response, and those other warning signs I mentioned earlier. That is what these entities are like, we tend to say—and sigh. But in fact these institutions are dynamic systems, having a particular organization which produces particular outputs. My contention is that they are typically moving into unstable phases, for which catastrophe is the inevitable outcome. And I believe the growing sense of unease I mentioned at the start derives from a public intuition that this is indeed the case. For people to understand this possibility, how it arises, what the dangers are, and above all what can be done about it, it is not necessary to master sociopolitical cybernetics. This is the science that stands to institutional behaviour as the science of hydrodynamics stands to the behaviour of waves. But it is necessary to train ourselves simply to perceive what was there all the time: not a monolithic entity, but a dynamic system; not a happy white crest, but the warning of catastrophic instability.

So far we have spoken a little of the nature of dynamic systems; but the other qualification that I used at the start was the word 'surviving'. The wave is not a *surviving* dynamic system, because its destruction is built into its organization. However, we certainly regard our institutions as survival-worthy. After all, they have survived until now, because they are capable of a trick we call *adaptation,* which waves are not. So why should there now be a fuss about instability and impending catastrophe?

Our institutions have already proven that they can survive, says the argument, and we can have confidence that they will continue to adapt successfully to change. Indeed, we insist that they must—for our institutions enshrine everything we hold most dear. Beginning with the family unit, based on love and mutual support; extending through the school—and perhaps that alma mater the university; bound together in the cohesion of the neighbourhood, the community, and the churches; ramifying into business and the growth of prosperity for all; exemplified, protected, and projected by the State; this—our society—is an entity that survives, albeit by adaptive change. And if this society embodied in its institutions is threatened by too rapid change, then the answer that many serious and concerned people give is to reinforce the rules of the society game, strengthen the institutions, tighten up the criminal, social and moral laws, and weather the storm. That is the conservative attitude. It is not mine. It is not going to work much longer.

Indeed, we ought to face the fact that this theory does not work now. People convince themselves that it does, because they see society as an entity, and its main characteristic is to be held most dear. Then they grit their teeth and declare that whatever is wrong with it must and can be put right again. Broken barriers, swept away by permissive morality, can be repaired. Departed children can be summoned home to eat the fatted calf. The majority of people, who do not attend a church, are still (surely to goodness?) fundamentally Christian. The starving two-thirds of the world will eventually be fed (well, not those two-thirds dying right now, but their descendants). And somehow a finite planet, with exhaustible resources, will be made indefinitely to support more and yet more growth. Oh no: this only even looks possible if we are dealing with a fixed entity, a society or a way of life that is held to enshrine eternal values, a golden ideal. If this has become rather tarnished, then it can be reburnished with a little elbow grease. So some people, and especially some politicians, seem to think.

But if society is a dynamic system all these phenomena are not simply blemishes—they are its outputs. These unpleasing threats to all we hold most dear are products of a system so organized as to produce them—to produce *them*, and not their contraries. These are not accidental; and they are not mistakes. They are the continuing output of a systemic conflict which is due to specific modes of organization. And those modes of organization have currently arrived at a stage in their inexorable pattern of behaviour which, like the wedge-shaped wave of 120 degrees, is incipiently unstable—on the verge of catastrophic breakdown. Or so I think.

I hope you will accept my invitation to investigate this hypothesis with me. And let me be more cheerful right away. These dire predictions I am making have to come about, which is why I said they were inexorable, if—but only if—we continue to support modes of organization into which these outcomes are inbuilt. We do not have to do that. We really can change the whole thing. But to succeed, we must first perceive the nature of dynamic surviving systems, and the conditions they must meet to remain stable yet adaptive.

In order to get rid of the concept of an institution as a fixed entity, we have to get rid of the classical picture of its organization. You know how this looks. The institution's activity is divided into chunks, which are also perceived as entities; these chunks are divided into smaller chunks, and so on. In every chunk there is a boss-man, with lesser bosses reporting to him and running the smaller chunks. This picture looks like a family tree, and it is useful for just one purpose. If something has gone wrong, you can use the picture to trace whose fault it is. In fact, this whole picture of an institution is just like a fault-finding chart that shows how an automobile is organized. Some people, and the channels connecting them, are shown in red (as if they were the fuel system), others are shown in blue (as if they were the electrical system), and so on. But nowhere on the automobile chart can you find such a thing as *speed,* which is what the automobile is all about.

What this orthodox organization chart leaves out of account, when it comes to understanding institutions, is that we are not dealing with pistons, pumps and distributor arms, but with people; and the connexions between the parts are not crankshafts, pipes, and electrical wires, but human relationships. What matters about the institution is not its set of dependencies but its performance—if you like, its speed. The organizational forces by which the whole institutional machinery is held together include psychological conflict, loyalty and perfidy, integrity of purpose, hard and lazy work. They also include all manner of special arrangements making cross-linkages between the cousins of the family tree, which are the formal boards and committees, the less formal liaison officers and advisory groups, the informal old-pals network—and even maybe secret connexions whose existence will be denied. How can we picture this dynamic system in our minds, and how contemplate its output and stability?

I will ask you to think first of a tennis trainer—two poles held in place by guy-ropes pegged to the ground, and connected by a piece of elastic from the middle of which hangs a tennis ball suspended by an elastic thread. Suppose that an institution has only two members. They are sitting on top of the poles—held firmly in place by the guy-ropes, which define their formal positions. What they must do between them is the work of the institution, and for this they need a connexion, which is the elastic thread. Now the role of the suspended tennis ball in this example is not too obvious, and it is vital to understand it. The ball stands for the *output* state of the system.

However complicated a system must be, there is one output state that defines it. That state is an output of the system—not in terms of what special things or detailed consequences are flowing from the institution's activity, but in terms of its total net performance. This is rather like saying that a human being, characterized as he is by all manner of detectable outputs, is in the net state of sleep—or violent effort, or concentration, or fighting. Or again we might liken the tennis ball to the net state of a game of chess at the (let's say) 26th move. There are all sorts of tensions implicit in the relationships of the pieces, and if the game were speeded up by cine-photography we really should see a dynamic system operating under its organizational conflicts. But if instead we take a still photograph of the board at the 26th move, then the output state is a single state, and it might be called 'white losing', or 'checkmate'.

If the men on top of the poles do their respective jobs properly, they will pull correctly on the elastic. The ball—which marks the output state of the system—will bob about for a bit, and then be still. The dynamic system is

THE THREAT TO 'ALL WE HOLD MOST DEAR'

doing its work, and producing stability. If the men are inefficient, and cannot make up their minds how to pull on the elastic (especially if they keep passing the buck), then the ball will bob about for ages, and may never settle. This system is unstable. However, if we assume goodwill and reasonable efficiency on the part of the two men, so that they behave like proper elastic connexions, the ball will soon stop bobbing about. The time it takes to stop is called the *relaxation time* of the system.

Well, this picture is a bit too simple for our needs. So let us erect a lot more poles (try to imagine about forty of them) arranged in a circle, where our original elastic connexion marks a diameter. Now let us join all the new men on the top of these poles to the system, by giving each one a piece of elastic and tying the other end to the central knot. These new members of the institution are not all equally proficient, or loyal, or hard-working; and we can represent that by giving some of them thin pieces of elastic, and some of them thick pieces. The ball was disturbed while we did that, and I think that we can bet that the relaxation time will now be extremely long. In fact, and this is really rather interesting: the harder all the men try conscientiously to manipulate the system so that it settles, the more unstable it is likely to become. Just imagine the chaos. 'Hey, George, stop pulling a minute.' 'Harry, you pull a bit harder.' And so on. In fact if all forty men are each trying to give instructions to each of the others, we shall have 1,560 communication channels trying to speak all the time. You are right: *it isn't going to work.*

The reason is that this system as a whole has too many possible states. I am not talking now about the solitary output state, but about the vast number of configurations which the organization itself can assume. Every one of those men on the poles may behave in a great many alternative ways: and these are permuted together to reveal the total richness of possible organizational behaviour. If we consider the total number of behavioural configurations that are possible, we have a measure of the system's complexity. Let us turn this perception into a formal definition. The number of possible states of a system is called its *variety*. This will be a most useful word for us, so may I repeat: variety means the number of possible states.

Suppose that each man can do only one of two things, which is an absurd simplification after all. Then between them they can produce more than a million million possible sets of conditions for the system. It is too many; and the tennis ball will never be able to settle. At least, it will in theory. But in practice the world is not going to leave the system alone for long enough. Just imagine those poor men feeling they have almost exhausted the possibilities after a week's work, when the cat comes into the garden, and takes a playful swipe at the ball with its paw. It is back to square one.

All our major societal institutions are high-variety systems; all of them need to have a finite relaxation time; but all of them are subject to constant perturbation—which is the word to use for the unexpected interference of the cat's paw. How do they cope? There is only one way to cope, and all institutions use it—although they use it in many forms. They have to reduce the variety of the system. Here are some of the ways.

They may put in four more taller poles, and connect ten of the shorter ones to each. The man on the tall pole gives instructions to his ten subordinates. That reduces the total system variety, but it also interferes with the short-pole men's freedom to do the best they can. It is in this way that freedom starts to be subordinated to efficiency; but the only alternative—which we must face—is total anarchy.

Second, they may put in a lot of rigid connexions, called rules, between the elastic threads, so that the system looks like a spider's web. That also reduces variety. But that confounded cat keeps coming around, and spoiling the whole effort. Or suppose that the child of the house comes into the garden and takes a tremendous crack at the ball with a tennis racket. Then the system may not have the resilience to take the strain, and may collapse altogether.

A third variety-reducing method used by institutions, for example banks and insurance companies, is to shoot the cat. This works, but is no fun if you are the cat. In any case, you had better not shoot the son of the house.

We have no time to go on exploring our model (for this is the name of our elastic network) but you can do that yourself. Remember these aspects of our work together so far. A dynamic system is in constant flux; and the higher its variety, the greater the flux. Its stability depends upon its net state reaching equilibrium following a perturbation. The time this process takes is the relaxation time. The mode of organization adopted for the system is its variety controller. With these points clearly in our minds, it is possible to state the contention of this first lecture with force and I hope with simplicity. Here goes.

Our institutions were set up a long time ago. They handled a certain amount of variety, and controlled it by sets of organizational variety reducers. They coped with a certain range of perturbations, coming along at a certain average frequency. The system had a characteristic relaxation time which was acceptable to society. As time went by, variety rose—because the relevant population grew, and more states became accessible both to that population and to the institutional system. This meant that more variety reducers were systematically built into the system, until today our institutions are nearly solid with organizational restrictions. Meanwhile, both the range and the frequency of the perturbations has increased. But we just said that the *systemic* variety has been cut. This produces a mismatch. The relaxation time of the system is not geared to the current rate of perturbation. This means that a new swipe is taken at the ball before it has had time to settle. Hence our institutions are in an unstable condition. The ball keeps bobbing, and there is no way of recognizing where an equilibrial outcome is located.

If we cannot recognize the stable state, it follows that we cannot learn to reach it—there is no reference point. If we cannot learn how to reach stability, we cannot devise adaptive strategies—because the learning machinery is missing. If we cannot adapt, we cannot evolve. Then the instability threatens to be like the wave's instability—catastrophic.

I said before that there are solutions, but I have also shown that they concern organizational modes. They concern engineering with the variety of dynamic systems. By continuing to treat our societal institutions as entities, by thinking of their organizations as static trees, by treating their failures as aberrations—in these clouded perceptions of the unfolding facts we rob ourselves of the only solutions.

In particular: by advocating a new insistence on variety reducing methods which worked in a bygone epoch, we advocate precisely the wrong thing, and seal our doom. THIS is the real threat to all we hold most dear.

Notes in support of the first lecture

Cybernetics

originally defined by the late Norbert Wiener as

*the science of control and communication
in the animal and the machine*

Cybernetics is exactly thirty years old; the name was added in 1947.

This original definition points to the relationship between control and communication, and to the existence of general laws affecting equally animate and inanimate systems. The first principle of such general importance to be recognized was the significance of *feedback* in all systems, whatever the fabric of their components.

Thirty years on, this new definition might be preferred:

Cybernetics is the science of effective organization.

Variety

is the measure of complexity in a system, defined as the number of its possible states.

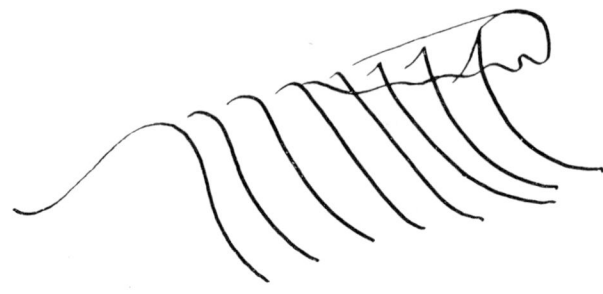

How the wave becomes unstable, and finally moves into catastrophic collapse.

after René Thom
   Stabilité Structurelle et Morphogénèse
   Benjamin, Massachusetts, 1972

The poles with their guy ropes define the formal positions that people hold in an institution.

The ball defines a point representing the net output state of a system.

The **relaxation time** of a system is the time it takes the **representative point** to reach stability after it has been **perturbed** (for instance, by the cat—which stands for an arbitrary interference).

THE THREAT TO 'ALL WE HOLD MOST DEAR'

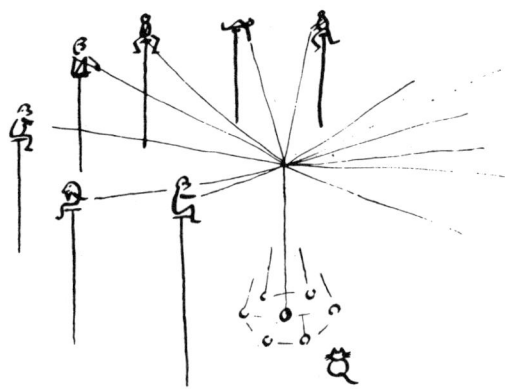

The larger the organization, the longer the relaxation time is likely to be. . . .

If everyone has complete **freedom** to do what he thinks is best, there will (unfortunately) be **instability**—which may feed on itself and become catastrophic.

If everyone is trying to communicate with everyone else, there will be n(n−1) communication channels open. When n=only 40, n(n−1)=40×39=1560.

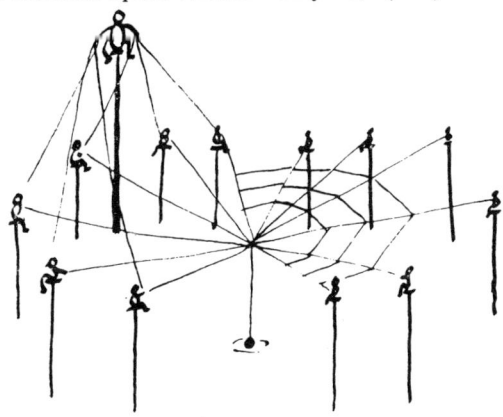

Three of the main ways by which institutions reduce their variety:

1. A boss constrains the freedom of his subordinates.

2. Rigid connexions called rules constrain the interactions of the elastic threads.

3. Someone shoots the cat: the institution does not accept arbitrary interference, and forces those with whom it interacts into stereotypes.

Proliferation of variety

If there are n people in a system, and each of them has variety x (each can adopt x number of possible states), then the variety of the total system thus defined will be x^n.

So if there are only forty people (n=40), each of whom has only two possible states (x=2), there are still 2^{40} possible states of the system.

$2^{40}=1,099,511,627,776$.

In the real world, we find that increased freedom (including new opportunities) proliferates variety to a point where our respected institutions cannot any longer cope with it.

Hypotheses

The relaxation time of the institutional system is now on the average longer than the average interval between perturbations, with the result that the institutional system is permanently unstable.

Since permanent instability feeds on itself (because there is no recognizable stable condition on which to base learning and adaptation), this instability is likely to become, like the wave's instability, catastrophic.

7 EVOLVING STRATEGIES

7.1 Systems Design

W. T. Singleton
Department of Applied Psychology, University of Aston, Birmingham

1 Men and Machines

The aim of technology is to provide man with a variety of devices which will increase his ability to control and manipulate his environment. The interdependence of these devices and their human operators has become one of the distinguishing characteristics of our civilization: men rarely work today without the help of machines, and, conversely, machines will not go on working for very long without some human intervention. Work is done by what are commonly known as 'man/machine systems'. The simplest system of this kind—comprising one man and one machine—is the basic production unit, the basic fighting unit and, often, the basic leisure unit.

The object for which any man/machine system is designed will be achieved only if all its components are matched to each other, and interact in ways appropriate to their common purpose. The properties and performance of each component can be properly assessed only in the context of the system. A speedometer which will serve its purpose for twenty years might be thought better than one which will do so for only five, but as a component of a low-price car which is itself designed to last only five years the second instrument will be the better, since it will be cheaper. Again, there can be no intrinsically 'best' seat: the best seat for the crane operator will certainly not be the best for the television viewer. Machines designed without due regard to the mental and physical capacities of those who are to use, control and maintain them are unlikely to be well designed—it is the performance of the man/machine system as a whole which is the measure of efficiency.

The need to assess components in their relationship to the systems of which they form part, applies no less to human components than it does to the mechanical components which they use.

Acknowledgement

Reprinted, by permission, from W. T. Singleton, 'Systems design' in *Applied Ergonomics,* Vol. 2, No. 3, 1971, IPC Science and Technology Press.

Systems design differs from engineering design in the importance it attaches to the human operator as an integral part of the system to be designed, and in the emphasis it lays on the suitability of all components for the functions to be allocated to them for the achievement of the overall purpose. This broader concept of the task, the growing complexity of equipment, the mounting cost of design errors and the need to develop new systems quickly all combine to demand a critical examination of the design process itself. The success of the systems approach to design depends on the close collaboration of the designer, the engineer and the human factors specialist (or ergonomist).

2 Aspects of the Systems Design Process

The logical approach to the design task is to break it down into a pattern of decisions which lays due emphasis on the complementary engineering and

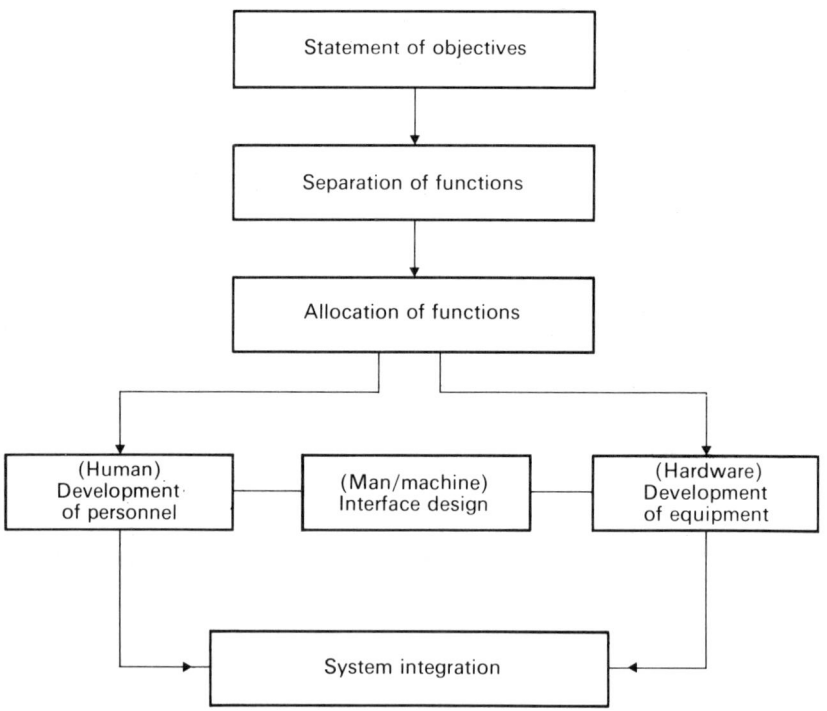

Figure 1 *The systems design process*

human factors, and which is applicable in principle to all systems design problems. This process, as outlined in Figure 1 may appear simple but will seldom prove so in practice: each of the many variables is likely to influence others, and decisions concerning the allocation of functions, interface design (i.e. the design of the connecting links), and training all interact to an extent which makes it necessary for the systems designer to evaluate many alternatives before reaching his final decision.

Allowance has often to be made for a number of conflicting requirements, and in the more complex cases it can be virtually impossible for the designer to envisage and evaluate the many alternative patterns which can result from the permutation of the possible solutions of the problems with which he is faced. For this reason research is being undertaken into methods of increasing his capacity to evaluate alternatives, by the use of computers and other aids in the designing of new systems.

Statement of objectives

The purpose of a system is to accept certain inputs and transform them into the required outputs. The ranges of acceptable inputs and required outputs, together with their time relationships, form a statement of the objectives of the system.

Even at this stage, compromises are already being made with engineering feasibility, cost and user requirements. Stating objectives may appear to be a straightforward logical exercise but it entails a very complex, essentially political set of decisions; which is why, in an industrial company, objectives are set by high level committees. This, of course, does not excuse needless vagueness; and the insistence on a specification, as for example in Figure 2, can help to exert a necessary discipline. There are always some aspects of the specification, e.g. aesthetic considerations, which cannot be stated numerically, but, fortunately, since the recipient of the specification is another human operator (usually with a title such as 'project engineer') these can be conveyed by verbal descriptions.

3 Separation of Functions

The systems designer must think in terms of functions; in terms, that is, of the activities required, as opposed to the ways in which they are to be effected by components. This ability is valuable in dealing with relatively straightforward systems, and becomes essential as they grow in complexity. For example, where power is required the amount necessary is initially more important than the means of obtaining it: diesel engines and electric motors are physical devices for transducing energy, and in designing a system the

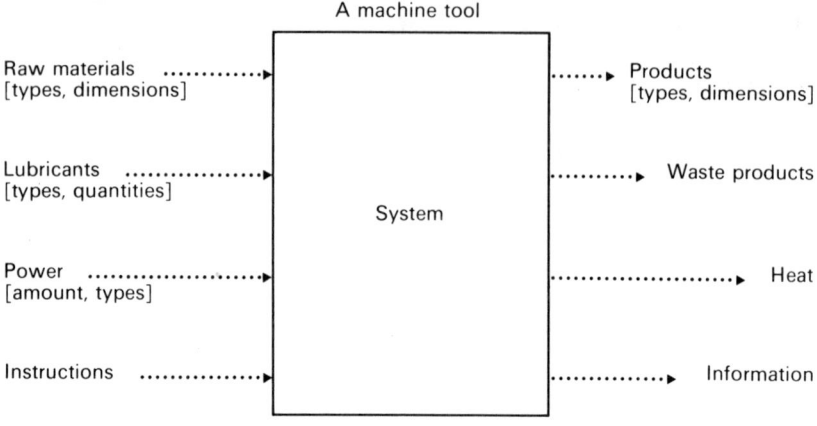

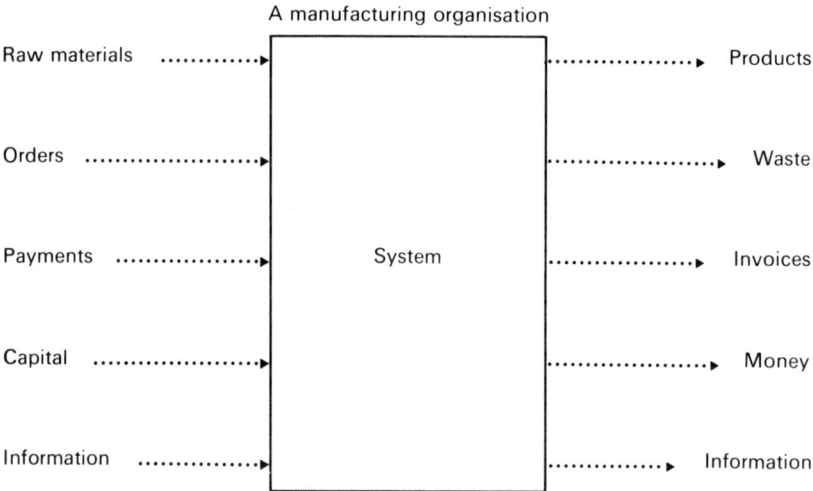

Figure 2 *Statement of objectives. The top diagram shows all the inputs and outputs to a machine tool. The designer must know or estimate all of these factors and the system he designs is, he hopes, the compromise best able to maximize the most wanted feature or features. For example, high versatility (many products) may be at the expense of high power requirement or high waste figures, and the best compromise must be achieved. The system can be much more complicated, for example a manufacturing organization as shown in the bottom diagram. Here the good manager still tries to maximize certain factors, e.g., money with fixed orders and capital.*

decision as to which should be used is best left for later consideration.

Again, the task of the designer of computers or other electronic circuits will be greatly simplified if he thinks in terms of 'logic elements' (e.g. and-, or- and no- elements) as his building bricks and does not concern himself overmuch with the electronic means whereby these elements do what is required of them.

Perhaps most important of all, initial analysis into functions simplifies subsequent decisions as to what the activities of the human and mechanical components in the system shall be. Figure 3 shows two illustrations of this separation of functions at a gross level. These would need to be further subdivided before the 'allocation of functions' could be made.

4 Allocation of Functions

It may be helpful at this point to trace the historical development of this approach to the problem of allocating functions between human and mechanical components. Until about 1950, military design was pursued in terms of simple on-line competition with the enemy, and the criteria for allocation of functions were based on the relative abilities of men and machines. This thinking was the origin of the *Fitts List* (produced by Paul Fitts, later Director of the Human Performance Centre, University of Michigan) illustrated in Table 1. It may be noted here that although the relative capacities of man and machine are apparent in broad outline, as indicated in this list, more research is necessary in order to express them in quantitative terms: at present the designer has often to resort to experiment to determine these factors in a particular system.

After 1950 the complexity of weapons systems increased to the point where cost became of critical importance, even to the larger nations, and a new criterion—the cost/value function—was added as a measure of the relative cost and effectiveness of performing functions with human operators or mechanical equipment. When these concepts spread into the field of industry, in about 1960, two further criteria were added. The first was the need for integrated tasks—that is, tasks which adequately utilize the abilities of human operators and, at the same time, make allowances for their limitations. The second was the need in large systems for graded tasks matched to the differing levels of ability and seniority to be found in every population. The whole philosophy underlying the allocation of functions is now increasingly centred on the human operator. However large or small the system, its objectives are achieved essentially by one man—the key operator. Other operators, and all the mechanical components used, serve to extend the key operator's capacities at three levels:

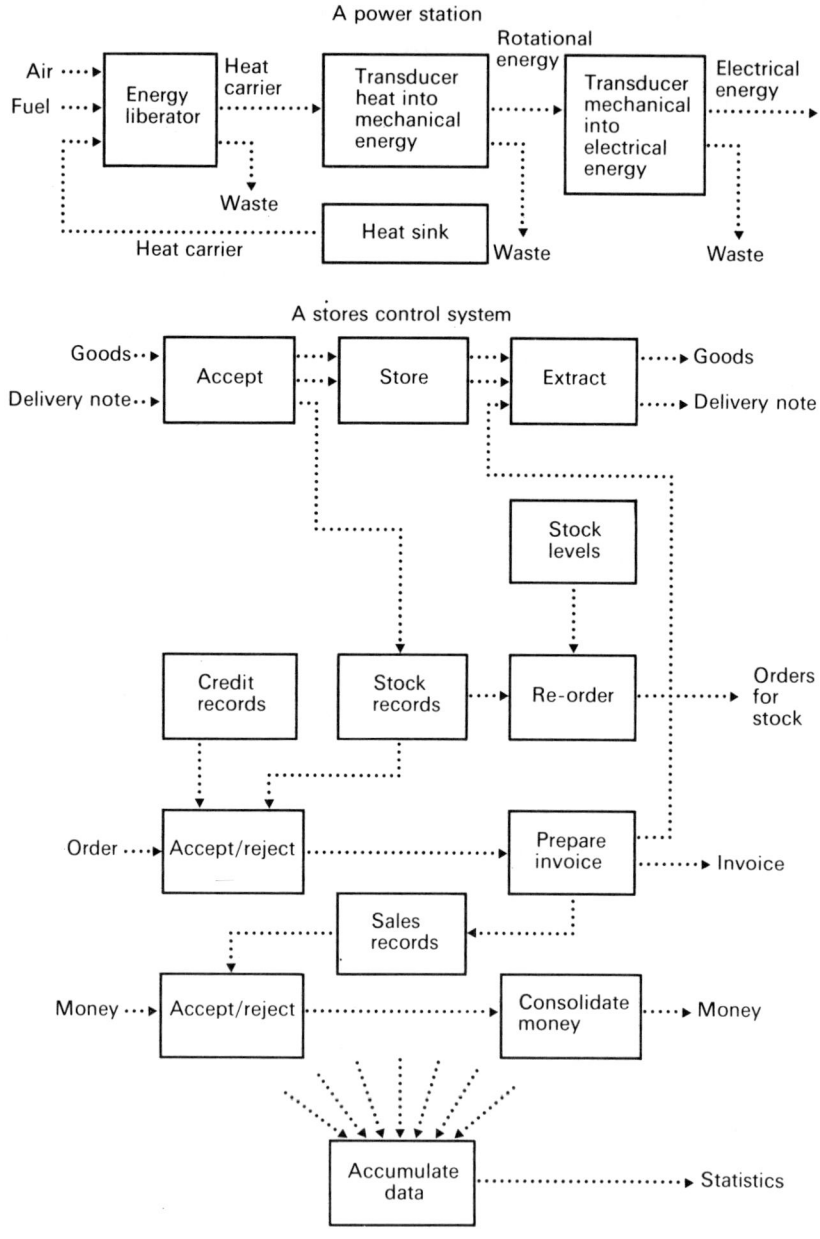

Figure 3   Separation of functions

1 Input—Instruments supplement his senses;

2 Decision making—Other humans, information storage and computer logic aid and his thinking processes;

3 Output—Other power sources supplement his muscles.

5 Personnel Aspects of System Design

Development of personnel

All the personnel decisions must be made in relation to the three main phases of activity with which human operators will be concerned: setting up the system, operating it and providing the maintenance it will invariably require. It may be noted that, although in so-called 'automatic' systems, the human operator is not employed on-line, he is still needed for the other activities: there is no basis in fact for the common assumption that all human factor problems can be eliminated by designing automatic devices.

The extent of the field covered by the human factors specialist in systems design is shown in Figure 4.

6 The Task Description

The basis and first step of all human factors work is the task description—that is, a simple statement of the functions which have been allocated to human operators. In the case of the design of new systems, this can be done at the initial stage by logically determining the job of individual operators from the demands of the system. In systems already in operation, the task descriptions are determined by observing and measuring what the operators in fact do.

The function of task description in co-ordinating the human factors information required in the system analysis, is outlined in Figure 5.

7 The Job Specification

The next step is to build up job specifications; that is, to determine how many operators will be required, what skills they must have to achieve the system's objectives, which of these skills are to be obtained by selection and which by training, and how the selection and training are to be effected.

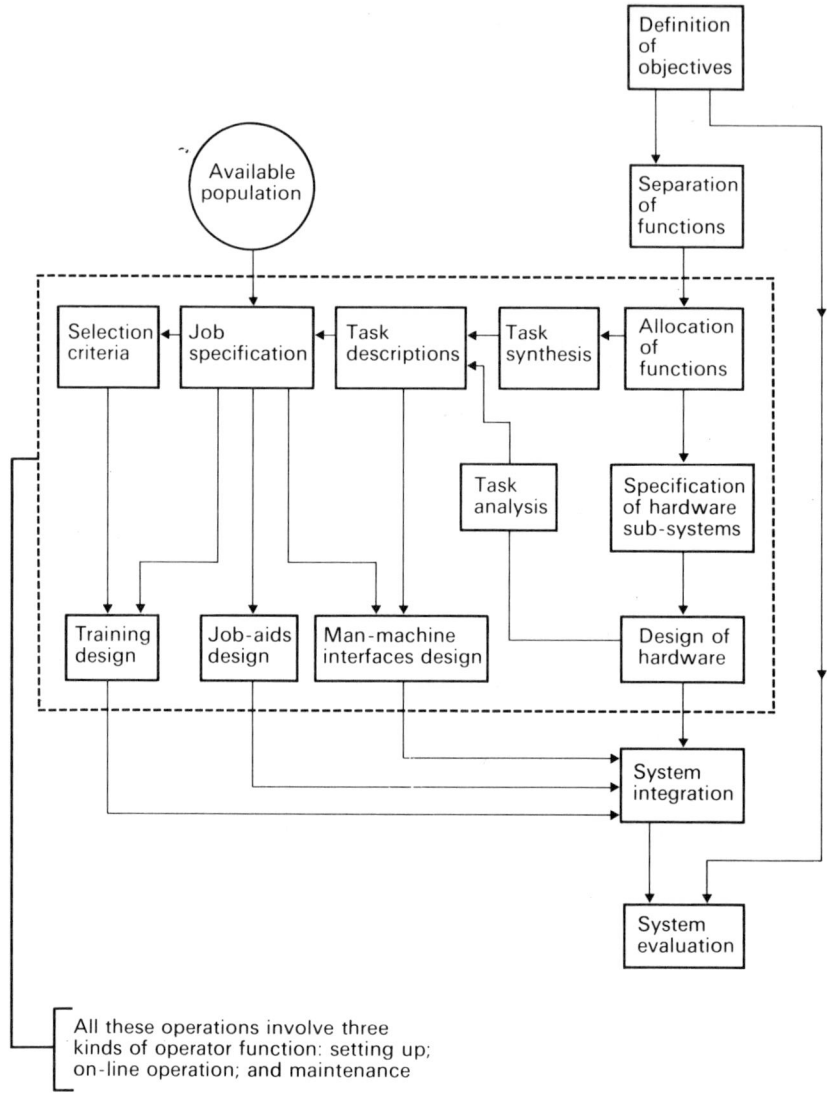

Figure 4 The role of the human factors specialists in systems design.

8 Interface Design

It is not usually difficult to meet the requirements of the human operator in the design of the work space and the environment.

SYSTEMS DESIGN

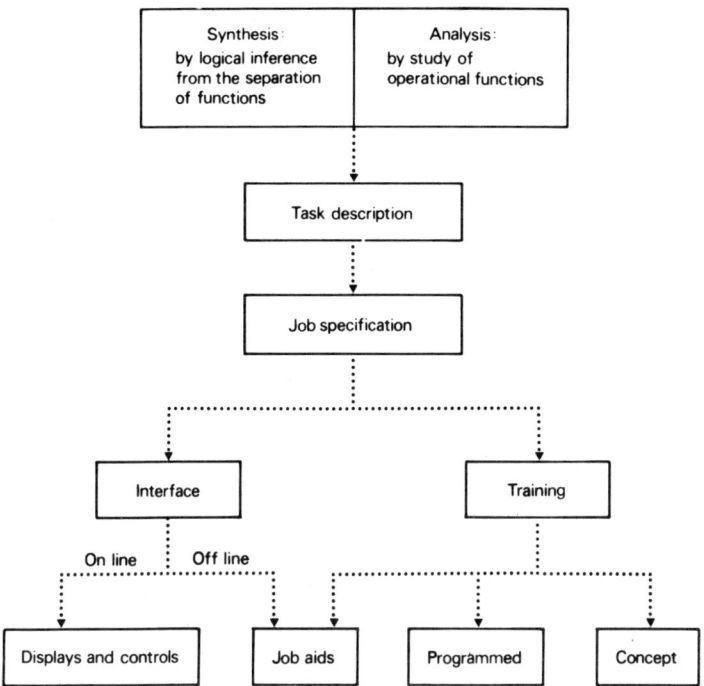

Figure 5 The coordinating role of task description

If machine and man are to be matched to form an integral working unit, close attention must be paid to the area of contact between them—the display and control interface—in order to reconcile their fundamentally different characteristics. The design of the one and the skills of the other must be such that the information output of the machine is adapted to the receptive intake of the man, and the physical output of the man to the control requirements of the machine. The number of variables involved makes this a difficult area of investigation, and there is no unique series of decisions which will lead to a solution: one of the arts of interface design is the consideration—in an order which suits the particular case—of all the variable factors as shown in Figure 6. For the successful design of the machine/man interface (to which the task description and job specification are essential preliminaries), the systems designer depends on the co-operation of the ergonomist and the engineer.

An interface design for a 'programmed' operator, that is the operator who has only to obey rules (for example, to press a switch when a pointer reading reaches a stated value—without knowing what the reading represents or

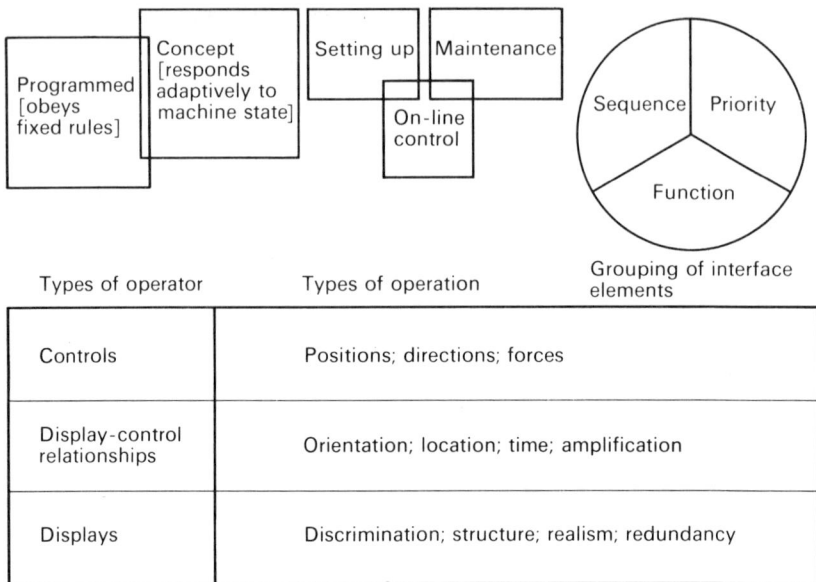

Figure 6 Interface design decision matrix

what the switch does) will differ from the interface required for a 'concept' operator, that is the operator who understands the system and can himself decide the control action appropriate to his interpretation of the machine state. Programmed operators are used considerably in modern systems, and although setting up and maintenance operations are now undertaken mainly by concept operators, there is a trend towards making maintenance a programmed operation (e.g., 'When red lamp lights up, replace component No. 74').

There must be a pattern in both the operator's search for information from the machine displays and his response to what they tell him. This can be established by reference to the sequence of operations (where this is fixed), the relative priorities of different display and control elements (as measured by either frequency of use or consequences of omission), and the functional aspects of the equipment (e.g., control of power or position). All these factors will influence the details of interface elements, including their positioning in relation to each other and the operator, the accuracy of the readings required and the levels of force necessary. Interface design demands far more than the provision of dials to suit the operator's eyes and controls convenient for his limbs. The most superficial study will show that his sense organs and muscles have their limitations, for which allowance must be made, but it is not so obvious that between sense organs and muscles he has computing devices which perform certain functions. It is these computing devices which give rise to the critical interface design problems. The presentation of the necessary data should require of the operator the minimum of thought and computation ('encoding'), and should guide him towards the correct decisions. This calls for consideration of the way in which he will organize the given information in order to reach his decisions, and requires that the data shall be organized as far as possible before it is presented at the interface—which is in effect an allocation of function.

The problems of control dynamics are often mathematically complex in that they require a statement of the time-relationship between control movements and the resultant changes in the state of the system. Large systems may have considerable inertia, resulting in a significant time lag between changes in control settings and the appearance on displays of their full effects. The sometimes impossibly high degree of anticipatory skill such systems require can be reproduced by the use of predictor displays.

9 The Design of Job Aids

The instructions to be provided for the operator are another aspect of the interface problem and close attention must be paid to the method of their presentation in relation to the information they are required to convey. Instructions may be given by legend plates on machines, by charts, diagrams or manuals—with which can now be classed film strips and teaching machine programmes. The design of such manuals and the like as used in British industry offers much scope for improvement (even in such basic aspects as the separation of setting up, on-line control and maintenance), and deserves more attention than it commonly receives. As shown in Figure 5, job aids comprise both training devices and interface elements.

10 Selection and Training

The criteria for selecting and training operators are based on the job specification and will depend on the type of operator required, the complexity of the interface and the availability of training facilities. Concept training, which is essentially education, will be necessary where the operator must understand the system sufficiently well to be able to interpret any development and formulate a method of dealing with the situation it indicates. Such training has little in common with that needed to enable an

Table 1 Fitts List: Relative Advantages of Men and Machines

	Machine	Man
Speed	Much superior.	Lag 1 second.
Power	Consistent at any level. Large, constant standard forces.	2.0 hp for about 10 seconds 0.5 hp for a few minutes 0.2 hp for continuous work over a day.
Consistency	Ideal for: routine; repetition; precision.	Not reliable; should be monitored by machine.
Complex activities	Multi-channel.	Single channel.
Memory	Best for literal reproduction and short term storage.	Large store, multiple access. Better for principles and strategies.
Reasoning	Good deductive.	Good inductive.
Computation	Fast, accurate. Poor at error correction.	Slow, subject to error. Good at error correction.
Input sensitivity	Some outside human senses, e.g. radioactivity.	Wide energy range 10^{12} and variety of stimuli dealt with by one unit; e.g. eye deals with relative location, movement and colour. Good at pattern detection. Can detect signals in high noise levels.
	Can be designed to be insensitive to extraneous stimuli.	Affected by heat, cold, noise and vibration (exceeding known limits).
Overload reliability	Sudden breakdown.	'Graceful degradation'.
Intelligence	None.	Can deal with unpredicted and unpredictable; can anticipate.
Manipulative abilities	Specific.	Great versatility.

operator to learn a series of predetermined patterns of action in response to specific states of the system.

11 Conclusion

It should now be apparent that it is impossible either to assign hard and fast priorities to the various interacting factors which the systems designer must take into account, or to specify the order in which he should make his decisions relating to the allocation of functions, interface design and training. The concepts described above are by no means fanciful, and nothing has been advocated which is not practised intuitively by the good designer. They derive from the fact that if the designer is to be successful in his solution of the range of problems with which he is confronted, he must have either a high level of innate ability and long experience or an understanding of the philosophy of systems design. Marked natural ability is rare, and the rapid emergence of new technologies exacts a heavy penalty for mistakes which may be made while experience is being gained.

Systems design is therefore to be regarded as an educational and disciplinary procedure which encourages a logical and systematic approach to the problems of making design decisions. It does not provide the answers to the questions, but it does define what those questions should be—and it emphasizes the fact that many of them relate to human beings.

Bibliography

de Greene, K. B. (1970) 'Systems psychology'. New York: McGraw-Hill.
Eckman, D. P. (ed) (1961) 'Systems: research and design'. New York: Wiley.
Flagle, C. D., Huggins, W. H., and Roy, R. H. (ed) (1960) 'Operations research and systems engineering'. Baltimore: John Hopkins.
Gagne, R. M. (ed) (1962) 'Psychological principals in system development'. New York: Holt, Rinehart and Winston.
Goode, H. H. and Machol, R. E. (1957) 'Systems engineering'. New York: McGraw-Hill.
Gosling, W. (1962) 'The design of engineering systems'. London: Heywood.
Hall, A. D. (1962) 'A methodology for systems engineering', Princeton: Van Nostrand.
Jones, J. C. and Thornley, D. G. (ed) (1963) Conference on design methods. Oxford: Pergamon.
Rosgrove, P. E. (ed) (1967) 'Developing a computer based information system'. New York: Wiley.

Singleton, W. T., Easterby, R. S. and Whitfield, D. (ed) (1967) 'The human operator in complex systems'. London: Taylor and Francis.

7.2 Human Error in Man-Machine Systems

D. Meister
The Bunker-Ramo Corporation

1 The Effect of Human Performance on System Effectiveness

Because system functioning is often critically dependent upon human activity, the effect of the human on the performance of the equipment he is operating and maintaining is highly significant. Any characteristic of the system which makes it difficult for operators and maintenance men to do their job reduces the efficiency of equipment functioning. This follows because the man and his machine are interdependent.

The way in which human inefficiency is indicated is through *errors* and *time* (delays). For the moment it is enough to consider an error as any deviation from the performance required of the operator to accomplish the system function. The deviation must, of course, impair system functioning if it is to be considered a meaningful error.

The error may reveal itself as:

(a) a failure to perform a required action—that is, an error of omission;

(b) the performance of that action in an incorrect manner—that is, an error of commission; or

(c) its performance out of sequence or at an incorrect time.

Time as an index of performance refers to the operator's failure to complete an equipment task *when* required by the system mission, or his failure to respond quickly enough to some signal or cue requiring an action. The time measure is an error also, expressed, however, in time.

Thus the operator's failure to perform correctly often degrades the performance of his equipment. For example, in the U.S. Post Office the average throughput of parcel sorting machines is 42 per cent of design capacity, of letter sorting machines, 40 to 77 per cent of design capacity (Communications and Systems, 1969). The major factor influencing that throughput is the operator input of parcels and letters.

Acknowledgement

Reprinted, by permission, from D. Meister, *'Human Factors: Theory and Practice'*, © 1971, John Wiley and Sons, New York.

The role of H* in system development is, among other things, to prevent the design of equipment whose characteristics may predispose to operator error. In that sense the analysis of equipment from the standpoint of those factors which could lead to error is an integral part of good design practice.

However, 'good' design practice by which engineers mean the electronic, mechanical, etc. principles which they ordinarily apply to solve design problems will not be sufficient to deal with most human factors design problems. Solutions to these problems require a special way of analyzing equipment—in terms of the effect of equipment upon the operator as well as the effect of the operator on the equipment—and special techniques. This is why a distinctive discipline devoted to solving problems of this sort has developed.

2 Types of error

Error has been previously defined as any deviation from a procedure required to operate or maintain an equipment. One should not assume from this, however, that all errors are alike in terms of their causes or their effects on the system.

Errors may be classified in various ways:

1 In terms of what caused the error.

2 In terms of what the error consequences are.

3 In terms of the stage of system development in which the errors occurred.

3 Error Causes

A distinction must first be made among what can be termed 'system-induced error', 'design-induced error', and 'operator-induced error'.

To design a system requires that one specify not only the individual items of equipment but also the number and types of personnel using the equipment; their background and training; appropriate data resources (e.g., technical manuals, instruction material, blueprints, etc.); logistics (e.g., correct number and type of spares and tools, properly stockpiled); and maintenance programs (e.g., preventive maintenance schedules, methods of malfunction detection and correction).

Human factors.

HUMAN ERROR IN MAN/MACHINE SYSTEMS

Errors may arise not only from inadequacies in the design of the individual equipment but also from inadequacies in the 'software' features mentioned in the previous paragraph; for example, specifying too few operational personnel or personnel with too little skill to perform required jobs will lead to error. Providing too few or inadequate tools or spares will also predispose to error. Such problems, which we term system error, cannot be blamed on the design of the individual equipment or on the operator himself; they reflect deficiencies in the manner in which the total system was planned. System-induced error, therefore, describes errors made by personnel which result from the inadequate design of the total system.

Design-induced error results from inadequacies in the design of the individual equipment. The resulting equipment characteristics create special difficulties for the operator which substantially increase the potentiality for error. Examples of improperly human engineered equipment are very common.

'The_____ ... (has) a diabolical arrangement of three identical knobs in a vertical row on the extreme left of the instrument panel.... None of the three controls is lighted and the vent pull is unlabelled. It would be quite easy for the_____driver to put out his headlights when he intended to close the fresh air vent or to cover his windshield with water when he needed lights.' (*CR*, January 1967, p. 35.)

'One drawback of_____'s ... styling is limited rear visibility. Its rear deck slopes too sharply to be seen from the driver's seat, making it difficult to judge distance when backing up.... In all ... of the speciality cars ... wide rear roof pillars create blind spots that we consider dangerous.' (*CR*, July 1967, p. 356.)

'_____has recessed controls so far into the instrument panel that operating them is difficult with a gloved hand, and the ignition key is difficult to turn bare-handed.' (*CR*, January 1968, p. 28.)

'... The speedometer's index lines were printed on the inner instrument face, but the indicating numbers were printed on a clear plastic lens at considerable distance out from the index lines, making the speedometer particularly difficult to interpret accurately.' (*CR*, February 1968, p. 88.)

Operator-induced errors can be traced directly to an inadequacy on the part of the individual who makes that error. Errors resulting from lack of capability (e.g., deficient vision) training, skill, motivation, or fatigue would be categorized as operator-induced errors. Driving the wrong way on a properly marked one-way street is an example of operator error that cannot be referred either to the system or the individual equipment.

301

In examining an error, therefore, we are faced with a number of possible causes. Assume for example, that a circuit is miswired during production. The error may have been caused by inattention or lack of skill on the part of the worker; by an incorrect blueprint, by inadequate lighting, by an improperly designed tool, etc.

A word of caution. It is often difficult to make an unequivocal assignment of error cause. Lack of training which produces an operator error may result in part from a deficiency in planning the system. This deficiency may have resulted in providing the operator with inadequate skill. Is this a system or an operator error? Hence all casual categories must be viewed with some scepticism. Moreover, to assign a casual classification does not mean that one has understood the error source or mechanism. The categories supplied above are merely a handy means of sorting errors into smaller 'bins'.

4 Error Consequences

The effect of an error is also a variable. Imagine that a timing circuit has been miswired. Depending on the function performed by the circuit and the system of which it is a part, the miswiring may simply cause the speedometer of an automobile to read 5 m.p.h. less than actual speed, or it may cause an autopilot to supply incorrect steering directions to an aircraft, leading to the latter's destruction.

Table 1 presents, among other things, a classification of potential error consequences, ranging from the relatively minor (delay in system performance) to the most severe (loss of life). Note that these consequences are affected by the stage of system development at which they occur: errors occurring in operation are more severe than those occurring in production and test, because in the former they are more likely to affect the equipment user.

A major distinction is between what we term 'human-initiated failures' (HIF) and human error. HIF is an error which results in an equipment malfunction. Hence, it is merely one subcategory of errors in general, many of which do not result in equipment failure. Because an equipment failure is a rather striking event, data on HIF are somewhat easier to collect than on errors which do not result in equipment breakdown. The data in Table 2 all deal with errors which resulted in one way or another in equipment failures.

There are other ways of differentiating error consequences. The effect of some errors is immediate, while that of others is delayed. The automobile driver who turns his steering wheel the wrong way in a skid experiences the

Table 1 Error Classification Categories

	Stage of System Development			
Design		Production	Test	Operation
Type of error				
Design error		Fabrication error	Operating error	Operating error
		Inspection error	Installation error	Installation error
			Maintenance error	Maintenance error
Casual Factors				
Inappropriate function allocation		Incorrect blueprints	Inadequate/incomplete technical data	Inadequate/incomplete technical data
Failure to implement requirements		Incorrect instructions	Inadequate logistics	Inadequate logistics
Poor human engineering design		Inadequate tools	Poor human engineering design	Inadequate training/skill
		Inadequate environment	Poor workplace layout	Inadequate motivation
		Inadequate training/skill		Poor human engineering design
		Poor human engineering design of equipment		Poor workplace layout
		Poor workplace layout		Inadequate environment
				Overload conditions
				Task complexity
				Poor personnel selection
Error Consequences				
Inadequately designed equipment		Scrapped/reworked equipment	Delay in system operations	Delay in system operations
		Production delays	Human-initiated malfunctions	Human-initiated malfunctions
		Higher cost	System breakdown	System breakdown
		Malfunctioning equipment classified as functioning	Failure to accomplish test	Failure to accomplish mission
		Good equipment rejected	Degradation in system performance	Degradation in system performance
			Possible danger and loss of life	Possible danger and loss of life

immediate effects of that error. The error of a production worker who makes a poor solder connection has no consequences until the connection ultimately breaks and fails the equipment.

Because of the relative immediacy of error effects, some errors are more visible than others. Many workmanship errors are difficult to discover even during inspection. Errors performed in equipment operation are usually quite visible because they affect the equipment or the equipment user.

Error visibility may also produce different error consequences. If the error is apparent to the man who made it, the chances of its being rectified are increased. This is one reason why errors made with discrete tasks (e.g., flipping the wrong switch) are more quickly corrected than those made with continuous tasks (e.g., tracking a moving signal).

Some errors are frequent, but minor in their effect; others are infrequent, but critical to system performance. In part, this is because error consequences vary as a function of the system in which they occur. Errors in firing a rifle at a target are frequent but will not lead (except in combat, and often not even then) to disaster. The pilot's failure to release his landing gear while landing an aircraft is infrequent, but invariably results in equipment damage.

Making an error need not necessarily lead to disastrous consequences. Many equipments are so designed that even if one makes an error, that error, once noted, can be rectified by performing the operation again. This is actually characteristic of much, if not most, of our equipment. If I turn my television set to the wrong channel, I still have the option of turning it to the right one. Error is, therefore, not necessarily synonymous with failure to accomplish the equipment's function. On the other hand, if I miscalculate my braking distance on a slippery street, my chances of rectifying the error (in time) are slight.

A great deal also depends on how one defines an error. In many military systems mission accomplishment requires such precise operation that error *may* be synonymous with system failure. If a bomb must be dropped no more than 100 yards from a target, then dropping it 105 yards from the target constitutes a system failure. On the other hand, as we have seen, many non-defence systems are quite forgiving of error. It is therefore necessary to determine the significance of the individual error and the means by which it contributes to mission failure before the piling up of error frequencies means a great deal.

5 Error in System Development

As Table 1 suggests, errors may also be classified in terms of the stage of

Table 2 System Failure as a Function of Human Error

Type of system	Type of failure	Number of Operations or time period	Failures resulting from human error (per cent)	Reference
'Defense'	System failures	4½ years	40	Cornell (1968)
X-15 Aircraft	Unsuccessful flights	164	12	Wilson & Gaffney (ND)
Missiles	Accidents	3 years	65	Willis (1962b)
Missiles/aircraft	Unspecified problems	Unknown	40	Willis (1962a)
Missiles Failure reports	548 failure reports	46		Willis (1962b)
Ships	Collisions, floodings, groundings	4 years	63.6	Willis (1962a)
Aircraft	Major accidents	47 accidents	51	Willis (1962a)
Missiles/aircraft	Equipment failures	Unknown	26–50	Willis (1962a)
Missiles	Human-initiated malfunctions	3829 failure reports	20–53	Shapero & Bates (1960)
Rocket engines	Human-initiated malfunctions	600 failure reports	35	Majesty (1962)
Missiles	Holds, postponements, aborts	Unknown	40	Majesty (1962)
Aircraft	Equipment failures	1642 failure reports	37	Meister (personal data)
Missiles	Failure reports	122 major system failures	35	Meister (1967)
Nuclear weapons	Production defects	23 000 defects	82	Rook (1962)
Three electronic systems	Human-initiated malfunctions	1820 failure reports	23–45	LeVan (1960)
Missiles	Equipment failures	1425 failure reports	20	Meister (1961)
Missiles	Human-initiated malfunctions	35 000 failure reports	20–30	Meister (1965)
Various	Engineering design errors	Unknown	2–43	Rigby & Cooper (1961)
Aircraft	Accidents	Unknown	60	Rigby & Cooper (1961)
B–52 aircraft	Human-initiated malfunctions and other human-related failures	552 failures	36	Meister et al. (1970)
Air-defense	Maintenance-induced malfunctions	2.3	11.7 (wholly) 14.1 (partially)	Robinson et al. (1970)

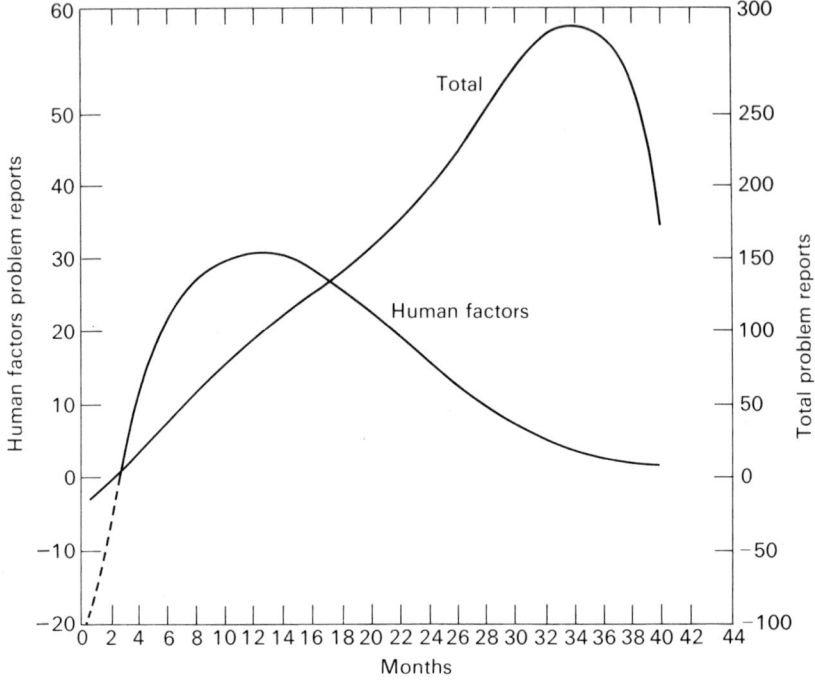

Figure 1

system development in which they occur. Traditionally, there are four stages of system development: *design, production, test,* and *operation*. Although the following simple definition fails to do justice to the complexities of each stage, it is sufficient to say that equipment is designed in the design stage, turned into hardware during production, tested to ensure that it meets specification during test, and operated by its users during operations. The phasing of these stages overlaps so that, in development of major systems, design of some assemblies or equipments may be going on while others are being produced and tested.

Errors of improper design can be termed 'design errors'. This type of error, illustrated earlier, occurs during the design of the equipment, but its effects are experienced only in operation of the equipment as an operator error.

Errors made in fabricating the designed equipment can be termed 'production' or 'workmanship' errors. Like design errors, the effects of production errors are delayed; they occur during fabrication but manifest their primary effect during test and operation.

Errors occurring during installation and maintenance of the equipment

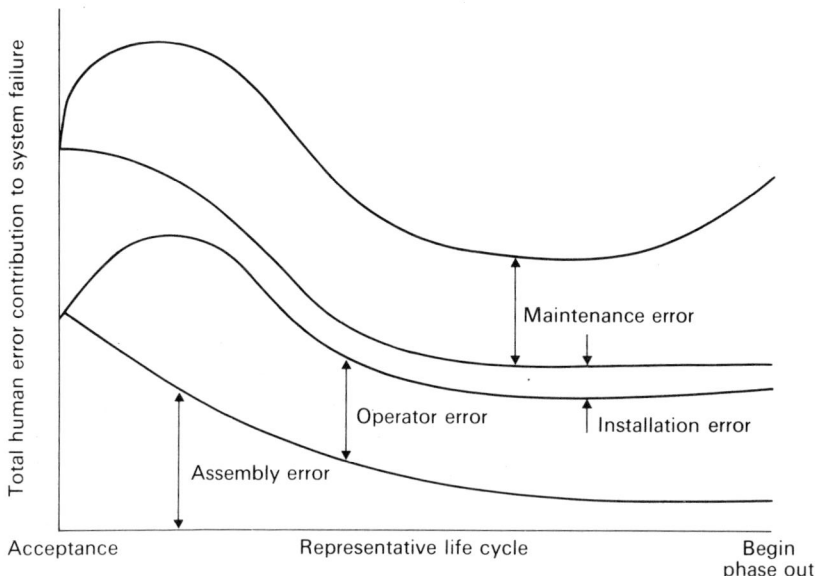

Figure 2

(which may occur either during test or operations) are 'installation' or 'maintenance' errors. These too have delayed effects.

Errors performed during testing are either operating, installation, or maintenance errors. Operating and maintenance errors recur, of course, throughout the period of system use.

The relative frequency of errors during system development is largely an unknown primarily because there are few, if any, efforts to collect error data by the contractor and the user (who might be embarrassed by such data). The lack of systematic efforts—either by the contractor or the government—to collect error data in terms of frequency, causal factors, and criticality is a serious deficiency. Without such data it is difficult to

(a) assess the importance of error in influencing equipment operations;

(b) pinpoint factors in system development which could be improved;

(c) predict the operational performance efficiency one can expect of a system, where that efficiency is influenced by personnel errors.

One piece of data does exist. Van Buskirk and Huebner (1962) have analysed the relative frequency of human-initiated failures (HIF) as a function of all the equipment problems reported in one missile system development program; their results are shown in Figure 1. Figure 2 indicates what one analyst considers to be changes in error frequency following acceptance of the equipment for operational use. Note that there is an initial build-up in error, followed by a progressive decline until a relatively stable frequency is achieved over the period of system use.

6 Error Importance

Despite the relative lack of data, there is substantial evidence to indicate that error is a crucial factor in system performance. This is shown by Table 2 which lists a representative sample of studies describing the frequency of error and its effect on equipment. Data on the specific systems or the time period described in the reports are sometimes lacking. The errors described are those which resulted in failure of the equipment to function (HIF), the scrapping of equipment components, or accidents. Obviously, this is mixing apples and oranges; scrapping components during production is not equivalent to losing an aircraft and crew. For this very reason, however, Table 2 presents a representative cross-section of the types of situations in which errors occur and their consequences.

The mean percentage of system failures (i.e., equipment disabled or prevented from accomplishing its function) resulting from these errors is about 40 per cent. Presumably, the remainder of these failures resulted from normal equipment wearout, non-operator-related design deficiencies, or other causes which can be ascribed only remotely to personnel.

The irreducible minimum of error to be expected even under optimal conditions—if there is such a minimum—is not known. However, an average of 40 per cent equipment failures resulting from human error, together with their effects, suggests that error is not only frequent, but significant for system performance—hence worth considering as a factor in equipment development. The study by Meister *et al.* (1970) indicates that HIF significantly reduced the mean time between failure (MTBF) of the equipments involved.

7 Design Error

Design errors are manifested in improperly designed equipment [as determined by H standards in MIL-STD 1472 (United States, 1969)], in failure to assign effective roles to equipment and personnel, and in failure to meet system requirements. We exclude from this definition those preliminary design efforts which are eliminated before final drawings or specifications are released. Obviously, many design errors are made while the engineer is considering a number of alternatives. Only those design errors which are *not* caught and which, appearing in the final design, remain to influence the operational usage of the system are within the definition of the term.

Functional allocation error

The first type of design error is to assign the man or the machine to a function for which it is not suited. This means either of two possibilities:

CASE I. The human is assigned to a function which he cannot perform or which could more effectively be performed by a machine component; for example, if a man were asked to time the speed of a 100 yard dash by counting his pulse-beats during the race, we would say that the function could better be performed by an electronic timer.

CASE II. A function is allocated to a machine component which might better be performed by the human. For example, a computer might be designed to make probabilistic judgments of the aesthetic value of paintings.

In the allocation of functions we assume that an error occurs when a function is assigned to a machine component when there is no significant advantage in having that function performed by the machine. In other words, the simplest and best design is always a manual one, provided that there are no significant advantages (e.g., performance capability, reliability, maintainability, and cost or convenience for the user) for automatic design.

The engineer may view this assumption as being unwarranted. However, the reason for selecting a human to perform a function over a machine, when all factors are essentially equal, is that mechanization has more complex consequences than does manual operation. Maintenance and logistics requirements, for example, are substantially increased by automatization. Unwarranted automation leads to unbridled technological proliferation. We recognize that this choice-principle may conflict with the engineer's design tendencies. Because of the engineer's training (and the average user's laziness), it is more natural for him to automatize whatever functions he can. The long-range effects of undisciplined technology (both ecological and psychological) are, however, beginning to become more painful to the user.

After system functions are defined, they must be allocated among machine or crew components (literally, who is to do what?). At the gross system level involving major functions, allocation is in part constrained by the nature of the function. For example, we would not ask the pilot to act as a jet engine, or demand of the operator that he act as an air defence warning station without radar. Thus, at the most molar function levels, the decision as to whether the man or the machine should perform a particular function is usually immediately apparent.

At more detailed function levels (corresponding perhaps to the sub-system and assembly level in equipment), the tradeoffs between man and machine are more molecular and less obvious. Often both the man and the machine can do the job; the question becomes, which can do it better? The analyst is concerned not with an entire system function but with such things as whether a series of manually timed operations (requiring a human to switch on a series of timing mechanisms) will be as effective as an automatic timing circuit which requires no human intervention. Naturally, multiple criteria are involved in making such decisions: cost, safety, performance reliability, maintainability, etc.

Because most function allocation problems are meaningful for H consideration only at relatively molecular levels, the lists of characteristics which differentiate men from machines (Fitts, 1951) (e.g., 'men are better at inductive reasoning, machines are better at monitoring') are of little practical value. These general characteristics apply primarily to top level system allocations which, as we have seen, are usually made on the basis of common sense or constrained severely by over-all design concepts.

Moreover, these 'men are better at . . ., machines are better at . . .' characteristics have other deficiencies: they are black or white and never any shade of grey; and they are non-quantitative, when the engineer making a trade-off wants to know, 'better by how much?'

Trade-offs at molecular decision points involve many parameters, while those at the top level usually involve only one overriding consideration; this is why top level function allocations are easier to make. The trade-offs between the manually operated switch and the timing circuit include such criteria as performance requirements (e.g., how precise must the timing be?); (which costs more?); reliability (probability of error *vs.* probability of circuit failure).

Since the decision involves a number of criteria, the proper combination of these criteria is quite complex. Because of this, allocation trade-offs are ultimately based almost invariably on purely intuitive methods. There are formal methods of making such allocation trade-offs (Teeple, 1961), but their validity is dubious and in actual practice they are difficult to apply. Usually they require more data than anyone could possibly have at the time the trade-off decision is required. A typical example is Barton's (1964) queuing technique for determining manpower in early system development, a technique that requires a minimum of eight data inputs, some of which cannot be determined until after the system is operational.

The H specialist's concern in such allocation trade-offs is to ensure that the human component gets a fair shake in the trade-off. The engineer's very natural tendency to select an automatic means of accomplishing a function in preference to a manual means (this is quite understandable; after all, it's his business to create hardware mechanisms to replace human labour) makes it possible that he will not pay full attention to the human side of the picture. Even when the engineer's allocation is justified, the H specialist wishes to ensure that a full hearing has been given to the possibility that a human component could or should do the job. In a sense, it is like being a lawyer for the human plaintiff; once the jury issues a verdict, the question is settled, but the defendant has a right to a full and complete hearing.

Once an allocation has been made, it is very difficult to determine whether it was or was not made correctly. Even when a machine component has been erroneously selected over one which is human, the machine component will probably function and may even perform relatively well; the cost the user pays because machine function is not as efficient as human function is often invisible. The reverse is also true, and the H specialist is just as interested in avoiding Case I errors as those of Case II. Deciding to include an unnecessary human function which requires an additional operator may cost a fantastic sum over the life span of a system. One estimate of overall human cost the writer encountered was $8.50 an hour per man. Thus over a five-year system life (2000 man hours per year) one unneeded man would add approximately another $85,000 to the cost.

Failure to implement human requirements

A second design error is failure to include in the design certain functions which are required if the operator is to perform in accordance with system requirements or at his maximum efficiency. For example, a display needed to warn the operator of a potential emergency condition may not be included in the design.

This type of error occurs most often when the function is only implicit in system requirements, and the designer fails to include the controls and displays needed to perform the function. Where the requirement is explicitly cited in the engineer's statement of work, he rarely ignores it. An example of an implicit requirement might be the need to provide a display to warn of an impending emergency when the emergency is only a potential one. Most statements of work (SOW) describe operating requirements rather completely but leave 'conditional' requirements (those dealing with situations which *might*, but do not necessarily *have*, to occur) to the imagination of the equipment designer. Such requirements may well become obvious if the system is analysed in depth. However, design, at least in its initial conceptual stages, proceeds very rapidly; by the time the implicit requirement is uncovered, the basic design concept may be so formalized that it is difficult to accommodate it.

Because of the way in which many SOW's are developed, with their concentration on major hardware requirements, the implicit human factors requirements are among those which tend to be overlooked. This does not mean that the system will necessarily fail because such implicit human factors requirements are late in being discovered. After all, the major system needs have usually been taken care of. However, the failure to implement implicit requirements means that the system contains a certain weakness which under great stress may reveal itself.

One example of such a design error is the following, reported by Gordon, 1964:

'During a silo missile accident, approximately 18 000 gallons of diesel fuel were gravity fed into the silo and became the main source of fuel for a follow-on 18 hour fire. There was no way to shut off the main feed line, since no one had provided an emergency cut-off valve for this auxiliary system.'

Obviously, no one had anticipated an operational problem in which an auxiliary fuel shut-off valve would have been necessary.

Human engineering design errors

A third very common design error is to fail to ensure that man and machine components interact effectively (inadequate human engineering of equipment). Specifically,

(a) failure to select the most appropriate control-display component for the particular operator function to be performed (e.g., selecting a bank of toggle switches to activate multiple step functions when a rotary control would be more efficient);

(b) failure to arrange controls/displays or other components (e.g., handles or access spaces) in a manner which will permit personnel to use them as rapidly and accurately as possible (e.g., placing a display and the control which is to be used in conjunction with it in widely separated locations);

(c) requiring the operator to use information or perform operations he does not need to accomplish his job (e.g., giving him a display for information on which he cannot act because the equipment for implementing that action has not been provided). Or the reverse—failing to give the operator enough information to do his job, an error often found in procedure development.

Because there are errors of detail, it is often difficult for the engineer to recognize their potentially damaging consequences. Why should the misplacement of a control or the selection of an improper display scale make that much difference to performance? The requirement to human engineer an equipment is even more conditional than the requirements discussed previously. In this third class of design error the engineer deals with a contingent, hence somewhat nebulous possibility; the effect of an improper design characteristic may or may not affect the operator, and even if it affects the operator's performance, the latter may or may not influence overall equipment functioning.

Examples of possible errors resulting from human engineering design deficiencies were given in the automobile examples cited earlier. These design deficiencies may lead to accidents, but, on the other hand, they may not. Inadequate rear visibility could lead to a backup accident, but maybe not. Misinterpretation of an inadequate speedometer scale may lead the driver to drive faster or slower than he intended, and that error could result in an accident, but only with a certain probability, never a certainty.

Are design errors frequent and significant enough that the reader is convinced that this is a factor to which he must pay attention in his design? Do such errors in fact influence equipment/system performance negatively? The evidence is less satisfactory than we would wish. Table 2 describes mostly workmanship errors because these are relatively easy to detect and describe.

It is much more difficult to tease out design errors in function allocation or in failure to include human requirements in equipment design. When these lead to failure or accidents, their causal relationship to the failure or accident may be difficult to establish. It must be emphasized that systematic studies of design error are the exception rather than the rule. Industries do not publicize their design errors; when they become aware of them, they attempt to conceal them. It is, moreover, very difficult to assess the significance of such errors. Obviously, no designer is perfect, and to that extent errors of judgement will inevitably occur. Design error becomes apparent only when there are major violations of design principles which lead to catastrophic consequences.

The factors which predispose to design error are the following:

1 Incomplete analysis of the requirements of the equipment and the total system.

2 Too hasty a design effort.

3 Predetermined attitudes or biases in the designer to one or other mode of design solution.

4 Excessive reliance by the engineer on his design experience to the detriment of design analysis ('shooting from the hip', so to speak).

8 Production Error

Many of the statistics reported in Table 2 refer to errors made in fabricating hardware: production errors. The great majority of HIF which comprise much of our statistical data on human error in system development involve production error. Of the 122 major system failures analysed by Meister (1967), the great majority resulted from production defects.

There are several reasons for the preponderance of production defects in our statistics. In contrast to records kept of human error in operational use of an equipment, records of components scrapped or repaired during production are usually very complete. Also, operator-induced HIF (resulting from human engineering design errors) are usually substantially less than HIF resulting from installation and maintenance. For example, only one HIF was reported in a two-month sampling of error data taken in missile test operations (Ehrlich and Horner, 1962).

A production error is actually a *workmanship* error, that is, an error made by the individual production worker which results directly in a failure of the manufactured article to meet a specified standard (usually blueprint). The 'visibility' of the production error arises from two sources: (1) to the extent that the standard is unambiguous, as in a blueprint, it is relatively simple to determine when a deviation from that standard exists; (2) a major part of manufacturing (inspection) has a specific responsibility for looking for and discovering such deviations.

Types of production error

In view of the variety of things that a production worker does in the course of fabricating equipment, he has many opportunities to make different kinds of errors. Table 3 lists a sample of workmanship errors reported by Rook (1962).

We may wonder how the small error rates reported in Table 3 can result in serious scrap/reject frequencies. There are two reasons: (a) several errors may be made in assembling an individual component; (b) considering the thousands of individual components assembled during a production run, the cumulative volume of these failures becomes impressive.

Table 3 Characteristic Errors Observed in Production

Definition of Error	Error Rate
Soldering operation results in solder splash	0.001
Soldering operation results in excess solder	0.0005
Soldering operation results in insufficient solder	0.002
Soldering operation results in hole in solder	0.07
Component is damaged by burn from soldering iron	0.001
Two wires which can be transposed are transposed	0.0006
A polarized component (diode, etc.) is wired backwards	0.001
A capacitor with preferred polarity is wired backwards	0.001
A solder joint is omitted	0.00005
A component is omitted	0.00003
A component of wrong value is used	0.0002
A lead is left unclipped	0.00003
Staking is omitted on fastener	0.00003
Staking omitted on adjustment	0.00003
Small item such as lockwasher is omitted	0.00003

Other errors which have been observed, but for which error rate data are presently unavailable, include the following:

1 Forcing parts together.

2 Cutting material to wrong dimensions.

3 Improper calibration of check equipment.

4 Holes mislocated, wrong size, or elongated.

5 Mismatched (e.g., incorrect cable connection).

6 Improper processing (heat treatment, aging corrosion treatment).

7 Cracked, torn, ripped, cut, warped, wrinkled, and anything else you can think in terms of bad treatment.

8 Defective potting.

9 Incorrect blueprints.

10 Wire not grounded or missing.

11 Debris found in equipment.

12 Wire pulled loose.

13 Excessive lubricant.

Causes of production error

Although some workmanship defects may be caused by worker deficiencies like lack of training or motivation, many are caused by situations external to the worker which predispose him to make the error (Meister and Rabideau, 1965):

Inadequate Work Space and Poor Work Layout. Highly precise motor manipulations require adequate work space and proper layout. Where containers for parts are not arranged, for example, in accordance with assembly procedures, the probability of selecting an incorrect part increases.

Poor Environmental Conditions (e.g., inadequate lighting, high temperature, and high noise level). Inadequate lighting increases the difficulty of positioning and wiring small components properly; high temperature and noise level reduce work effort.

Inadequate Human Engineering Design (machinery, handtools, and checkout equipment). This factor affects production equipment just as it does operational equipment; for example, in one equipment used to check out autopilot amplifiers in the factory, investigators found test accessories which took up most of the working area, difficulty in hooking up the unit, and poorly laid out control panels (Urmston and Cutchshaw, 1960).

Inadequate Methods of Handling, Transporting, Storing, or Inspecting Equipment. The author recalls an instance of one production department that had an exceptional failure record for one type of highly expensive electronics component until it was discovered that the components were being transported in carts which permitted them to slip off on to the floor. Redesigning the cart cut the failure rate to an acceptable level.

Inadequate Job Planning Information (inadequate or unavailable operating instructions or blueprints). It is not unheard of to find components being fabricated to out-of-date instructions because the information has been delayed in reaching the worker.

Poor Supervision. One production department had a very high defect rate until it was discovered that the supervisor refused to allow his people to sit at the benches at which they worked.

Another factor which cannot be ignored is the complexity of the equipment design which the worker must fabricate. Where design is complex, the difficulty of fabrication presumably increases. [Experimental data on this factor is unavailable, except in the case of inspection processes, where complexity has been shown to be a significant factor affecting inspection accuracy (Harris and Chaney, 1969)]. Designs which are unnecessarily complex represent a distinct form of design error. One of the functions of liaison engineers attached to manufacturing is to make the difficulties of fabricating equipment known to the design engineer. Although it is impossible to ascertain quantitatively the contribution of design complexity to production error, it is probably substantial.

The effect of these factors is to create a work situation favourable to the commission of production errors; that is, the probability of error increases as a function of inadequate production characteristics. Obviously, if one had a factory area with poor lighting, incorrect blueprints, and poor human engineered handtools, the result would be a serious defect rate.

Note that only one small part of this list of factors involves motivation. There is a general tendency to blame fabrication errors on inadequate 'worker motivation'. In part, this is the reason for the widespread popularity of the 'Zero Defects' programme and other production improvement programmes. Presumably, if one could increase the worker's motivation, his error rate would decrease correspondingly. However, as Rook (1965) says, '... Most errors result from SCE (situation-caused errors) rather than from HCE's (human-caused errors). People who continually make goofs tend to be eliminated'.

If one assumes that the factory is a system like any other, in the sense of having a goal (mission), equipment and personnel components, and logistics, maintenance, and communication functions, then the same requirement exists to tailor the factory to the capabilities and limitations of its personnel in order to accomplish production goals.

Historically production has not utilized human factors techniques, nor, for that matter, has **H** been much concerned with improving the production line. There are several reasons for this: (a) the predominance of the work/motion study or industrial engineering discipline within the factory; (b) the factory's traditional emphasis on rather simple, discrete elements (hence work/motion) rather than on consideration of production as a system, which is the way **H** specialists tend to view it; (c) the traditional concentration of **H** on prime equipment development.

The effect of production error can be extremely serious not only in the cost of rework and scrapping but in terms of failures of the operational system. Since the inspection function is only partially successful in screening for defects, inadequate components fail when they reach operational use.

9 Installation/Maintenance Error

Installation and maintenance error both involve behavioural and causal factors similar to those found in production error. The kinds of error situations that arise are exemplified by the following extracts from records (Ehrlich and Horner, 1961):

'The quick disconnect covers on the "mixture ratio control fuel" side and the "fuel and lube flowmeter" outlet fittings were reversed. 510–570 psi was trapped in the flowmeter fuel outlet line'.

'"An 8" section of tubing was welded on the assembly. No weld is called out for this assembly'.

'Tube assembly installed in four sections instead of three as required'.

'Panel is located approximately 14" lower on wall than called out on blueprint'.

Installation errors are short-term errors; that is, they occur primarily when a new system is being installed in a fixed site. Once the system has been installed and bugs worked out, the incidence of such errors should decrease markedly. They are, however, costly until they are removed; 42.9 per cent of all HIF's reported over a twelve-month period in the early part of a missile test programme (Meister, 1961) consisted of assembly and installation errors.

In contrast, maintenance errors persist throughout system life and may in fact increase as the system wears out (see Figure 2), thus increasing the opportunity for maintenance (and consequently error) to occur.

10 Inspection error

Another category of error related to manufacturing, but also to be found in lesser degree in test and operations, is inspection error. The inspector's task is to uncover and prevent from entering into operational use any equipment which is defective, that is, does not meet the standards required by blueprints or instructions. Most inspection is performed during production; however, new components and equipment arriving at a test or operational site are often inspected again prior to their being placed in use.

Theoretically, if inspection were completely effective, there would be no need for anyone to be concerned about production error affecting operational system performance; all defective items would be caught and eliminated. The problem then would be only the reduction of the expense involved in scrapping or repairing defective equipment.

Unfortunately, inspection is not 100 per cent accurate. McCornack (1961) reported an average inspection effectiveness of about 85 per cent. However,

Harris and Chaney (1969) report that on the basis of their data 'variations due to product complexity alone can cause a range of average inspection accuracies from 20 to 80 per cent.' They point out 'it is seldom that we find over 50 to 60 per cent of the defects being detected at any point in time by a single inspector.'

The same factors that were considered responsible for production error are also responsible for inspection error. The inspection process makes great demands on behavioural processes. The very name, inspection, implies visual examination and judgement. The inspector scrutinizes the physical characteristics of the equipment; he measures its performance; he compares equipment-induced values with numerical standards. The accuracy of the inspection process can, therefore, be improved by methods of increasing the discriminability of defective equipment. Some of the improvements in inspection efficiency produced by human factors methods are described later.

11 Operator error

The kind of error we are all familiar with is that made by the equipment user in the course of a programmed operation. Although a great deal of data is not available, the following trend seems reasonable. Operator error is first noted in the test phase when equipment is first exercised; it gradually builds up and reaches a peak in the initial phase of user operations (see Figure 2) when the engineers who designed the system are replaced by its intended users. As user personnel become more familiar with the equipment, the curve of operator error decreases and then levels off. This asymptote (level of continuing error) depends on many factors including the inherent difficulty, level of operation and personnel turnover (new operators). However, it appears not to be related to operator experience level once the new personnel entering the system have reached a minimum level of skill. The study by Meister *et al.* (1970) on operator-induced HIF found no significant relationship between the frequency of that error and experience level.

Although consumer errors are frequent, most of them have few serious consequences (except in terms of accidents); for example, I am in a hurry to make an appointment, and I push the wrong elevator button. As soon as I do, I recognize it and push the correct one. My error has cost me a fraction of a moment, at most a slight delay if I get off at the wrong floor.

With major equipment systems such as those ordinarily developed for the military, errors are less frequent; system personnel are specifically trained for their jobs, and many fail-safe precautions are included in design and procedures. However, when errors are made, they are inherently more serious. Military combat systems tolerate much less error than do civilian systems. Their goals demand more precise accomplishment. It may be insignificant to push the wrong button in an elevator but disastrous to do so in a missile launch. The following examples (Meister, 1956) are characteristic:

... 'A missile was being landed under automatic control (this was before the development of inertially guided missiles). It appeared to the observation pilot to be coming in too fast. The pilot radioed to the telemetering trailer that the missile should be switched to ground control. In the excitement the control operator missed the correct sequence for transferring control and the missile remained in automatic, except that now it became erratic and nearly crashed into a populated area.

... 'In one case of a missile misfire, the operator on the tracking panel turned his control to the local (manual) control to stop automatic tracking. The launcher immediately slewed to zero elevation angle, damaging the launcher and endangering the ship and its crew.'

The causes of operator error fall into two categories: *idiosyncratic* (operator-determined, e.g., aptitude and motivation) and *situational*, produced by system inadequacies, such as inappropriate procedures or poor training. The operator is directly responsible for the former; system developers are responsible for the latter. Of the two categories, the situational is obviously easier to modify; inadequate training or environment can be improved; poor procedures, revised.

Any individual error is probably multidetermined; that is, more than one factor predisposes that error to occur. This is the reason why, when we backtrack from the error to determine its causes, it is sometimes difficult to pinpoint these causal factors.

It is often assumed that there is an irreducible component of error which will inevitably manifest itself in humans. The author cannot subscribe to that position; **H** assumes that errors (or any other performance deviation) are caused by a 'mismatch' between the capabilities of the operator (idiosyncratic factors) and the demands of the job (situational factors). The human who is required to perform a job brings to that job certain aptitudes and skills for the job (assuming he has been trained). The job itself imposes certain demands upon those skills. An error will occur whenever the balance of demands and capabilities is disturbed. That balance is disturbed whenever one or more of the predisposing error factors listed in Table 4 exist.

Table 4 Predisposing Operator Error Factors

Situational	Idiosyncratic
Poor human engineering/workplace design	Lack of motivation
Inadequate environmental conditions	Lack of skill/training
Overload conditions	Lack of capability
Improper personnel selection	
Task complexity	
Inadequate technical data and logistics	

In other words, there is an *error potential* in man which is not realized until a predisposing condition, creating a mismatch (e.g., poor human engineering design), permits the error to occur. The predisposing condition is the catalytic agent which translates a potential into an actual error. From this standpoint, there is nothing inevitable about error.

Theoretically, error can be prevented completely because if we eliminate the predisposing factor the potential error will never be realized. This, of course, remains only an ideal, a 'design gaol'.

The number of predisposing situational factors in Table 4 suggest that we cannot rely on training alone to overcome inadequate situational factors. Since training is directed at modifying the individual, it only indirectly reduces the impact of situational demands by enabling the operator to cope with them more efficiently. Hence additional training or better personnel selection will never completely catch up with the situational demands. It is possible by training to mitigate the negative effects of poor human engineering or excessive task complexity, but it is impossible to eliminate these effects completely. Although we would never suggest reducing training (which is, in any case, needed to perform the job), it is apparent that only by reducing job/equipment demands (e.g., simplifying design) can the balance between situational demands and personnel responses to these demands be accomplished.

References

Altman, J. W. (1967) *Classification of Human Error,* in W. B. Askren, *Symposium on Reliability of Human Performance in Work,* Report AMRL–TR–67–88, Aerospace Medical Research Laboratories, Wright-Patterson AFB, Ohio, May.

Barton, H. R., *et al.* (1964) *A Queuing Model for Determining System Manning and Related Support Requirements,* Report AMRL–TD4–46–21, Aerospace Medical Research Laboratories, Wright-Patterson AFB, Ohio, January.

Chase, W. P. (1969) *Implementing Human Factors Test Results,* in M. T. Snyder *et al.* (eds.), *Proceedings of the Human Factors Testing Conference,* 1–2 October, 1968, Report AFHRL–TR–69–6, Air Force Human Resources Laboratory, Wright-Patterson AFB, Ohio, October.

Christian, J. F. (1962) Ergonomics—Palliative or Definitive, *Ergonomics,* vol. 5, pp. 279–284.

Communications and Systems Inc. (1969) *System Description Report,* System Engineering Program, Report 105–68–1–1. Washington, D.C.: U.S. Post Office Department, 24 March.

Cornell, C. E. (1968) Minimizing Human Errors, *Space/Aeronautics,* 71–81, March.

Ehrlich, J. and Horner, D. R. (1961) *Human Engineering Discrepancy Reports of OSTF–1 Aerospace Ground Equipment.* General Dynamics/Astronautics, San Diego, California, 28 April.

Ehrlich, J. and Horner, D. R. (1962) *Personnel Subsystem Reliability During Category II Test Series I OSTF–1 Test Operations.* Report REL–R–146–7–022, General Dynamics/Astronautics, San Diego, California, 13 February.

Fitts, P. M. *et al.* (eds) (1951) *Human Enginering for an Effective Air Navigation and Traffic Control System.* Washington, D.C.: National Research Council.

Gordon, R. B. (1964) *Engineering Safety into Missile-Space Systems,* Presented at the SAE–ASME–AIAA Aerospace Reliability and Maintainability Conference, Washington, D.C., 29 June–1 July.

Harris, D. and Chaney, R. (1969) *Human Factors in Quality Assurance.* New York: Wiley.

Koskela, A. (1962) Ergonomics Applied to Office Work. *Ergonomics,* vol. 5, pp. 263–264.

Lacy, B. A. (1967) The Design of the Operator's Tasks in a Tea Blending Plant, *Ergonomics,* vol. 10, pp. 266–270.

LeVan, W. I. (1960) *Analysis of the Human Error Problem in the Field,* Report 7–60–932004, Bell Aerosystems Co, Buffalo, New York, June.

Majesty, M. S. (1962) *Personal Subsystem Reliability for Aerospace Systems,* Presented at the National Aerospace Systems Reliability Symposium, Salt Lake City, Utah, 16–18 April.

McAbee, W. H. (1969) *Category I Personnel Subsystem Test and Evaluation on the C–5,* Minutes of the Second Tri-Service/NASA Personnel Subsystems Human Factors Test and Evaluation Conference (TESCON), Lockheed Missiles & Space Co, Sunnyvale, California, 3–5 December.

McCornack, R. L. (1961) *Inspector Accuracy: A Study of the Literature,* Report SCTM 53–61 (14), Sandia Corporation, Albuquerque, New Mexico.

Meister, D. (1956) *The Effect of Human Errors on Missile Test Performance,* Report ZX–7–015–T.N. Convair, San Diego, California, 9 April.

Meister, D. (1961) *Analysis of Human-Initiated Equipment Failures During Category I Testing, OSTF–1,* Report REL R–054, General Dynamics/Astronautics, San Diego, California, 21 November.

Meister, D. (1962) *Individual and System Error in Complex Systems,* paper presented at the American Psychological Association meetings, St Louis, Missouri.

Meister, D. (1967) *Applications of HUman Reliability to the Production Process,* in W. B. Askren, *Symposium on Reliability of Human Performance in Work,* Report AMRI–TR–67–88, Aerospace Medical Research Laboratories, Wright-Patterson AFB, Ohio, May.

Meister, D., Personal data.

Meister, D. (1965) Human Factors in Reliability, Section 12, In W. G. Ireson, *Reliability Handbook.* New York: McGraw-Hill.

Meister, D. and **Rabideau, G. F.** (1965) *Human Factors Evaluation in System Development.* New York: Wiley.

Meister, D. et al. (1970) *The Effect of Operator Performance Variables on Airborne Equipment Reliability,* Final Report, RADC–TR–70–140, Rome Air Development Center, Griffiss AFB, New York, July.

Peters, G. A. and **Hall, F. S.** (1963) *Missile System Safety: An Evaluation of System Test Data,* Report ROM 3181–1001, Rocketdyne, Canoga Park, California, 1 March.

Rabideau, G. F. et al. (1961) *A Guide to the Use of Function and Task Analysis as a Weapon System Development Tool,* Report NB–62–161, Northrop Corporation, Hawthorne, California.

Raffle, A. and **Sell, R. G.** (1969) The Victoria Line—Passenger Considerations, *Appl. Ergonomics,* vol. 1, pp. 4–11.

Rigby, L. V. (1967) *The Sandia Human Engineering Rate Bank (SHERB),* Paper presented at the Man–Machine Effectiveness Analysis Symposium, Los Angeles Human Factors Society, University of California at Los Angeles.

Rigby, L. V. and **Cooper, J. I.** (1961) *Problems and Procedures in Maintainability,* Report ASD–TNN–61–126, Aerospace Medical Laboratory, Wright-Patterson AFB, Ohio, October.

Robinson, J. E., Deutsch, W. E. and **Rogers, J. G.** (1970) The Field Maintenance Interface between Human Engineering and Maintainability Engineering, *Human Factors,* vol. 12, pp. 253–259.

Rook, L. W. (1962) *Reduction of Human Error in Industrial Production,* Report SCTM 93–62 (14), Sandia Corporation, Albuquerque, New Mexico, June.

Rook, L. W. (1965) *Motivation and Human Error,* Report SCTM–65–135, Sandia Corporation, Albuquerque, New Mexico, September.

Shackel, B. (1962) Ergonomics in the Design of a Large Digital Computer Console, *Ergonomics,* vol. 5, pp. 229–241.

Shackel, B. (1969) Work Station Analysis—Turning Cartons by Hand, *Appl. Ergonomics,* vol. 1, pp. 45–51.

Shapero, A., Cooper, J. I., Rappaport, M., Shaeffer, K. H. and **Bates, C. J.** (1960) *Human Engineering Testing and Malfunction Data Collection in Weapon System Programs,* WADD Technical Report, 60–36, February.

Teeple, J. B. (1961) *System Design and Man–Computer Function Allocation,* Presented at ORSA–TIMS Meeting, 19–21 April.

Teel, K. S. *et al.* (1968) Assembly and Inspection of MicroElectronic Systems, *Human Factors,* vol. 10, pp. 217–224.

United States, MIL–STD 1472 (1969) *Human Engineering Design Criteria for Military Systems, Equipment and Facilities.* Washington, D.C.: Department of Defense.

Van Buskirk, R. C. and **Huebner, W. J.** (1962) *Human-Initiated Malfunctions and System Performance Evaluation,* Report AMRL–TDR–62–105, Aerospace Medical Research Laboratories, Wright-Patterson AFB, Ohio, September.

Urmston, R. E. and **Cutchshaw, C. M.** (1960) *Human Engineering Principles Applied to the Design of Factory Test Equipment. 1: TET–704,* Report AE60–0290, Convair/Astronautics, San Diego, California, 11 April.

Willis, H. R. (1962) *The Human Error Problem,* Report M–62–76, Martin/Denver Co, Denver, Colorado, June.

Willis, H. R. (1962) *Human Error—Cause and Reduction,* Presented to the Joint Meeting of the Midwest Human Factors Society and National Safety Council, Chicago, Ill., November.

Wilson, R. B. and **Gaffney, J. L.,** *Man's Reliability in the X–15 Aerospace System,* undated.

7.3 Human Factors: Micro to Macro

Alan L. Porter

University of Washington, Seattle, Washington

Introduction

The genesis of this paper was a simple observation that two areas of study with much in common ignore each other. The one area, Human Factors (HF), focuses on the interactions between man and machine; the other, which can be called "Technology Policy Assessment" (TPA), focuses on the interactions between society and technological systems. They thus share interests in the interactions between humanity, i.e., people, and technology, i.e., machines. Moreover, HF and TPA share both the objective of the effective management of machines for the benefit of people, and methods of study pertaining to topics such as environmental effects, organizational behaviour, information processing, and system characteristics. Despite such common ground, there is a lack of evidence that either group is seriously aware of the other.

Despite the apparent lack of attention to the scholarly efforts regarding technology policy assessment, there are strong indications that the Human Factors community is evolving in the directions of increased involvement with civilian applications and with scaled-up systems. Seminara (1973) compared the technical program content between the 1966 and 1972 HF annual meetings to show a reversal from a 70% DOD/NASA orientation to over 70% civilian applications. A tabulation of the 1961 International Ergonomics Congress and the 1972 HF annual meeting (see Table 1) indicates an increase in reports pertaining to more aggregated levels from 10% at the 1961 meeting to 31% in 1972. Deutsch (1973) likewise notes a shift among HF specialists toward work on large technological systems, such as urban systems and health care delivery programs. Given these developing interests, it becomes important that HF acquaint itself more fully with the efforts taking place in the area of TPA.

The following sections pursue this theme through a comparison of these

---

Acknowledgement

Reprinted, by permission, from A. L. Porter, 'Human Factors: Micro to macro' in *Proc. 17th Annual Meeting Human Factors Soc., 1973* Copyright Human Factors Society Inc.

areas of study, the "micro", Human Factors, and the "macro", Technology Policy Assessment. Based on this comparison, two kinds of interaction between HF specialists and this so-called "macro" level, TPA, are suggested.

Technology for man

Concern over the interface between people and machines is both deep and broad. The popularity and controversiality of such works as "The Technological Society" (Ellul, 1964), "Future Shock" (Toffler, 1970), "Where the Wasteland Ends" (Roszak, 1972), and "The Limits to Growth" (Meadows *et al.*, 1972) attests to this. Current policy issues reflect heavily on the impacts of technology on mankind, for instance, disarmament, environmental protection versus industrial development, the energy crisis, trade balance problems, and governmental invasion of privacy. All contain dilemmas revolving around the uses of technologies for human advantage.

The use of technology by and for man is a concern that increasingly dominates the national goals (IEEE, 1972). The issues span the spectrum from one man with one machine to mankind in a pervasively technological world (Figure 1).

Approaches to the solution of problems involving the interaction of humanity and technology likewise run a gamut from basic scientific research; through practical engineering, business management, and political science; to philosophical musings. Witness the vitality of Human Factors; the flourishing of social science investigations related to technology (e.g., Helmer, 1966; Sheldon and Land, 1972); broadening engineering curricula (e.g., Alfred P. Sloan Foundation support to ten engineering schools to enhance the social responsibility of engineers); and a blossoming of "Technology and Society" programs (e.g., "Science, Technology, and Society" at Cornell; "Science, Technology, and Public Administration" at Berkeley; "Policy Studies in Science and Technology" at George Washington University; "Social Management of Technology" at the University of Washington; and at least twenty-five others). It remains to be shown that there are useful interactions to be realized between the poles of the scholarly spectrum involved with the interactions between technology and man, i.e., HF and TPA.

Two+ interdisciplinary areas

Figure 1 depicts two interdisciplinary areas concerned with the confluence of humanity and technology: Human Factors and Technology Policy Assessment. The illustration of an area of study, such as HF as the study of individual man-machine interactions, is not meant to exclude other interactions from its realm; rather it is a perceived relative emphasis. One could well choose to analyze other sets of human-technological interactions, such as the effects of single pieces of technology on society (e.g., the first atomic bomb), or of multiple technological systems on an individual (e.g., psychological alienation in an increasingly technological American society). In addition, it turns out to be useful for the purposes of this exercise to distinguish an area intermediate to HF and TPA, which could be said to concentrate on the interactions between groups of people and machines. While exhibiting great overlap with both HF and TPA, and most often considered as a general research approach not limited by a subject focus, "Systems Science" is a useful designation for such an area. At this point it is useful to set forth definitions of the areas of interest.

Definitions

While the terms "technological system" and "society" are subject to discussion, for present purposes it suffices to consider them as the more aggregated ends of the respective axes (Figure 1). The highlighted interdisciplinary areas are defined as follows:

Human factors. The systematic application of knowledge about human characteristics to the design of man-made facilities; particularly that knowledge concerning man's relation to his machines and his environment. The objectives are enhanced utilization of equipment and facilities, and increased human satisfactions (based on McCormick, 1972). This definition could not wholly describe the actual approach and research of a HF specialist, because HF is an interdisciplinary area drawing upon both the relatively basic sciences (experimental psychology) and the relatively applied (medical engineering). The real and imagined differences among Engineering Psychologists, Ergonomists, Human Engineers, Biotechnologists, *et al.* do not seriously alter the thrust that HF concerns itself with the individual man as opposed to society, with the individual machine as opposed to large technological systems.

Technology policy assessment. An interdisciplinary area of study that emphasizes understanding of (1) the decision processes and institutional structures involved in the formulation and implementation of public policy concerning technology; (2) an evaluation of the effects of technologies; and (3) the relationships between the factors determining technological policies and the resultant effects (based on E. Wenk, Jr., personal communication, and Flajser, 1973). The objective of TPA is a better utilization of technological potentials for society through improved policy-making. TPA is a subset of the Policy Sciences (for overview, see Dror, 1971) focused on technology; from another aspect, it is an elaboration of Technology Assess-

Table 1 Classification of Report by Source

Source	Level of Focus (number of reports)		
	Man-Machine (individual focus)	Men-Machines (systems focus)	Society-Technological Systems (public systems, policy focus)
Human Factors			
1961 First International Congress on Ergonomics (*Ergonomics*, **5**, No. 1, 1962)	37	4	0
1972 HFS Annual Meeting	72	30	3
Human Factors, **14**, Nos. 3–6, 1972	22	8	0
Systems Science			
IEEE Systems, Man & Cybernetics Symposium, 1971	24	40	24
RAND Corporation Systems Analysis Reports to 1970 (SB–1022)	9	46	32
Technology Policy Assessment			
RAND Corporation Policy Sciences Reports to 1972 (SB–1037)	0	14	85
Policy Sciences, **3**, Nos. 1–4, 1972	1	4	26
Technology Assessment, **1**, Nos. 1–3, 1972–73	0	1	18

Table 1 (Explanatory Note)
Classification was performed by the author; specific examples include:
Man-Machine Level: target detection, individual decision-making, stress effects on man, control and display;
Men-Machines Level: interactive communications, hospital patient care, submarine escape, logistics, systems analysis, mathematical aspects of systems theory, military gaming;
Society-Technological Systems Level: health care delivery systems, PPB, use of technology in Columbian education, future values, policy analysis.

All technical reports and workshops were counted, except for the RAND bibliographies, for which the initial 100 entries were tabulated. Reports were excluded if they did not pertain to interactions of humanity and technology. Journal issues were chosen to be comparable in number and vintage (c. 1972). Certain classifications were particularly difficult to pigeonhole; for instance, market effects on vehicle safety improvements (society-technological systems) or decision-making regarding public policies (man-machine). These examples clearly draw on multiple levels, as many studies do to a greater or lesser degree.

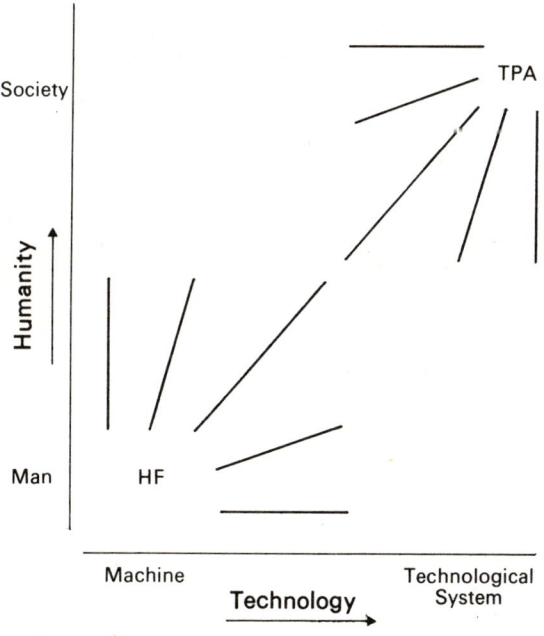

Figure 1 A humanity-technology interface

ment (for overview, see Kasper, 1972 and Jones, 1971). The research interests included under such titles as Technology Assessment, Policy Sciences, Policy Analysis, Management Sciences, and assorted "Science, Technology, and Society" efforts tethered to such disciplines as business administration, engineering, law, and political science are not differentiated for present purposes. [As yet, there is no consensus as to a cover term for these areas of study; TPA is suggested as descriptive of the two prime orientations.] The single categorization as TPA is based on a shared emphasis on more aggregated considerations regarding the management of technology for the benefit of society.

The additional area introduced as "Systems Science" is taken as an emphasis on the design of a configuration of men, machines, and procedures with the objective of the highest expected pay-off, i.e., the best system performance obtainable. It is a research strategy with a focus on the concept of a system, employing various analytic methods to enhance decision-making (based on Hollander, 1971, and Quade, 1968). This interdisciplinary category is meant to include Systems Analysis, Systems Engineering, Operations Research, and Decision Analysis, not speaking to the differences among the various-labelled practitioners, but rather noting a degree of common emphasis on the level of aggregation of "men and machines."

Patterns of interaction

Indications are that the interaction pattern includes minimal communication between HF and TPA, but a considerable dialogue between Systems Science interests and both HF and TPA. A scanning of references cited in the literature of the respective areas supports this conclusion. However, the nature of each area is so broad in itself, draws in turn from multiple disciplines, and pertains to such varied applications that interpretation of this cross-citing is necessarily limited. An alternative indicator of the degree of shared interest is the number of reports corresponding to the three levels: "man and machine", "men and machines", and "society and technological systems,' presented to each of the respective audiences. [A preliminary effort at categorization led to the inclusion of the intermediate level with the related classification "Systems Science" because of the large number of reports not fitting smoothly into the two polar categories.] Counting of several sources from HF, Systems Science, and TPA yields Table 1.

The table indicates that papers presented in a HF forum emphasize the man-machine level, rarely reaching to the society-technological systems level; TPA shows a converse distribution. In contrast, Systems Science forums respond to both polar levels, and the level of "men and machines" is well-represented in both HF and TPA forums. This demonstrates that Systems Science, in a sense, provides a bridge between HF and TPA, but neither HF nor TPA apparently pays direct attention to the other.

The next section compares HF and TPA in more detail. The Systems Science aspect is not pursued in the belief that it is sufficiently familiar to HF personnel to offer effective access to them and is not a focus of this paper. This does not necessarily imply sufficient interaction; Chaillet (1967) argues that the participation of HF engineers in systems analyses is inadequate.

Comparison of human factors and technology policy assessment

Areas of study can be characterized in various ways, but the "reporter's questions" of "who, what, when, where, why, and how" provide a reasonable handle. Table 2 presents brief responses by this author along these lines, thereby setting out objectives, research interests, methods, participants, settings, and histories for HF and TPA.

Both the similarities and the differences are worthy of note as they indicate potential grounds for communication. To summarize from Table 2, there is considerably indicated commonality in approach, including a practical problem-solving orientation to many similar research interest, social science interchange with engineering, shared methods, and youthfulness. The methods and research interests also indicate possible complementary relations. Nonetheless, the subject matter varies considerably because of the level of focus, i.e., emphasis on individual man-machine versus society-technological system. While this difference in research interests is significant, there are ample possibilities for useful HF inputs to TPA, and reciprocal exchange.

In light of the attractiveness of interaction between HF and TPA, why do they remain aloof from each other? Both fields draw from numerous disciplinary and interdisciplinary sources; the scope of inputs to each is broad, not provincial. Therefore, it is reasonable to assume that the lack of interaction between HF and TPA is due to either (1) unawareness, as both are rather small, young areas of study, and/or (2) perceived irrelevance because of the difference in focal level. The former appears to be the main factor at this time, but the latter may prove to be a significant barrier to full interaction in the future.

A second look at the data of Table 1 was undertaken to probe the characteristics of TPA. A further breakdown of each cell in terms of the type of report involved as (1) abstract or general analysis, (2) methodological or

Table 2 A Comparison of Human Factors and Technology Policy Assessment

Question	HF	TPA	Parallels	Differences
Why? (Objectives)	Design to optimize system performance and human satisfaction (individual level)	Policy analysis to optimize system performance and human satisfaction (social level)	Applied Objectives (problem-focused)	Scale of focus (scope)
	Solve practical applied problems	Solve practical applied problems		
	Solve private and public problems	Satisfy public policy concerns		
What? (Research interests)	Man-machine interaction (assignment of functions)	Society-technological system interaction (assignment of responsibilities)	Multiple	Scale of focus
	Human characteristics (psychological, biological)	Social characteristics (social, political, legal)		
	Machine characteristics	Technological characteristics		
	Sensory-motor processes	Problem awareness		
	Information processes (individual)	Information processes (institutional)		
	Communication systems	Communication systems		
	Environmental effects (on man)	Environmental impacts (on the environment and on mankind)		
	Safety analysis	Risk analysis		
	Organizational behaviour (work group)	Organizational behaviour (large group)		
	Systems (small)	Systems (large)		
	Decision-making	Policy-making		
	Control processes	Social and system feedback		

	HF	TPA	Comments
How? (Methods)	Task analysis	Performance determinant analysis	HF has a stronger experimental basis, more concrete inputs for analysis
	Experimentation (field and laboratory)	Theoretical analysis	Rational, systematic approaches
	Controlled observation	Uncontrolled observation	
	Simulation, modeling	Primitive modeling and computer simulation	
		Forecasting	TPA includes future interests per se
Who? (Participants)	Social scientists (experimental psychologists)	Social scientists (sociologists)	Emphasis on applied social science/engineering; TPA is more diffuse
	Engineers	Technical experts (engineers)	
		Political scientists, lawyers, decision analysts	
Where? (Setting)	Military	University	Relative frequencies in various locations
	University	Think tank	
	Industry	Government	
When? (History)	Youthful (post-World War II)	New (late 1960s)	Not widely recognized; Less established areas
	Oriented toward general (timeless) and current problems	Oriented toward current problems, also general and future	Major interest in current problems

gaming reports, and (3) specific applications or case studies, demonstrated a relatively abstract TPA emphasis. For example, for the RAND Corporation Policy Science reports relating to society-technological systems ($N=85$), this author classified 46% as abstract, 39% as methodological, and only 15% as relating to specific applications. This contrasts, for example, to the comparable RAND Systems Analysis reports at the men-machines level ($N=46$), for which only 17% are abstract, 59% are methodological, and 24% relate to specific applications.

The indicated relative data-poverty of TPA is an invitation to cautious extrapolation of relevant HF experimental findings. Generalization from the individual to the aggregated, always requiring care, is exacerbated by the size and complexity of the systems involved, their dynamic environments, and problems of data access. For instance, in the case of the SST (Supersonic Transport), what were the flows and influences of technical information on policy-making? What were the determining factors on the vote of a particular California Senator? Principles of information processing and decision-making could provide a beginning framework for response to such questions. The description of possible specific arenas for relating HF and TPA is the next task.

Avenues of interaction

The first observation is that an increased mutual *awareness* is essential to the development of any useful interchange between HF and TPA. This paper addresses itself to the HF side, but it is reasonable to expect that increased activity on one side would generate reciprocal interest. It is asserted that (1) HF has something to contribute to TPA, and (2) HF, in turn, can be enriched from TPA.

HF contributions to TPA

HF has a general expertise, specific findings, and the abilities to research important questions, all of potential value to TPA.

Impacts of public policy decisions on major technological delivery systems, such as the SST, Cable TV, nuclear power plant moratorium, or an Alaska pipeline, involve all citizens directly or indirectly. But, in addition, there is an expertise in the HF community which could provide inputs to policy-makers as to the accuracy of assessments which draw upon HF specializations (e.g., human implications of SST noise patterns), integration of such details into a composite picture, and the methodological propriety of policy assessments (e.g., are assumptions of social feedback incorporation consistent with basic control theory?). HF has a special voice on TPA issues in respect to its direct focus on the interactions between man and machine. The HF focus on the individual could add an important emphasis to the aggregated TPA arena. In these days of concern over technology-induced alienation, it would be well for policy analysis to touch back to the "micro" level of the individual person.

Specific HF findings should be scrutinized to determine which can be usable in various aspects of TPA. Communication of such findings requires translation into a form digestible to the TPA practitioner, i.e., bearing on problems of current concern. For example, someone pursuing a technology assessment of offshore oil production would be potentially interested in HF data on characteristics of platform work environments on men, safety factors, effects of oil-production-generated pollutants on man, or a function analysis of oil processing. A policy evaluation of offshore oil production would be particularly involved with aspects of decision-making, information-communication processes, organizational behaviour, and control systems, all candidates to draw on HF expertise (see Kash and White, 1973; Crutchfield et al., 1973; Coates, 1972; and Breslow et al., 1972).

A truly mutual benefit can be foreseen in HF attention to TPA issues leading to specific research on areas of high policy priority. There are a number of such "macro" areas which warrant inputs in the form of "micro" research-generated knowledge. These will be explored in more detail as a subset of benefits which the HF community could expect to draw from TPA.

TPA contributions to HF

The flip side of the coin are those benefits HF can anticipate from TPA. These are chiefly a result of a broadened perspective and awareness of areas where research is in demand, rather than as specific inputs to HF research problems. While there are TPA methods from which HF could enrich itself (e.g., impact analysis, risk analysis) and specific findings (e.g., as to organizational behaviours) of possible value to HF, these are not central.

A perspective on current and future policy issues is absolutely essential to an area such as Human Factors. As Don Price (1965) has said, "Science can insist on ignoring questions of purpose in order to be objective and precise; the professions cannot." The highway engineer has awakened to discover that his artifacts are no longer desired in the old, successful format of the 1950's; changed social preferences are reflected in broadened highway design criteria. Similarly the nuclear engineer and the M.D. are no longer left to their own devices; technological policy concerns are shifting. Interest in such measures as the developing social indicators (Sheldon and

Land, 1972) may even prove useful for day-to-day design in terms of how people are responding to environmental features today. The importance of HF attention to such "macro", value-laden considerations has been noted (e.g., 1968 HF Society presidential address, Lyman, 1969.)

TPA can be a valuable guide to important areas for research, in that it reflects national policy considerations. This has been recognized by Congress in establishing its first new staff organization in years with the Congressional Office of Technology Assessment, through P.L. 92-484 in October, 1972. Specific suggestions for needed HF research are not hard to come by. The implications of the Occupational Safety and Health Act of 1970 (P.L. 91-596) are quite familiar to many HF specialists. The SST controversy underscored knowledge gaps regarding stratospheric ozone sensitivity to disruption, which then might affect radiation levels. A key question is what would be the likely human consequences of long-term alterations in various radiation levels?

An example of a technology assessment procedure which places demands on HF is the preparation of "102C's", the environmental impact statements required in Section 102(2) (C) of the National Environmental Policy Act of 1969 (P.L. 91-190). This thriving business now emphasizes social as well as natural environmental impacts; furthermore, the Environmental Protection Agency (EPA) is preparing broader and more comprehensive guidelines. Particular aspects of the impact statement process may elicit interests among the HF community. Are national ambient air quality standards (Federal Register, April 30, 1971, 8186-8201) realistically based on human effects as a function of various combinations of pollutants over various time periods? Or, how complete are HF inputs to the settings of noise control standards? EPA is required by the Noise Control Act of 1972 to publish by November, 1973, information on the levels of noise consistent with the public health, including standards for motor vehicles and construction equipment. While the setting of such standards if of HF interest, there is a continuing feature in that all proposed projects will be required to provide information on noise impacts in terms of: affected human activities sensitive to noise, noise levels (of what mix of frequencies and intensity) at alternative sites, and an evaluation of how tolerable predicted noise impacts will be and what abatement means could be utilized.

Environmental statement requirements are multi-faceted. For example, Northwest Region guidelines (U.S. Environmental Protection Agency, 1973) for highway projects presently require information for the project and alternatives as to factors such as traffic flow patterns; interchange designs; air quality implications; noise measures; litter control procedures; urban transportation control strategies; secondary impacts such as additional houses, industries, and recreation uses; effects on sensitive populations including occupants of schools, hospitals, or nursing homes; and short- versus long-term tradeoffs.

While the previous examples have been presented as indicating opportunities for HF, it is clear that they also represent areas in which TPA could benefit from HF. Such possibilities for mutual advantage are the promise held forth in encouraging mutual awareness.

Conclusions

The theme of this conference, the consumer factor, reflects a movement of Human Factors interests toward the "macro" social aspects of technology. Both specific HF applications to consumer problems and general HF concern with the implications of consumer issues are included. Other indications have been noted of a shift in the scope of HF toward certain aspects of more aggregated interactions, i.e., toward the society-technological system end of the spectrum. HF is involved with a "macro" world, whether that be in terms of a parent organization incorporating HF data into its project decision-making or a nation striving to define and fulfill its social goals.

TPA is a "macro" interdisciplinary area sharing interests with HF in the interactions of technology with humanity. In light of a present lack of communications between HF and TPA, it is suggested that both HF and TPA could benefit from an increased HF awareness of technological policy issues and practices, based in part on familiarity with the literature of TPA. There is a need both for specific research inputs to TPA and for a personal interest in policy issues from a critical HF perspective. This is not to equate the areas of HF and TPA, suggesting a direct interchangeability of participants or results, rather it suggests a complementary relationship between them, beneficial to both.

One possible step which could further such a relationship would be to maintain a HF voice to the new Congressional Office of Technology Assessment (COTA) to formulate needs for and mobilize HF expertise as pertinent to particular assessments which arise. The Human Factors Society might wish to consider a recommendation along those lines to COTA in its present formative period.

References

Breslow, M., Brush, N., Giggey, F., and Urmson, C. (1972) A survey of technology assessment today. Report by Peat, Marwick, Mitchell & Co. for NSF (Contract No. NSF–C631).

Chaillet, R. F. (2967) Human factors requirements for the development of U.S. army material. In W. T. Singleton, R. S. Easterly, and D. C. Whitfield (eds.), *The Human Operator in Complex Systems.* London: Taylor and Francis, Ltd.

Coates, V. (1972) Technology and public policy: The process of technology assessment in the federal government. A report of The Program of Policy Studies of The George Washington University (available from NTIS).

Crutchfield, J., Flajser, S. H., Stokes, R., and Parlette, R. (1973) Petroleum production, consumption, and the marine environment. A report of The Program on the Social Management of Technology, University of Washington.

Deutsch, S. (1973) The changing face of societies. *Human Factors Society Bulletin,* Jan., vol. 16, p. 1.

Dror, Y. (1971) *Design for Policy Sciences.* Elsevier (Policy Sciences Book Series), New York.

Ellul, J. (1964) *The Technological Society.* Knopf, New York.

Flajser, S. H. (1973) Technological delivery systems in the social management of technology. Paper presented to the *27th Annual Meeting of the Western Political Science Association.*

Helmer, O. (1966) *Social Technology.* Basic Books, New York.

Hollander, G. L. (1971) Synthesis of major systems: An open challenge. In *IEEE Systems, Man and Cybernetics Group: Annual Symposium Record,* pp. 3–5.

IEEE Workshop on 'Toward a framework for national goals', *IEEE Transactions on Systems, Man, and Cybernetics, SMC–2,* (1972), vol. 5, pp. 565–629.

Jones, M. V. (1971) *A Technology Assessment Methodology.* Washington, D.C.: The MITRE Corporation.

Kash, D. and White, I. (1973) A draft report of a technology assessment of outer continental shelf oil and gas operations. Report by the Technology Assessment Group, Science and Public Policy Program, University of Oklahoma, Norman, Oklahoma, April.

Kasper, R. G. (1972) *Technology Assessment.* Praeger Publishers, New York.

Lyman, J. (1969) Measuring metafacts. *Human Factors,* vol. 11, pp. 3–8.

Meadows, D. H., Meadows, D. L., Randers, J., and Behrens, W. W., Jr. (1972) *The Limits to Growth.* Universe Books.

Price, D. K. (1965) *The Scientific Estate.* Oxford University Press, New York, p. 123.

Quade, E. S. (1968) Introduction. *In* Quade, E. S. and Boucher, W. I. (eds.), *Systems Analysis and Policy Planning: Applications in Defense.* Elsevier, New York, pp. 1–19.

Roszak, T. (1972) *Where the Wasteland Ends: Politics and Transcendence in Postindustrial Society.* Garden City, Doubleday.

Seminara, J. L. (1973) Change in emphasis. *Human Factors Society Bulletin,* vol. 16, p. 1.

Sheldon, E. B., and Land, K. C. (1972) Social reporting for the 1970's: A review and programmatic statement. *Policy Sciences,* vol. 3, pp. 137–151.

Toffler, A. (1970) *Future Shock.* Random House, New York.

U.S. Environmental Protection Agency, Region X (1973) *Environmental Impact Statement Guidelines.*

GLOSSARY

Amnesia   Loss of memory
   Post traumatic amnesia   Loss of memory for events occurring after the time of onset of amnesia. (cf. retrograde amnesia)
   Retrograde amnesia   Loss of memory for those events and experience preceding the cause of the amnesia. (cf. post traumatic amnesia)

Anthropometry   The measurement of physical dimensions of the human body, such as the strength, length, relative positions and possible movement paths of its components.

Arthritis   Inflammation of a joint.

Ballpark estimates   Very rough order-of-magnitude estimates.

Bandaid   American term for an adhesive plaster (e.g. for a cut).

BART   The San Francisco Bay Area Rapid Transit System, a suburban railway system opened in the early 1970s.

Bits   A bit is a unit of information content equal to one binary decision or the designation of one of two possible and equally likely values or states of anything used to store or convey information.

Chance, departures from chance, and non-chance variance, see *Significance* and *Predictable variance.*

Control-display ratio   The ratio of the movement of a control device to the corresponding movement of the display indicator to which it is linked.

Correlation   A statistical measure of the degree to which two or more variables tend to be systematically associated or opposed in a population. For instance, if taller people tend to be heavier, then height and weight are positively correlated. If people who have high incomes tend to spend less time unemployed then income and duration of unemployment are negatively correlated. Perfect positive and negative correlations are indicated numerically as correlations of $+1.0$ and -1.0 respectively. 0.0 indicates total lack of correlation.

Cybernetics   The scientific study of control and organisation in biological, machine and social systems.

Decibel   A unit of sound intensity measured on a ratio scale.

Dementia   Non-specific but lasting deterioration of emotional, intellectual or judgemental powers, as a result of certain types of damage to the brain (organic dementia) or old age (senile dementia).

Distal criterion   The ultimate criterion or overall policy for the whole system, see *Proximal criterion.*

Dyspepsia   Indigestion.

Electromyography   The tiny electro-chemical changes involved in neural and muscular activity can be detected by placing electrodes on the skin and connecting them to powerful amplifiers, usually driving a pen-recorder.

Muscular activity then appears as a burst of oscillations of the pen.

Electroplexy   Electro-convulsive treatment in which electric current is applied to the brain.

Experimental psychology   The employment of systematic, controlled, scientific methodology to analyse human (or animal) behaviour and inferred mental processes, usually for individuals, rather than groups.

Feedback   The return of information about the output of a system for use in controlling the preceding processes in the system.

Fiducial approach   Attempting to calculate limiting cases (worst or best possible) rather than estimating the most likely case.

Field studies   Research carried out 'on site' (e.g. in a factory) on ongoing activities as they occur, rather than in a laboratory.

GNP   GNP or Gross National Product is the main official economic measure of the total national output and can be broadly defined as the total value of all the goods and services produced in the country in a single year.

Herpes simplex   An acute infectious virus disease characterised by groups of watery blisters on the skin and mucous membranes.

Hypoglycaemia   A condition caused by low levels of glucose in the blood, the symptoms for which include nervousness, profuse sweating and dizziness.

Iteration   Repeated cycling round the whole or part of a sequence of operations so as to approach nearer and nearer to some goal which cannot be achieved exactly by any single non-repeating sequence.

Job enrichment   Techniques for improving worker satisfaction by including aspects of self-supervision and management functions in tasks, and avoiding highly repetitive short-cycle tasks.

Knowledge of results   Letting experimental subjects know how well they are doing as they go along, or at intervals, and possibly allowing them to compare their results with those of others.

Lability   Instability.

Long term memory, see *Memory.*

Mean time between failure   A measure of reliability: the average operating time between failures of an item which is repaired or replaced each time it fails.

Mediating processes   Internal mental processes which cannot be observed directly, but have to be hypothesised to explain the observed behavioural relations between measurable stimuli and responses.

Memory

> *Long-term memory*   The ability to respond to a stimulus, recite a list, remember an association, and so on, a long period of time after the material was presented. It seems to be functionally separate from short-term memory since information can take much longer to be entered into it or retrieved from it, and it has a slow rate of decay and

an immense capacity.

Short-term memory   The correct recall of, or appropriate performance of material immediately or shortly after its presentation. This appears to be mediated by a separate mechanism from long-term memory, distinguished by its very rapid access, rapid decay and small capacity.

Mission   Because of the military links of early reliability studies, the ultimate purpose that an operational system must achieve is sometimes called its 'mission'.

Motor output   Nothing to do with cars. It means muscular activity.

Multiplication probability model   The overall probability of some device failing in *either* Mode A *or* Mode B *or* Mode C *or* Mode D *or* . . . etc., where A, B, C, D, etc. are independent failure modes, none of which has a high probability of occurring, is approximately:

(Probability of A) x (Probability of B) x
(Probability of C) x (Probability of D) x . . . etc.

Nervous debility, see *Neurasthenia*.

Neurasthenia   A psychoneurotic reaction characterised by chronic aches and pains, and physical and mental fatigue, believed to result from sustained emotional stress which the individual cannot cope with.

Noise   Any disturbance in a received message which does not represent part of the original message as sent. Often used to refer to random disturbances, but in fact includes any unwanted additions.

One-way screen   A device such as a semi-silvered mirror arranged so that someone on one side of the screen cannot see someone on the other side.

Optimization   Finding the 'best' solution or situation in terms of some stated criteria.

Overload   Information overload is a condition where the rate of information input to a system exceeds the processing capacity of that system, causing either rejection or loss of a part of that input or a total breakdown of processing.

Paradigm   A pattern to be followed. A general model or representative example.

Parameter   Loosley, the same as a variable (q.v.); but can also be used to indicate a control variable (q.v.) which is being held constant while other variables are allowed to change.

Percentile   The nth percentile of a set of numbers arranged in ascending order of magnitude is that number below which n per cent of the numbers fall.

Phlebitis   Disease causing inflammation of the veins.

Phoria, Lateral phoria, Vertical phoria   Apart from the necessary differences in visual field due to stereopsis (q.v.) the two eyes have to be correctly aligned with one another. Phorias are incorrectly aligned with one another. Phorias are incorrect alignments of the two eyes, in vertical, horizontal, and rotational terms.

Post-traumatic amnesia, see *Amnesia.*

Predictor In areas such as accident research, much effort has been spent trying to find measurable characteristics of people that can be used to predict whether they are likely to have an accident. Such 'predictors' are very rarely perfect—all they show at best is that a person with characteristic X is slightly more likely to have an accident than someone without it. However, when a battery of such predictors is collected together, the overall accuracy is likely to be much greater.

Product rule of reliability engineering   See *Multiplicative probability model.*

Proximal criterion The immediate, local, short-term criterion for the next manouevre. See *Distal criterion.*

Redundancy/redundant The fraction of the gross information content of a message which can be eliminated without loss of essential information or meaning. Redundant information repeats or reinforces the meaning of a message without adding substantially to it.

Refractory period This is a brief period of time following one stimulation of a system when the system is either completely unresponsive, or requires a stronger than normal stimulus to respond to a second stimulus.

Regression analysis A statistical technique for fitting a straight line to represent the principle axis of the oval cluster of points that tends to appear when two imperfectly correlated (q.v.) variables are plotted against one another. The line is often thought of as indicating the "underlying" relationship between the two variables when random variations are removed.

Reliability (in the statistical sense) Test/re-test reliability is the degree to which two identical applications of the same test produce the same results. Inter-observer reliability is the degree to which two observers, both independantly recording the same events, agree in their records.

Reliability engineering The branch of engineering concerned with ensuring that products (e.g. TV sets) or systems (e.g. Nuclear Power Stations) will not fail more frequently than is acceptable.

Retrograde amnesia, see *Amnesia.*

Short-term memory, see *Memory.*

Significance (in the statistical sense) Where there is a substantial random element in measuring variables, there is always a chance that a particular set of measurements will appear to vary together, or to differ consistently from one another, for purely chance reasons—the 'luck of the draw'. To reduce the chance of being caught in this way, there is a large battery of statistical techniques which can tell you the odds of your particular set of measurements having turned out as they have done purely by chance. In the behavioural sciences measurements are very rarely accepted as worth considering unless the odds against their being chance results are at least 20:1, and preferably at least 100:1. These odds are usually called the 'significance' of the data, typically expressed as a probability (e.g. '$p < 0.05$' or '$p < 0.01$').

SST   Super Sonic Transport. The equivalent British project is Concorde.

Standard Deviation   The square root of the Variance (q.v.). The commonest statistical measure of variation.

Stereopsy   Depth perception using the fact that the two eyes are separated and therefore see slightly different views of the world, as in a stereo-scopic slide viewer.

Stimulus-Response and *Stimulus-Organism-Response*   In the first half of the century, strictly Behaviourist psychologists determined to be rigorously scientific, attempted to model behaviour entirely in terms of the variables they could record directly—the stimuli presented to the individual, and the externally detectable responses they produced, without hypothesising any mental Mediating Processes (q.v.). It soon became apparant that this strict Stimulus-Response approach could not successfully model all behaviour, and that mediating processes had to be invoked; this development was sometimes called the Stimulus-Organism-Response approach. Cognitive psychology (q.v.) is the logical outcome of this latter approach.

Taxonomy   Classification scheme.

Validity   See Section 2.

Variables   A descriptive dimension of some class of things which in any individual case can be assigned one of a set of values by some defined process of measurement or categorisation. For example height, eye-colour, weight, sex, level of school education, date of birth, name, are all variables that could apply to people.

> *Control variables*   These are variables whose values are kept constant, or within acceptable ranges, throughout an experiment, so that changes in the dependent variables (q.v.) can be related unequivocably to changes in the independent variables (q.v.).
>
> *Dependent variables*   Variables, usually in an experimental setting, whose values are to be measured to see how they are affected by controlled adjustments in the independent variables (q.v.).
>
> *Independent variables*   The variables which an experimenter pre-selects or controls in an experiment, so that he can observe how the dependent variables (q.v.) behave under these conditions.

Variance   One of the standard statistical measures of the amount of variation found when each member of a population is measured in respect of some variables (q.v.). The average of the squared deviations of each individual measurement from the average value for the population as a whole is known as the variance.

Vigilance tasks   Tasks involving prolonged attention to some display or activity to detect infrequent but important incidents—e.g. scanning radar, watching over a super-market for shop-lifters. Industrial inspection tasks can be similar, though they usually involve much subtler and more complex discriminations.

Visual acuity   Accurateness or sharpness of perception of black and white detail.

Waiver of legal responsibility   A document stating that in the case of an experiment, the experimental subject will not hold the experimenter legally liable for any accidents happening during or any subsequent ill-effects resulting from that experiment.

Worker participation   Involvement of workers in the design of their own jobs, setting of rates of pay, working hours etc.

Zero defects program   Propaganda designed to induce workers and other to reduce the number of errors they commit. Its first major use was in the American space programme where unusually high reliabilities were required.

INDEX

absenteeism, 45, 189ff
acceleration, 145, 151, 152, 184
acceptability (credibility and risk), 13, 35, 40, 41, 122, 123, 189, 210ff, 246, 265
accidents, 6, 55, 145, 152, 157, 159, 173–187, 210–229, 305, 308, 313, 319; analysis, 12, 34, 181; causes, 175, 176, 183; data, 55, 173, 174, 175, 181ff, 210ff, 225ff; investigation (*see also* public inquiry) 176, 183, 185; potential, 179, 214, 313; prevention, 12, 34, 173, 185; proneness, 34, 160, 162, 170
accountability (*see also* responsibility), 205, 250, 255ff
Adams, S. K., 12, 13, 32, 33, 36, 40, 143ff
adaptation, 207, 269, 270, 276, 281, 284
advertizing, 222, 225
aerospace, 31, 133
aesthetics, 145, 152, 287
age, 38, 146, 149, 151, 153, 158, 170
aggregation, 16ff, 327, 330, 337
aircraft (*see also* pilots), 46, 55, 173ff, 217, 220, 226, 228, 230ff, 273, 302, 304, 305, 308, 334
air quality (*see also* dust, odours, pollution, ventilation), 102, 144, 145, 336
alcohol (*see* drugs)
alertness (*see also* arousal, attention, relaxation), 100, 102, 109, 166
alienation, 327, 335
Allnut, M. F., 184
allocation of functions (*see also* Fitts list), 50, 51, 126, 180, 286ff, 303, 309ff
Altman, J. W., 40, 116, 117, 122, 123
ambiguity (*see* confusion)
amnesia (*see* memory)
analysis of variance, 75
anatomy (*see* anthropometry)
anniversary, 159
Anthrobus, J. S., 86
anthropometry, 17, 21, 37, 38, 47, 48, 51, 67, 71ff, 144, 146, 154, 236, 237, 340
anxiety, 99, 145, 159, 160, 162, 168, 170, 176, 183, 184, 190, 243
aptitude, 84, 320
APU (Applied Psychology Unit), 46, 47
arousal (*see also* alertness, attention), 18, 99ff, 234
Ascot Ltd., 76
assessment of personal performance, 250
atomic power (*see* nuclear energy)
attention (*see also* alertness, arousal, relaxation), 98, 102, 105, 106, 110, 159, 165, 171, 180, 302
attention: narrowing under stress, 180

attitudes (*see also* values), 32, 151, 184, 190, 193, 194, 239, 263, 264, 266, 270, 271, 313
authority and power (*see also* control), 203, 204, 205, 206, 214, 249, 250, 251, 254, 257, 260, 263, 264, 266
automation; of jobs, 34, 49, 180, 189, 191, 197, 291, 309, 311; of skill (*see also* skill), 10, 18, 98, 99, 103
automobile (*see also* car drivers), 143, 190ff, 213ff, 225ff, 273, 277, 278, 285, 301, 302, 313, 336
autonomy, 205, 264ff
availability, 145, 153
aviation (*see also* aircraft, pilots), 220, 221, 222, 223, 226
Ayers, A. W., 83
Ayoub, M. A., 17
Ayoub, M. M., 17

Bahrick, H. P., 98
Bakan, P., 84
Baker, C. H., 83, 84, 85
Baker, J. D., 24
Balle, J., 10, 11, 12, 13, 20, 26, 34, 41, 247ff
Barlay, S., 173
BART (Bay Area Rapid Transit System), 143ff, 340
Barton, H. R., 310
Bates, C. J., 305
Bauer, H. J., 144
Baumol, W. J., 265, 268
Beer, S., 10, 13, 20, 21, 38, 273ff
benefits, 20, 144, 210ff, 245
Bergum, B. O., 85
bias, 23, 24, 83, 158
Bilodeau, E. A., 111
Bilodeau, I. A., 111
Binet, A., 44
biomechanics, 6
biological sciences, 17, 45
biological characteristics, 21, 332
biotechnologists, 327
Birmingham University Department of Anatomy, 76
Black, H. C., 174, 181, 182
Blau, P. M., 249
blueprints (*see* specifications)
Board of Trade, 174
boredom (*see* monotony)
Bouwcentrum, 76
Bradley, J. V., 59, 60, 62
Branton, P., 17
Bratton, E. C., 76
Breslow, M., 335
British Standards, 22, 35, 36, 38, 76
Broadbent, D. E., 96
Brown, S. C., 12, 44
Brown, I. D., 99, 103
Brown, L. D., 109
Bursill, A. E., 106

INDEX

business management, 326, 330
Byrne, D. E., 151

Cambridge cockpit, 47
Canty, E. T., 153
capital, 264, 266
Capwell, D. F., 191
car drivers (*see also* automobiles), 93, 96, 98, 99, 103, 105, 313
catastrophe and natural disasters, 36, 176, 224, 228, 265, 275, 277, 281, 282, 284, 304, 320
Cattell, R. B., 44
Chaffin, D. B., 147
Chaillet, R. F., 331
challenge (*see* motivation)
Chaney, F. B., 87
Chaney, R., 316, 319
channel capacity and limitations (*see also* information handling capacity), 97, 99, 103, 176, 180
Chapanis, A., 23, 88, 133, 138, 140, 141
Checkland, P. B., 29
choice, 94
Chidsey, 148
Childs, M. J., 25
circadian rhythms, 184, 340
civilian applications, 48, 81ff, 230ff, 325, 333
clothing, 102, 148, 150, 301
climate (*see also* weather), 125, 150
coalitions, 203
Coates, V., 335
Colquhoun, W. P., 84, 87
comfort and convenience, 145
communication (*see also* information transfer), 13, 29, 40, 41, 49, 52, 137, 139, 184, 214, 248, 279, 281, 283, 317, 332, 337
communism, 268, 269
community, 271
compatibility, 116, 178, 188, 207, 208, 311, 320
competition (*see* market)
complexity, 19, 20, 21, 24, 28, 32, 37, 46, 51, 84, 87, 100, 116, 181, 212, 215, 233, 279, 286, 287, 289, 296, 303, 316, 319, 321, 334
compromise (*see* optimization)
computers, computer models, 18, 28, 35, 96ff, 126, 287, 291
'concept' operators, 286, 294, 295
conditioning, 47
conflict, 49, 51, 201, 203, 205, 207, 260, 261, 262, 275, 277, 278, 287
conformity (*see also* social factors), 202
confusion, 59, 165, 184
Conover, D. W., 141
consultants, 230ff, 260, 261
consumers and consumer demand, 31, 49, 263, 301, 319, 337
Consumer Reports, 301
contracts, 137, 140
control (*see also* authority), 205, 251, 264, 281, 285, 295, 320, 325, 330, 332, 334; dynamics, 295; loop, 19, 32; of tasks, 10, 18, 98, 231ff, 240; of technology, 211, 214, 325ff; , theory, 334
controls (*see also* displays, interface), 32, 47, 48, 54ff, 117, 119, 120, 170, 176, 181, 236, 293, 294, 295, 301, 312, 328; control-display relationship, 54, 294, 312, 328, 340; identification and coding, 55ff; layout, 48, 165, 236, 313; types, 54, 117; uses, 54
cooker, 65ff
Cooper, J. I., 305
Cornell, C. E., 305
Corporate image, 271
corporations (*see* organizations)
cost-benefit; including trade-off (*see also* cost-effectiveness, optimization), 13, 20, 36, 126, 210ff, 310, 311, 337
cost-effectiveness, (*see also* cost-benefit, optimization), 189, 190, 192, 194, 195, 210ff, 245, 246, 289
costs, 20, 25, 28, 65, 126, 127, 144, 192, 193, 210ff, 246, 267, 271, 287, 289, 303, 309, 310, 319
Council of Scientific Management in the Home, 76
Crannel, C. W., 61
credibility, 13, 40, 41
crime (*see also* vandalism), 145, 152, 214, 274, 276
cross-over point, 205, 206, 256, 260, 262
cross-referencing, 134
Crutchfield, J., 335
culture, 143, 151, 211, 234, 269
Cutchshaw, C. M., 316
cybernetics, 276, 281, 328, 340

data banks; Data Store, 26, 27, 28, 39, 40, 52, 116ff
Damon, A., 146, 151
Davis, D. R., 10, 11, 12, 18, 23, 34, 157ff, 183
Davis, L. E., 34
Davis, R., 97
death, 20, 210ff, 273
decision analysis, 330, 333
decision making, 20, 22, 29, 41, 93, 104, 110, 180, 214, 237, 243, 247, 248, 264, 268, 286, 291, 294, 309, 327, 330, 332, 335, 337
decrement (*see* vigilance)
Deese, J., 85, 101
dehumanization, 34, 190ff
Department of Health and Social Security (*see also* health care), 248, 253, 254
depression, 159
design, 6, 30, 51, 137, 150, 176, 213, 222, 230, 246, 285ff, 300, 306, 308ff
Deutsch, S., 325
development time (*see also* technological

347

INDEX

development), 51, 136, 286,
Dhesi, J. K., 24
Dickson, W. J., 24
disability (*see* handicap)
disaster (*see* catastrophe)
discretion, 250, 254
discrimination; tactile, 56ff; visual, 84, 87, 97
disease and mortality risk (*see also* health), 18, 218, 219, 220, 221, 271
disorientation, 176, 177, 178
displays (*see also* control-display relationships, interface), 32, 47, 48, 84, 86, 88, 104, 117, 164, 171, 176, 179, 183, 286, 292ff, 301, 311, 313, 328
display layout, 171, 236, 311
distraction, 102, 161ff, 183
division of labour (*see* job fractionation)
documentation (*see* manuals, specifications)
Doob, A. N., 151
doom, 274
Dror, Y., 327
drugs, 18, 102, 108, 110, 161, 212, 266
Dunlap, J. W., 85

Eames, R. D., 133
Easterby, R. S., 141
Ebbinghaus, H., 44
ecology (*see also* environmental protection), 309
economics, 10, 20, 30, 154, 211, 263, 264, 267, 271, 273; economic factors, 52, 137, 139, 144, 151, 153, 154, 173, 189, 191, 210, 211, 224, 251, 265; growth, 35, 211, 267, 268, 269, 311
education, 211, 269, 271, 273, 295, 327
efficiency and effectiveness, 99ff, 102, 109, 127, 170, 173, 181, 188, 254, 279, 285, 299, 311, 319
Ehrlich, J., 314, 318
electricity, 217, 227, 229, 290
electromyography, 37, 70ff, 340
Elliot, E., 82
Elliott, L. L., 110
Ellul, J., 326
emergency provisions and reactions, 145, 164, 165, 184, 185
emotions, 52
engineering, 6, 23, 44, 47, 136, 140, 286, 293, 300, 303, 309, 311, 312, 317, 319, 326, 327, 333; human engineering (*see* human)
entrepreneur, 266, 270, 271
environment, 18, 20, 33, 46, 48, 125, 144, 145, 152, 177, 184ff, 211, 273, 285, 292, 303, 316, 320, 321, 325, 326, 327, 332, 335, 336
environmental protection (*see also* ecology), 326, 336
epidemiology, 31
Epstein, M., 86
equipment reliability (*see* reliability)

ergonomics (*see* human factors); classical, 48ff; Ergonomics (Research) Society (*see also* Human Factors Society), 47; error, 51ff; interface, 48; knobs-and-dials, 33; systems, 50ff, 285ff
Eriksen, C. W., 95
error, 6, 19, 22, 45, 51, 52, 99, 102, 103, 104, 108, 114ff, 137, 157, 159, 160, 166, 169, 171, 173ff, 271, 299ff; cause removal programme, 194; causes, 28, 129, 170, 174, 300ff, 307, 316, 317, 320; consequences, 28, 52, 123ff, 175, 286, 300, 302ff, 308, 317, 319; correction, 304; criticality or importance, 114, 175, 211, 302, 304, 307, 308; definitions, 114, 129, 299, 304, 314; estimates, 116, 121; frequency (*see* error rates); immediacy or lag, 304, 307; potential, 122, 318, 321; prediction, 115, 124; probability, 52, 116, 310; rates, 52, 115, 122ff, 304, 307, 314, 315, 317, 319; taxonomy, 28, 300ff; types, 28, 29, 299, 300, 302, 303; visibility, 304, 314; of commission, 114, 299; of ommission, 114, 294, 299; assembly error, 307, 318; design, design-induced or design-stage error, 170, 286, 300, 303, 306, 308ff; fabrication error, 303, 306; human caused error (HCE) and human error, 173, 175, 302, 317; human engineering design error, 303, 312ff; idiosyncratic error (*see* individual factors); inspection error, 303, 318ff; installation, maintenance or test-stage error, 303, 305, 306, 317ff; operator, operator-induced or operating-stage error, 121, 122, 170, 300ff, 306, 319ff; production stage, fabrication or workmanship error, 303, 304, 306, 313ff, 319; situation caused error (SCE), 317, 320; system induced error, 300, 301, 302; timing error, 114, 169, 171, 299
ethics (*see* morals)
Etzioni, A., 249
evaluation (*see* cost-effectiveness, validity)
excitement (*see* arousal)
executive hierarchy, 249, 251, 252, 259, 261, 277
expectations, 19, 143, 161, 165ff, 183, 189, 200ff, 295
experience, 11, 23, 30, 104, 175, 176, 178, 181, 183, 193, 214, 314, 319

failure (and faults), 19, 51, 87, 100, 114, 124ff, 173, 268, 304, 305, 308, 312, 313, 314, 316, 317; definitions and taxonomy, 87, 176; prevention, 265; probability, 310; rates, 26, 127, 225, 317; failure to implement human

requirements, 303, 311ff; fail safe, 319; fail dangerous, 157ff
family ties and pressures, 162, 167, 202, 273, 276
Farnborough, 47, 48, 173
fatigue (*see also* sleep, workload), 38, 45, 47, 176, 234, 301
fault trees, 27, 125
fear (*see* anxiety)
feedback (and knowledge of results), 85, 98–100, 108–110, 195, 212, 214, 281, 332, 334, 341
fiducial approach, 126, 341
field data, 40, 83, 116
field studies, 11, 23, 24, 26, 245, 247ff, 333, 341
field testing, 212
Firebaugh, F. M., 24
fitting trials, 67ff
Fitts, P. M., 61, 97, 98, 289, 296, 310
Fitts list (*see also* allocation of functions), 289, 296, 310
Fitzgerald, T. H., 196
Flajser, S. H., 327
Ford, R. N., 189, 191, 194
Ford, T. E., 176
forecasting, 333
Fox, R. H., 102
Fraser, D. C., 85
Freedman, J. L., 151
freedom, 283
Fuchs, A. H., 104

Gaffney, J. I., 305
Galbraith, J. K., 10, 12, 20, 35, 263ff
Galton, F., 44
gaming, 328, 334
Garvey, W. D., 104
gas industry, 76
generalizability, 13, 24, 39, 49, 88, 125, 144, 146, 224, 334
General Systems Theory, 21, 273ff, 328
geographic factors, 52
ghettos, 274
Gilbreth, F. and L., 44, 51, 76
goals, 18, 263ff, 317, 337
Goldsmith, R., 102
Golob, T. F., 153
Gooding, J., 190, 193, 196
good practice (*see also* standards), 23, 134, 139ff, 250, 300
Gordon, R. A., 265
Gordon, R. B., 312
government and state (*see also* authority), 214, 224, 266, 307
Gowers, E., 32
Gross National Product (GNP), 268, 269, 274, 341
grievances (*see* job satisfaction)
Gustofsen, R. L., 153
Gutman, E. M., 150

Hackman, R. C., 192
Hall, F., 191, 192, 193

Hampton, I. F. G., 102
handbooks (*see also* instructions, manuals), 133, 144
handicap, 38, 145, 147, 149, 150, 151, 154, 192, 215
Harabedian, A., 84
Harris, D. H., 87, 316, 319
Hatcher, J. F., 84
Hawkins, R. R., 76
Hawthorne studies/effect, 24, 45
Hays, W. L., 37
health (*see also* disease, injury), 31, 38, 45, 145, 161ff, 211, 213, 218, 266
health care, 247ff, 325, 328
hearing, 161
heat (*see also* temperature), 48, 102, 184, 185, 236, 296
height (*see* anthropometry)
Helmer, O., 326
Herzberg, F., 191, 196
highway code, 97
Hill, C. E., 191
Hird, J. F., 189, 193
history, 44ff, 289
Hockey, G. R. J., 105, 106, 107
Hollander, G. L., 330
Hopkin, V. D., 179
Horner, D. R., 314, 318
hospitals, 251, 254ff, 328, 337
housewives, 32, 65ff
Howell, W. C., 88
Huddlestone, H. F., 185
Huebner, W. J., 307
human; human caused error (HCE) (*see* error), element, 31, 124, 128; engineering, 6, 301, 303, 312ff, 321, 327; failure potential, 114, 176; human initiated failures (HIF), 302, 305, 307, 314, 318, 319; performance capabilities, 46, 47, 176, 177, 186, 188, 289, 301, 309, 317, 320; performance limitations, 46, 47, 176, 178, 186, 188, 289, 294, 317; reliability (*see also* reliability engineering), 52, 114, 122, 128, 173, 296, 309, 310; requirements, 303, 311, 313; sciences, 6, 52
human factors; expertise limitations (*see also* lack of data), 9, 13, 23, 29, 30, 36ff, 48, 52, 144, 189, 196, 292, 325ff; knowledge, 9, 46, 327; origins, 44ff; Society (*see also* Ergonomics Society), 336, 337
humidity, 102, 145
Hunt, D. P., 57, 58, 61

ideology (*see also* values), 30, 41, 268
idiosyncratic factors (*see* individual factors)
IEEE, 326, 328
illness (*see* health)
illumination (*see also* lighting and visibility), 45, 48, 62, 63, 145, 160, 302, 317

INDEX

illustrations, 135
impact analysis, 335, 336
incentives, reward, punishment and earnings (*see also* motivation), 34, 85, 140, 191, 215, 264, 270ff
income (*see also* incentives), 153, 211ff
individual factors (*see also* personality), 84, 115, 129, 152, 320
industrial relations and labour policy, 6, 20, 188ff, 244, 245, 265, 267
information, 12, 19, 134, 178, 180, 232, 233, 243, 248, 312, 316, 334, 335
information handling capacity (*see also* overload, spare capacity), 101, 177, 178, 180, 233, 285
information processing (and mediating processes), 96, 117, 120, 176, 177, 291, 294, 295, 325, 332, 335
information transfer (*see also* communication), 47, 135, 140, 145, 184, 294, 295
injury (*see also* health), 18, 20, 31, 157, 218
inputs, 19, 48, 95ff, 117, 120, 291
inspection (*see also* vigilance), 82ff, 86ff, 195, 303, 304, 314ff
installation, 51, 241, 242, 291, 294, 295, 306, 307, 314
institutions (*see* organizations)
instructions (*see also* manuals), 19, 23, 51, 85, 86, 133ff, 295, 300, 303, 316, 318
intelligence, intelligence tests, 44, 45, 84, 296
interdependence, 125, 129
interdisciplinary, 28, 49, 51, 52, 327, 330
interface (*see also* controls, displays), 33, 286, 287, 292ff; man–machine, 12, 32, 35, 48, 50, 51, 325ff; society–technology, 12, 34, 35, 325ff
International Ergonomics Association, 47, 325
interviews, 23, 157ff, 195, 230, 233, 239, 243, 247
'Inverted U' hypothesis (and Yerkes-Dodson Law), 100, 101
investment, 264
Ireland, R. H., 133, 138, 140
Irwin, I. A., 121
iteration, 246

Jamieson, G. H., 87
Jenkins, H. M., 83
Jenkins, W. O., 56
Jerison, H. J., 84
job aids (*see also* labels, manuals), 51, 87, 286, 292, 295
job analysis (*see* task analysis)
job description, 29, 50, 286, 291ff, 311
job design, 12, 34, 188ff, 237, 243, 321
job enrichment, 34, 40, 191ff, 341
job fractionation, 194, 317
job rationalization, 194

job rotation, 192
job satisfaction, 34, 162, 191ff
job simplification, 49, 188ff
job specification (*see* job description)
Johnson, E. M., 24
Jones, M. V., 330
Jordan, N., 51
judgement, 87, 88, 159, 176, 181, 313

Kappauf, W. E., 84
Kash, D., 335
Kasper, R. G., 330
Kaysen, 265
Kellen, M. L., 83
Kerslake, D., 102, 106
keyboards (*see* controls)
Kibler, A. W., 88
Kirk, N. S., 46, 47
kitchen, 65ff
Klein, L., 11, 12, 13, 27, 28, 33, 36, 39, 41, 230ff
Knaff, P. R., 85
knobs (*see* controls)
Kogan, M., 10, 11, 12, 13, 20, 26, 34, 41, 247ff
KOK, 76
KOR (knowledge of results) (*see* feedback)

labels (*see also* job aids), 51, 63, 117, 295, 301
laboratory research and its limitations, 49, 82ff, 118, 121, 144, 333
lack of data (*see also* human factors expertise limitations), 24, 27, 83, 116ff, 129, 133, 137, 139, 144, 154, 195, 215, 217, 218, 224, 307, 308, 310, 313, 316, 319, 334
lag (*see also* psychological refractory period), 54, 176, 177, 180, 295
Lamb, G. B., 23
Land, K. C., 326, 336
Langdon, J. N., 83
Lansing, J. G., 153
Lappin, J. S., 95
law, 23, 250, 251, 254, 330, 332
Lawshe, C. H., 83
layout of equipment (*see also* control layout, work station), 48, 243, 316
Lazarus, R. S., 101
learning (*see* information transfer, skill)
Lee, A. M., 178
legend plates (*see* labels)
Legge, D., 111
Lehr, D. J., 85
Leister, D., 26
Le Van, W. I., 305
Lewis, H. E., 102
lighting (*see also* illumination, visibility), 118, 152, 236, 302, 316, 317
Lindsley, D. B., 82
Linton, R., 200
logistics, 300, 303, 309, 317, 321, 328
Long, J. 76

350

loyalty, 278, 279
Lucaccini, L. F., 11, 13, 25, 38, 39, 40, 81ff, 85
Lyman, J., 85, 86, 336

Mackworth, N. H., 81, 82, 83
McCormick, E. J., 12, 32, 54ff, 327
McCornack, R. L., 82, 318
McDonald, W. F., 152
McFarland, R. A., 55, 146, 151
McGrath, J. J., 83, 84, 86
McGregor, D., 196
McKenzie, R. E., 110
McLaughlin, G. M., 133
Mahaddie, C., 78
Maine, 200
maintenance and repair, 51, 145, 175, 188, 232, 285, 291, 294, 295, 299, 300, 306, 307, 309, 310, 314, 317
Majesty, M. S., 305
management, 6, 23, 138, 140, 189ff, 212, 231, 239, 240, 245, 247ff, 255ff, 264, 268, 271, 326
management science, 330
man–machine systems, 6, 32, 50, 51, 114, 115, 126, 127, 129, 173, 285ff, 299ff, 325, 327, 332, 334
manuals (*see also* handbooks and instructions), 7, 22, 23, 27, 51, 133ff, 177, 195
Marans, R. W., 153
market, 265ff, 329
Marris, R., 265, 267
Marshall, T. H., 200
Martin, J. B., 147
Marx, K., 201
Maslow, A. H., 196
Mason, E. F., 265
Mausner, B., 191, 196
maximizing return, 263ff
Mayo, E., 45
Meadows, D. H., 326
Meadows, D. L., 326
mediating processes (*see* information processing), 341
medical factors, 160
medicine (*see also* health), 17, 34, 46, 47, 48, 157ff, 327; industrial medicine, 31, 47
Meister, D., 11, 12, 13, 21, 26ff, 33, 39, 40, 114ff, 299ff, 305, 308, 314, 316, 318, 319
memory and amnesia, 19, 47, 95ff, 161, 162, 181, 233, 237, 243, 296, 340, 341
mental health (*see also* psychiatry), 18, 192, 211
mental retardation, 192
Merton, R. K., 10, 13, 19, 38, 200ff
methodology, 11, 29ff, 123ff, 128, 129, 192, 211, 217, 225, 230ff, 247ff, 285ff, 334
military, 20, 31, 46, 47, 48, 81ff, 137, 144, 146, 151, 174, 188ff, 289, 305, 312, 319, 320, 333

Millar, A. E., 144, 152
Miller, R. B., 136, 138, 141
mining, 215, 218
Ministry of Transport, 97
Ministry of Transport Road Research Laboratory, 47
misinterpretation (*see* confusion)
Misner, G. E., 152
models, 7, 9, 11, 16, 18, 19, 20, 21, 26, 28, 39, 41, 95, 114ff, 123, 126, 127, 129, 154, 211, 267, 280ff, 328, 333, 342
multiplicative probability model, 342
MOHLG (Ministry of Housing and Local Government), 76
Mohn, G., 121
monitoring, 82ff, 99
monotony and boredom (*see also* fatigue, vigilance decrement), 84, 145, 192
Montague, W. E., 86
morale, 45, 86, 271
morals, moral expectations, 41, 201, 207, 276, 277
Morgan, C. T., 141
Moses, L. N., 154
motion studies, 44
motivation (*see also* incentives), 32, 33, 34, 52, 83ff, 115, 125, 127, 138, 188ff, 203, 212, 218, 234, 269, 271, 301, 303, 316, 317, 320, 321
motor capacity (*see* sensory motor)
MRC (Medical Research Council), 45, 46, 47
MTBF (mean time between failure), 308
Munger, S. J., 119, 121

National Environmental Policy Act, 336
negotiation, 20, 28
Neisser, U., 18, 111
Noble, M. E., 98
noise; audible, 48, 102, 106, 108, 109, 144, 145, 152, 184, 233, 236, 245, 316, 336; statistical, 296, 342
nuclear energy, 35, 195, 222ff, 229, 273, 305, 334, 335

obesity, 161
objectives and mission, 249, 263ff, 287, 288, 317
O'Brien, R., 146
Occupational Safety and Health Act, 336
O'Connor, P. J., 173
odours (*see also* air quality), 145, 151, 152
O'Hanlon, J., 84, 86
operation, 51, 236, 285, 291ff, 299, 300, 306, 307, 309, 318, 319
operations research, 127, 128, 330
optimization (*see also* cost-benefit, cost-effectiveness), 10, 17, 20, 75, 76, 99ff, 100, 126, 148, 205, 210, 212, 213, 214, 221, 233, 265, 287, 288, 308, 310, 330, 342

351

INDEX

organizations, 6, 10, 12, 20, 34, 35, 40, 200ff, 247ff, 264ff, 273ff
organisational analysis, 248
organisational behaviour, 20, 52, 264ff, 273ff, 325, 332, 335
organisation structures, 20, 35, 200ff, 247ff, 264ff, 273ff, 327
orientation, 31, 176, 177, 178
Ormond, E., 85
Osler, S. F., 101
outputs, 19, 48, 98, 117, 120, 291
overload (*see also* information handling capacity), 101, 103, 177, 178, 180, 233, 296, 303, 321, 342

panic, 164, 165
paramedical, 254, 261
parsimony, 17, 19, 342
Parons, H. McI., 28, 201
participation, 30, 190ff, 218ff, 225, 243
Patridge, D. M., 84
Payne, D., 121, 123
perception (*see also* senses, visual perception), 47, 48, 152
personality (*see also* individual factors), 52, 84, 168, 184, 190
personal space, 145, 151
personnel, 46, 50, 51, 117, 138, 140, 188ff, 291, 301, 308, 317, 319; selection, 31, 46, 47, 51, 84, 191, 192, 197, 256, 292, 295, 303, 321
perturbations, 280, 282
Peterson, R. O., 191, 268
Phillips, B. S., 23
philosophy, 326
physical factors (*see also* anthropometry), 146, 147, 154, 177, 185
physical sciences, 17
physiological factors, 46, 100, 152, 160, 177
physiology, 31, 45, 46, 48, 65, 100
pilots, 31, 32, 45, 47, 128, 136, 173ff, 304, 309
poison, 18, 31, 274
policy; analysis, 328, 330, 335; making, 6, 12, 34, 35, 248, 249, 265, 266, 327, 330, 332ff; science, 327
political, 6, 30, 52, 211, 212, 214, 277, 287, 332; science, 326, 330, 333
Pollack, I., 85
pollution, 31, 145, 211, 274, 335, 336
Porter, A. L., 12, 35, 52, 325ff
post office, 299
Poulton, C., 10, 13, 18, 19, 21, 38, 85, 93ff, 95, 97, 99, 100, 102, 104, 106, 110, 111
Powe, W. E., 84
power (*see* authority)
practice and rehearsal, 95, 98, 104, 181
pregnancy, 151
preoccupation, 166, 184
Price, D., 335
privacy (*see also* secrecy), 145, 151, 204, 205, 326
probability, 27, 123ff, 213, 215, 313
procedures, 133ff
product rule (reliability), 115, 121, 343
'programmed' operators, 286, 293
project organization, 234ff
psychiatric conditions, 18, 34, 159ff, 170
psychological factors, 45, 46, 143, 144, 151, 177, 332; refractory period, 97, 180
psychology, 6, 18, 45, 47, 48, 117, 130, 157, 164ff, 309, 327; cognitive, 18; educational, 44; engineering, 327; environmental, 46; experimental, 44, 327, 341; human, 20; industrial, 6; occupational, 239; organizational, 6; personnel, 44; social, 19, 52; vocational, 44, 51
psycho-physical, 152
psycho-physiological, 10, 17
psycho-somatic factors, 23, 163ff
Public Inquiry (*see also* accident investigation), 23, 176

Quade, E. S., 330
quality of life, 210ff
questionnaires, 230, 239, 246

Rabideau, G. F., 316
radar, 81, 82, 88, 179, 309
RAF (Royal Air Force), 47, 173, 181, 186
railways, 143ff, 157ff, 183, 223, 226, 272, 273
RAND, 328, 334
reaction times and response lags (*see also* responses and lags), 44, 47, 97, 108, 119, 180, 295, 299
redundancy, 62, 178, 343
reference points, 281
refuelling, 230ff
Regan, R. A., 88
rehearsal (*see* practice)
relationships (*see also* role relationships), 247ff, 250ff, 263, 278; attachment, 258; collateral, 256, 257, 261; coordinating, 255, 257; monitoring, 255, 257; prescribing, 251, 254, 261; service giving, 251, 257; service seeking, 251, 257; staff, 251, 256, 257; superior–subordinate (*see also* cross-over point), 250, 254, 255, 260, 261
relaxation, 159, 168, 169; time (*see also* lag), 279, 280, 282
reliability; engineering, 26, 41, 115ff, 195, 225, 343; of evidence, 13, 18, 24, 27, 37, 38, 121, 122, 123, 128, 145, 153, 343; equipment, 114, 123, 126, 128, 195, 296, 305, 310, 315; human, 114, 122, 123, 128, 173, 188, 296, 305, 310; system, 116, 124, 126, 180
religion, 52, 270, 277
repair (*see* maintenance)

INDEX

research and development, 270, 336
resources, 136, 137, 210
responses (*see also* reaction times), 19, 117, 167, 169, 171, 180, 181, 294, 297
responsibility (*see also* accountability), 195, 250, 267, 326, 332
rest pauses, 110, 240, 244
reward and punishment (*see* incentives, motivation)
Ridgeway, S., 67
Rigby, L. V., 305
risk, 20, 31, 35, 145, 185, 210ff, 246, 265, 268; analysis, 332, 335; risk-benefit analysis (*see* cost-benefit); occupational, 218; public awareness of, 222, 229; voluntary/involuntary, 213ff, 225
Roberts, J., 146
Robinson, J. E., 305
Roethlisberger, F. J., 24
Rogers, H. B., 83
role, 19, 20, 21, 22, 26, 28, 30, 200ff, 239, 249, 250, 254ff, 271; expectations, 202, 204, 207; set, 200ff, 207; relationships, 26, 200ff, 254; of the ergonomist, 29, 49, 188, 189, 292; multiple, 201
Rolfe, J. M., 12, 32, 33, 173ff, 185
Ronan, W. W., 128
Rook, L. W., 191, 305, 314, 317
Roszak, T., 326
rules, 280

Saballus, D., 193
sabotage, 189, 191, 197
sacking (dismissal), 190, 267
safety, 32, 49, 52, 125, 145, 152, 173ff, 185, 210ff, 225, 232, 266, 310, 329, 335
safety analysis, 332
sailors, 105
Salmon report, 257
Salpukas, A., 191
sampling, 24, 68, 84, 123, 144, 146, 157, 158, 314
sanitation (*see also* health), 145
Sargant, W., 101
satisfaction (*see also* job satisfaction), 332
SCE (*see* error)
Schacter, S., 151
Schultz, V., 194
scientific method, 17
Scott, W. R., 249
Scucchi, A. D., 180
seating, 145, 147, 153, 233, 285
secrecy (*see also* privacy), 204, 205
self interest, 20, 267, 269
self respect, 271
Sells, S. B., 180
Seminara, J. L., 325
senses, 61, 98, 177, 294, 295
sensitivity of models, 39

sensory; input, 19, 44; motor processes, 44, 47, 332; threshold, 84, 87
separation of functions, 286ff
sequential activity sampling, 65
Shackel, B., 11, 12, 13, 27, 28, 33, 36, 39, 41, 148, 230ff
Shapero, A., 305
Shaw, L., 34
Shef, A. L., 211
Sheldon, E. B., 326
Shelton, W. C., 146
Sheppard, N., 78
shifts (at work) (*see also* sleep deprivation), 102, 236
Shipley, 148
Sichel, H. S., 34
Siegel, S., 37
signal detection, 84, 88
signal-to-noise ratio, 87
signals (railway), 157ff
Simmel, 201
Simmonds, D. C., 103
simulation, 11, 28, 39, 47, 82, 125, 183–185, 230, 237ff, 246, 333
Singer, J. L., 86
single channel input selector (*see also* inputs), 97, 180
Singleton, W. T., 11, 29, 50, 285ff
sink, 65ff
Sipowicz, R. R., 84, 86
situational variables, 115, 129, 320, 321
skill, 19, 47, 93ff, 103, 181, 192, 254, 291, 293, 301–303, 319–321
sleep deprivation (*see also* fatigue, workload), 102, 105ff, 176, 184
Sloan foundation, 326, 335
Smith, E. M. B., 181, 182
Smith, R. L., 11, 13, 25, 38–40, 81ff, 84, 85, 86
Snyderman, B., 196
social factors, 32, 144, 145, 332; interactions, 10, 19, 52, 151; mechanisms, 201, 202, 207; norms, 204; science, 235, 262, 326, 333; stratification, 203; structures, 11, 29, 200ff, 207, 251, 262ff, 274
socio-economic, 151, 211
socio-political, 276
socio-technical systems, 30, 274, 325ff
sociology, 6, 19, 29, 200ff
Solandt, D. Y., 84
Sommer, R., 151
sonar, 88
SOW (statement of work) (*see* job description)
spare capacity (*see also* information-handling capacity), 99, 101
specifications, 138, 140, 287, 302, 303, 311, 314, 316, 317, 318
speed, 94, 116, 145, 181, 296
Spencer, H., 201
Sperling, G., 95
sport, 31, 217, 219, 220, 222, 226, 227
staff turnover, 138, 140, 189, 190, 192,

353

INDEX

194
standards (*see also* good practice), 22, 24, 35, 138, 140, 170, 174, 266, 308, 314, 319
Starr, C., 10, 12, 20, 35, 210ff
Starr, J., 133
starvation, 277
state (*see* government)
statement of objectives, 287, 288, 292, 293
statistics, 20, 37, 55, 73–75, 116, 153, 173–175, 181, 214, 215, 220, 224, 225, 269, 314, 342–344
status, 200, 201, 207, 248; set, 201
Steidl, R. E., 76
Stein, A., 141
stimulus, 117, 180
stimulus–organism–response paradigm, 117, 344
stock control, 290
storage, 147, 316
Stoudt, H. W., 146, 151
strategies, 21ff, 104
strength (*see also* anthropometry), 146, 149
stress, 17, 18, 21, 34, 36, 46, 48, 93ff, 100ff, 115, 125, 128, 159, 168, 170, 177, 183, 184, 188, 233, 234, 243, 273, 312, 328
combinations of stress, 108, 110
strikes, 45, 189, 191, 197
Stump, N. E., 60
subjectivity; subjective preferences, 72, 75, 144, 152, 154
subordinate, 250ff, 263, 266, 267, 271, 280, 281
supervision, 233, 316
Swain, A. D., 12, 13, 34, 40, 123–125, 127, 128, 188ff, 190–192, 194
systems; analysis, 35, 285, 291, 328, 330, 334; approach, 197, 328; design, 285ff; development stages, 28, 51, 193, 241ff, 291, 303, 304, 306; dynamic properties, 274ff; engineering, 330; instability, 275, 283; methodologies, 29; science, 12, 35, 325ff; theory (*see* General Systems Theory)

task; analysis, 50, 51, 120, 124, 125, 192, 193, 237, 252; complexity, 87, 303, 321; continuity, 304; description, 117, 251, 286, 292, 293; design (*see* job design); diversification, 192
Taylor, F. V., 104
Taylor, F. W., 44, 51
Taylor, J. C., 34
techniques, 21ff
technology, 31, 35, 130, 143, 210ff, 265, 325, 337; assessment (*see* TPA); development, 40, 210ff, 270, 271, 309, 326ff
technostructure, 263ff
Teel, K. S., 87

Teeple, J. D., 310
Tehan, D., 152
telephone, 101
temperature (*see also* heat), 145, 316
templates in the memory, 98
test, 303, 306, 318, 319
THERP (Technique for Human Error Rate Prediction), 21, 39, 40, 41, 123ff
Thom, R., 282
threat, 100
Tickner, A. H., 103
Tiffin, J., 83
time and motion study, 44, 46, 51, 317
time study, 44
Tinkham, M. L., 192
Toffler, A., 326
tools, 303, 317
top event (systems failure), 124
TPA (Technology Policy Assessment), 12, 35, 212, 213, 325ff
TPA curricula, 326
tracking, 94, 104, 105, 106, 122, 304
trade-off (*see* cost-benefit)
traffic, 214
train drivers, 157ff
training, 28, 29, 46, 47, 51, 175, 176, 181, 184–186, 191, 192, 197, 286, 291ff, 300, 301, 303, 316, 321
industrial training, 31
transfer of training (positive and negative) and habit interference, 64, 181
transportation (*see also* aviation, airplanes, automobiles, railways), 32, 143, 173, 217, 336
trial and error, 211
Tuttle, H. C., 193, 195
typing, 93, 189

uncertainty, 180
unemployment, 45, 46, 211, 267, 269
unions, 190
United States Transportation Safety Board, 174
Urmston, R. E., 316
user preferences, 143, 144, 152
utility, 210ff

validity (evaluation and assumptions), 13, 21, 32, 37, 38, 49, 65, 82, 121, 123, 127, 128, 153, 154, 192, 195, 210, 217, 218, 222, 230, 239, 242ff, 269, 287, 292, 327, 335, 344
values (*see also* attitudes, ideology), 52, 151, 201, 207, 210, 213, 214, 225, 249, 264, 328, 336
Van Buskirk, R. C., 307
vandalism, 11, 12, 13, 22, 23, 32, 37, 133ff
variability, 19, 27, 28, 37, 51, 151, 344
variety, 279ff, 282ff
variety reduction, 280, 283
Veniar, S., 82
ventilation (*see also* air quality), 236

vibration, 48, 144, 145, 152, 296
vigilance; research (*see also* inspection), 25, 38, 81ff, 345; decrement, 81ff
violence, 274
visibility (*see also* illumination, lighting), 159, 162, 164, 175, 176, 179, 303, 313, 316
vision, 152, 170, 178, 301; colour, 158, 160; acuity, 158, 160, 170, 178, 319, 345; contrast, 178; cues, 47, 179; discrimination, 84, 87, 97; perception, 47, 319
Vitt, J. E., 153

Wachs, M., 152
Waldron, M., 133
Walley, J. E., 76
Wallis, R. A., 84
Walvekar, A. G., 17
war, 44–46, 48, 50, 55, 82, 214, 220, 227, 273, 326, 333
Ward, J. S., 10–13, 17, 22–25, 32, 35–38, 40, 41, 65ff, 67, 146
Ware, J. R., 84, 85
weather (*see also* climate), 159, 160, 164, 179, 180
Webb, W. B., 84
Webber, C. E., 86
Weitz, J., 62
welfare, 49
Welford, A. T., 97, 111, 133

Wenk, E., 327
Wherry, R. J., 84
White, I., 335
White, R. M., 146
Wiedenfeller, E. W., 84
Wiedman, T. G., 133, 138, 140
Wiener, E. L., 86
Wilkinson, R. T., 102, 108, 109
Williams, H. L., 115
Wilson, R. B., 305
Willis, H. R., 305
Woodson, W. E., 141
workload (*see also* fatigue, rest pauses), 45, 48, 103, 178, 233, 242, 243
work station (*see also* layout of equipment), 12, 33, 48, 50, 65ff, 230ff, 292, 303, 316, 321
work study (*see also* time and motion study), 47, 51, 317
work surface, 65ff
worker participation, 30, 191, 193, 345
Wraith, R. E., 23
Wyatt, S., 83

Yerkes-Dodson Law (*see* 'Inverted U' hypothesis)

zero-defects, 52, 179, 190, 191, 197, 317, 345
Zehner, R. B., 153
Zeller, A. F., 173